PHYSICIAN

OF THE

SOUL

Exploring the mystical meaning of the life of

DR. ALBERT SCHWEITZER

Letters from a Journal

Renate zum Tobel

authorHOUSE™

1663 LIBERTY DRIVE, SUITE 200
BLOOMINGTON, INDIANA 47403
(800) 839-8640
WWW.AUTHORHOUSE.COM

First published by AuthorHouse 07/21/05

ISBN: 1-4184-7618-8 (e)
ISBN: 1-4184-7619-6 (sc)

Library of Congress Control Number: 2004094633

Printed in the United States of America
Bloomington, Indiana

This book is printed on acid-free paper.

Cover photograph by Renate zum Tobel,
Cover design by Teina Tallarigo, Graphic Designer/Illustrator

For

Alexandra, Marco, Ava, William,
Maximilian and Valentina

with Love

In memory of a great teacher with deepest gratitude

Dr. Albert Schweitzer
January 14, 1875 – September 4, 1965

Dedicated to the fellowship of those who are suffering, for we are
all brothers in spirit.

The 'light' of his soul brings clarity on what is essential in life. May
his healing energy spread to all of us reading about him as we begin
to appreciate, love and know ourselves on a deeper level.

Acknowledgements

I thank Dr. Albert Schweitzer for having taken the time out of his very busy life to write: '*Out of my Thought and Life*', '*The Mystery of the Kingdom of God*', '*The Quest for the Historical Jesus*', '*The Mysticism of Paul the Apostle*', '*The Light within Us*', '*Out of my Childhood and Youth*', '*Indian Thought and its Development*', '*The Psychiatric Study Of Jesus*', '*The Philosophy of Civilization*' and '*Pilgrimage to Humanity*", only to mention a few.

I respect his life of compassion, his wisdom and love. Most of my resources are based on his words, having become a large part of the legacy he left for us to ponder. He encouraged me to become and to remain a free thinker. He encouraged me to be strong, forgiving and loving. He is an example for me of what it means to be kind, humble and to practice harmlessness. He came to my rescue when I least expected any help from outside. He made it possible for me to take a look at myself and to make the monumental decision to change my life. He became my light on the path, a messenger of life, a messenger of love, and a messenger of hope and inspiration. I allowed him to become the physician of my soul. Oddly enough, he would be the first to say, "I didn't heal you, you healed yourself." That's humility in action!

I thank Erica Anderson for her compilation of Dr. Schweitzer's words in the book 'Albert Schweitzer: Thoughts for Our Times'.

I thank Norman Cousins for having given us the inspirational book '*The Words of Albert Schweitzer*', without which I would not have been able to get so deep into the mind and spirit of the man.

I thank Jacqueline Berrill for her passion in writing, '*Albert Schweitzer: Man of Mercy*' in which she describes this giant of a man's state of consciousness, igniting a spark in my heart, which turned into a burning flame. This woman, a housewife with a passion for gardening and writing, had unknowingly become a role model for me.

I thank Earlyne and Dr. Robert Chaney for opening my heart and mind. Their knowledge and dedication accelerated my understanding of the Ancient Wisdom Teachings. For this I am deeply grateful.

I am indebted to all the courageous authors who inspired me, including Ken Keyes Jr., Maurice Bucke MD, J. Krishnamurti, Goethe, Annie Besant, Alice Bailey, Ralph Waldo Emerson, Rudolf Steiner, Manly P. Hall, Elisabeth Kübler-Ross MD, Joseph

Campbell, Deepak Chopra MD, Evelyn Underhill, Joy Mills and Helena Petrovna Blavatsky, only to mention a few. Some of these authors are not with us today, but their work lives on. All are examples of using the written word for the benefit of humanity. All have become examples for me, encouraging me to be courageous and to tread 'the road less traveled'.

This page would be incomplete without a 'thank you' to my teacher and friend, Anthony Fisichella, a metaphysician of extraordinary talents and vision. Thanks Tony, for your dedication to the advancement of human thought and for furthering the divine potential inherent in each of us for spiritual development. You never missed an opportunity to challenge us and to confront us, being a signpost on the path, knowing deep inside that you couldn't do more than that.

I thank my friend Karin Querfeldt for offering to read and edit these letters. Her talents for language and her deep insight were very helpful during the final stages of editing. Without her support, her encouragement and her dedication to the education of humanity this book would not have become a reality for me. Thank you for being my guardian angel and for giving me the ultimate push during moments of fear, doubt and procrastination.

I especially thank my three children for offering to be my teachers in this life. Without their love I could easily have disappeared into the sea of people who live lives of 'quiet desperation'. They have put up with my notion that there must be more to existence than meets the ordinary eye. I ask them to forgive me for having been absent while searching for love in all the wrong places. I am so very grateful for having been blessed with their presence in my life, and the presence of my grandchildren. I express my most heart-felt gratitude to them.

R. z T.

February 3, 2004

Table of Contents

Foreword

Freeing your mind past the *'thinking'* stage and pressing on to the *'being'* stage is the ultimate purpose of this unique book.

Probably there is no other like it. The spiritual philosophy of Albert Schweitzer is explored by the author in a series of letters she has addressed to the deceased genius.

Thus the premise of the book is unique along with its presentation. What would *you* say to the revered genius? Renate's book really includes you in her conversations with the man for the ages.

Robert G. Chaney
March 12, 2003

Introduction

This story developed from one particular letter in my personal journal. Before writing this letter, I was deeply frustrated and stuck in a mode of just getting up and coping with life's many daily challenges. The joy of life had somehow escaped me. I was tired of being a slave to crippling fears, which is often the cause of the symptoms of emotional pain and suffering. I started to ask, 'Where do fears originate?' There must be more to life than this! There must be some way I can overcome the effects of what seemed like a roller coaster ride of pleasure and pain. What is the secret to being happy? I had so many questions and decided it was time I started a dialogue with Dr. Albert Schweitzer, whom I had allowed to become my spiritual teacher.

I see myself as an average person who has always been curious and interested in learning. My early circumstances had not allowed me the privilege of a formal higher education. My best and most *formative schooling, seen only in hindsight, has been life and the many experiences* that were presented to me on my path.

My diplomas are the books I have written and the books I have read, understood and applied to my life. It is my deepest desire to be of help. This story may lead us to wake up to who we really are—souls, seeking experiences that will lead to recognition and growth on the path, leading us to a deeper awareness. Recognizing our own ignorance and fears, replacing them with love, reverence, tolerance, humility, faith, hope, gratitude and finding the courage to take responsibility for our experiences, is part of the process. This process will eventually lead us to self-mastery, to more freedom and independent thought, and finally, to a deeper understanding of our selves and others, through compassion and love.

While writing I recognized that 'Know thyself', is the message, the path, the way and the goal. It is the first step we will eventually take—it is also the beginning of understanding the Laws of Life. Looking outside for life's answers by choosing glamour, excitement and material possessions had become less and less fulfilling for me. It kept me aimlessly running in circles. I discovered that until we make the decision to investigate the physical, emotional, mental and spiritual aspects of our own nature, many answers to this puzzle elude us. Often, this stage is preceded by asking ourselves a few fundamental questions about life, including: "Is that all there is?" There is an inherent magic in asking ourselves these and other questions. Once the internal curiosity is aroused and a dialogue is established, the answers appear all by themselves, seemingly out of nowhere. Will more of us eventually gain the insight and courage needed to look at our selves and ask some questions?

An internal revelation occurred. Slowly at first—I began to see a process. My soul started to stir and my intuition gave me a glimpse of the meaning of the phrase, '*the peace that passeth all understanding*'.

When this inner peace is *experienced* even once, we start searching. We discover that all the tools are inside. As we tame our small ego and still our restless mind, we discover that we are more than our external personality. We are something far greater, far more beautiful and far more powerful. We are individual souls seeking experiences through which to grow and eventually obtain liberation. Only then do we begin to recognize the value of transcending our fears, our lower nature, our lower mind and our lower personal self. We begin to see that a large part of the secret of life is found first in self-observation, which eventually turns into self-realization. This includes the recognition of the value of wisdom, leading us to an internal transformation. I found that the spiritual aspect of our nature, our soul, is often neglected and misunderstood, and it is always trying to get our attention—to guide us. All we have to do is become still and listen!

As we allow our soul to become the driver of our physical vehicle, one moment at a time, we discover powers inherent and hidden in all of us.

The power to love.

The power to see with new eyes.

The power to be inspired.

The power to aspire.

The power to create.

The power to become more than we are presently aware of reveals itself as we open the door to a new level of '*Being*'. How often had I heard the words, 'The teacher appears when the student is ready', yet, not fully understood this phenomenon. The message is heard when the student is ready to hear the message, not a moment sooner and not a moment later.

The message has always been there as part of the Ageless Wisdom Teachings. It can be found in every religion, providing we look deep enough. It can be found in every mystery school, in every ancient myth and in every experience we encounter. It seems to be waiting for us to reach a certain level of dissatisfaction, discontent, disillusionment and disappointment. Until then, even if the message is shouted from the highest rooftops, we will not hear it.

The teachers are already there, waiting for us to find the courage to reach out and start to ask ourselves some of the more profound and deeper questions about life. All a teacher can be is an example, or a signpost on the path. The path must be understood and walked voluntarily by each student.

This is a story about a teacher and student relationship. It is a story about where this relationship has led me, and where it continues to lead me today. This is the essence of this personal journey, captured in my journal. A true teacher can inspire and become an *ideal*, leading by example *only*. This is not to be confused with the word idol, which is an empty lifeless symbol. A teacher is like an older brother who has walked and lived through life's experiences. He understands our daily struggle—yet, he knows that he can't do the needed work for us. He can only give us encouragement and support. A good teacher knows he can lead us to the water, but he can't make us drink. A teacher helps us to help ourselves. A good teacher will *not* give us a fish if we are hungry, he will teach us how to fish.

For me, Dr. Albert Schweitzer exemplified all of these human qualities. He was a mystic with a highly developed sense of self. Yet, he was above all, what we would call a 'practical' man, a man ruled by reason and a keen intellect. He understood our struggle.

As we awaken, we begin to see that learning and growing are our own responsibilities. This recognition is a huge step towards our freedom and independent thinking. Looking at myself was the most painful and yet, the most liberating experience I encountered. Therein lies the paradox, the riddle we must solve.

I began to see that all growth is spiritual. The spark, the momentum, the energy—the life force—the will to live—is in everything and in everyone, and can be found in all of the kingdoms of nature. They are the mineral, plant, animal and the human kingdom. Are there still higher kingdoms? Isn't it only our present limited perception and old conditioning which keeps us from recognizing the divine? If, 'as above—so below' is true, it stands to reason that there must be still Higher Kingdoms, higher dimensions and realms beyond the human, Kingdoms we are not as yet aware of. Do only enlightened beings or mystics get a glimpse of these

Kingdoms, or will all of mankind eventually evolve, increasing our vibrations enough to allow entrance to these realms?

I believe that 'Beings' like Dr. Albert Schweitzer are sent to humanity from time to time, whose primary aim is to aid humanity in its evolution.

The following letters are a part of my personal journey, indicative of where I've been and how I got to where I am today, thanks to teachers like Dr. Albert Schweitzer.

The Truths inherent in ancient teachings are experienced relative to our growth, relative to the stages of an individual's awareness along the evolutionary road of life. I see changing attitudes, leading to deeper perceptions all around me. I see it in some current movies, in the new resurgence of spiritual books and movements dedicated to finding the High Road, to elevating our human consciousness and to piercing the veil of ignorance. There is no right or wrong path, there is only the path.

Contemplation and self-reflection are the first step. This reflection must be experienced in the deepest recesses of each person's heart. Everything in nature evolves and is governed by Universal Law. This Law governs all that exists in our manifested world, including nature, science, religion, space, mathematics, physics, philosophy and our physical body.

In our essence we are spiritual and only by going within do we discover this knowledge. Getting to know *who* we are, what our purpose is, and where we are going. This becomes the 'quest'. This inner evolution commences once the search to know who we are has begun. It is the search for the beloved, our true self—our spiritual Self—our Real Self. Furthermore, our level of recognition, perception and understanding is relative to our soul growth. Yes Dr. Einstein, in the finite world we live in "it is all relative"! The first grade is not better than the ninth, both are needed to complete the curriculum. It is not better or worse, only different.

It's as if a spark in my heart had been ignited and turned into a flame, becoming the light within showing me the way. The desire 'to know' has been awakened, becoming my light in the darkness. That's when I discovered that I and humanity are one, comprised of individual spiritual beings on an evolutionary journey, having an individual and a collective earthly experience in order to grow and evolve. Through each painful experience a lesson is recognized. On some level we begin to sense the need for transformation, felt as the need for freedom, wholeness, self-reliance and liberation.

We are all interconnected on this journey and will ultimately recognize that we must first heal ourselves in order to experience an inner level of peace. Only then can we help and encourage others with our passion to know Truth.

I propose the idea, that soon more and more people will begin to understand this process and humanity will reach the point of 'critical mass' needed to change our collective consciousness. Until then, peace can only be obtained one person at a time and I know that the process starts with me right here—right now.

Publishing this material was not my reason for writing. Only after showing this journal to a friend and being encouraged to do so, did I take this step. My fears and shyness will have to take a back seat, as I have decided that it may help others, who just like me, may be struggling with certain painful issues in life. To help and share is my only motivation. If it resonates with something in your own heart, use it. Become a free thinker and please remember to allow your heart to decide what is right and true for yourself. What the heart will recognize, can't be captured with words.

R. z T.
January 14, 2004

Preface

Dear Dr. Schweitzer,

Today is Sunday. I got up especially early this morning and decided it was the right time to start a dialogue with you. I want to tell you so many things, and just don't know where to begin. My mind is flooded with inspiration and gratitude. The time for procrastination is behind me. As I stare at the blank pages I notice that the fear of failure is leaving me, because life is not about failure or success, it's about doing your best! Did you feel this sense of surety when you embarked on your new journey in life? My mind is filled with a sense of purpose and confidence. I have not always felt this way, and this is actually part of my story.

Like many new students of metaphysics, I stumbled and fell on numerous occasions. The growing pains at times seemed unbearable. Where did I get the courage to dust myself off and start again? The path to awareness is not always paved with smooth stones; nevertheless, here I am, wanting in my own way to give homage and meaning to your life and your healing message.

I discovered so many interesting things about you on my path. Others may find this information helpful and noteworthy, and begin to experience something new internally, by having gotten to know you. This is certainly true for me.

Your life has inspired so many, and I feel it is time to rekindle your spirit for a new generation. Our generation is largely unaware of the great accomplishments of your life. I find that many, even of my generation, have somehow forgotten or only dimly remember you.

What is my objective in looking at your words and the example of your life— again? After all, you must be aware that there are already several biographies of your life in existence. My story does not focus on your life as a doctor alone, so in this respect some will call it different.

I found myself puzzled as to what motivated you. What or who inspired the many volumes you wrote on the state of civilization and humanity? What is the mystery you left for us to ponder?

My objectives are as follows:

First and foremost I want the world to see the other side of your personality. The mystical or transcendental aspect is often overlooked or forgotten when viewing your accomplishments. You followed your intuition on most occasions, allowing yourself to be led to a destiny that even you had not imagined for yourself. What is intuition? It will be my great challenge to further examine this peculiar ability, as it becomes clearer in my own mind. You called it by a different name. You referred to this phenomenon as your 'small inner voice'. We in America refer to it as intuition. It is only a word, but do people really understand its meaning? I will examine your charisma, your powerful will and magnetic personality. What is charisma?

One of the enigmas of your life is the great turn you took at the age of thirty. What happened to you then? You had several doctorate degrees. Why did you give up a career in the fields of theology, philosophy or music? You had studied and researched these subjects so diligently and with great integrity. Most of the books you wrote on these subjects are still in print today. Yet, at the age of thirty you decided to become a medical doctor and devoted your life to healing the less fortunate, the ignored and much exploited people of Africa.

Your writing clarifies your understanding of the Laws of Nature and the Laws of the Cosmos, such as: 'The more you give—the more you receive' and 'He that loses his life shall find it'. I will look at the wisdom of some of these laws and show how you practiced them. Was it your intent to teach us a part of the mystery?

Second, I want you to see that your efforts in teaching and writing about your Truth, as you had discovered it, have not been in vain. I studied your books to the best of my ability and must admit to being filled with awe and humility as I begin to understand the immensity of what you had *thought* about and *created* in your lifetime.

The moments of doubt, fear and weakness still rear their ugly head on the odd occasion, but you certainly have taught me to think freely, to think deeply and clearly, eliminating these feelings more and more from my consciousness. You also taught me to embrace uncertainty and to remain flexible.

One of your great contributions to mankind has been your constant reminder for us to *become* and *remain free thinkers*, to take responsibility for our own life, and not to blindly accept the dogma and conditioning we are exposed to. You questioned everything and were never afraid to form your own conclusions and to share your truth, as you discovered it. Did you see a bigger picture?

I wondered and became curious about so many things in life. You have led me to independent thought and actions. You had recognized that service to humanity is a law of life. Is that a part of the secret? What are these Universal Laws, where are they hidden? I felt so small while viewing your accomplishments, yet, I became more and more curious.

You are, and will always be my hero, my inspiration and mentor. It is my intention to dedicate this journal to you, and to all the dedicated individuals who volunteered to work by your side, some even without monetary rewards.

My third objective is to tell the story of your life from my personal perspective, as it has taught me so much about myself over the years. What you did for me can't be measured in ordinary terms. It is my deepest wish to touch the minds and hearts of others, who just like me, may be searching for the deeper meaning of life. Perhaps I will ignite a flame in the heart of others, creating the desire to want to know more about you and your life.

You have become a perfect example for me. Your speeches and sermons had left an impression on all fortunate enough to be present at their delivery. I can only surmise at this point what the people had felt by examining their responses in hindsight. You are my inspiration during the process of writing this journal and I thank you from the bottom of my heart. You had walked the path leading to the temple of Wisdom. This will be the story of how I got to know you and my quest to understand the *meaning* of your life.

My fourth objective is to show how your compassionate and humanitarian nature liked to appeal to the 'average thinking' person. I am motivated by the same desire. I want to present your discoveries again, this time for my grandchildren and those, who just like me may be interested in unraveling the mystery of the life of Jesus. I am not a religious person in the usual sense of the word, because I realize that religion is man made. Therefore, I use the word with great hesitation and trepidation. Words—can be so limiting and can be easily misunderstood, yet words, is all I have at my disposal at the present time.

I became a student of metaphysics, which lead me to the question, 'Is there a deeper meaning, an *esoteric meaning* behind the life of Jesus?' Is his message fully understood by the clergy of Christianity today? Was Jesus a man or was he a God? While searching for the truth about your faith you studied this subject and came to certain conclusions. Could the message of the life of Jesus have been about the future evolution of humanity? If so, it behooves us to take another look at what religion is and how religion is taught today.

My fifth objective is to show that we are all evolving on several levels simultaneously, on the emotional, the mental and the spiritual. Who were your teachers, who were your role models, your ideals? Who inspired you in order for you to become a living example for us, a role model for what the future man will be able to perceive and accomplish?

Knowing the truth about creation and humanity as the foundation is not enough. This truth must be lived and experienced. I know this knowledge will be sought out by every individual himself—through experience—recognition—and going within for the answers. Yes, it means we are alone on this path, this journey of discovery when we start to ask the following questions:

Who am I? Where did I come from? What am I doing here? Where am I going? How do I get there?

My sixth objective is to show that it is possible to access a deeper level of understanding without a collection of degrees or diplomas.

I, like you, struggled with ideas and concepts that only became clearer once I freed my mind from 'thinking' and experienced 'being'. I am self-motivated, self-taught and self-educated, only driven by my desire to grow spiritually, to know and experience the meaning of life and its purpose on this plane of reality—our world.

Your statement, **"I've made my life my argument"** had for some time been a puzzle to me. Only now do I recognize what you meant.

My quest is not for happiness in the usual sense. Happiness, like everything else in the finite world, has a beginning and an end. Happiness is just another emotion that is subject to change.

My seventh objective is the one that is closest to my heart. It is to mature spiritually, to take responsibility for my life and to make service my goal. But first I want to know myself, become honest with myself, heal myself and be true to myself. I want to know and experience peace and feel joy more often. *'The peace that passeth all understanding'* is often talked about and referred to in your writings. Will I ever experience this peace?

All I know is that I am on the path of self-discovery. A path that is at times hard and painful, sometimes filled with joy and laughter.

A path sprinkled with contradictions and magic at the same time. I would love to become an instrument of that peace.

What tools will I employ? Thoughts and Words? You had inspired me not only with your thoughts and words, but I was most inspired by your ethics, your character, your values and your courageous actions. Knowing words are limiting in describing certain experiences, it becomes my greatest challenge to describe what I am referring to.

Some of the ancient knowledge as I discovered it, is timeless and eternal and it has had a wonderful healing affect on my body, emotions, and my mind. I have already created a new life for myself by writing you this letter, opening my heart, my mind and soul to you.

Independence and freedom—before only dreamt about—is now becoming a reality in my life. I am referring to independent thoughts and actions. Dare I spell it inde PEN DANCE...?

In closing this letter I would like to express my deepest gratitude to you for not only inspiring me at this crucial juncture in my life, but for also inspiring millions of people before me. Did they feel the same passion for learning as I did? It seems at times as if my hair is on fire, wanting to know the many secrets still hidden from my view. The secrets not only of science and nature, but also the secrets of *Life, Light, Wisdom, Love and Compassion*. Could they possible be connected?

Your love and compassion moved mountains in your time. Perhaps it is time for humanity as a whole to expand our awareness and raise our level of consciousness. You have certainly proven that it is possible! As I review the immense body of your earthly accomplishments it is my intention to contribute to someone who may read these journal entries. For instance, give encouragement to someone—who just like me—was searching in the dark. I didn't start reading your words until twenty years after you passed to the other side.

As I begin to get a glimpse of the unity of all existence I find that your quest is not so unique after all. The discovery that this is the journey of every man and woman, the journey of every soul, almost takes my breath away.

I ask that you be with me while I write you these letters, and please continue to inspire me, as your great teachers inspired you. For this I give thanks, as in great humility I will attempt to tell the story of how you came to be part of my life and inspiration, and to prove that the light of your soul is still burning brightly. Could this be my SUNday?

Your forever grateful student, *R*
Sunday, July 22, 2001

Part I

Experience

"Never say there is nothing beautiful in the world any more. There is always something to make you wonder in the shape of a tree, the trembling of a leaf."[1]

Albert Schweitzer

"True knowledge leading to wisdom can only be found in experience, everything else is just information."

Albert Einstein

1

Remembering

Dear Dr. Schweitzer,

Today is Monday, July 23rd, in the year two thousand and one. Coming in from watering my plants on the terrace at this early hour, it is 4:30 A.M., I can already feel the Florida humidity building. Just another hot and sticky Florida summer day, or is it? As I review my letter to you yesterday, I feel my life is changing.

The idea for the story I am about to tell you was originally conceived in the spring of 1999. It was a story about you. A story about your life, and what you were able to create in the ninety years you spent on this planet. A lot has happened to me since. Life seems to change very quickly for me now. Life is teaching me to be more flexible. Is this what these letters will be about? Nothing ever stays the same?

On this Monday morning, I have decided to start my letter with a quotation I read a lifetime ago, or so it seems at times. I read Jacquelyn Berrill's book, entitled '*Albert Schweitzer: Man of Mercy*', for the first time in the spring of 1986. This book is now out of print. I will take the liberty to quote from the first page in chapter one. When I first read these words they fanned my imagination and curiosity. I would like to share her words with you now:

"The time had come. The train from Copenhagen pulled into the Eastend Station at Oslo, in Norway, and a large man, stooped with age, stepped out into the raw, cold November air. The excited murmuring of the crowd rose momentarily and then ceased entirely. Albert Schweitzer, the famous doctor of the African jungle, the man of mercy, carrying his old, familiar, battered, metal suitcase, had come to receive the Nobel Peace Prize. The station was packed with people, rich and poor, old and young, who had gathered to see the man who had given up a life of ease to devote his great talents to the welfare of the natives of Darkest Africa, a man who had received his doctor's degrees in theology, philosophy and music before he even began to study for the medical degree which he was required to secure if he was to serve his fellowmen in the way they most needed. The crowd saw a powerfully built man with a large, untrimmed mustache and unruly hair, now snow white. His eyes were wise and piercing, his smile friendly, and the people were deeply moved. Applause filled the station as he stepped forward to shake hands with everyone who was there."[2]

As this scene becomes clear in my mind's eye, I can almost feel the cold Norwegian air while sitting here at my desk in Florida. I can feel the awe and respect that transfixed the crowd and know how those people must have felt.

I have decided not to follow in the footsteps of what is considered to be the 'conventional' style of writing. I am new at this, and presently don't consider writing my vocation. Writing is my hobby at the moment. Ever since I wrote my first poem in 1985, I have had this wish to become a writer. However, I discovered that a wish alone is not enough, when it comes to desiring a change and having a new vision.

What follows is a list of your accomplishments, compiled and condensed, at the beginning of my story, so whoever may read this letter will get a glimpse of the meaning of the words 'higher consciousness.' Perhaps, this will shed some light on my motivation for writing to you, brighten the way for others not familiar with you and your chosen life path. Here is the list, a condensed résumé of your life in chronological order:

1875 January 14

You were born in Kaysersberg, a small medieval village, which before World War I was part of Germany. During the year 1875 your father became pastor at Günsbach, located a few miles south of Kaysersberg in the Munster Valley. He moved the family to this location when you were only six months old. You were a sickly infant and your mother spent many sleepless nights watching over you. In this picturesque valley, which is now part of Alsace, France, you experienced your childhood and youth before the turn of the century.

You were born under the astrological sign of Capricorn. In my mind I picture the symbol of Capricorn. A mountain goat, climbing sure footed up a steep and rocky mountain, searching for food, somewhere between earth and heaven. Combining the numbers of your birth date I arrived at the number nine, which in esoteric numerology is the number of completion, the number representing the eventual attainment of man and humanity. The meaning of this number, only became clear to me very recently.

1880

You attended the Günsbach village school followed by primary school (Realschule) in Munster. Your mother shed many tears over your poor grades, wondering whether you would ever mature. You were a young dreamer, and found school difficult during the first few years. It wasn't until a teacher took you under his wing, teaching you how to study, that you became interested in academic pursuits, fueled by your early curiosity and your own imagination. You may not have shown great initial enthusiasm for schooling, however, you soon discovered that one of your talents was music. You learned to play the piano at the age of five then graduated to mastering a more challenging instrument, namely the organ. You gave your first public performance during your father's church services, filling in as a substitute for the organist at the age of nine, in the village church in Günsbach. J. S. Bach was the composer of many spiritual works for various instruments, including the organ. Included in Bach's immense body of compositions are many inspirational hymns. Your natural talents and your affinity for the organ began at an unusually early age. Not only the sounds—but the vibrations produced by this magnificent instrument left an impression on you at that early stage of your development. What is *vibration*? What are *frequencies*, and what is *resonance*? Just the other day someone told me that the sound of the organ is the closest sound to the human voice.

1893 June 18

After eight years of schooling at the Muhlhouse Secondary School, at eighteen you passed your matriculation examination for the University of Strasbourg.

October

You took your first trip to Paris, where you chose to study the organ under Widor.

November

You began your study at the University of Strasbourg choosing *theology, philosophy and musical theory,* along with the study of languages, namely Latin, Greek and Hebrew while living in the theological Seminary of St. Thomas. You were already fluent in German and French. While at this university you wrote your first book, a small brochure in French, based on the life and activity of Eugene Munch, your former organ teacher at Mulhouse, who died of typhoid fever at the beginning of your career. It was the beginning of the pursuit of one of your passions—writing. Amazingly, you were only eighteen, an age when most teenagers are confused about what they want to be, not knowing which goals to pursue.

1894 – 1895

Since military service was mandatory in your time, you entered the service at nineteen, joining the infantry regiment 143. Not leaving your books behind, you used this time to study and formulate your ideas about the Bible, the Gospels of the New Testament in particular.

1896

At the age of twenty-one you already knew what your future path would be, and said:

"I would consider myself justified in living until I was 30 for science and art, in order to devote myself from that time forward to the direct service of humanity."

1897 Autumn

You wrote a thesis required of all candidates for the first examination in theology using the topic prescribed by the faculty. "The Idea of the Last Supper in Daniel Schleiermacher, Compared with the ideas of Luther, Zwingli, and Calvin." You were already digging deeper than most students, searching for the truth behind the Gospels. You were a free thinker, finding your own truth and forming your own conclusions. As a result of your inquiring and open mind, you studied philosophy, perhaps to gain a deeper understanding, searching for the missing pieces of the puzzle, as presented to us in the Gospels.

1898 May 6

At the age of twenty-three you passed your first theological examination before the faculty, keeping some of your newly discovered ideas to yourself, knowing that this was not the time to rock the boat. You had to conform in order to pass these tests. Did you know that certain truths would reveal themselves eventually? You somehow knew that this was not the appropriate setting and the appropriate time to voice your findings—your discoveries. Had you started to question the authority of the church? Had you discovered a fallacy in our historical conception of Jesus?

Summer

You continued to study philosophy at the University of Strasbourg under professors Ziegler and Windelband. At the end of the summer you proposed to Professor Ziegler the theme of your doctoral thesis: *"A study of Kant's philosophy of religion in relation to the different stages of what seemed to him its constant evolution".*

From the beginning of October you spent six months in Paris where you had an active social life and received organ tuition form Widor, secretly enhancing your technique with piano instructions from Marie Jaell.

1899 Autumn-Spring

You studied at the Sorbonne in Paris, in your spare time devoting yourself to further organ studies under Widor.

April-July

You spent these months in Berlin for the study of philosophy and spent many hours honing your skills on the organ.

End of July

You received your Ph.D. at Strasbourg after the examination in philosophy.

December

You were appointed Lehr-Vicar (*curate*) at the church of St. Nicholas in Strasbourg, in compliance with the rule that required a student to serve in a church for a period between his first and second theological examinations.

End of December

You were only twenty-four when your book entitled *'The Religious Philosophy of Kant from the 'Critique of Pure Reason'* *'Religion Within the Bounds of Mere Reason'* was published by

J.C.B Mohr at Tübingen. Did you understand this *early* that religion must be harmonized with philosophy in order for it to make any sense to us on a deeper level? You dared to ask fundamental questions such as, 'What was our faith based on?' and 'What is the truth behind our old belief systems?'

1900 July 15

You passed the second theological examination before a commission of learned pastors.

July 21

You obtained your doctorate degree (*licentiate*) in theology with your study of the Last Supper.

September 23

You were ordained at St. Nicholas as a regular curate.

1901 May 1-September 30

You received the provisional appointment as Principal of the Protestant Theological Seminary.

Your book entitled *'The Mystery of the Kingdom of God'* was published by Mohr at Tübingen, and ignored by most scholars and theologians—the 'intelligentsia' of your time.

1902

You were a lecturer in the faculty of theology in Strasbourg and began writing a study of the life of J.S. Bach and his music.

1903 October 1

You received a permanent appointment as Principal of the Protestant Theological Seminary, and moved from the city to their official quarters on the Embankment of St. Thomas. You searched for a life that has purpose, hoping to adopt orphaned children neglected by society. You searched for your own field to be of service.

1905 January 14

Around your *thirtieth birthday,* you decided to devote the rest of your life to the service of others. Your chosen field of service was to help the natives of Equatorial Africa, having been inspired by an article written by the French Missionary Society. In order to accomplish this you had to become a doctor of medicine, because doctors were desperately needed in this part of the world. You did not say that your decision was based on 'enlightenment' and any particular experience. However, all I have researched and learned about this phenomenon, point to this event very clearly. You immediately notified relatives, friends and acquaintances of your intentions. They were dumbfounded and tried to influence you to change your mind. To no avail! You were very sure of your path and your strong will made itself known to others. You were aroused by feelings of *deep compassion* for the suffering of humanity, the plight of the native African in Equatorial Africa, having been moved by a statue in the city of Colmar. In your youth you had been deeply affected by your visits to a statue, by the sculptor Bartholi, of an African male revealing a tortured expression.

You not only thought about it, you actually took the necessary physical action to follow your feelings. You allowed no one and nothing to interfere with your convictions. This shows me the strength of your character and the strength of your will. You became a powerhouse of determination. Others may not have agreed with you, but you had earned their respect. Your ethics based on a higher core value system was functioning perfectly, directing all of your thoughts and actions.

Your book *'J.S. Bach'* was published by Costallant in Paris.

October 13
You made known your decision to serve as a missionary doctor and entered into discussion with the Paris Missionary Society. Your books, *'Indian Thought and its Development'* and *'The Philosophy of Civilization'*, are among the most visionary and profound books I've ever read. The ideas for the books *'The Mysticism of the Apostle Paul'*, and *The Philosophy of Civilization'*, must have already been brewing in your mind.

1906
You resigned from the directorship of the Theological Seminary and began your studies as a medical student at the University of Strasbourg. Your second book *'The Quest of the Historical Jesus'* which was a further explanation of your first book, was published by Mohr at Tübingen, and your treatise *German and French Organ-Building and Organ-Playing* was published by Breitkopf and Hartel in Leibzig.

1909 May
You gave an address to the organ section of the third Congress of the International Society of Music in Vienna, and played a major role in formulating the International Regulations for Organ Building recommended by the organ section.

1911
Your book *'Paul and His Interpreters'* was published by Mohr in Tübingen.

Autumn

You played the organ for Widor's '*Second Symphony for Organ and Orchestra*' at the Festival of French Music at Munich.

Autumn-December

You passed your examination in medicine at Strasbourg at the age of thirty-six, followed by a period of complete exhaustion. You had accomplished what you needed to do in order to be of service to humanity.

1912 Spring

You resigned from your post as instructor at the university and as preacher at St. Nicholas.

June 18

On this date you married Helene Bresslau, the daughter of a Strasbourg historian. Afterwards, you retired to your father's house in Günsbach to work on the second edition of '*Paul and His Interpreters*', assisted by your wife Helene. Helene, a nurse by training, was the perfect partner. Having served as the editor and proofreader of your manuscripts she was later to work at your side in the hospital. Friends and family began to support your unusual efforts with donations, gifts of money and their time. Your demonstration of values was so noble and so admirable, that everyone found you hard to resist.

1913 February

Having completed your year of internship, and having finished your thesis, you received your degree in medicine.

March 21 Good Friday

When you and Helene departed from Günsbach, the train station was filled with friends and well-wishers. The next day you embarked from Bordeaux for Africa, where you arrived on April 16. You established a hospital on the grounds of the Lambaréné station of the Paris Missionary Society. Your book '*The Psychiatrical Study of Jesus*', was published. This book, which was the thesis you submitted for the needed medical degree, reveals your field of interest and explains your keen interest in the search for the spiritual nature of man, which was so instrumental in shaping your destiny. These values became the essence of your character. The second edition of '*Paul and His Interpreters*' was published by Mohr at Tübingen.

1914 August-November

Seventeen months after arriving and establishing a clinic in Africa, during the outbreak of World War I, you and your wife

Helene were interned at Lambaréné as enemy aliens, because you were both still German subjects in a French Colony. During the leisure time forced upon you, you began your work on *The Philosophy of Civilization*.

1915 September

While on a 200-kilometer journey up the Ogowe River to N'Gomo, the words **"Reverence for Life"** suddenly came to you as the elementary and universal conception of ethics (values) for which you had been searching. Your whole philosophy of civilization was subsequently based on this principle.

1917 September

You and your wife were transferred back to France as prisoners of war, held in military barracks in Bordeaux, then transferred to a civilian internment camp at Garaison (Upper Pyrenees). You had an attack of dysentery, which you treated yourself with what was available, but which left after-effects, later necessitating surgical operations.

1918 Spring

You were transferred to St. Remy de Provence, and served as a doctor during the daytime, working on your book *The Philosophy of Civilization* during the evening hours.

End of July

You were able to go back to Alsace under an exchange of prisoners program and you returned to Günsbach.

October

You were very aware of your responsibility to earn money for your family and for the venture in Africa, accepting a position as assistant at the dermatology clinic. You were also re-appointed to your post as curate at St. Nicholas in Strasbourg.

1919 January 14

Your daughter Rhena was born on your forty-fourth birthday. You gave your first sermons on the theme of '*respect for all life*'.

1920 Spring

You delivered a series of lectures at Uppsala in Sweden, using as your subject '*The problems of world and life affirmations*' and '*Ethics in philosophy and world-religions*'. You gave further organ concerts and lectures in Sweden to pay off the debts you had incurred for the hospital in Lambaréné.

You also received an honorary doctorate degree from the Theological faculty in Zürich, Switzerland and were offered a position which you declined. Your book '*On The Edge of the Primeval Forest*' in which you described your first impressions and experiences of Africa was published at Uppsala, Sweden.

1921 April

You gave up both positions in Strasbourg and returned to Günsbach, where you were appointed vicar to your father. This allowed you to work quietly on your book '*The Philosophy of Civilization*' and to continue your study and writing about music.

1923 Spring

You gave lectures on philosophy at Prague University. Your book '*The Philosophy of Civilization*' was published by C.H. Beck in Munich and by Paul Haupt in Bern, in two volumes, entitled '*The Decay and Restoration of Civilization*' and '*Civilization and Ethics*'. In the same year, your book '*Christianity and the World-Religions*' was published by Allen and Unwin in London.

1924 February

'*Memoirs of Childhood and Youth*', giving us a glimpse into your inner world of childhood experiences and your early environment, was published by Allen and Unwin in London, that same year.

February 14

You left Strasbourg for Africa, while your wife Helene and your daughter remained in Europe. The internment had left its mark on your partner's health and compelled her to recuperate in Europe. She stayed there until the advent of the Nazis in 1933.

April 19

You began your second sojourn in Africa, which lasted until July 21, 1927. You needed to reconstruct the hospital, which had fallen into ruin, and later you transferred the facility to a new and larger site at Adolinanongo, where the new buildings were constructed of hardwood and corrugated iron. During this period of rebuilding you had to abandon all your literary work. In the morning you worked as a doctor and in the afternoon as a common laborer and carpenter.

The number of your patients constantly increased and you were obliged to ask for two more doctors and two extra nurses. You were able to keep up your musical practices on your piano with organ pedals. Reports of your work in Africa were sent to Europe in the form of letters to friends and supporters. These letters were published, in three small volumes, by Beck in Munich and Haupt, in Bern.

1925

You received the honorary degree of doctor of philosophy from the University of Prague in absentia. In Africa, you started clearing the land for a larger hospital. You planted fruit trees and vegetables in order to provide the nutrition so often lacking in the diets of your patients. The jungle had to be cut back every few months as it repeatedly threatened to encroach and overtake your garden. You could be found engaged in this physical labor during the short growing season.

1927

Your new hospital was set up 3 kilometers upstream from the Ogowe River.

July

You returned to Europe giving concerts and lectures in order to raise funds to cover the operating expenses of your jungle hospital. Your patients not only received free medical care, they also received free food while under your care. You gave lectures and concert tours in Sweden, Denmark, Holland, Germany, Switzerland, England, and Czechoslovakia. Recordings for gramophone were made in London. During this time you devoted all your spare time to your next book, *'The Mysticism of Paul the Apostle'*. This book was completed on the boat that carried you back to Africa in December 1929.

1928 August 28

You received the 'Goethe Prize' from the City of Frankfurt and delivered an address in which you describe your indebtedness to Goethe. Many scholars later believed Goethe to have had extraordinary insight into the human psyche and often referred to him as being 'mystical'. You decided to build a home in Günsbach with the prize money, but only after you had raised the equivalent amount for the hospital in Africa.

1929 December 26

You began your third sojourn in Africa, which ended on January 7, 1932. During this period you wrote your autobiography, *'Out of My Life and Thought'*, which was first published by Felix Meiner in Leipzig in 1931.

1931

You received the honorary degrees of Doctor of Divinity and Doctor of Music from the University of Edinburgh.

1932

You received the honorary degrees of Doctor of Philosophy from Oxford University and Doctor of Laws from St. Andrews University.

February

You returned to Europe, giving lectures and concerts in Holland, England, Sweden Germany and Switzerland. You worked on the third volume of '*The Philosophy of Civilization*'.

1933 April 21

You began your fourth sojourn in Africa, which lasted until January 11, 1934. All of your *leisure* time was devoted to the third volume of your book on philosophy.

1934 Autumn

You gave the Hibbert lectures at Manchester College in Oxford, under the subject '*Religion in Modern Civilization*'.

November

You gave the Gifford Lectures in Edinburgh, in which you endeavored to trace the progress of human thought from the great thinkers of India, China, Greece and Persia. Your chapter on the evolution of Indian thought grew to such an extent that you decided to publish it as a separate book. '*INDIAN THOUGHT AND ITS DEVELOPMENT*' was published by Beck in Munich in 1934.

1935 February 26

You began your fifth journey to Africa, which ended August 22, 1935.

November

You gave your second course of Gifford Lectures, followed by lectures and concerts in England.

1936

Your treatise '*INDIAN THOUGHT AND ITS DEVELOPMENT*' was published in English by Hodder and Stoughton in London.

You worked on your philosophy book, and in October recorded organ music for Columbia Records in London on the organ of St. Aurelias's at Strasbourg.

1937 February 18

You began your sixth journey to Africa, which ended on January 10, 1939. You had carried with you the manuscript for your philosophy book, believing that now at last you could finish it, but the increasing responsibilities of the hospital left you little time.

1938

You wrote the book *'From My African Notebook'* filled with anecdotes based upon the ideas and the lives of the natives, which was published by Meiner in Leipzig that same year.

1939 January 10

You left for Europe in the hope of completing your third volume of *'The Philosophy of Civilization'*.

February

You arrived in Europe, staying only for twelve days, because you sensed that war was unavoidable and might break out at any moment. You had just enough time to organize the supply of medicines and settle the urgent matters of equipment before returning to Africa.

March 3

You began your seventh sojourn in Africa, which lasted ten years, ending in October 1948. During the first two years of the war, you were able to work continuously on your writings but afterwards the scarcity of hospital personnel made it necessary for you to devote yourself almost exclusively to the care of the sick and to other hospital duties. The fighting factions in Lambaréné respected the hospital's neutrality. Towards the end of 1945 you wrote an account of the war years at Lambaréné 1939-1945.

1941

Your wife was able to escape from Europe, now under Nazi control, and joined you in Africa after a difficult journey.

1948 September

You returned to Europe, visiting your wife at Königsfeld, seeing your four grandchildren for the first time. You spent the rest of your time in your home in Günsbach, working on a theological book and on the third volume of *'The Philosophy of Civilization'*.

1949 June

You arrived in New York for your first visit to America, during which you received an honorary degree of Doctor of Laws from the University of Chicago in the Rockefeller Memorial Chapel. You also visited Boston and a few other cities, after which you returned to Günsbach. In the USA you were recognized as **"the greatest man of the 20th Century"**.

October

You began your eighth sojourn in Africa, which ended in May 1951. You had intensified your work for those afflicted with leprosy, using the discoveries of American medical science.

1950

You were made a Chevalier of the Legion of Honor. Your book *'Story of my Pelican'* (Ein Pelikan erzählt aus seinem Leben) was published.

1951 May-December

On September 15th you received the Peace Prize in Germany. The 10.000DM prize was given to you by the West German Association of Book Publishers and Book Sellers at Frankfurt, in recognition of your efforts in promoting world peace. You turned this money over to German refugees and destitute writers.

December

You were elected to be a member of the French Academy of Moral and Political Sciences.

December

You embarked on your ninth voyage to Africa, which ended July 1952.

1952 February 27

You were awarded the Prince Charles Medal by King Gustav Adolf of Sweden, for your great humanitarian achievements.

November

You began your tenth trip back to Africa, which ended in May 1954. You began the construction of a new village for Africans suffering from leprosy and dedicated this village to the memory of your mother and father.

1953 October 30

At the age of seventy-eight you won the Nobel Peace Prize. The Nobel Peace Prize was awarded to you in absentia, and was accepted on your behalf by the French ambassador to Norway. You announced that the prize money, roughly $36,000 would be used toward the expenses of completing the construction of the leprosy hospital, a project you had started in the spring of 1953.

1954 May

You returned to Europe for six months. At the end of July you gave your last official concert in homage to Bach at the Church of St. Thomas in Strasbourg. You were made a foreign honorary member of the American Academy of Arts and Sciences.

May-December

You were in Europe, ending your journey with a visit to Oslo, Norway on that cold November day. On November 4, 1954, you finally accepted the Nobel Peace Prize in person. You then delivered the long awaited acceptance speech in the presence of King Gustav Adolf of Sweden, entitled *'The Problem of Peace in the World of Today'*.

1955

On January 14th, your 80th birthday, congratulatory messages arrived from all over the world. In the fall you visited Paris, Great Britain, Switzerland and Germany.

1957 Spring

On April 23rd your talk on *'The Problems of the Atom Bomb'* was broadcast by Oslo radio in several languages. Your wife, and loyal companion Helene, passed away on June 1st in Zurich. She was 78. Helene was a very special woman who worked by your side and understood your need to educate and heal the less fortunate. Her body was laid to rest in Lambaréné.

1958

You made three more appeals against the danger of nuclear tests, which were broadcast by Oslo radio.

1959

After a short stay in Europe you left for Lambaréné, which became your 14th and final stay in Africa.

1963

On the 18th of April you celebrated your 50 years in Africa.

1965

On January 14th you celebrated your 90th birthday. Visitors arrived from all over the world. In the spring and summer of that year you worked at the hospital and handled all of your own correspondence, which grew every year. You personally responded to every letter received, and were especially touched by letters from school children. You also completed your annotated edition of *Bach's Organ Works*. Your strength was in decline.

September 4

Shortly before midnight you left the physical plane of existence, leaving the rest of us in awe of your earthly accomplishments, allowing us to ponder the meaning of your words: **"My life is my argument"**.[3]

In your last years you set yourself the final task of awakening humanity to the insanity of developing, testing and employing nuclear weapons. Your correspondence reached out from the jungle hospital in Lamberéné to world leaders of that time. Dwight D. Eisenhower, Jawaharlal Nehru, Nikita Khrushchev and later John F. Kennedy were recipients of your letters, your appeals for sanity.

You had spent the later part of your life not only as a physician in Africa, but attempting to elevate the consciousness of humanity through your prolific writing. You made, what to us looks like the ultimate sacrifice—giving yourself—your life—to the people who needed you most. At your level of awareness it was the most natural and only thing to do. You had *realized yourself*.

You lived a life filled with purpose, love, light and compassion. You lived what you knew and believed to be your truth, becoming an example, showing 'the way' to the rest of us.

After your passing, a book of your philosophical ideas appeared in print entitled: *'The Light Within Us'*. The original German edition *'Vom Licht in Uns'* was published by Verlag J. F. Steinhopf, Stuttgart. Your insights have changed my life and serve in keeping your spirit alive. It is now so worn that some of the pages have separated from their original binding. Only now, in remembering do I get a deeper understanding of the meaning of those words.

Your physical body was laid to rest in the small cemetery near the jungle hospital beside your wife and life partner, Helene, in Lamberènè, Africa.

Thank you dear Dr. Schweitzer for the light that you shed on our level of human consciousness. I would hereby like to tell you that this light is still burning brightly and is shining on my path today. My heart is filled with a deep gratitude today as I remain,
Your devoted student, *R.*

Dear Dr. Schweitzer,

I have become very aware that the mystery of life and the spiritual evolution—often known as the spiritual *awakening* of mankind—had been of great interest to you all your life. Your philosophical ideas, including your early discoveries about human nature, have been of interest to me for the last sixteen years. As a result, I started asking myself a lot of questions.

Does that qualify me to become a biographer of your life? No—and that's not my intention. What I wish to accomplish by writing to you, is to let you see the effects your life, your thoughts and actions have had on me personally. This involves talking about how I got to know you and to discover my own purpose.

I first met you in the summer of 1985. However, it isn't wise to talk about this incident—this mystery—as yet. Getting to know you better has taught me that the only real teachings are to be found in our personal experience. Since I can only talk about my growth through my own experiences, I must therefore go back in time, start at the beginning and review the early experiences of my own life. Knowing we are all created equal, having many qualities in common, my experiences are not so different from the experiences of others. I also found, that in order to understand myself in relationship to others and to the universe, I must look back.

What or who is this *self* I am referring to? Philosophers have wrestled with this question for thousands of years. I am sure you are familiar with this question, since philosophy was a subject of great interest to you. I began to see that religion, I prefer to call it spirituality, philosophy and science, must be looked at together. You understood this and had the foresight not to study theology alone. You knew that the subjects of philosophy and science were closely linked to the understanding of our spiritual nature and its evolution.

I prefer not to use the word 'religion' too often, because I am beginning to see that what we refer to as religion, has been created by mankind. Religion is man's attempt to come to grips with and explain mystic visions and experiences of seers and prophets, which resulted in the immense subject of spirituality and mysticism. We can't come to grips with the idea that certain things are still incomprehensible and therefore will remain a mystery.

You often used the word 'Truth' in your writings. You were looking and searching for a deeper truth behind the many different spiritual teachings of the great masters. This led you to study other religions and belief systems. What did you find? Is one *unchanging* aspect or *thread* of 'Truth' to be found at the core of all of these diverse teachings? What is Truth?

You were known to be a free thinker, so I know you won't object to my questions. I would like to qualify my truth, the truth as I am experiencing it, by saying that my truth is relative and not concrete, because my awareness is constantly shifting and growing. In other words, everything is in a constant state of change. This is certainly true for me.

I have learned through experience that the more I *think* I know, the more I recognize that I know nothing. I have experienced the validity of the statement: "A fool thinks he knows, but a wise man *knows* that he knows nothing." It appears that you found a huge part of the puzzle by concentrating your research on the life of your master teacher, the man known as Jesus.

In order for me to understand the path that I have chosen to experience, to understand the changes that have taken place in my awareness, I have to go back to the beginning. I've often read that man is the microcosm, a miniature of the macrocosm. In order to understand the Macrocosm do I have to look at myself? As above so below...?

If the finding of 'as above—so below' is true, are we all a reflection of this macrocosm, a mirror of the creative force? The miracle of life will elude us until we examine ourselves? 'Know thyself' rings in my ears. This admonition is at the core of the ancient mystery schools and philosophical teachings, and is therefore a very good start. Is there a difference between *knowing* and believing? Your friend and contemporary, Albert Einstein, once said and it bears repeating: *"Knowledge turns into wisdom only through experience—everything else is just information."*

While I am on the subject of mysteries, the mystery of your appearance in my life and the changes that this meeting has brought about, is becoming the essence of this story—which is my story. Will it remain a mystery? I wonder...
Your devoted student, *R.*

Dear Dr. Schweitzer,

The story I am about to tell is a new beginning for me. People may ask, 'What inspired you?' There is no simple, one-sentence answer to this question. Looking back, there were many books I read that led me in this direction, however, I believe it was my curiosity and sense of wonder that started my personal search for higher knowledge.

It wasn't one particular magical book that started me on the journey I am about to tell you about. What I am referring to, of course, is my life *before* that fateful day in August of 1985. My life until then was a collage of pictures and events, which only make sense as I look at them in hindsight. Some of the meanings of the early experiences in my childhood and youth are slowly beginning to make sense to me now, therefore a look back at my childhood and youth seems like a good idea.

As I remember my childhood years I ask myself, 'Where is the innocence I enjoyed as a child?' 'Where is the joy we often experience as children?' 'Where is the feeling of freedom?' 'Why do we get a glimpse of it so rarely?' As children we often experience this freedom, because when young we often live in the present, the *now* moment, unconcerned with our past or our future.

When do we start closing ourselves off to these experiences of complete joy? When does our child-like delight in the world and its magic disappear? When do trust, fearlessness and faith, get replaced by mistrust, fear and doubt? Why do we change? When do we enter the darkness of fear and insecurity? During adolescence? Why? Is it because as children we are still able, on rare occasions, to remember our previous existence—our existence in spirit form? If fear represents darkness, where and what is this light we are all seeking?

I was born in the month of October in 1944. The war in Europe was almost over. Both of my parents were German. During the end of the war my father was stationed in what was then Yugoslavia, now a separate country named Slovenia, adjoining Austria to the north. This country has seen many wars and much strife. It is a part of the world that often became the battleground between the Christian and Moslem faiths. The grievances go back many centuries, not unlike the constant territorial eruption between Israel and Palestine.

My mother and father moved our family to Austria right after the war, where we lived for two years, followed by a more permanent move to Germany. The city of 'Düsseldorf on the Rhein' became my home. This is where I remember growing up. I was too young to remember anything before this time, so I will only discuss what I do remember about my childhood.

For instance, as a young child I had the recurring dream that I could fly. These dreams persisted, and I remember not wanting to wake up. The sensation was so light and beautiful, viewing the landscape and people from above... I must have been around ten or eleven when this particular dream dissipated.

While remembering certain times in my childhood feels good, other memories bring back pain. One of the greatest joys in my life then, I must have been around seven years old, was asking Santa Claus for a pair of skates. The ones with white leather boots. Skating on frozen rivers and ponds with a pair of screw on blades was for the little children. I was becoming grownup and my ultimate desire at that time was receiving a pair of *real skates*.

That's when I realized Santa did not really exit. My parents were not rich, so buying this kind of impractical gift was considered a luxury, meaning sacrifice on their part. I guess being selfish came naturally to me at that age.

After reading about your childhood, I must admit that my level of consciousness was certainly not equivalent to yours. However, this is not the only difference between us. I will elaborate on this a little later.

Sure enough, that Christmas I found a pair of skates with white leather boots under the tree. For months that winter, and many winters to follow, I was in seventh heaven. Since I was not old enough to take the streetcar on my own, my sister had to accompany me on the first few trips to the indoor ice arena. Soon, after a lot of begging, I was allowed to make this trip on my own. The arena was in the center of the city, and it was not an easy undertaking. The route was not direct, which meant waiting in the cold and transferring streetcars two times. Coming home in the dark on those cold winter nights, my feet damp and my face glowing from the workout, is a very happy memory—still to this day.

I dreamed of becoming a figure skater. My mother kept saying: "You want to become a figure skater—a star?" That was completely out of the question, because we were poor and there would never be enough money for skating lessons. That was considered a luxury reserved for others. Who knows where I would have ended up had they been able to afford this tutoring.

Undaunted, I looked forward to these escapes from my routine of school and homework. The anticipation and feelings of joy were evident every time I ventured out into the cold winter nights. What was this feeling? Did the gliding, twirling, jumping—feeling the wind in my hair, remind me of flying? I found complete joy in those moments of being alone on the ice.

I remember reading that you also found great joy in being alone. You looked forward to those long walks home from school, hoping deep in your heart, the other boys would not join you. This gave you time to think, time to absorb the serenity of your beautiful surroundings. Yes, you were already aware of the necessity of being alone with your thoughts. Were you aware of the power of meditation as a boy? I wonder...

Remembering my school days from 1950-1956 brings to mind two teachers who left a lasting impression on me. Fräulein Liselotte Haferburg was a spinster, as we called every woman not married by the ripe old age of thirty-five. She was truly devoted to her students and took her vocation seriously. I admired everything about her. I never saw her wear make-up, yet she was beautiful. Her nature was kind and gentle, always ready with a smile and a few encouraging words for her pupils. Seldom did I see her in a sullen mood. Fäulein Haferburg had a very young face, although the war years must have deepened the few lines she did have.

She taught the first, second and third grade grammar and writing. On many occasions, instead of scolding or punishing me for a mediocre performance, she encouraged me to do better. She always saw room for improvement, and made me feel that I had some sort of hidden potential. Under her tutelage I learned how to play the flute, and before long I was in the school orchestra. Her patience was legendary, considering the cacophony of sounds coming from the instruments of beginners. I still thank her today for making the extra effort needed to listen to us youngsters and for respecting the needs of children just starting out on the journey through life.

Dear Dr. Schweitzer, I know you had teachers in your youth who left a lasting impression and I will ask you many questions about your own childhood later on. Until tomorrow,
Your devoted student, R.

Dear Dr. Schweitzer,

A funny thing happened yesterday, Tuesday. I just remembered that you might find this amusing as well, since your dry and ironic sense of humor is legendary.

It was my day off from work. I decided to visit my youngest son's new offices. His name is Steven, and he has been quite successful in his pursuits of financial freedom. At the ripe age of 34 he decided to escape the corporate ladder and go his own way. Before this, he was the president of a brokerage firm. It was his idea to take this company public and he was instrumental in its success. He is quite the visionary, arranging for mergers and the expansion of branches into Europe. He has become a .com success, which is the term we use today to describe these young entrepreneurs.

A few weeks ago he told me that he never bought a lottery ticket in his life, feeling that a windfall of this sort would rob him of many necessary life *experiences*. Yes, our society would call him exceptionally smart. His latest desire is to go back to university for another few years and earn his doctorate degree. He would love to become a teacher. The following poem just entered my mind. I wrote this poem in the month of March 1996 when Steven was entering a new phase in his life. He had earned his MBA in finance and opened an independent accounting office. It shows my inner feelings at the time. Had I engaged my intuition? I now wonder...

The Conductor
I have this son who came early
Premature and eager to start
Bright, sunny—reaching his goals yearly
With a smile—he played each part.

He is a quick learner—I found
Always achieving more
Making me laugh—making me proud
After a rough journey—landing safely on the ground.

After only one year, he's reaching still further again
He'll be on his own—no more protectors
Being independent—that's my train
"I'd like to be my own conductor..." his refrain.

Success—is the taste he's after
Big ideas—he'll be fantastic at the game
Never forgetting that—laughter
Is part of his steam—not just his name?

He sees the big picture unfolding...
His energy and drive are hard to miss.
I see his big heart while he is holding—his dog,' Schatzi'
Asking, "Can I have a big kiss?"

This combination of heart, mind and brain
Will serve him well—the secret of his success?
He creates a fire—people will jump on his train.
Hold on! This ride they don't want to miss!

Fear—yes—before the train is boarded
As it starts to roll... faster...
His eyes are opened—and he sees
Just another test to be mastered!
RzT 1996

"What is it you would like to teach?" I asked him on several occasions. Albert Einstein taught at Princeton didn't he? Education is the most important pursuit I can think of, yet, how many highly educated people are still ignorant when it comes to life skills, or searching for the deeper meaning of life? More information does not necessarily makes us wiser. When and how often do today's educators ask us to look at ourselves? How many of our intellectual pursuits lock or box us in, instead of setting us free?

You are a perfect example when it comes to the pursuit of knowledge and wisdom. More about that later, I am getting away from the funny event.

Around noon yesterday, I went to an arts and craft store looking for a few items to make a collage for my grandchildren for Christmas. Yes, I do think ahead, don't I? It is now the month of July and I am already preparing for Christmas. My mind does have a tendency to jump into the future, but I am learning more and more to appreciate the joy of the present moment, finding it brings the greatest joy!

The idea occurred to me to bring Steven a gift for his new office. While browsing the store, I allowed my intuition to guide me to the appropriate selection. Something made me stop in front of a group of posters. I was attracted to the larger than life face of Dr. Albert Einstein. The caption underneath his name read: *"Great spirits have always encountered violent opposition from mediocre minds."*

Guess who this inscription reminded me of? Yes—you, of course. I was delighted with this selection and looked forward to presenting it, as the appropriate present from a mother to her smart son.

Here is what happened next. The poster was about 24"x36" wrapped in cellophane with a stiff cardboard backing. It almost flew out of my hand a couple of times as I crossed the street from the parking lot to the office. It was a sunny Florida day, however the wind was unusually strong. I had trouble keeping this poster in my hands, smiling to myself as I pictured Albert's face being caught in a gust and flying through the air.

Upon entering the lobby of Steven's building, several people grinned at me after noticing the face I was carrying. It was noon and the elevator became crowded. I had nowhere to put this poster so I lifted it up to make room for more people. The group of men, who immediately recognized the famous face I was carrying, broke out in applause.

Upon exiting the elevator and trying to find the right door, it happened again... A young man looked at the picture, and although he was more than 30 feet away, he gave me a 'thumbs up'. I could hardly believe what had just happened. The people I encountered could not help but respond. After all these years, people will never forget the face of a great genius. My grin turned into a silent chuckle.

Steven took one look at the poster and smiled, thanking me with a kiss. "I will find a spot for this on my wall", he said as I was leaving.

Had I been lucky enough to find a poster with your face, I would have bought that instead, of course! I just want you to know where I stand when it comes to loyalty and interest! Knowing you, your response would have been the old maxim, *Great minds think alike.*

What strikes me now, as I look at your face, which is framed and has a prominent place on my writing table, is that there is a slight resemblance! You both had the same unruly bushy hair, and were sporting the same long drooping mustache. What response would I have gotten had I carried your face under my arm? Your features are just as memorable. However, there would be many in this age group who would not remember you. This makes my writing to you even more meaningful and fulfilling.

Something else just occurred to me. The similarity with Einstein does not end with outer appearances. You both studied some pretty heavy universal concepts, approaching this subject from two different angles. You each experienced a different facet of the same prism. To top it all of, you both won a Nobel Prize.

Einstein studied science, mathematics and physics. He found the underlying reality of the unity of all existence! He discovered that on the sub-atomic level, the underlying reality is not matter, or energy, but consciousness or an intelligence that is the *source* of all of them. This reality cannot be contained in our thoughts or described with our words—but it can be *experienced* directly, because it is the ground of all being.

You, Dr. Schweitzer, discovered this unity through your study of theology, music, philosophy and science, including your study of the life of a great Master Teacher, the great metaphysician—Jesus.

I must run now, so I won't be late for work. I hope you see the humor in yesterday's incident. May it bring a smile to your face, like it did to mine. The poster was the perfect gift. My intuition had served me well.

Your devoted student, *R.*

Dear Dr. Schweitzer,

To continue the story about important teachers in my life, there is one teacher I must not overlook.

Herr Hans Jeratsch was a man equally dedicated. His sense of humor and enthusiasm helped with the dry subject of mathematics. Math was my least favorite subject. We had to memorize the multiplication table and stand up in front of the class reciting these tables as part of a test. I was so nervous, that my palms were often hot and sweaty. I had this great fear of being in front of an audience. Some people call this stage fright. I had become very *self-conscious.* I know that this fear kept me from doing my best in those subjects, although I did not see it as clearly as I see it now—in hindsight.

He also taught history, which became my favorite subject. Instead of teaching us about recent history, such as Napoleon, the First and Second World Wars, he told us stories of ancient Greek myths and legends; the legends of the Greek gods and how they related to the ancient belief systems. The stories puzzled me and aroused a curiosity that has never left me.

The legends of Zeus, Hermes and Apollo, gods, or god-like emissaries, who were known to be feared and loved at the same time. Mercury or Hermes, was depicted wearing a helmet and sporting wings on his heels. He was recognized as the 'divine messenger'. I found out later, that the Romans had the same gods—only, Zeus was referred to as Jupiter and Hermes, was known to the Romans as Mercury. There was much thunder and lightning if the gods were not pleased with the behavior of their offspring. These beings were always depicted as existing in the clouds, some sporting shields, magic staffs, wings and helmets. The Nordic races have similar myths and legends, dating back to a time no one can remember. The characteristics and attributes are the same in each case—only the names are different.

Rereading some of these legends not only confirmed my curiosity, but it reminded me of my teacher. As children, we often joked about his enthusiasm. One sign of his excitement was the small amount of white foam collecting at both sides of his mouth when he spoke. Once in a while he would become aware of this and hastily wipe his mouth. We all grinned in delight.

I loved my teacher's idea of history and later found certain operas very appealing. Richard Wagner for instance, set many of these old legends to music. His heroes were Siegfried and Parsifal. Some of the heroes developed supernatural, often magical powers of one kind or another.

I find that because we don't understand something we call it magic. Once we understand it, it becomes science.

The heroes portrayed are searching for the Holy Grail. I am also reminded of King Arthur and The Knights of the Roundtable. Was the dwarf and alchemist Alberecht in Wagner's themes, the same as —Merlin? I wonder...

Thinking of Richard Wagner, I understand that you met his life companion Cosima. I will elaborate on this a bit later, since I don't want to jump ahead.

I wonder now at all the similarities of the ancient teachings and legends. All the archetypes had similar qualities of power and magic. The plots of these stories always revolve around larger than life aspects of our own human nature. Worth mentioning are greed, jealousy, hate and power—the antithesis of good—such as the virtues of charity, love, hope, honesty, faith and compassion, which are the moral and ethical values that we all hope to attain in the end. They depict the struggle we are all faced with in life. I am referring to the struggle between good and evil, ignorance and knowledge, light and darkness. Are we all eventually going to search for a deeper understanding of ourselves, leading to wisdom? Throughout history there has always been this struggle between light and darkness, restlessness and serenity, war and peace. Is this struggle necessary? Does this struggle symbolize the evolution of mankind? Since I am referring also to peace of mind, can this all be happening in our minds as well? I wondered... What I intend to write about, aroused my interest only after reading your words and after I had gotten to know you better.

One of the many subjects that captured my imagination concerned the ancient mystery schools often mentioned by the early Greeks and the Egyptians. I searched for answers and looked in many directions. I read and studied, seeking a deeper understanding of what was meant. I looked back at some of the great teachers. Going back to ancient Greece, I found Orpheus, Pythagoras, Herodotus, Plato and Socrates. Later I learned that Plato, born in 428 B. C., was the favorite pupil of Socrates and established the first place for higher learning. Plato's Academy is sometimes called the first university in history. Being curious I read that:

"Plato was not fully satisfied with the knowledge which he secured from Socrates, and determined to perfect himself in a diviner form of wisdom.

Having dedicated his life to the discovery of truth, Plato was resolved to travel into any country where wisdom might be found, even if it be to the furthermost parts of the earth. Therefore it was natural that he should go to Italy where he could attach himself to the disciplines of the Pythagoreans. There is evidence that from the Pythagoreans he gained much of natural and divine philosophy. He discovered that the Pythagoreans in turn had gained much from other nations, so he traveled to Cyrene where he studied geometry with Theodorus.

"Next he went to Egypt to study astrology with the priests, for Cicero says, "he learned from the barbarians (Egyptians) arithmetic and celestial speculations." Having surveyed the whole of Egypt he settled finally in the province of Sais, where he studied with the wise men concerning the origin of the universe, the immortality of the soul, and the transmigration of the soul through earthly bodies. This accomplished he returned to his

own nation, regretting that the Eastern wars had prevented his journey to India."4

It's been acknowledged that Plato did not obtain his knowledge only through the reasoning power of his rational mind. Did his illumination proceed from his own soul?

I became interested in the ancient texts in Sanskrit, in the ancient legends of India, Mesopotamia and Persia. What was the mystery? Do they all depict the journey of man and the journey of the soul?

These countries are considered to be the cradle of civilization. Iraq and Iran in particular are currently countries in chaos, appearing to be going back to the values and human restrictions the West left behind during the Middle Ages. What did religion accomplish, if anything? Did you ever think about these things? Did Zoroaster and Mohammed really profess women to be second class citizens? Or did we as humans, considering our comprehension is so limited, misunderstand, and therefore, misinterpret and misuse some of the wisdom passed down by the prophets and sages throughout the ages?

I am certainly not sparing our Western religions and thought processes in this observation. We have created the same mess. You saw this already as a student, before the turn of the century. You had an inquiring mind. You were looking for some of the answers—seeking a deeper truth. You had remained a free thinker despite all the opposition your ideas must have created. You stood strong, steadfast in your observations and beliefs about what you uncovered, including the mystery of the life of Jesus.

You studied theology first. What follows, are some of your recollections after one year of university, as retold in your autobiography '*Out of my Life and Thought*':

"Thus, at the end of my first year at the university, I was troubled by the explanation then accepted as historically correct of the words and actions of Jesus when He sent the disciples out on their mission. As a consequence of this, I also questioned the interpretation that viewed the whole life of Jesus as historical. When I reached home after maneuvers, entirely new horizons had opened up for me. Of this I was certain: that Jesus had announced not a kingdom that was to be founded and realized in the natural world by Himself and the believers, but that

was to be expected as coming with the approaching dawn of *a supernatural age*.[5] (My italics)

Further down I read:

"In my remaining years at the university I pursued, often to the neglect of my other subjects, independent research on the Gospels and on the problems of the life of Jesus. Through these studies I became increasingly convinced that the key to the riddles awaiting solution is to be looked for in the explanation of the words of Jesus when He sent the disciples out on their mission, in the question sent by the Baptist from his prison, and, finally in the way Jesus acts upon the return of the disciples."
"How grateful I was that the German university does not supervise the student too closely in his studies, nor keep him breathless through constant examinations, as is the case in other countries, but offers him the opportunity for independent scholarly work!"[6]

That's why you are my hero. Dr. Schweitzer, the world has not forgotten you. What you already knew as a student, I only just now begin to understand.

While I am touching on the subject of religion I must mention that my childhood, in this respect, was vastly different from yours. I did not have any formal religious training, nor was I given any spiritual direction in my youth. Unlike your father, who was the local pastor of your church, my father was a non-practicing Catholic, who only attended church on important occasions. His sister, my aunt was the *good* Catholic in the family.

My mother was a Protestant who did not really believe in formalized religion either. Seeing all the horrors of war had left her with many sad and bitter memories. Did she question the existence of God? I never asked her this question—I was only a small child. My mother was born in 1911. She lost both her mother and father when only six, due to the influenza epidemic of 1917. Her maternal grandmother raised her and her younger brother. Could this have been the original cause of her constant restlessness and melancholy? I wonder...

I viewed my mother as strong willed and courageous. For me she was an example of what it means to be charitable. She never compared herself to people who had *more* possessions or a *higher* status in society. She always reminded us that there are a lot of people in this world who were *less fortunate* than we were, and she never turned her back on a beggar. If her money ran out, she gave food. I fondly remember the snippets of wisdom she passed out in the form of sayings or maxims.

The one I remember most often is: "Es ist nicht immer Gold was gläntzt", which translates into: 'All that glitters is not always gold.' She also said, "People who live in glass houses should refrain from throwing stones", and reminded me of the inherent wisdom of, "Don't cry over spilled milk" or "It takes one to know one." There was one I didn't understand until now: "Du kannst nicht über Deinen eigenen Schatten springen", which means, 'You can't jump over your own shadow'. How many people can relate to the truism found in these small phrases and contemplate the deeper meaning?

Often I found myself being dragged to church services by my cousins, who considered themselves to be the *right* Christians being Roman Catholics. The sermons were often given in Latin and I left, not being any wiser as to what it all meant. The aroma of incense had penetrated my clothes and often lingered long after I left the church.

My mother often talked about the hypocrisy found in some peoples' character. People who considered themselves to be 'good Christians', often lied, cheated and robbed others. Not to mention the atrocities committed in the name of God during the Inquisition, and the systematic slaughter of the *earlier or primitive* Christians, known as the Cathars and Gnostics. These people were hunted down and killed on the instructions of the Pope, because they were considered heretics or pagans. Their beliefs did not conform to the Church of Rome. What happened to 'Thou shallt not kill?' History shows that many people were massacred or persecuted because they had a different belief, a different 'religion'. Isn't the same still true today?

I can see why you studied theology. You had a different example! Your father valued *aspiration*, knowing that we can all become more than we are. That's what I call true spirituality. Your father *truly believed* and *lived* what he preached, resulting in his ability to inspire others. I quote your experiences with sermons:

"In my first years in Mülhausen I suffered a lot of homesickness for the church in Günsbach. I missed my father's sermons and the services familiar to me since my childhood. These sermons

made a great impression on me because I noticed how much of what my father said in the pulpit came out of his own experience. I became aware of how much effort—and even struggle—it was for him to lay open his heart every Sunday to the members of his congregation. I clearly remember today sermons of his that I heard while I was still attending village school.

"I liked the afternoon services most; I almost never missed one when I was in Günsbach. In these intimate devotions, my father's unpretentious way of preaching was at its best. The melancholy feeling that the festive day was approaching its end gave these services a peculiar solemnity.

"From the services in which I participated as a child, I took with me into life a feeling for the solemn and the need for stillness and spiritual concentration. I cannot imagine my existence without this feeling."[7]

I do not recollect ever being inspired by any church service I attended as a child, so in this respect our experiences with religion where very different. However, I was also not brainwashed into believing that one religion is right and others are wrong. Knowing that this kind of conditioning often leads to *narrow thinking* and can take years to undo or overcome, I am now very grateful for my mother's stubbornness.

The extent of my religious training was trying to be a good person, and allowing my conscience to be my guide.

I remember an incident during the early 50's that left a deep impression on me. During the summer months a band of what we called 'gypsies' used to roam through our neighborhood. There must have been twenty or thirty people, all family members, or so it appeared, who came through our part of town to sell trinkets and to beg. They were so different from us, that many people became scared and locked their doors whenever this group appeared. These gypsies had very black hair, which was often worn in braids and decorated with colorful scarves. Their form of dress was also very unusual in that the women wore long skirts, which had seen better days, while the current fashion was knee length. Mothers came with children in tow. These people only spoke the most rudimentary German, having a heavy eastern accent. On their carts were bolts of colorful cloths, dolls and cheap trinkets. A lot of the local people were afraid because these people appeared to be so different and somehow aggressive in their begging.

My mother gave whatever she could spare at the time, taking a particular interest in the little children. She always did what she could, no matter how small her contribution, or how great her sacrifice. Her remarks were: "These people are only trying to survive in a strange country." I see now how my mother had the courage to act on her beliefs and convictions, as I remember my girlfriends and I pressing our noses against the windowpane, wondering where these people might have come from. My mother told us later that these people came from Romania and as far away as Turkey. This reminds me of an experience you had in your youth and I quote:

"A Jew from a neighbouring village, Mausche by name, used to come occasionally through Günsbach with his donkey cart. As there was at that time no Jew living in the village, this was always something of an event for the boys; they used to run after him and jeer at him. One day, in order to announce to the world that I was beginning to feel myself grown up, I could not help joining them, although I did not really understand what it all meant, so I ran along with the rest behind him and his donkey cart, shouting: "Mausche, Mausche!" The most daring of them used to fold the corner of their shirt or jacket to look like a pig's ear, and spring with that as close to him as they could. In this way we followed him out of the village as far as the bridge, but Mausche, with his freckles and his gray beard, drove on as unperturbed as his donkey, except that he several times turned round and looked at us with an embarrassed but good-natured smile. This smile overpowered me. From Mausche it was that I learnt what it means to keep *silent* under persecution, and he thus gave me a most valuable lesson. From that day forward I used to greet him politely, and later, when I was in the secondary school (the Gymnasium) I made it my practice to shake hands and walk a little way along with him, though he never learnt what he really was to me. He had the reputation of being a usurer and a property-jobber, but I never tried to find out whether this was true or not. To me he has always been just 'Mausche" with the tolerant smile, the smile which even to-day compels me to be patient when I should like to rage and storm."8

This incident shows how your conscience was already fully aroused as a youngster. Our conscience is the part of us that always *knows*, reminding us of the right thing to do in situations, including unjust persecution and discrimination.

There is one other thing I must mention while I am talking about my childhood. I was never formally baptized. My mother resisted my father's demands; she was becoming stronger in her convictions that this is not necessary for a baby. She later told me that she wanted me to decide about matters of religion for myself. What did this make me—a heathen in the eyes of the Catholic church? Are you smiling? Yes, I was young and naïve—back then.

You, on the other hand, were exposed to many devotional and religious observances. Prayer—just to mention one. In a small book edited by Erica Anderson, I read that you were aware of things normally not found in the consciousness of a young boy. Even as a small child you followed your usual evening prayers by *silently* adding a special blessing for all of God's living creatures, including all the animals:

"It was quite incomprehensible to me—this was before I began going to school—why in my evening prayers, I should pray for human beings only. So when my mother had prayed with me and had kissed me goodnight, I used to add silently a prayer that I had composed myself for all living creatures. It ran thus: *'Dear God, protect and bless all beings that breathe, keep all evil from them, and let them sleep in peace'.*[9] (My italics)

Yes, it is obvious that our childhood was quite different in many respects. One thing we did have in common was our love for nature. Now back to my school days...

Along with Greek history, we were taught about ancient Egypt. Egypt, a land of mystery, where Pharaohs were gods and the priests or Hierophants, were also the educators. I read about the ancient mystery schools in existence then, and continued to wonder, what's the mystery? Egypt is a land of many unsolved mysteries. Who built the pyramids and what were they used for? What do the elaborate burials mean? Why do the ancient hieroglyphs depict some gods with animal heads? What is this symbolic of? What secrets does the Sphinx keep hidden? Why did this highly advanced civilization disappear? Was initiation a common ritual then? What is initiation? Where the pyramids necessary for this ritual? Who were the gods or beings they worshipped and communicated with? Who were Toth, Hathor, Osiris, Isis and Horus?

These studies awakened my deep interest and passion for archaeology. Learning about any ancient civilization kept me spellbound. In my youth, had someone asked me: "What will you be when you grow up"? I would have proudly answered, "An archaeologist!"

To me, men in the desert sporting pith helmets, searching for ancient treasures while trying to uncover the mystery of a long forgotten civilization, were the ultimate symbol of the romantic journey into the ancient past. What is just now entering my mind is quite astounding. Am I *becoming* an archaeologist of sorts? Digging up old truths, looking at them from different angles—trying to put the pieces together? Hmm...an interesting idea!

Dear teacher, I must get ready for work since it is now 7 A.M. Funny how time flies when I am enjoying myself. Until tomorrow I remain,
Your devoted student, *R.*

Dear Dr. Schweitzer,

Today is Friday. I thought about your childhood and your experiences on several occasions during my working hours yesterday. I actually experienced some absentmindedness. My mind was occupied with thoughts about you and Einstein. I pondered on some of the similarities in your lives. Your quest was to understand the spiritual aspect of man leading you to philosophy and science. His initial quest was to understand the laws of nature through science, leading to the unknowable aspect, which is spiritual. Did both of you come to the same conclusion?

Another incident kept my mind wandering. A friend called, telling me that her mother passed away yesterday. Her mother had been suffering from cancer. My friend is aware that only the body dies—not the soul. Yet, as humans we feel a deep loss when our own mother leaves, creating a deep pain and void. I remember my own mother's death and how it had affected me. I was relieved that her suffering was at an end, followed by the realization that we will all die—eventually. How can my words possibly be helpful in a situation like this?

What had you discovered about disease? Do we really cause our own sickness? Does it all start in the mind or perhaps in our *subconscious mind?* If this is so, and modern science has finally come around to acknowledging this, how do we explain this

impersonal—yet, very personal reaction? Therein lies a paradox.
If our minds affect our emotions—which then in turn affect our
bodies, does it all come back to the fundamental, the absolute
Universal Law? Is it the law of cause and effect? I see that it is very
impersonal. Is our pain and suffering self-induced? Created by our
selves? Does this process start in our mind, is then communicated
to our emotions and finally manifests in the physical body? Do all
thought patterns eventually manifest in this way? Does it behoove
us to examine this process?

I spoke to my friend about dying a few weeks ago. She, like me,
also believes in reincarnation. Does this make it easier to bear the
pain of loosing a loved one? I know it is true for me.

Still, the pain experienced is real. I will try my best to find some
words that will help her during this first week of bereavement. As
I think about what to tell her, I am reminded of your words to the
grieving:

"We must all become familiar with the thought of death if we
want to grow into really good people. We need not think of it
every day or every hour. But when the path of life leads us to
some vantage point where the scene around us fades away and
we contemplate the distant view right to the end let us not close
our eyes. Let us pause for a moment, look at the distant view,
and then carry on.
"Thinking about death in this way produces true love for life.
When we are familiar with death, we accept each week, each
day, as a gift. Only if we are able thus to accept life—bit by bit—
does it become precious."[10]

Thank you from the bottom of my heart for your help and inspiration
today.
Your devoted student, R.

Dear Dr. Schweitzer,

It is Saturday night and I just returned from a very special
concert. Going to bed at this time would be completely useless, since
I have to share an important revelation with you. The performance
I attended tonight was the grand finale of the symphonic series
'Beethoven on the Beach'.

Every night this week a different piece of music was presented, shedding light on Beethoven's work and his life journey. I only had tickets for this one, the last performance, *Symphony No. 9 in D Minor, Opus 125*, also known as the *'CHORAL'*, his last and final contribution to humanity, one of my favorites.

You, being an accomplished musician would understand my complete elation after the *'Ode to Joy'*, a choral piece that dominates the conclusion of Beethoven's Ninth Symphony. All of a sudden while closing my eyes I felt I knew what Beethoven had experienced and was able to pass on to us in his genius. He had experienced a personal revelation or transformation not unlike what you must have experienced.

Since this was his last symphony, becoming one of his most powerful, it must have been frustrating, if not painful for him, not to be able to *hear* the individual instruments come together—the way I experienced them coming together tonight. There is no doubt in my mind that he saw—the ideal of brother and sisterhood—the unity of humanity, despite its enormous diversity. This theme is at the root of the poet Schiller's *'Ode to Joy'*. This ideal, with which Beethoven readily concurred, is shown in the final crescendo becoming...*a hymn to the ideal of human perfection.* I was deeply moved and felt as if I were walking on clouds when I left.

I remember reading that you had a similar experience in your student days after a performance of Wagner's *'Tannhäuser'*. You wrote that the 'high' lasted for several days. You described being 'overwhelmed' by an emotion that is so powerful, yet so difficult to explain. You wrote about the effect this music had on your feelings. You were only sixteen years old at that time in 1891. Another one of your favorites was Wagner's *'Parsifal'*, which depicted the story of man's quest for the Holy Grail.

Your love for music started early. At sixteen, I listened to rock and roll. Although my mother had loved any opera by Verdi, she considered Wagner's music heavy and complicated, clearly not understanding the underlying genius of the man. Therefore, I never even attempted to listen or find pleasure in his music. Many things have obviously changed, including my taste in music.

You were responsible for this change. Yes, it was only after knowing that you studied Johann Sebastian Bach, and the organ, that I actually bought several recordings of Bach, including the famous compositions for the organ. The Toccata & Fugue in D Minor has become one of my favorites.

I also experienced this 'high' you talked about. I experienced it this evening, on my way home, while coasting along I-95, listening to classical music playing softly in my car. The traffic was light at this late hour and I was surprisingly aware of the mechanics of driving and very alert.

Yet—suddenly—completely out of nowhere, I saw my letters becoming a story, perhaps a book not just about you, but also about me. It came to me like a bolt of lightning. Your life unfolded in my mind's eye and—in one instant—I knew what I needed to learn and write about.

Tonight in the car I was not 'thinking'. I felt very relaxed—very elated. I embraced a moment that was free of thoughts—just 'being'—in the *present* moment. This is hard to describe in words. Is this similar to the state of peace you often referred to?

I was still in complete reverie about the symbolic power of Beethoven's vision, which rises above the narrow confines of race, nationalities and patriotism, when your life became clearer to me as well. I contemplated what Beethoven had experienced as an 'ideal' inspiration for all people and all time, when my thoughts drifted back to you. I felt the true impact your life has had on many people, including myself. The inspiration emanating from your spirit is very powerful. That's why I could not go to bed this evening without sharing this extraordinary experience with you. As I am about to go to sleep, I remember what you said to someone about the subject of music:

"Joy, sorrow, tears lamentation, laughter—to all these, music gives voice, but in such a way that we are transported from the world of unrest, to a world of peace, and see reality in a new way, as if we were sitting by a mountain lake and contemplating hills and woods and clouds in the tranquil and fathomless water."[11]

This subject, the mysterious state of meditation, a state arising from the quieting of the mind, you called it 'contemplation', or the experience of the now moment, will surely surface again in later letters.

Yes, you certainly had gained a larger view of life in its varied manifestations. Glancing at the clock, I realize that it is now well past midnight. Thank you so much for your words of inspiration and wisdom. Now I can sleep peacefully and say, " Good Night."
Your devoted and grateful student, *R*.

Dear Dr. Schweitzer,

I am sorry for not writing yesterday. Sunday was a hectic day for me and I found myself in a funky mood all day. The music of Beethoven was still in my head, and I thought about going to the mall to buy the CD version of Beethoven's 9ᵗʰ Symphony, wishing to replace my worn audio tape. I never made it to the mall.

As I looked through my selection of music this morning, I always play music while writing to you, I found that I already had the CD. It is a recording with George Solte conducting the orchestra. I don't remember purchasing it, but I must have thought ahead—coincidence? Now that you know what I am playing, can you hear it?

Beethoven's nine symphonies depict his journey through life. Anyone, who has listened to his symphonies in sequence, will understand what I am alluding to. His music depicts the struggle, recognition, suffering, pain and breakthrough, the triumphant joy he experienced at the end of his life. His symphonies are numbered from one to nine. This is also symbolic. Each number has its own vibration, nine being the number of completion. As his life journey neared the end he experienced a transformation, embracing the recognition that we are all one, that we are all brothers, resulting in his grandest accomplishment. He, like you, lives on. We still experience you through the creations you left behind for us to ponder.

Early this morning I thought about the mystery of my existence. I picked up a book edited by Erica Anderson. She had compiled some of your memorable thoughts into a book entitled *"Thoughts of Our Times"*, after returning from observing you in Africa. I randomly opened it, wanting to refresh my inspiration, as these words flew off the page:

"We find ourselves in a new movement of thought. In a movement where, through science and through the searching of our hearts, everything has become mysterious. Science has led us from knowledge to knowledge but also from mystery to mystery. Mystery alone can lead us on to true spirituality, to accept and be filled with the mystery of life in our existence."[12]

Strangely, we see mystery surrounding each and every one of us on a daily basis. The mystery of a tree blowing in the wind; the mystery of a flower; the mystery of electricity; the mystery of radar; the mystery of magnetic fields; the mystery of gravity and motion; the mystery of our life energy; the mystery of an orange tree; the mystery of seeds; the mystery of life; the mystery of thought. The mystery of our breath and the mystery of our pulsating hearts—only to mention a few.

Erica Anderson visited you on several occasions in Africa. I just recently learned that she was instrumental in creating the only documentary film in existence showing your life and activity in Africa. From what I heard, this movie was nominated for the Oscar in 1958, and won in the category of best documentary film. To this day I have not been able to obtain a copy of this film. To actually see real (reel) footage of you and see the jungle hospital you created in Africa would be the greatest thrill I can imagine at this moment! Until then, the movie that was made about a small part of your life, the movie 'The Light In The Jungle' will have to do

I didn't like the movie all that much, because it concentrated only on your work as a doctor, omitting the most important part of your life's work, namely your philosophy. No one seemed to have taken your wishes into account. Here is what you said to the film biographer who filmed the *original* documentary:

"When you portray me it should be not as the doctor who ministers to the sick. It is my philosophy of reverence for life that I consider my primary contribution to the world."[13]

My mood has improved considerably since I started writing to you today. What caused this 'poor me' attitude to arise so suddenly? Looking back on yesterday I see that I picked up, or had tuned into the stressful activity of my work environment. Perhaps the negativity of some person around me had rubbed off or attached itself to me. Was it attracted to me because I felt sad, tired and cranky? I felt alone, wondering why I am always trying to figure things out by myself—struggling with every emotion that comes up—alone. That's when your words came to my rescue.

Your feelings on this matter where pretty obvious when you picked up a disappointed man hitchhiking in Europe. You don't condone whining and complaining about one's situation and lot in life, as can be observed by your answer to this man:

"You must not expect anything from others. It's you, yourself, of whom you must ask a lot. Only from oneself has one the right to ask everything or anything. This way it's up to you—your own choice. What you get from others remains a present, a gift!"[14]

Yes—words of true wisdom. The words are *choice* and *gratitude*. Thank you so much for your kind, and always timely words. Am I correct in assuming you expect people to make their own decisions, take responsibility for their own learning, thereby create their own experiences? Learning everything your own way, through experience, is the only real knowledge and wisdom that will last. Where did I hear the words, 'the burnt hand teaches best?'

I had a great day off, loved talking to you and will close with a big thank you. With deep gratitude for everything I remain,
Your devoted and grateful student, *R*.

Good Morning Dr. Schweitzer,

The movie 'A Light In The Jungle' is still on my mind. I found the casting of actors quite good. The actor portraying you had the same hair and the actress Susan Strasberg, who played your wife, is also of Jewish heritage and has a certain resemblance to your life partner Helene. I wondered whether you would be pleased with this rendition of your life. So many things were not shown.

Perhaps I will bring this movie with me tonight. Perhaps—my son Steven would like to watch the story of your life? We'll see! I certainly will not push my ideas on him. I learned lately that this is completely counter-productive. People find their own way of learning and seek out the best tools for themselves.

There is one other incident I now remember and must mention, before leaving the memories of my childhood. It is rather odd and quite mysterious. I was given the name Renate at birth. This is pronounced Renata in German. My mother had wanted to name me Monica, however my sister had just read a novel in 1944 and the heroine of her story was named 'Renate'. She liked the name and pleaded with my mother to consider giving me this name.

Throughout my childhood I was often asked, "Do you know what your name means in Latin?"

The first time this happened, I replied, "No" shaking my head. When this question came up again and again I felt proud to know the answer myself and replied: "Yes, the name Renate originates from the Latin words *re nata* meaning reborn—or born again." No, I am not associated with or a member of the fundamental Christian group known as 'born again Christians'. That is obvious! Just in case, I feel the need to clarify this. As I remember these encounters now, I am filled with a strange amazement. Do we always get these messages, but are too dense or too asleep to notice them on our journey through life? Or are we only able to see the true meaning of certain choices in hindsight? I wonder...

I just looked up what the name Albert means. It is a version of the old Germanic name, *ADALBERT*. Athal—means NOBLE, perhaps even ROYAL and bertha—means BRIGHT. Your parents certainly chose correctly. Noble and bright, is a very good description of you. Your intentions and thoughts were always noble and bright.

Math and science were not my favorite subjects as I mentioned earlier. It's only now that I recognize the importance of these subjects. I can certainly understand how a physicist can become totally fascinated and engrossed in the mystery of numbers and mathematics.

Some have called me a late bloomer. Was it Jane Fonda who said: "It's OK to be a late bloomer—as long as you don't miss the flower show?" In closing this part of my recollections I wish to thank you for your patience while I rambled on about my life, remembering the early years. They were so average—so ordinary, when compared to your childhood, but one of the big lessons I am learning in my growth is never to compare myself with anyone else!

Is that a part of the puzzle in the game of life? This reminds me of a poem I wrote in the beginning of August 1985, that fateful summer in the steamy Florida heat, after a day of daydreaming on the beach—before my trip to Georgia.

Pieces
Where is my place?
Hey—wait a minute
Who shuffled this deck?

Where is my piece of the action?
Do you feel cheated and alone...?
Relax—now is the time to think and reflect.

What have I done
To isolate myself
Why don't I feel—I belong?

Do I have to be the winner
At all cost?

Child, —listen
It's really very simple...
You are where you are—for a reason.

When all is said and done
Take a good look at yourself.
Can life be trying to tell you something?

Life is a puzzle—but relax
You have your own niche
Once calm and still—you will find

Your piece of the puzzle.
RzT August 17, 1985

It is now sixteen years later and this poem has helped to transport me back in time.

Thank you so much for inspiring me during the hours of writing. You are my hero. With love in my heart I say "Auf ein baldiges Wiedersehen."

Your devoted and grateful student, *R.*

Sources Chapter 1:

1 P. 25 *The Words of Albert Schweitzer*, Norman Cousins
2 P.1 *Albert Schweitzer:_Man of Mercy*, Jacqueline Berrill 1956, Dodd, Mead & Company, New York, NY.
3 P. 97 chronology adapted from *the Words of Albert Schweitzer*, Norman Cousins.
4 P. 147-146 *Twelve World Teachers*, Manly P. Hall 1965, The Philosophical Research Society, Los Angeles, CA.
5 P.9 *Out of my Life and Thought*, Albert Schweitzer, re-published in 1998, The Johns Hopkins University Press, Baltimore, MD.
6 P.10 *Out of my Life and Thought*, Albert Schweitzer.
7 P.55 *Memoirs of Childhood and Youth*, 1997 Syracuse University Press, Syracuse, NY.
8 P.7 *The Light Within Us*, Albert Schweitzer, Philosophical Library Inc., New York, NY.
9 P.9 *ALBERT SCHWEITZER· Thoughts of Our Times*, Erica Anderson, Pilgrim Press, New York, NY.
10 P.58 *ALBERT SCHWEITZER: Thoughts of Our Times*, Erica Anderson.
11 P.73 *The Words of Albert Schweitzer*, Norman Cousins.
12 P.23, *ALBERT SCHWEITZER· Thoughts for Our Times*, Erica Anderson.
13 P 37 *ALBERT SCHWEITZER: Thoughts for Our Times*, Erica Anderson.
14 P.33 *ALBERT SCHWEITZER: Thoughts for Our Times*, Erica Anderson.

"As we acquire more knowledge, things do not become more comprehensible but more mysterious".[1]

Albert Schweitzer

2

Searching

Dear Dr. Schweitzer,

This morning I woke up to a heavy downpour. It is storming outside. This kind of rain is very typical for Florida in August. I tend to forget that hurricane season is upon us. On this rainy day I chose the music of Brahms to accompany my writing. My mood is mellow as I remember the difficult period of growth during my teen years and the years of my marriage. The music is somewhat melancholy creating the right mood to take a reflective look back.

Every day is enjoyable for me, now that I have found a hobby. It seems like a miracle, but I know deep inside it is not. Did you know there are no such things as miracles? You knew better, didn't you? I better not jump ahead again, and will go back to the proper sequence of events.

My parents separated in 1957. My mother decided to take me with her to Canada in the hope of starting a new life.

I was twelve years old when our plane landed in a new country. I only knew a few words in English, such as 'please' and 'thank you very much'. Many of the sudden changes took place during the onset of my teenage years. During the years of 1957-58, I experienced new customs, a new language, new schools and new friends. All this coincided with the physical changes taking place in my body.

I missed my father terribly, but decided to keep these emotions inside, knowing my mother had her own pain to deal with. She expressed a lot of anger and resentment towards my father. Their marriage had been turbulent. I had witnessed many fights. More often than not, they were based on my mother's jealousy and the fact that my father spent less and less time at home. From what I gathered, he had another lady friend. He had supported us financially, but that was it.

During this time of transition I didn't have many friends. In school I was treated like an outsider because I could not speak the language. Also, the Second World War was still fresh in many peoples' minds and the fact that I was a German did not endear me to many classmates. This may not have been true, but that's how I felt.

My mother, who only spoke a few words of English herself, accepted a position as live-in housekeeper for a wealthy Jewish family. They could communicate in Jiddish, which is very similar to German. Her kind employer soon agreed to allow me to live with her. This is something not often heard of today, but my mother was big hearted, strong willed, very capable and a very good cook. In order not to loose such a 'gem', this family agreed to allow me to share a room with my mother. My mother was restless and changed positions every year. This meant a new environment, new schools, and living with a new family. At a young age I was forced to become flexible, having had to get used to change quickly. I did not have a choice in the matter and suffered silently, knowing my mother did this just to survive.

I suffered alone, because most of the other kids in my class had rich parents and wouldn't understand what I was experiencing. As soon as I had mastered the English language enough to read, thanks to a pedantic English teacher, I retreated into a world of books. I had discovered my love for reading!

It became an escape from the circumstances that surrounded me. I read many romantic novels and yearned to experience the feeling of 'falling in love'. I could hardly wait to grow up, hoping things would be better once I had a job and was on my own. I was secretly hoping the fiction I was reading about would materialize in my life. Those years are filled with painful memories. It is only now that I am able to recall those times. Had I shoved these memories under the rug in order not to re-experience or relive this pain again? I wonder...

In retrospect, I see that the pain and suffering of my adolescence and youth actually forced me to grow up quickly. My carefree childhood years had come to an abrupt end. In order to earn some pocket money for movies and books, I looked for a job. The owner of an antique store nearby offered me my first part-time job. I cleaned and polished old silver in a cramped and dusty shop, filled with wonderful treasures. The store was so crammed with inventory, that there was hardly enough space to walk. All the while I dreamed of growing up fast. I knew I needed to finish the minimum of schooling in order to get a clerical job.

After completing my junior matriculation I went to a special secretarial school to learn typing and shorthand skills. I wanted a better life than my mother had. Hoping not to follow in my mother's footsteps, I wanted to work in an office. Becoming a housekeeper was not part of my dreams. In 1961, at the ripe age of 17, I accepted the first full-time position I applied for. I became a filing clerk for the electric utility company of Ontario. Being a quick learner I soon found myself climbing the 'corporate ladder' accepting a clerical job in the engineering department. I smile as I remember my simple ambitions at the time...

A year later, being not quite eighteen, I met a man who appealed to me because he seemed very mature and different. He was almost twelve years my senior, which is a lot when one is still a teenager. I was impressed with his confidence, his self-assurance and his knowledge.

Certain things must have appealed to him about me as well. I wonder now, whether the fact that I was still a virgin had something to do with his attraction. He was what we now call a 'Renaissance man', a man with varied talents and interests, someone who always considered his opinion on everything to be the right one. He was very different from the boys I knew at the time. Today in psychological terms we would label this type of person as being 'self-righteous'. I, of course, had no clue what that word meant, saw no warning signs and fell head over heels 'in love' with what I saw as his genius.

He was considered successful and we liked many of the same activities such as camping and skiing, and he had a pilot's license. Shortly after I lost my virginity he suggested I move in with him. I thought I died and went to heaven. In the late summer of 1963 I found myself pregnant. When I told him the news his romantic reply was: "I did not take any precaution on purpose, I wanted to

see if you were able to have children, so now let's get married."
That's how I came to be married before the age of nineteen.

My daughter Eve was born the following May. A year later my
son Marc was born, closely followed by my youngest son Steven,
born in the early part of 1967. Suddenly, I was the mother of three
little ones at the ripe old age of twenty-two.

My spiritual quest took several unexpected turns, starting with
Yoga classes I attended in the 1960's. Then a few years of utter
turmoil followed. My marriage had more than its share of turbulent
and emotional moments, and soon I found myself completely
miserable.

One of our main differences was his attitude towards sex. My
husband saw sex as a natural human function and demanded I look
at it the same way. There was never any romance or love involved
in this act for him. For instance, he never said the words 'I love
you'. This resulted in a growing resentment, which I began to feel
on a deep level inside. Since the word love never crossed his lips,
I believed it to be my fault. There must be something wrong with
me. I felt trapped. I had no money, no courage, no self-esteem and
no power. I justified my decision to stay by thinking, in time he will
change, in time he will grow to love me. On the plus side of this
equation I had three beautiful children.

It never got any better. My notion that he could change soon
led to many arguments. His yelling and screaming, those strange
temper tantrums, are now only a distant memory. I never knew
what mood to expect. Sex was not romantic or loving, never even
once. He expected me to perform even though he may have hurled
degrading insults at me only moments before. After an encounter
of fierce yelling and screaming I had no desire, no tender feelings
for this man. He blamed me. He often told me that I was frigid and
very provincial in my outlook in life.

My husband never once told me I was pretty or special. On the
contrary, he used every opportunity to put me down, often in a mean
and degrading way. I already sensed his strange and often violent
disposition after the birth of my first child. Why did I stay and have
two more children with this man? I was scared and frightened. I
couldn't breathe. I lived in the dark. I felt as if someone had turned
out the lights!

I was too young to know any different and too scared to make a
move to change my situation. He had all the money, all the control,
and the fact that everything we owned was in his name left me

completely dependent on him. Looking back now, I do not regret anything, as I would not have had my three beautiful children. What about my learning experiences? I would not have had those either. Things tend to work out the way they are supposed to. Any change I desired had to come from me.

My desire to be independent first became apparent in early 1974. Enrolling in a Real Estate course seemed to me a solution. The children were in school and I could make my own schedule. To my own surprise I passed the exams and found a position right away with a reputable company. At home, the emotional abuse continued and I slowly found myself faced with having to make the big decision. Stay and die inside—or leave. The pain was at times unbearable. Sometimes it was so bad that I thought I would suffocate. I felt like a root-bound plant. Yes, the leaves were still green and I bloomed on schedule, but there was no growth. My life course had become stagnated. I needed to move on. I intuitively knew that in order to grow I needed to leave. The direction this growth would take was not clear to me, but I knew inside that I needed to unbind or uproot myself. The years I told you about are still hard for me to remember and talk about. During this time I found that selling real estate was what I needed to do—my route of escape!

Soon, I found myself living two lives simultaneously. I just realized this now, in hindsight. My life at work was filled with accomplishments and a certain level of success. My boss thought I had potential. There is that word again, so often used by my teachers.

At home, I was constantly told how stupid and incompetent I *really* was. I can almost compare it now to night and day—negative and positive—darkness and light. I guess I chose the light didn't I? That's strange, I never looked at it this way before... What is light? Are we always faced with similar choices in life?

Guess where I preferred to spend my time? My growth was now my responsibility. Was I becoming more mature at the age of thirty-two? I separated from my husband in September 1976 and experienced many years of guilt, suffering and sadness.

I had three beautiful children. I decided, and my husband agreed with my decision, to put the two boys into a full time boarding school. I thought that this would be good for them, since the shock of moving to my first tiny home, coupled with a painful separation, would be too much for me and for them to handle. At the age of eleven for Marc, and ten for Steven, they were enrolled at Upper Canada College. I also felt it was good for them to be together, since they were inseparable as boys growing up.

I remember the scene of my first visit to the school that chilly early fall day. Steven had caused a commotion at school and I was called to calm him down. I arrived with my girlfriend, who had brought several chocolate bars. She found chocolate to be good medicine for many of *her* life situations. It didn't work!

Steven kicked and screamed at me. He hated being away from home and hated everything about this school. Marc on the other hand just stood back. He suffered in silence. I was too dense to see that they were deeply hurt and needed my love and attention. I left feeling depressed and guilty. The guilt I felt was so bad, that I am ashamed to admit now that I even thought about suicide during that first year of separation. I experienced a deep pain, worse than anything I had ever experienced before or since.

My daughter Eve came to live with me at the age of twelve. Then again at fourteen, after her father could not handle her temperament. She was going through her own growing pains of becoming a teenager and we had many tough moments together. She was a lot more head strong and rebellious than I remember being at that age. So, I had my hands full—not to mention that my mind was often stressed out—stretched to the limit.

I gave you an earful didn't I? I am so sorry, it was not my intention to ramble on about this part of my life at all, but it is part of my experience and growth. I would not be the same person today without those painful experiences. I can look back now with a certain amount of gratitude, even for the painful experiences I encountered in my marriage, although at the time I felt angry and depressed. I had no idea what I was searching for.

Dear Dr. Schweitzer, you more than anyone understand human nature and our underlying struggle for freedom. You had a higher view of things.

Your devoted Student, *R*.

Dear Dr. Schweitzer,

The rain is continuing, causing havoc on some roadways. The rainy season in Florida often creates flooding in low-lying areas.

Even an umbrella seems futile during these storms. I heard there is a small disturbance brewing in the Gulf of Mexico. Tropical rains, are something you know a lot about.... I read how you had to cope with and endure many heavy rainy seasons in Africa. Not to mention insects, clammy humidity and lack of electricity and air conditioning... In other words, all the comforts we today take very much for granted, you had to do without. Today I'd like to continue telling you about a few of my experiences during the late 1970's.

The Real Estate firm I had chosen to align myself with was sponsoring a weekend seminar entitled *'Adventures in Attitude'*. The year was 1977, or was it 1978? I remember living in a tiny house, having left behind the stately seven-bedroom Tudor home we had lived in. It had certainly not brought me happiness! I felt alone and depressed in that big impressive house on many occasions.

The seminar was a turning point in my life. It brought me face to face with a new way to look at my life, revealing the power of the mind, and how we as humans often *automatically* re-act to situations we experience in life.

The facilitator, who was also the district manager of our company, approached me the next Monday and said: "Would you like to give the next seminar, scheduled for two weeks from now? I think you are one of the few who really *got* it!" Meaning what? Had he recognized how I responded to this information? Does a sponge soak up water?

Yes, that is a good analogy. As a matter of fact, I could not understand why everybody else did not 'get' the message or had not experienced the same feelings I had experienced. What was that feeling? What was the message? It was as if a light had been turned on in my head. I just opened a book at random and stopped finding your words:

"Not less strong than the will to truth must be the will to sincerity. Only an age which can show the courage of sincerity can possess truth which works as a spiritual force within it."[2]

How sincere was I in the pursuit of knowledge? I was sincerely seeking and this was my first experience of opening my mind to a new way of looking at life situations, leading me for the first time to look at myself truthfully. The whole weekend was spent on exercises and examples of looking at *myself*—not others—for solutions to life's problems. When asking me to be the facilitator for the next seminar, it was obvious that he did not know about my stage fright. I guess it did not show outwardly.

Being on a 'high' about learning and life in general, I agreed in a moment of absolute confidence, thinking to myself, "If he believes I can do this—I guess I can!" My nature had been painfully shy. The thought alone gave me the chills and sweats. "Me—in front of an audience?" I almost picked up the phone on more than one occasion to tell him he had picked the wrong person. But I didn't... Something *inside* gave me the courage to say yes to this challenge and to over-ride my anxiety and fears, just this once. The whole weekend was like an out of body experience for me. I must admit that public speaking is still one of my small phobias today. Where does this come from?

The seminar was a success and it was the first time I played the role of teacher or facilitator. Not only was I teaching, I was learning something about myself at the same time. Is that how it works? The subject of '*attitude*' had me spellbound. What had I learned?

Our perceptions, which are interpreted by the mind, create our emotional experiences and reactions to life situations. To my amazement, I discovered that our personal view is not always correct. Our opinion is often distorted by our limited personal experience and by our limited perception. Our reactions are triggered by previous experiences, more often than not coupled with previous conditioning, based on false beliefs we still cling to and carry around in our mental and emotional nature. We see things and situations not how they really are—but how *we* are or how *we* feel. Most of our judgments are relative to our level of awareness and understanding at any particular moment in time. I discovered that we make all sorts of judgments on a daily basis, about all kinds of situations, pretending to *know*. Know what? Why do we label everything as good or bad? I will use the weather as an example... The weather just IS. A farmer will be happy when it rains, and someone who had planned a picnic for that day will be sad. Therefore, the weather is not good or bad, it just IS. However, we tend to interpret it according to our present state of mind and emotions.

Isn't our evaluation of things and situations often based on how they make us *feel* at that moment? It has nothing to do with whether this evaluation is true or not. Our feelings (emotions) are caused by thoughts. Who is in command of our thoughts? We are! Who is in charge of our mind? We are, at least we like to think we are and believe this to be so! I am jumping ahead again, and will return to the important subject of the power of thoughts later.

I mention this experience now, because it was a turning point in my life. This became the first of many experiences that started my quest to know more about my own nature and about human nature in general. Once I discovered that my 'self' created the unhappiness, I was hooked on the subject and became fascinated. I began searching...

I started reading. My interests were quite diversified and I found myself devouring many different books. Among my favorite books were stories about discoveries, such as the journey of Heinrich Schliemann, a wealthy German industrialist who around the turn of the century left his normal life behind to discover the truth behind the '*Legend of Troy*' and the city of Mycenae. Schliemann became fascinated by Homer's '*Iliad*' and the stories found in '*The Odyssey*'. How did he know that Homer's Troy was not just a legend shrouded in myth?

Schliemann, a man wearing a pith helmet in the heat of Turkey, followed his dream, becoming an archaeologist. I had learned about the legend of Troy, and the wooden horse used in the Trojan War in my long forgotten history classes. Schliemann successfully excavated the ancient city of Troy. He proved to himself that many of the long forgotten legends were based on events that actually occurred, even though many myths had been passed down verbally through the generations that followed. At times these myths were presented in the form of parables and dramas. Is the same true for the Greek legends?

This past summer I finished reading a book entitled '*Secret Wisdom of the Great Initiates*' by Earlyne Chaney, a modern day mystic. Reading this material reminded me of my school days fifty years ago. I will quote you one paragraph from her introduction:

"The greatest philosophers the world has ever known have declared that if the religion of the Mystery Schools had been properly interpreted and understood, it would have been—and still would be—the noblest tradition ever given to the world. The teachings of Greece's greatest philosophers revolve around the Mystery religions."[3]

Thank you Earlyne for this book. It further confirmed what I had wondered about all these years, as she reveals:

"These philosophers and mystics were fully aware that the legends of Greece were thinly veiled myths concerning matters of incomparable importance. They were aware too that the highest instruction of the Mystery schools was taught often through symbols, allegories or parables. Even the greater Mysteries were often presented in the form of drama—dramas depicting the creation of the universe, the coming of the gods, the divine government of cosmic laws, the salvation of the soul and the soul's ultimate return to its home in the worlds beyond the earth plane."[4]

I read that Plato and Socrates taught by asking their students questions, thus stimulating each one to think for themselves. Plato's answers were given in the way of stories or myths. This also reminds me of the music and operas written by Richard Wagner. The fascination with archaeology did not leave me, although I became very interested in other subjects along the way. For instance, I had discovered that looking at 'myself' was not an easy task. My ego fought very hard to defend my trivial thoughts and justified every wrong road and every stupid action. Then I discovered that there is no such thing as a wrong road. I soon saw that my road had been my choice, my way of experiencing the world around me—this time around—experiencing the law of karma, which is the impersonal Universal Law of cause and effect. After all, it was my painful experiences that made me stop and—think. I just glanced at your words for a moment, searching for the appropriate inspiration and read:

"As soon as man does not take his existence for granted, but beholds it as something unfathomable and mysterious, thought begins."[5]

My thoughts had begun to shift. Then I read your words:

"Truth has no special time of its own. Its hour is now—always."[6]

Dear Dr. Schweitzer, thank you for bringing me back to the *now* moment. The story of how my journey started is almost over. It is time for me to get ready for work. It is nearing 7:30 A.M., and the candle I had lit in front of your picture is still burning. Yes, it has become my habit to light a candle before I sit down at the computer each morning. This helps me to focus my attention and concentration. It is becoming harder and harder each day to leave this writing desk and go to my regular job. However, I am grateful because it does pay the bills. I sincerely thank you for entering my thoughts again today.

Your devoted student, *R*.

Dear Dr. Schweitzer,

The rain has finally stopped. It was a nice day yesterday—all around. I thought of time, and how it seems to fly. Here it is— another Sunday! What is time? How come there never seems to be enough of it for me lately?

During this past week, my son gave me a book. While visiting his office I saw it lying on his desk. It's entitled *'Life's Little Instruction Book'* and proudly announces on the cover that it has become a #1 New York Times Bestseller. This morning I opened it at random guess what jumped out at me?

"Don't say you don't have enough time. You have exactly the same number of hours per day that were given to Helen Keller, Pasteur, Michelangelo, Mother Teresa, Leonardo da Vinci, Thomas Jefferson, and Albert Einstein."[7]

Marc said, "I can see you like this book, please take it with you." Then he added with a smile, "It also says, 'Don't buy a beige car'—guess what mom, the person who gave me this book, drives a beige car." We both broke out in laughter.

Since then I have found many examples of truth and wisdom in this book. Such as, "Evaluate yourself by your own standards, not someone else's" and, "Never eat the last cookie." I am not surprised that it became a bestseller.

Yesterday, instead of going straight home after work, I found myself in the company of a dear friend who is experiencing a lot of turbulence in her life at the moment. She is faced with a crisis and feels alone and depressed. The pain was clearly visible in her eyes and face.

Her husband of thirty years has announced that he wants a separation. He needs to find his own path, which he said was a spiritual path. He told her he must be alone. My friend is experiencing a deep pain, feels hurt and is very depressed. I just sat and listened, although she could not get herself to be fully open and talk about it. I reminded myself to be still and just listen. At the present she is in a *blaming frame of mind*, blaming her husband, blaming other people and the world in general for her situation. She was looking outside, in other words she was looking in the wrong direction. I could see that her attitude was keeping her stuck and contributing to her misery.

An incident earlier yesterday morning had taught me not to open my mouth too freely. At the usual Saturday morning meeting held at my place of employment, my exuberance and joy for life came through somehow. I must have said something, or acted in a certain way, because a colleague turned to me and laughingly said: "Are you on drugs or something?"

This taught me to be quiet and not talk about some of my observations and experiences. So, with this new lesson fresh in my mind—I just sat and listened to my friend, knowing that I could not really help her. Or could I?

It was a beautiful balmy Florida evening and we were sitting out by the pool. The Florida humidity can be stifling during the summer, so sitting outside during the month of August is rare. As I sat there staring at the three candles I had lit, a thought crossed my mind. My friend has been a Roman Catholic for all of her forty-nine years, and at one time she revealed to me that she had taught Sunday School. What has the teaching of the church done for her? What information, what knowledge and wisdom does she have to draw on to console her at this crucial point in her life?

Is religion becoming obsolete in the way it is being taught? What has been lost over the years? What have we done to the 'words' of Jesus? The churches have created a dogma that very few people can relate to. Heaven and hell are a good example. Why does the church still promote this kind fallacious picture instilling the masses with fear? We are taught to recite prayers and the 'Hail Mary' by rote. Why aren't we taught the meaning and power behind these exercises of meditation? I see the bumper sticker 'Jesus Saves', and wonder how many people really understand the true meaning of those words.

I think of how often I have heard rituals performed during a church service and heard the verses repeated by a congregation as if spoken by mechanical robots. Was the message, often disguised in parables, really sinking into our consciousness? Have the words of the Master teacher been understood? Have we ever really examined them or shown a personal interest in his mysterious life, works and words, or has it all become just background noise to ease our conscience? Can the masses, going to church only on Sundays, identify with what is being taught on the pulpit? Does it evoke a certain inner feeling of truth? If so, the church is serving them well. I also see a dichotomy in going to church on Sundays and believing in science the rest of the week.

If we are asked to believe that Jesus will do all the hard emotional and mental work for us, does it really serve our best interest and further our growth? How illogical is that? Am I supposed to believe, that all I have to do is go to church and sit with my mind and heart closed, and all my trespasses will be forgiven? Doesn't this perpetuate and foster the false belief that the answers are to be found *outside* of ourselves?

Jesus was a great Master, a teacher beyond the normal scope of our comprehension. He showed us the way, but we must learn to listen—learn to feel—and *want* to understand—what he is really saying to us. Then we begin to understand that he was, and still is, a signpost on our path to higher learning and to a new way of perception, but he can't *walk* the path for us.

It is not faith that is harmful. It is our false beliefs that perpetuate fear, insecurity, helplessness and confusion. In this respect we create our own prison. I had learned over the years that one of the ways out of the prison of fear is to start to pay attention to my thoughts, since thoughts create my internal dialogue. Some people find it so much easier to blame others—looking outside of themselves—for the root cause of their suffering, actually getting stuck in this frame of mind for a long time. Faith, on the other hand, results from an *inner knowing* and is the direct result of personal *experience*.

The day I realized that no one had the power to make me unhappy, and that I was actually creating this emotion myself—my eyes were opened to a new reality. By agreeing to take responsibility for my inner state, I had tapped into a new sense of freedom. A form of independence dawned on my horizon. This shift in awareness has shed light on one part of the big mystery. I knew intuitively that further investigation into my own nature would change the way I experience others and myself. I also knew that I must remain flexible to new ideas and remain open to change.

We are creatures of habit and hate any form of change. We resist looking at ourselves at all cost. We are afraid! Yes, fear is the biggest obstacle encountered while aspiring towards inner growth. Our fear only delays the inevitable; it does not remove our duty to ourselves, which is to take full responsibility for our inner state whatever that state may be. It helps to admit to ourselves that we are confused, it helps to admit that we are scared, at least we are being honest. That is the first step out of denial of our condition.

I could feel that my friend was not ready to hear what was on my mind. I certainly did not want to cause more pain at this particular moment. I did not ask her the questions forming in my mind, because I knew that this would not be a good idea. My intuition told me to keep quiet. Instead we sat in silence—a silence which became deafening—yet was pregnant with opportunity! What should I say?

Slowly, I started to tell her about my experiences with deep disappointments and depression. I thought back to those years of pain and suffering, the years I just talked about in an earlier letter. What helped me then? Who threw me the life preserver? All I could think of was, that what finally helped me the most was writing. Looking back, I remembered that I had read somewhere, I don't remember where, that starting a journal is very helpful during the experience of depression. I thought at the time, "Why not try it, what do I have to lose?" That was in the early 1980's—over twenty years ago.

I shared these thoughts and moments with her to the best of my ability, feeling her fear, sadness and stress! What did I remember about those moments? Everything! I remembered starting to write in a journal. I told her that it would be easy for me to just give her one of my many blank journals, but that's not how it works. When she is *ready*, she will make the effort and buy this journal herself. It must be her decision, her choice, and her money. It must become a sincere desire on her part to want to help herself that will motivate and prompt this action, not mine.

Making a list, of what she is *grateful* for in her life—at this time, right now—no matter how faint this gratitude presently is—would be a good idea. That's how I got started. This list, quite short at first, became longer and longer each passing day, because a shift of perception is experienced. I also shared how good it felt to write. In hindsight I have recognized that releasing my innermost feelings on paper, became the first step I took towards healing myself. It was truly therapeutic and had worked for me.

Writing was my special time of learning something about myself. I said, "You know, as I sometimes look back at the entries of my first journal, I discovered that I am not the same person any more." Was she truly listening? I don't know...

Before she left with eyes red and swollen, I hugged her and said, "This pain is your biggest chance for growth, if only you could grasp its significance. Perhaps you are just not ready to see at this present moment that this is your biggest opportunity in disguise. You and your husband had been leading separate lives for quite some time now. You just chose to ignore this. The time has come to let go! So, go home and cry until there are no more tears left."

How much of what I said to her last night registered with her? Does it matter? I often heard the words, "When the student is ready, the teacher appears." How true this is. Hitting someone over the head with a two by four isn't going to get the message across if the student is not ready. However, when the time comes and the student is ready and makes the *effort*, the touch of a feather will wake her or him up. Until then the choice to move on and let go must remain her choice.

I had let go of so many things in my life. Life appears to be a series of lessons and many of them deal with letting go. I find it true that when faced with moments like this, it is absolutely essential to let go voluntarily, otherwise, it will be ripped from us violently. The rug will be pulled from under us—metaphorically speaking. I did not say any of this to her, of course, but those were my thoughts yesterday evening, sitting outside on a warm Florida evening.

Now, do you understand why I did not write to you last night? After my friend left I went to baby-sit my grandson. On my son's coffee table I found a book entitled 'Beethoven'. I read this picture book cover to cover, while my grandson was quietly sleeping in his crib. I glanced at the beautiful paintings of Vienna and the surrounding palaces. They did not have cameras in Beethoven's time, so a painter must have been part of the court entourage. Included in this version, a condensed life story of the great artist, are pictures of Napoleon. Beethoven was born at the end of an era known as 'the Enlightenment' and lived through the French Revolution and Napoleon's Wars. His third symphony *'Eroica'* was originally dedicated to Napoleon, in celebration of one of his many conquests. Was Beethoven aware of the importance of the historical events he bore witness to? Most of the time he was so preoccupied composing and transferring his visions into the musical compositions he heard in his head, that he couldn't even remember to clean his chamber pot.

I learned more about Beethoven than I had previously known. For instance, he was a contemporary of the poet Goethe, and had enjoyed a relationship with him mainly through correspondence. They did meet and I would love to have been a fly on the wall on such occasions. Wouldn't you?

Was it a coincidence that I happened to find this book, after just having attended the concert the previous week? Is this an example of synchronicity? I looked at the clock and seeing it was only ten, kept on reading.

When I finally got home, shortly after eleven, my body felt tired. I went to bed with the book currently capturing my attention. It is the life story of Richard Wagner. There are several other books currently on this table waiting to be continued. Among this collection of books, some of which were written by you, are 'Conversations with Goethe' and 'Francis of Assisi a Revolutionary Life' written by Adrian House.

I gave you quite an earful this morning. Thank you so much for being in my thoughts last night. What would you have said or done for a friend in a similar situation? That's when I saw your words:

"The most valuable knowledge we can have is how to deal with disappointments."8

Do you know how hard it was for me to remain silent? Did you ever have a similar experience? Knowing what I know now, about the journey of the soul and the gathering of experiences, I could have said a lot more, but I didn't. Was this a test of sorts?
Your devoted student, *R.*

Dear Dr. Schweitzer,

Before going back to my experiences of the late 1970's, I will tell you about my visit to my son's home last night. My daughter-in-law had given a birthday party for her mother in the afternoon. I was invited, but could not join them until after I left my place of business around five. My ex-husband was among the invited guests. We talked for a while and I could feel myself reacting in my usual way to some disparaging and hurtful remark he made about a mutual acquaintance. I became angry. Yes, my buttons can still be pushed.

Arriving home, instead of going straight to bed I went outside to sit on my terrace in the darkness. I looked at the luscious tropical scenery surrounding the moonlit lake. I was struck with the thought, 'why is there so much suffering in the world?' I hope my fleeting comment had not caused my ex more suffering, than he is already experiencing. I also thought about his childhood. He had never discussed that part of his life very much. Was he put down or abused emotionally or mentally in some way? Or was he born with this anger, choosing this time around to learn a bit more? I really don't know...

Did you see this kind of suffering also? You couldn't have been concerned with the suffering of the physical body only. As I read your words:

"The fellowship of those who bear the Mark of Pain. Who are the members of this Fellowship? Those who have learned by experience what physical pain and bodily anguish mean, belong together all the world over; they are united by a secret bond. One and all, they know the horrors of suffering to which man can be exposed, and one and all they know the longing to be free from pain."[9]

Yes, I see now that a lot of our pain is also often emotional and mental. I find it difficult to look back on my years of struggle and pain. At times I feel overwhelmed as I discover how much there is still for me to learn!

Coffee is brewing, filling my apartment with its delicious aroma. I will be here at my computer for a while, I presume. Now it is time to get back to my story.

The earlier mentioned seminar *'Adventures in Attitude'* was my first experience at looking at *myself*. I only understood a very small part of what was happening to me, however, a *seed* must have been planted in my mind. It was therefore, only a matter of time until this seed sprouted and bore fruit. That's how it works, doesn't it? Did I water this seed often enough, or did it lie there neglected and dormant for many years?

What did I do during those years? What did I learn? In hindsight—as usual—my vision becomes 20/20. I will spare you all the details and just touch on the highlights. Yes, I did become the facilitator for the next weekend seminar in 1978 and experienced a strange elation. For a few days after, it felt like I was walking on cloud 9. I couldn't get over the fact that I was able to focus and concentrate for this length of time. It appeared as if my shyness and inferiority complex had taken a back seat for the time being. Shortly after this episode, however, I found myself back in my usual routine. I have never attempted public speaking again!

The years passed, my ex-husband moved to Florida. I allowed him to take my two sons with him, because of my fear of not being able to adequately provide for them. He also threatened never to give me a divorce unless I agreed to this arrangement, and I was naïve enough to believe his threat. He had a very violent temper, and his outbursts often paralyzed me. The pain was terrible. I was living in a small home, never knowing where my next dollar would come from. Fear? Definitely! I rationalized my decision to allow the boys to live with him in the following way: 'One day when they are old enough, I can explain my fear based decisions and feelings much better'. I knew that he would be a good father to the boys in particular, and that I needed to grow up. I also rationalized that Florida is only a three-hour flight from Toronto, with many direct flights available.

Guess what happened...? I missed them terribly. My daughter and I went to visit frequently, almost every few months. I wrote this poem in early August of 1985. This explains where I found myself at the time.

The Roller Coaster
Dear God, where am I
Up or down?
Slow down—my head is spinning
I want to get off—but don't know how...

That was my life
Not too long ago
Loss of control—fear—panic.
Blaming other people—like a manic
Drifting to and fro.

Was it yesterday,
Or the day before
I decided to get off
I wanted more?

After a long hard look inside
I found an awareness...
Was it the real me?
Can peace and love—be my new harness?

My fellow travelers
Please give it a try
Once you get started
It's easy as pie!
RzT Aug. 1985

The only thing I must add to this, is the fact that it wasn't all
that easy. I still experienced many moments of confusion and
doubt, causing pain and suffering. Yet I received a glimmer of hope
through my poetry. I would like to elaborate on the phenomenon of
starting to write poetry, but want to stay on track, and will find the
occasion to explore it again.

In 1984 I frequently felt despondent. I searched for a way to be
with my children, but Real Estate was the only way I knew how to
earn a living, or so I believed at the time. Money was in short supply
and I was always catching up. I spent it on trips, choosing to spend
a lot of time in Florida during those years. The moment I arrived
back in Toronto I could hardly wait to return. My friends at work
teased me by saying, "Now that you've sold this property are you off
to Florida again?" Yes, my job gave me the freedom to travel. As
long as I performed my duties no one seemed to care. My position
was commission based only.

One day, I must have experienced the *need for change* acutely
in my soul. I somehow found the courage to call a developer,
an acquaintance of mine, asking if by chance, he might need an

experienced sales person for their Florida development. I had heard that a property, located in Florida, had been giving them problems.

Guess what? Within two months I found myself traveling to Florida, with only a few of my belongings in tow. The few items I did pack were necessities or of sentimental value to me, such as my books, rugs and paintings. I sold most of my other accumulated material possessions to friends, and had a garage sale for the rest. Whatever would not fit into the small trailer I had rented was given away. My friends admired my courage to leave a good job and a certain amount of financial security behind. I don't know where I got the courage to make the choice to uproot my fairly comfortable existence.

It was spring, a good time for new beginnings. I left at the end of May, looking forward to starting my new job of selling ocean front condominiums on June 1st. My son Marc, the middle child, had offered to fly up and help me with the move. He was eighteen and about to start college. What a journey that was! We laughed and joked the whole way to Florida. I was so happy to be leaving my old life behind, and my son said that he was happy knowing his mom would now be living nearby.

The feeling of love I felt in my heart for my children was like a magnet. I missed them terribly! Having given myself huge guilt trips during all these years of separation had worn me out. No more, I thought, as we drove throughout the night, not even stopping to sleep in a hotel. We did stop at a rest stop to doze for a couple of hours, because I could see Marc's eyelids beginning to droop. As soon as we crossed the border into Florida and I experienced the heat of the Deep South, I felt even happier.

I am about to tell you my experiences of the two years spent in Florida, so I will stop in order to regroup my thoughts and emotions. The next part will need my serious focus and attention.

Dr. Schweitzer, I thank you for being my friend, mentor and my inspiration. I could never have found the courage I have now without you. Before I go, I will share the last line of a movie I watched last night. It was a story written by Jane Austin and the heroine at the end of the movie said, "It could have all turned out differently—I suppose—but it didn't!"
Your very grateful and devoted student, *R.*

Dear Dr. Schweitzer,

Allow me now to reflect on the years 1984 to 1986. After starting my new position which had the fancy title of 'Director of Marketing', I found myself sitting in an almost empty building. I kept busy planning a new advertising campaign for the upcoming winter season, decorating a new model suite, and reporting my observations, along with certain recommendations to Head office. After completing my duties, I spent a lot of my time staring out at the ocean, which was right outside my office window. The view was absolutely mesmerizing. I considered myself very lucky to have been given a rent-free apartment with this assignment. Is there really such a thing called—luck? I wondered...

The few people who had purchased residences in the building were for the most part snowbirds from New York City and the southeastern coast. Since I could not leave the building during the day, I again started to read.

My choice of reading material was very diversified to say the least. The local library was within walking distance from the building, which is an absolute rarity in Florida. A coincidence? I found myself interested in books that even astounded me. Included in the stack collecting on my office desk and night table were subjects on Metaphysics, Quantum Physics, Einstein's Theories, Reincarnation, Philosophy, Hindu Beliefs and Religion, Buddhism, Egyptian Civilization and History. My favorite light books were biographies. I loved reading about famous or infamous personalities, their motivations, their inspirations, their sense of values, their adventures, their accomplishments, and often wondered whether they had an early sense of their later destinies.

Many of the earlier mentioned books were over my head and I admit to understanding and absorbing only a fraction of the information. However, they stimulated and satisfied my curious nature.

I just remembered a passage in a book I read about your early years as a student. The book I am referring to, and will at times be quoting from, is '*Albert Schweitzer: Man of Mercy*'. I will explain later how this book came into my possession. There I found the following passage:

"The field of science also became a favorite, particularly chemistry, physics and geology, although Albert was not satisfied with the answers his textbooks gave him. Everything seemed to have a ready-made answer, all things were satisfactorily explained, and nothing was left of the mystery of nature. He found this idea ridiculous! Who could really explain hail, snow, rain and wind? He felt that a snow crystal or a rain drop, were beyond explanation. They were miracles, as they remain to this day. As a matter of fact, he began to see miracles everywhere and to dream about their wonder. His dreaming now, instead of interfering with his schoolwork, only quickened his mind, so that he was even more alert."[10]

I can see from this passage that your curiosity about the nature of life and the various manifestations of nature—visible to us—the sense of the miraculous—were already present in your consciousness at an early age. Now, I am ready to tell you more about my stay in Florida.

A few days after starting this position, I was introduced to the resident manager, who had her apartment on the main floor. We took a liking to each other almost immediately. Since I had a secretary performing a lot of the work I had outlined, she often came up to my office and we took time out to chat. We had very little in common, or so I thought at first. She was brought up Roman Catholic, yet was intrigued by the book titles on my desk.

Our topic of conversation concerned philosophical and esoteric issues including, life after death, spirituality, ghosts, channeling and other psychic phenomena. We shared part of our life story that summer, going out together to local restaurants. She filled me in on the history of the building and how it came to be sold to my boss.

The summer of 1984 turned into fall. That October, I turned forty. During the winter months of 1985 my routine was broken by a few visits from my boyfriend. You might say, that we had started a long distance romance. Shortly after our meeting in Toronto in 1982, this man took on an assignment in Saudi Arabia. He was a medical doctor, specializing in high-risk pregnancies. His motivation for taking the Saudi assignment was clear. He needed to make extra money to pay off his debts. What had attracted me to him?

Through this relationship I discovered that I enjoyed being a 'rescuer'. Although he was very educated, another appealing feature, and much older than I, he tended to whine about the circumstances of his life. In hindsight, I now see that he too was blaming everyone and everything—but himself.

He had a keen interest in history and I kept thinking that he could have chosen to become a historian, since this was obviously his favorite subject. Military History in particular, including the naval battles of the First World War, held a certain fascination for him. He knew every captain by name, especially the names of German captains and could recite details of every major naval battle. Not only that, he had taught himself how to speak German. I often teased him by saying, "Maybe you were a German naval officer in your past life."

Instead of pursuing a career in the field of history, this man felt obligated to follow in his father's footsteps, becoming a medical doctor. He mentioned that it was expected of him. Was that part of the reason for his suffering? It's not that he wasn't brilliant. He certainly was. That's what attracted me to him, but he always considered himself to be a scientist rather than a medical doctor.

By not following his own heart and his own passions he saw himself as a victim, resulting in self-pity. I sensed a lot of resentment and anger towards his parents, yet—he revered them both. What responsibility did he have in making his life choices? Was his anger not directed towards himself, resulting in the symptoms of self-pity and depression? This reminds me of something I wrote that summer, after one of his visits.

Growth
Why do we pattern our life
After our parents beliefs?
What are we afraid of?

They were no different from us,
At one time—searching in the dark
For certain answers.

They've given us life—yes!
Nurturing and love
Meaning well, they don't like to see us fall.

"Step into my shoes—my son"...
Seems to be a favorite expression,
"Take over what I've started—and run."

How sad and most unfortunate
Our parents try to save us from 'mistakes'.
Control our destiny—if we let them.

We can't live our lives—like them.
We are who we are—different.
We do not want to hurt them, by letting go.

Our growth is our responsibility
NOW
Although we owe them everything...
Rzt August 1985

You were faced with the same dilemma. You were expected to become a theologian, a pastor, just like your father had been. However, history shows you took a different path. You not only took full responsibility for your decisions, but you must have had to face many other obstacles, including the opinions and advice from friends and relatives. Their opinions were well meant. All thought they knew the right thing for you to do. You announced your decision to attend medical school to family and friends, with the intention of serving as a doctor in Africa. I quote from a booklet "Albert Schweitzer World Citizen:

"Of course he expected some protest and objection. But his unexpected decision raised a real storm. His closest friends reproached him for having kept them in the dark about such an important step. Was it because he had not gained enough, quickly enough in his career that he was now throwing everything away? Schweitzer did not deign to reply. Later in one of his books he was to write: 'There was not the slightest reason for making such a suggestion. For at that time I had reached an unlooked-for level of success for a man of thirty, a level that others would have earned only after years and years of struggle.' He laughed heartily, on the other hand, with those who called him "a bull in a china shop". There were also those who quoted from the Bible the parable of the man to whom God gave talent so that he should use it and not so that he should squander it.

Some asked him why he wanted to throw away years on medical study: 'You are already a Minister of the Church. Why not simply go out there and preach?'
"Because I want to bring help there that is more than just words".
Another friend confronted him with one of the better arguments: 'You wish to bring medical help? Right. Then stay in Europe, give lectures, give organ recitals, write books. They will earn you a lot of money and you will be able to send twenty doctors out there instead of going there yourself'.
He might have been swayed by these arguments had his decision not been already taken irrevocably."[11]

Sure of yourself as ever, you informed your family and friends that there were hundreds of square miles in Gabon, Africa without a doctor. Some must have seen your particular quality—your deep sense of duty and responsibility—as a fundamental part of your character.

Your musical friends were just as insistent, saying that a talent like yours does not come along very often, it is a gift from God and should not be rejected, just like a painter does not have the right to blind himself. Although you warned these friends that any musical instrument would be reduced to powder because of the climate and the destructive insect population, they insisted on giving you a piano with pedals which you could not avoid accepting.

You were incredibly mature at an early age. You listened and had begun to trust your inner voice allowing it to guide you. I see you as following your intuition. Had you recognized that this would never steer you in the wrong direction? I wondered...

Oh, how time flies again. I may have forgotten to tell you that I'll be going to Europe in September. My planned trip is only four weeks away.
Your devoted student, R.

Dear Dr. Schweitzer,

Rather than leave the subject of our parents choosing our lifetime profession, I will continue the story about the doctor. I saw first hand how his choice of profession affected him. I see how giving in to someone else's wish, as to what is right for us, and not following our own heart, is very destructive to our later happiness and sense of fulfillment.

By not following our bliss—the soul's yearning—we cause misery, not only for the people around us, but mostly for—*ourselves*.

I met this man in the spring of 1982. Shortly after our first date, he told me that he had decided to accept a two-year contract and would have to leave for Saudi Arabia in a few months. Jeddah would be his destination. These Middle Eastern locations, including Saudi Arabia, sounded romantic and exotic to me. Were these foreign and mysterious places appealing to the hidden archaeologist in me? He promised to write and said, "Wouldn't it be great to meet in Europe during my leave?" It sounded good to me. We entered into a long distance relationship. I kept ignoring the fact that you can't get to know someone via letters and the odd phone conversation. His letters were long and interesting, as a war was in full swing between Iran and Iraq. He wrote about his first encounter with camels and described them as having a certain majestic bearing, which he admired.

His services were in high demand in this developing country. He told many stories, some of which were very humorous. One such story sounded so ludicrous, I didn't know whether to believe it or not. You, Dr. Schweitzer, may find this amusing

During the construction of a hospital there were several things the decision-makers had not taken into consideration. For instance, in their desire to copy the latest American trend of wall to wall carpeting, they installed it in the operating rooms. Other follies followed, such as making the elevators too small to accommodate the hospital beds. Yes, they were blessed with lots of oil money, but lacked practical experience. Are you smiling?

His letters kept me spellbound. To some degree his interesting letters satisfied my curiosity about this strange and mysterious land. He always ended his letters with how much he looked forward to coming home, followed by how much he missed me. Sometimes I got the feeling that he considered this assignment as a form of punishment, much like serving time in prison. No matter how many letters I wrote telling him to enjoy his stay, to look at these experiences as an opportunity to learn new things about a different culture and lifestyle, his misery and whining could be read between the lines. He felt that the Saudis considered the presence of foreigners, especially Americans and Canadians, as a necessary evil. They needed the training and expertise, but considered the foreigners *infidels* under Islamic law.

When the time arrived for his vacation, he planned an elaborate trip for us to Austria, Germany and Switzerland. I was overjoyed! I looked forward to seeing this part of the world again, having spent most of my life in North America since 1957.

We embarked on our trip in the spring of 1983. The glorious scenery of Salzburg and Vienna seemed to be wasted on my friend. His depression was keeping him stuck in a *'poor-me'* mood unable to fully enjoy the present moment.

I, on the other hand, soaked up the sounds, sights and aroma of Vienna. We visited the Emperor's summer palace. Schönnbrunn was a splendid example of the decadence and overwhelming material wealth of that era. Napoleon had stayed in this stupendously opulent residence, the summer retreat of the Emperor. The splendor and wealth of the ruling class just took my breath away. The infamous Marie Antoinette was an Austrian princess.

We took carriage rides through the streets of Vienna visiting the stables of the Lipizzianer, a breed of horses used for ceremonial dressage. The Viennese coffee is world famous and I looked forward to our morning ritual of hot coffee and delicious pastries. I could not understand my friend's depression and his constant anxiety. At that time I did not understand the difference between anxiety and depression. How could you feel sorry for yourself in these surroundings?

He did perk up when we took a boat trip up the Danube and arrived in the medieval town of Dürnstein, staying in a medieval monastery, now a five-star hotel. The name of this hotel is 'Richard Löwenherz'. It is nestled in a hill overlooking the Danube. In the distance we could see the ruins of an ancient castle. While walking the narrow streets, we came across a restaurant with the sign 'Sänger Blondel' prominently displayed. My friend got very excited. "Could they be referring to the minstrel Blondel?", he asked.

As we looked up at the ruins he exclaimed, "This must be the fortress where 'Richard the Lion-Hearted' was held prisoner during the crusades!" "Oh my God, do you know where we are?" "Now I know why our hotel is named 'Richard Löwenherz'." The history buff in him came out again and I became thoroughly delighted with his enthusiasm. His mood changed, as he talked to every passerby about the legend of how Richard heard the music being played by a troubadour, a singing poet, the minstrel Blondel. Richard heard the music in the valley below. This is all part of the history of this quaint part of the world. I then remembered some of this being taught in my grade school in Germany many years ago. Following this incident, Richard was found by his sympathizers and released.

What was this crusade all about? Who were these minstrels, the traveling poets who cloaked ancient wisdom in poetry and song? I wondered... I will continue this story tomorrow. Good bye for now, I have to run, my other duties are calling me.

Your grateful and devoted student, *R*.

Good morning Dr. Schweitzer,

Recalling this episode is becoming longer than I had anticipated. This morning my curiosity about the crusades of the 11th and 12th Century led me to my Encyclopedia Britannica. There were not only thirteen pages on the crusade, but also one full page dedicated to Richard I, King of England. The French referred to him as "Coeur de Lion". He was the hero of countless romantic legends. Richard was the third son of Henry II and Eleanor of Aquitaine, born on September 8, 1157. He led what had become known as the Third Crusade.

I opened the Encyclopedia this morning and found the information I sought regarding the crusades, now part of our history. I say 'our', because although we may be American or Canadian now, our ancestors mostly came from this part of the world. This is becoming a quote because the book describes it so much better than I can:

"The term crusade is commonly used to refer to military expeditions organized by Western Christians against Muslim powers in order to take possession of, or maintain control over the Holy City of Jerusalem and the places associated with the earthly life of Jesus Christ. Between 1095, when the First Crusade was launched, and 1291, when the Latin Christians were finally expelled from their bases in Syria, historians have formally enumerated eight major expeditions. Many other lesser ventures also took place, and even after 1291 there were attempts to recover what had been lost."

"This period of roughly two centuries was one of significant social, economic, and institutional growth in Western Europe.

As a consequence, each of the Crusades reflected the particular conditions prevailing in Europe at the time, and their impact on Europe varied as new situations developed in the East."[12]

In my history classes I had learned that Europe at that time consisted of various feudal kingdoms ruled by individual monarchies. Especially significant for the Crusade was a general overhaul of the ecclesiastical structure, which enabled the *'popes'* to assume a more active role in society.

In 1095, for example, Urban II, although still meeting resistance from the German Emperor, who opposed papal reform policies, was in a strong enough position to convoke two important ecclesiastical councils. I found a whole discourse dealing with Richard I, also known as 'Richard the Lion-Hearted'. I quote:

"The English king was never to reach Jerusalem. He won a victory at Arsuf in 1191, but reoccupied Jaffa as a base, and took Daron in 1192 but failed to progress further. Messages from home were urging his return. He had been in constant communication with Saladin and his brother al Adil, and various peace proposals were made, which included marriage alliances. In fact, there seemed to be warm cordiality and considerable mutual respect. Finally, on September 2, 1192, the two opponents signed a treaty of peace to last five years."
"The coast of Jaffa north remained in Christian hands, but Ashkelon was to be demolished. Pilgrims were to have free access to the holy places. On October 9 Richard left. He was shipwrecked and finally fell into the hands of Leopold of Austria, who had not forgotten the slight at Acre. The most lasting achievement of the Third Crusade, however, was Richard's capture of Cyprus. In succeeding decades it gained in importance, not only as an outpost of the coastal possessions but also as a base for future crusades and finally as a kingdom in its own right."[13]

I found more on Richard in the same book and I quote:

"Richard sailed home by way of the Adriatic, because of French hostility, and a storm drove his ship ashore near Venice. Because of the enmity of Duke Leopold of Austria he disguised himself, but was discovered at Vienna in December 1192 and imprisoned in the duke's castle at Dürnstein on the Danube. Later he was handed over to Henry VI, who kept him at various

imperial castles. It was around Richard's captivity in a castle, whose identity was at first unknown in England, that the famous romance of Blondel was woven in the 13th century."14

To refresh my memory about this part of the story, I looked for the booklet I had kept as a souvenir of this trip, describing the hotel in Dürnstein:

"In addition to being a lovely medieval village along the Danube, Dürnstein is also infamous because England's King Richard, known as 'The Lionhearted' was imprisoned in the castle on the hill above this village. The castle is now in ruins, but the romantic story of how his faithful minstrel Blondel, rescued the King still lingers on. The hotel was once a monastery and like so many old church properties it occupies the 'choice' site in town. The hotel is perched high on a cliff overlooking the Danube with a fabulous view. To capture the beauty, there is a terrace which stretches alongside the hotel—a favorite place for guests to sit and sip some of the local wine and watch the boat traffic on the river far below."

Yes, Dr. Schweitzer, we sat on this terrace, sipping the local wine while glancing up at the ruins of this castle, as I in my mind relived a part of history. I became very curious about the *early* Christians, who's belief in 'the Christ' and his message was so strong, that they risked their lives during the crusade in order to secure Jerusalem, which had become the symbol of their faith. What else did the mystery of the life of Jesus have to teach us?

Even today I am inspired to take another look at what his life is all about and what legacy he left for us to ponder. I am looking at his words now and see a much deeper meaning than I had ever thought possible. I remember this trip fondly because the experience in Dürnstein exposed me to a history long forgotten by so many people. I thanked my friend for having taken me to such a beautiful place.

Dear Dr. Schweitzer, I hope I did not bore you with this slight digression. You loved the subject of history as well, especially when it concerned the *early* Christians, their belief systems and movements. You took on an enormous task and researched the life of Jesus, resulting in your book '*The Quest for the Historical Jesus*'. This book must have ruffled many theological feathers in your time. A more faint-hearted man would never have attempted such a project. But, as we already know, you were anything but faint-hearted. You could also have been described as 'lion-hearted'.

In esoteric literature a lion's face is often used to symbolize the sun of our solar system.

Let's see, how would I describe you? Fearless, openhearted, kind-hearted or better still—'Albert the Compassionate'? Every book ever written about you and your life seems to give this description of your character and personality. I totally agree with their recognition of your exceptional ability to put *yourself* into another person's shoes. Yes, this title seems to suit you much better. You not only saw the pain of others, you *felt* their pain in your own heart as well.

You traveled to Vienna during your lifetime. I also became aware that you spent some time in Southern Germany and Switzerland, writing and recuperating from having contracted dysentery while being a prisoner of war. The First World War, that is. I wonder about so many of your life experiences and adventures, as I now remember some of my own. I just remembered another stop on that particular trip through Europe; my visit to 'Schloss Neuschwanstein', the famous residence of King Ludwig of Bavaria. This is the castle after which all the Disney insignias are fashioned. Most of the commercial phenomena of Walt Disney happened after your passing.

The castle is spectacular. I later learned that the structure and its interior were completely inspired by the genius of Richard Wagner. Most murals depict scenes from mythology. King Ludwig of Bavaria was completely enamored with Wagner, his poetry and his talent for musical creations. He had commissioned the building of a huge room, several hundred feet in length, known as the 'Sängerhalle' to house the choir for a performance of *'Tannhäuser.'* It appears, looking at the stage settings, that this castle was built to pay homage to all of Wagner's works. We stayed in a hotel that overlooked the temporary residence of Richard Wagner.

Wagner used this home during the years he performed and staged his operas in the castle. Wagner's later residence near Bayreuth was christened 'Wahnfried'. How can I possibly translate the meaning of this word? The word 'Frieden' means—*peace.* The word 'Wahn' stems from the word 'Wahnsinn' meaning—*madness or insanity.* So the correct translation is—peace of mind or freedom from insanity.

You had recognized the genius of Wagner. Wagner was quite temperamental and was often described as being a pleasure seeking character. You were only sixteen in 1891, when you heard your first performance of Wagner's work, and described how you felt:

"My veneration for Bach was matched by the same feeling for Richard Wagner. When I was a schoolboy at Mühlhausen at the age of sixteen I was allowed for the first time to go to the theater, and there I heard Wagner's Tannhäuser. This music overpowered me to such an extent that it was days before I was capable of giving proper attention to my lessons in school."
"In Strasbourg, where the operatic performances conducted by Otto Lohse were outstanding, I had the opportunity of becoming thoroughly familiar with the whole of Wagner's works, except, of course, Parsifal, which at that time could only be performed at Bayreuth. It was a great experience for me to be present in Bayreuth in 1896, at the memorable new performance of the tetralogy, the first since the original in 1876. Parisian friends had given me tickets. To pay for the journey I had to content myself with one meal a day". 15

As you know, *Parsifal,* which deals with man's quest for the 'Holy Grail', the holy chalice or cup and the deeper mystery of our earthly existence, was Richard Wagner's last musical work which he staged himself at the Bayreuth Festival Theater in 1882, the year before his death in Venice on February 13, 1883. Wagner knew that in the story of *Parsifal*, every person would recognize himself. It reveals man's eternal quest for truth, salvation and freedom. Is this what all the ancient myths depict? I wondered...

Dr. Schweitzer, did you know that Wagner's following is now stronger than ever? Many of Wagner's fans consider a trip to Bayreuth a special annual event—comparing this trip to a pilgrimage—paying homage to a great genius and his life's work. During your frequent travels to Strasbourg, you remembered meeting Wagner's widow, Cosima, in this way:

"Cosima Wagner, whom I had met in Strasbourg while working on my book on Bach, made a deep impression on me. She became interested in my idea that Bach's music is descriptive. Once, when she visited the eminent church historian Johnnes Ficker in Strasbourg, she asked me to illustrate my view by playing some of Bach's choral preludes on the fine Merklin organ in the new church. She also, on that occasion, gave me interesting details about religious instructions she had received in her youth, and later, after she had decided to convert to

Protestantism. However often wc mct, I was never able to overcome my shyness in the presence of this noble, highly artistic, extraordinary woman."16

Wagner's son, Siegfried, was the conductor and producer of Wagner's operas from 1896-1906, which coincided with the time of your visit. You must have known that it was Cosima, who staged *Tannhäuser* in 1891, *Lohengrin* in 1894 and the complete *Ring of the Nibelungen* in 1896. I can see why you were deeply impressed with this extraordinary woman.

What I found very interesting, is the fact that Cosima Wagner, Richard's last love, was the illegitimate child of the composer Franz List. Her first husband, Hans von Bülow, was the court conductor for King Ludwig. She left von Bülow to become Richard Wagner's life companion.

King Ludwig certainly recognized talent and surrounded himself with very exceptional people. He especially revered Wagner, whom he describes as having bocomo his obsoonion and deep love interest Wagner's music is not for the fainthearted. It is not for someone who's taste in music leans towards background music. Wagner's genius lies in following his passion, his ingenious way of creating verse and music and of creating operatic masterpieces inspired by the old Germanic and Nordic myths and legends.

Many people saw him as selfish and egotistical. I see him differently and prefer to call him 'self-aware'. He was a visionary with a very sure sense of his own special talent and ability. He felt inspired and motivated by an *elusive inner power*. Richard Wagner, like J.S. Bach, Mozart and Beethoven before him, *had* to write verse and music. These composers heard the melodies in their inner being. Creating music was as necessary in their life, as breathing is to us. It was in their blood. Wagner knew his talent, he knew his purpose and he knew his destiny. His grandiose personality may have ruffled some meek feathers, but the fact remains that he was a genius.

Yes, I see the difference. How else, pray tell, could he possibly have created these incredibly powerful and moving masterpieces? Is that the secret? Be true to yourself?

You were also self-aware. Does having this kind of self-awareness hurt anyone? Yes, perhaps this is true to a certain extent. Only those are hurt, however, who do not understand what this really means; only those are hurt who *expect* you to follow a certain path, which may not be your path. They feel hurt by your being different, by your demonstration and desire to be independent and remain very much an individual. The question entering my mind is, "Would Dr. Schweitzer and Richard Wagner have accomplished anything had they sought everyone's approval?"

Approval
Criticism—oh, how we shudder and shake
Taking it personal
Is our biggest mistake.

Criticism—if meant well
Is for our growth
A chance to tap the big well—of knowledge?

Look at it this way
Does it hurt—to see yourself
Through someone else's eyes?

Do you seek their approval? Why?
Are they at the helm
Of your ship?

What a waste—can you afford it?
The answer for me
Is a simple—no!

Criticism—keep what will help you
Let the rest go.
No one is perfect—that we all know.
RzT August 1985

Although Wagner's personality was not in anyway like yours, he did feel inspired, and like you, he listened to his inner guidance, which he called 'his daemons'. This word is often misunderstood. It does not mean demon; on the contrary, Socrates often used this word to describe his 'genie', and gave the credit of his inspiration to this entity. The word originates from the Greek mythologies and means 'guardian spirit'.

Wouldn't you and Richard Wagner have remained ordinary citizens leading lives of quiet desperation, had you not followed your dreams and inspiration? What is inspiration?

Your pursuit of *independent thinking* would have been stifled had you sought every person's approval. A preoccupation with seeking validation, approval and self-worth outside of yourself would never have led you to your extraordinary life of *selfless* service to humanity.

This has turned into a much longer letter than I had expected. Maybe tomorrow I will get back to my fateful experience of meeting you in the summer of 1985.

Your faithful and devoted student, *R.*

Dear Dr. Schweitzer,

I am listening to Wagner's prelude to 'Tannhäuser' on my stereo this morning. Glancing at my calendar, I realized that this is day twenty of my daily writing to you.

Is it true that we learn the most from our intimate relationships? My doctor friend taught me a lot—yet, I felt no real passion for this man. In my mind, during the early part of our relationship, I had pictured this man as the perfect partner to eventually retire with. I saw him as the 'professor type' I had yearned for, affording me the intellectual stimulation I had not experienced in any previous relationships. Was I replacing one wishful thinking with another? As mentioned before, we only had a long distance relationship. This is certainly not the way to fully get to know someone. Not the way I had known another man during a previous passionate love affair, which had run its course and ended in 1982.

Letting go of this earlier relationship was not easy. I cried myself to sleep many nights! The move to Florida helped me tremendously in that respect. After letting go of this painful, yet exciting affair I threw myself into my new relationship with a vengeance. Coming to the rescue of this poor doctor, who in his words 'had messed up his life', was the perfect preoccupation and diversion for me at that time. He was codependent and needed me to mother and protect him—something my previous lover would have completely rejected. Was that the main difference? I now see codependency as the *opposite* of self-reliance and independence.

This brings me back to the summer of 1985. My friend's assignment was to be completed that fall, and he had suggested we plan a life together on his final return from Saudi Arabia. At the time, I felt this could be a possibility and flew to Toronto, proceeding to get my divorce finalized. Nine years of separation was long enough, and there was no chance of me going back to my husband. The children were grown. All three had completed high school and were on their way to college. We were all living in Florida, which was great.

My days were spent reading, rising early to watch the sunrise, followed by walking on the beach. On rainy days off, I curled up on the terrace and read or dreamt of another life while looking at the ocean. I certainly had a lot of time to reflect. The summer months turned into the steamy heat of August, reminding me that hurricane season was approaching.

After a few scary encounters with nature the previous year, we thought of several things that would help the building weather the heavy rains and winds forecast for that season.

The regular staff had become quite friendly and one woman in particular frequently stopped at my desk to talk. On one particular day she stopped and gave me a present. It was a book entitled 'Handbook to Higher Consciousness' authored by Ken Keyes Jr.

This lady must have looked at some of the material I was then reading. Why else would she think I might be interested in this book? Was it pure coincidence? This again reminds me of the phrase, 'When the student is ready the teacher appears.'

I found the title intriguing because it dealt with 'how to obtain peace and happiness'. I thought—this is what I need to learn right now, and found myself absorbing this book immediately. Everything I read made absolute sense, yet I did not quite understand it fully. For instance, the name God was never mentioned, yet the subject matter was very spiritual in that it dealt with levels of awareness and consciousness, some of which seemed very lofty and definitely unobtainable in one lifetime. Practicing unconditional love was the main theme. All progress seemed to begin with looking at myself honestly. This included my attitude and my belief systems. This book somehow reminded me of 'Adventures in Attitudes', so I kept reading and followed some of the instructions, knowing this would help me in creating a new outlook on life.

Included were some references to Buddhism, reflected in thoughts and parables, which I had recognized to be very helpful before, in creating a deeper psychological insight. I had studied Buddhist philosophy to some extent and had found it to have many practical applications to some of my life situations. I chose to see them not as problems any more, *preferring* to see them as challenges. Were these challenges absolutely necessary for my personal growth and the shaping of my character? I continued searching...

Many questions had already started to form in my mind about the *effects* of changing one's outlook on life. Change is good, not something to be feared. Change is absolutely necessary for growth. How can we expect different results while thinking the same thoughts, leading us to the same results over and over? Einstein supposedly said: *"Doing the same things over and over and expecting different results—is insanity."*

That was my big revelation after reading and *experiencing* the feelings this book evoked in me. As a matter of fact, I did not just read it like other books, but made it a point to study it and to experiment with it, seeing myself on every page. At times I drifted into a meditation. Closing my eyes, I started to experiment with thinking of '*nothing*', which for me was one of the hardest things to do. I've heard it described as entering the space between thoughts. I paid particular attention to the advice of living in the NOW moment, and started to have some magical experiences. I am so grateful for receiving this book.

Moments
There have been moments
When I wanted to scream and shout.
There have been moments
When I just pout.

There have been moments
That were—absolute bliss...
Then there were moments
I'd just as soon have missed.

There are some moments
Of complete sunshine and joy
Those are the moments
Which make my heart pine.

Why, what's going on?

What are these moments...
Of—sorrow and pain?
I've learned to hug them—and learn
They are my LIFE—don't you see?
RzT Aug. 20, 1985

I experienced a lot of mixed emotions while *honestly* contemplating my own life. This book helped me to begin to see myself as responsible for all of my own predicaments and feelings. For the first time in my life I asked myself the question: "Who am I?" and "What could be life's purpose?"

That summer, in the early part of August, I started to keep a journal. After my usual mundane entries, I put the journal away, and one day started to write poetry. Me a poet? That was very funny, or so I thought at the time. Are you smiling? Dr. Schweitzer, thank you for listening to me today!
Your grateful and devoted student, *R.*

Dear Dr. Schweitzer,

The book *'Handbook to Higher Consciousness'*, once I experienced and began to understand the premise, not only opened my mind, it also opened my heart. It was as if a switch had been turned on. Where there was darkness before, I now experienced a glimmer of light.

I recognized the wisdom of detaching from my emotions. These emotions were running my life back then. I was on an emotional roller coaster without being aware that I had any other choice. It's as if I had been a puppet or robot all my life, tossed around by the emotions of other people and my own, creating further turbulence. I had never taken charge of or examined these emotions before, never questioned the effect these emotions and thoughts had on my life.

As I remember those summer days, living in complete solitude on the ocean, I know that this was a distinct turning point in my awareness. Although I did not understand all I was reading, some of it must have hit home, becoming a revelation of sorts. I not only took long walks on the beach early each day, but I also frequently sat on the beach at night, staring at the starry moonlit sky—and wondered... Observing the stars and seeing the different galaxies in space made me feel insignificant. On one balmy hot afternoon I saw the ocean differently. It felt more like being on a huge lake. Instead of the usual pounding surf, I experienced only ripples on the surface of the water.

That afternoon I was released from my regular duties and I took this opportunity to relax on the beach. I felt like floating on an air mattress and that's exactly what I did. There was hardly a breeze. As I lay back and closed my eyes, I had a most unusual experience. I seemed to drift up and see myself from above. I floated further up and saw the whole beach, then the state of Florida, followed quickly by a view of the whole planet earth. What was this? This must be how the astronauts see our beautiful planet. I experienced seeing the blue of the ocean and the green of the vegetation, broken only by white puffy clouds. I had no idea how long this lasted, or why this had happened. The moment I started 'thinking' again, I found myself back on the air mattress and felt the cooling sensation of the water on my feet. I do remember seeing myself as small as a grain of sand and having experienced a feeling of 'oneness' with this planet we call earth.

I assumed that everyone at one time or another has had these experiences, and promptly forgot this incident. This experience was a bit more profound in that I saw the whole planet, feeling myself somehow merged with it. I was no more than a speck or minute particle. This quickly put my problems and worries into a whole new perspective. Not only that, I knew the book I had been reading must have left a deep impression. What had I learned, if anything? I would like to only touch on the main points.

They are as follows:

First, our mind is programmed by what we put in—by what we have experienced, and how we *interpret* this experience. Second, I came to the realization, that the mind is much like a computer. If I change my programming, (change my thoughts) I can change my life. Providing I wanted to—of course—I always had a choice in the matter. Do I have free will? That's one of the questions I am presently struggling with. If my choices can only be based on all of my previous experiences, which have formed my personality and character, how much free will is there? Yes, I have choices, but do I have free will? Where has my *will* led me? Have I used it at all, or have I allowed myself to just drift? I wonder... Third, I realized that we all search for love and *respond* to love. Not the usual human love, but Love of a different nature. I am talking about unconditional Love; the Love that does not judge or critique, the Love that is *all-inclusive,* the Love that allows me to see others as myself. Where has this love been hiding? We often associate love with the organ in our body called the heart. Once I opened my spiritual heart and used my higher mind, I saw everyone and everything differently—including myself. How come I never loved myself *this* way before? Why did I only give my so-called love to others, forgetting to love myself? Who am I?

The fourth revelation was the absolute power and control of the (lower case) *ego.* It can misguide us, always finding a rational answer for wrong or irrational thinking. This ego often encouraged poor judgment—and at times—even justified and rationalized unethical behavior. Who was this 'I' the *ego* I was so strongly identifying with and protecting? What was meant by 'I AM THAT I AM?' Was there a lower and higher ego or self? What about my soul? Did I have a separate soul, or was it all part and parcel of the material or physical me? I still had strong desires and ambitions. At times I found it very hard to uplift these emotions and desires to preferences, as was suggested. At other times I experienced the wisdom and freedom of doing so. I started to practice letting go of wanting to control everything, allowing situations and people to be. In other words I accepted what IS.

The fifth truth revealing itself was also quite profound. I realized that I—and I am sure a lot of other people—did not know, how to live in the present moment. What was so important about this revelation? I observed in myself how my thoughts were constantly occupied with either the past, which is *dead*—or the future—which is only *imaginary.* Both are not real in the sense that they do not exist. This led me to the question: "How often was I really present?" This deep realization, more than anything else, seemed to expand my awareness of how we operate. I say we, because—am I not so different from others. What had I discovered by experiencing the NOW moment and being fully *present*? Was that part of the secret? The truth of this revelation could not be ignored. I tried to practice being in the now moment and found this to be a very difficult thing to master—at first. However, since I had recognized the wisdom and experienced the power to be found in this truth, could I afford to ignore this new information?

I had certainly bitten off a huge chunk of information... Now, I needed to chew on this, then swallow and digest it, making it my own experience. I began to practice what I had learned. I somehow *knew* this information to be true. Yet, I was scared because my old way was much more familiar to me. I did want to grow and change. Why? Because I was not happy. I was very discontent. I was very fearful. Yes, fear is an emotion facing everyone, at one time or other. What was I afraid of losing? My 'self?' Which 'self' was my ego so busy protecting?

Yes, at first it was just information, because I had not *experienced* it. Then, very slowly at first, it dawned on me. In moments of complete solitude and contemplation I started to feel at peace. I also began to feel more at ease. Feelings of real joy and a new sense of freedom seemed to envelop me in those moments. I started to see the absolute necessity of being alone for a while. Was this the reason I had chosen this job? Had the universe provided me with this respite, this opportunity to experience silence and grow?

I bought a deck of Tarot Cards at that time. As I glanced at the scenes depicted in the Major Arcana, I got the feeling that this may be showing me the path of the soul. A path we must all eventually walk and discover on our own. Did these cards depict the trials, tribulations and temptations we are all faced with during our incarnation on earth? Was I experiencing a revelation? Who invented these cards, where did they first originate? Were the deeper mysteries about life handed down from generation to generation, throughout the ages, depicted in pictures, symbols and shrouded in myths? The first card of the major Arcana pictures the fool, and the last card is the universe, often shown as a woman surrounded by stars. Do some of these pictures relate to what Carl Jung referred to as Archetypes? What does this mean? How does this relate to the science of astronomy and astrology? Does it show the eventual path of the evolution of man? Does it depict the influences encountered and the stages on the path we as humans tread and must somehow master?

The instruction book that came with the cards suggested that the cards be looked at intuitively. I allowed my intuition to lead me to the deeper meaning behind the symbols. The elements of nature such as earth, water, air and fire for instance, represent the physical, emotional, mental and spiritual nature of man. As I contemplated the Tree of Life, I realized how little I knew about the

Kabbalah and the ancient Judaic mystical teachings. The pentacles represented the energy of our physical/earth nature. The cups represented the energy of our emotional/water nature; the swords depicted the energy of our lower and upper mental/air nature, and the wands/fire depicted the energy of our spiritual nature. These suits represented the four bodies we all use to operate in this worldly existence. Our modern playing cards are fashioned after these ancient cards.

Who was directing me to these experiences? I had no idea, and just sat down one evening and started to write down some of my very private inner feelings. That's how my writing continued. One of the first poems I ever wrote comes to mind. Perhaps I wrote this after my afternoon experience on the ocean.

Waves
I feel so lucky and grateful
The ocean is just at my door.
The sounds so familiar and soothing...
Who could possibly?
Ask for more?

Waves—can be pounding and threatening
But those days are few
All I think of—are the days
When a walk on the beach
Makes me feel fresh—as dew?

The water is alive and beckoning...
It calms my frazzled nerves.
I drink in the comforting motion—caressing me...
Aware that I am part of this universe.

This heavenly pleasure is mine
Why me?
Could the COSMOS
Be trying to
Tell me something?
RzT August 1985

I didn't question where the sudden urge to write poetry came from. Instead, I looked forward to writing each evening. I, of course, liked to egotistically believe that it was 'I' who was writing, not knowing what or whose energy was flowing through me. I did not understand this energy at the time. Could this be what is called creativity?

It seemed so simple. All I did on those occasions was to completely relax, take a few *deep* abdominal breaths and focus on one thought or one feeling at a time. I loved the wisdom and truth that stared me in the face, but must admit to being a bit confused— to say the least. Were these poems all lessons for me alone? Or could I share them with others? What was their purpose? I did not analyze this too much at the time. Instead I just read my books, started to experiment with meditation and left it at that.

Meditation was something new to me. I found it very hard to follow the directions given. Instructions such as—still your mind, relax and concentrate on breathing only, focus your attention on nothing. Yet, wasn't that what I was experiencing during writing?

Why was I doing all this? What would be the results of such effort? Who were the Yogis, or other ancient teachers of enlightenment? What was enlightenment and expanded awareness all about? I admitted to not having a clue. I tried all of the above mentioned exercises because I was not really happy. How many of us are really happy, all of the time? I had accepted the states of unhappiness, sadness and confusion labeling them as the 'human condition.' Dare I ask or search for anything more? Why was I asking myself so many questions? In hindsight, the answers to some of these questions did not arrive all at once. Some answers only came many years later, some are still left unanswered today.

Could there be a different way to experience the world and myself? What are happiness and the state of bliss, often referred to as Nirvana? Isn't happiness just another emotion that comes and goes? Some people have searched for a different state and called it 'experiencing the peace that passes all understanding.' Was there really a God?

Dear Dr. Schweitzer, I remember that you had often referred to this exalted state as *peace of mind*. Did you experience this peace? Did you search like me—in the dark—looking for truth and answers to some of the most profound question in life? *Why had Truth and Love become your religion*? I wondered...

During this summer in Florida I found myself searching—asking myself many profound questions—about relationships, about life, about it's purpose, about fate and destiny.

Searching
Where am I going?
Where have I been?
The life force is flowing
Without it being seen.

What's written in the cards?
Our minds want to know
A life filled with adventure—or shards?
Will it make me grow?

There is this quest
Happiness, peace, satisfaction and love
A need to leave the nest
Gathering experiences like a lone dove.

Is it all already written?
Us, just filling in the blanks—just so, so?
Or is our destiny hidden
Creating this desire to know?

To know—may not be the answer
The daily toils and laughter—may be
All there really is—like a dancer balancing
Being in the moment—feeling free?

Creating—allowing inspiration
To make you feel worthwhile.
Allowing love and perspiration
To linger for a while.

Enjoying the moment—so hard to do
Relaxing into a feeling
Letting go of wanting to know
What is a life—what is its meaning...?
RzT 1996

Oh my—it is almost eight. I must leave this letter and get dressed. My dear friend, I am getting close to telling you about the trip I took to Georgia, at the end of August that year, but—I must run now in order not to be late for work. Until tomorrow then... Your grateful and devoted student, *R.*

Sources Chapter 2:

1   P.26 *The Words of Albert Schweitzer*, Norman Cousins.
2   P.19 *The Words of Albert Schweitzer,* Norman Cousins.
3   P.1 *Secret Wisdom of the Great Initiates*, Earlyne Chaney, 1992 Astara Publishing, Upland, CA.
4   P.2 *Secret Wisdom of the Great Initiates*, Earlyne Chaney.
5   P.22 *The Words of Albert Schweitzer*, Norman Cousins.
6   P.19 *The Words of Albert Schweitzer*, Norman Cousins.
7   #322 *Life's Little instruction Book*, H. Jackson brown Jr., 1991, Rutledge Hill Press, Nashville TN.
8   P.24 *The Words of Albert Schweitzer*, Norman Cousins.
9   P.44 *The Words of Albert Schweitzer*, Norman Cousins.
10 P.56 *Albert Schweitzer-Man of Mercy*, Jacqueline Berrill.
11 P.10 *Albert Schweitzer, World Citizen*, Jean Christian.
12 P.297 *Encyclopedia of Britannica.*
13 P.305 *Encyclopedia of Britannica.*
14 P.827 *Encyclopedia of Britannica.*
15 P.12 *Out of my Life and Thought*, Albert Schweitzer.
16 P. 30-31 *Out of my Life and Thought*, Albert Schweitzer.

"Where there is power, there some result or other is produced. No ray of sunlight is ever lost, but the green, which it wakes into existence, needs time to sprout, and it is not always granted to the sower to live to see the harvest. All work that is worth anything is done in faith."[1]

Albert Schweitzer

3

The Visit

Dear Dr. Schweitzer,

Today is Sunday. I have the luxury of being at home all day, having asked for an extra day off during the slower summer months. This allows me some time to think about my upcoming vacation. This afternoon I plan to attend a lecture. The subject will be 'The Teachings of Pythagoras'. Along with Socrates and Plato, he is said to have had a great impact on civilization. Why else would we still be talking about him today?

Pythagoras, also known as the sage of Krotona, was born on the island of Samos in the Aegean Sea around 586 BC. He was an older contemporary of the Buddha. He lived almost a hundred years. Wasn't it during the sixth century BC that Gautama attained enlightenment? This century was a remarkable period of mental and emotional revolutionary changes in the life wave of our civilization. Along with teachers such as Shankaracharya and Mahavira in India, there was Zoroaster and the ancient deity known as Ahura Mazda in Persia—while Lao Tse and Confucius enlightened China with Taoism.

This will surely be a very interesting afternoon and I look forward to anything new I can learn about this man, a Master and teacher who lived during a great period in our history. Pythagorian teachings have been handed down through the ages by a select group of his students. Nothing was ever written down by the teacher himself. For instance, Pythagoras, along with his discovery of geometry, also taught that all numbers have a vibration. He seemed to know more than is commonly understood about the mystical aspect of numbers and nature. We now refer to his teachings as sacred geometry. What else did he know and teach? I wonder...

I must not get carried away with this subject today. You see, foremost on my mind this morning is to describe to you what led up to my visit to a spiritual retreat—exactly sixteen years ago this month. I can pinpoint the dates correctly because, for some strange reason, I had dated my poems.

My new friend had established a habit of coming up to my office during the summer months in Florida. We discussed many different subjects, including metaphysics and reincarnation. During one of our discussions she told me of a trip she was planning, and shared some of her past experiences with a spiritual teacher. The teacher she referred to had lived in Miami several years ago, filling a need for many spiritual seekers. She later moved to Georgia.

My friend inquired, 'would you be interested in a journey to a retreat in Georgia?' It was summer, and I had not taken a break from my job since I started in June the previous year. There was the odd business trip to Toronto, but that was not considered time off. After a few days of consideration and asking the corporate channels for permission, I thought, 'Why not?' I found myself being very curious about so many things. I had so many questions...

Shortly after the decision was made, we found ourselves heading north. In my suitcase were a journal and the poems I had written—since I expected to continue writing. The thought had occurred to me, "Who in their right mind drives to Georgia in the blistering heat of summer?" Justifying my actions was not difficult. This was the perfect time to leave. Summer was not a busy time for luxury real estate in Florida. Our prospective buyers were most likely enjoying themselves on the beaches of Long Island or on Martha's Vineyard.

My friend and I shared the responsibility of driving. By late afternoon we could be found on I-75 heading north through the interior of the Florida countryside. The drive was uneventful except for one incident. We stopped at several gas stations and at one particular stop, while browsing through the usual Florida gift shop items such as T-shirts, seashells and bags of oranges and grapefruits, I spotted a post card. This postcard had a particular appeal for me. On the front picture was a huge hot air balloon. The caption read: *"Our minds are like parachutes—they only function—when open!"* I loved this motto and on impulse purchased the postcard, using it as a bookmark for my journal. Once inside the air-conditioned car, I smiled and thanked the universe for this little treasure. Glancing out the car window I saw the landscape change, from the usual miles and miles of deep green orange groves, to moss covered live oak trees. Seeing the sandy Florida soil change to a reddish clay color, was a sign that we must be close to the state line of Georgia.

We arrived later that evening and were led to our rooms. I found the accommodations a bit strange, but did not care too much since I was very tired and just glad to be finally out of the car. The next morning found me up early. I was greeted by a beautiful sunrise and chose to walk the grounds. In front of the group of cottages, which were actually large trailers located on a slight hill, I saw the main house. This must be were the teacher lives, I thought, as I enjoyed the peaceful stroll through a luscious countryside. There were real trees here—how lovely!

The trailers housing the students were as big as a three-bedroom home. There was a living room, dining area and a kitchen, and our particular trailer had a fireplace and a large Jacuzzi tub. Our rooms were modest but adequate. There were no telephones or televisions. Near the back of the large main residence was an outdoor swimming pool. The cuisine consisted of various vegetarian dishes, prepared by the teacher's grown daughters. 'So, this is a family business', I silently observed.

We had planned to stay a total of six days, including the two days spent driving. This left four days for relaxation and learning. Actually, as I remember it now, there were no definite lectures or instructions given. We were pretty much left to our own devices. Since I had no agenda or expectations of what this was to be all about, I read, continued writing poetry, and simply relaxed into each day, enjoying the change of scenery. Looking at the ocean had its charm, now I soaked up the new atmosphere of being in the forest.

I met and talked to several interesting women. They were from different parts of the country, and some, like my friend, had been at this retreat before. I observed them while they were drawing, reading or swimming in the pool. "Is that it?" I thought—"just a place to completely unwind from the normal activities and stresses of everyday life?" I had already experienced this for some time in Florida and silently wondered why my friend had suggested I come to this place. Now, of course, I know the value of a retreat. The purpose clearly is to allow me to get in touch with, or to retreat into 'myself'.

During a particular discussion with the other women, I heard about a *treatment* that was being offered. It had something to do with balancing the chakras, which I already knew were the energy centers of our etheric bodies. We all have this energy field consisting of magnetic ether surrounding our physical body. Supposedly, people who have obtained the psychic ability of clairvoyance can see this energy field.

The ancient cultures had known about this a long time ago. Eastern disciplines—such as yoga and meditation—make us aware of this energy and show us how to use it properly. I had already learned the importance of breathing during yoga and meditation. One of the questions I had asked myself often was, 'Why did it take our Western civilizations so long to discover this? Why had we blocked out this important part of learning? What were our scientists in the West doing? What were they currently researching? Were they figuring out how to better serve humanity? Or were they too busy learning how to make new nuclear devices so we can blow each other up faster? What about our modern medical experts?'

Some of our doctors are beginning to accept the eastern tradition of the scientific application of acupuncture—finally! My doctor friend did not believe in the benefits of meditation. He was very much against this kind of mental and emotional exploration. What was he afraid of? Is looking at yourself that painful? Yes, for certain people it is almost too painful. He had preferred to keep the venerable profession of medicine out of the field of esoteric teachings. How many other professionals in science and theology are stuck with this outdated and limiting mind set? Why were we in the West so far behind in any kind of research dealing with the subject of energy, thoughts and emotions? This kind of research is now considered to be the 'new frontier'. Why was the medical profession so against this kind of exploration back in 1985?

For instance—take the discovery of the mind's influence over the physical body, and the discovery of the power behind our thoughts. Why had no one looked at this power? Yes, I must admit there are a few brave souls who did dare to shake the proverbial boat, and some of these individuals are, or were medical doctors. Deepak Chopra, Andrew Weil, Elisabeth Kübler-Ross and Maurice Bucke were trained physicians, respected professionals in the field of medicine. Did their curiosity and open-minded inquiry lead them to new experiences and important discoveries? Why aren't more people curious?

As a matter of fact this may be a good time to mention that I did not have an extensive formal education. I had discovered that intellectual pursuits give me a lot of information, but they don't make me a wise human being. Only understanding and experience can do that...

Perhaps this is why I spent so many years reading books. I was trying to catch up to what I thought everybody else already knew. Sorry, Dr. Schweitzer, please forgive this digression.

Why did I have this sudden urge to vent my spleen? Perhaps I have memories make me frustrated with the scholars and experts who for years have carefully skirted around the idea of the research of energy, thoughts—and soul experiences. Did they consider this a subject to be isolated and therefore to be filed under *philosophy, religion* or *mysticism*—subjects not to be confused with science? If they can't explain something it does not exist? How do you explain the mind? How do you explain electricity? How do you explain radio waves, vibration and frequency? How do you explain nature? How do you explain the formation of a snowflake?

Maybe it is a good idea to stop writing for today. I am getting a bit too emotional. Time to cool off and time to reflect on what I am about to tell you next. I am ending this letter with lots of love in my heart for you. As I tackle the mundane task of cleaning out my closet and my apartment, I am sure you will enter my thoughts again. Things will flow better with less clutter around me. I find this activity to be helpful in clearing my mind as well.

The sun is out now, and I plan to spend a few quiet moments at the pool, before getting ready for the afternoon lecture on the mysterious Pythagoras.

Your devoted student, *R.*

Dear Dr. Schweitzer,

This morning I woke earlier than usual. As I glance at my clock radio I see the numbers 3:30. I wasn't quite sure whether to get up or not, since today is Monday, my day off. Experience has taught me that if I go back to sleep, I will wake up tired and groggy. So here I am. I paced the floor this morning, not wanting to start writing right away. I was still digesting yesterday's lecture on Pythagoras. Is that it, or is it because I had a great revelation about you? Feelings of gratitude for the ancient teachings overwhelm me at times. I will tell you about the insight gained yesterday afternoon at a later time, preferring to continue the story about my experience in Georgia.

After being told that a balancing of the chakras would have a healing effect on several levels, namely emotional, mental and physical, I made the decision to undergo this healing therapy. It was our last day, so procrastination was not an option. I really did not want to spend the money. The cost would be around $200, which was a lot of money for me then. I also found myself a bit apprehensive, since this was all new to me. Putting aside my fears, I agreed to experience this therapy.

My appointment was set for 2 P.M. It was a balmy summer day in Georgia. The therapist had prepared the room by lighting a candle. I smelled the aroma of incense. A stereo was playing soft, almost angelic music. In other words—the mood was very relaxing. In the center of this room I saw a table very similar to what a massage therapist would use. She asked me a few questions, then suggested I place myself on this table, lying down face up. I had no idea what to expect so after taking a few deep breaths, she suggested I relax.

She asked me to close my eyes and to breathe deeply, extending my abdomen with each intake and lowering it as I breathed out. The musical sounds, the aroma and the soft humming of the air conditioning almost put me to sleep. The therapist spent a few minutes explaining what she was about to do. I honestly do not remember exactly what she said. I do remember that she told me she would be working with the energy field around my body. In other words, she would not be physically touching me. After granting her my permission to go ahead, she asked me to keep my eyes closed during this session. By this time I was so relaxed that I expressed my concern about falling asleep. She assured me that this would not happen.

She must have started at the lower end of my body, because as she reached my stomach area I felt some warmth, as her hands passed over my solar plexus. As she reached my heart center, which is located in the upper chest, she asked me to picture a scene from my childhood. I pictured a scene when I was around four or five years old, sitting on my father's knee. I had not seen my father since I arrived in Canada at the age of twelve. He had passed away at the age of fifty-four in 1965.

During these few minutes, I remembered that he did love me and I felt more at peace. Elisabeth said, "It's all right if you want to cry," but I did not shed any tears. I just felt he also knew I loved him. After giving him a big hug, I said a farewell, thanking him for having given me a lot of happy memories during my childhood.

Her hands must have also stopped over my throat chakra, but I honestly don't remember any particular experience or sensation there. Perhaps I have forgotten that part because my *next experience was so memorable*. As her hands reached the area of my forehead, Elisabeth asked me to picture a television screen. I tried to follow her instructions and pictured a blank black screen. She asked me to turn this screen on. What happened next is so incredible, that I will never forget this moment as long as I live. What I experienced is the following:

I saw a large face, at first I was not sure to whom this face belonged. Then it dawned on me! **It was your face**! I recognized the unruly head of white hair and the drooping mustache from pictures I had seen in my childhood. Then, as if in a flash, I saw you standing next to what appeared to be, an old piano. I saw a room in which the walls looked a bit rough and primitive, in that the wooden beams or upright studs on the walls were exposed. There was a table or desk in this room filled with many papers—a certain clutter, if I may be so bold—consisting of sheets and sheets of papers. Not only that, there were sheets and notes of papers tacked all over the wall, fastened with nails or string. Everything was seen crystal clear, as though I was watching a movie. My attention turned back to you, leaning against this piano. Your attire was a white, short sleeved open necked shirt and loose fitting trousers. You just looked at me. I will never forget your kind, yet penetrating eyes. There was something mesmerizing about your eyes. I was so startled and puzzled that I told the therapist what was happening.

She advised me to ask you a question. I remember thinking, 'What should I ask?' Finally overcoming my shyness and surprise

I dared to ask, "Why did you appear to me this way?" Then you started to speak. I can still hear your words clearly in my head:

"Please learn all you can about me. Familiarize yourself with my work!"

Your expression was serious, yet your eyes were filled with a genuine kindness, as I felt them penetrating my being. Then in a flash you were gone.

Tears welled up in my eyes, and I could not speak. The therapist must have felt my emotional state as she continued her work in silence. I had no idea how long this scene lasted, whether it was a few minutes or a few seconds. I just remember being completely puzzled and confused. As I sat up, I told her what I had just experienced. She asked me how I knew you. I replied, "I don't know anything about him at all, except what my mother had told me in the early 1950's, when I was only seven or eight years old."

"My mother had told me that Dr. Albert Schweitzer was a great humanitarian, having dedicated his life to establishing and operating a hospital in the jungle of Africa," I mumbled. Followed by, "She seemed to have great admiration and respect for this man."

That was all I knew about you—then, that summer afternoon in Georgia. The session ended with the healer's admonition: "You must take this great man's words very seriously, he must have had a reason to come to you like this! Nothing like this ever happens without a reason." "Why me?" were the only words I could think of. This was all too strange and weird for my limited comprehension— back then. What did I do next? Absolutely nothing!

I went back to my room finding it hard to contain my tears. Why? Because I felt so stupid and so small, totally ill equipped to handle any task given to me by such a great historic figure as you. You were a person not only held in great esteem and admiration by my mother; the whole world must have known all about you. Why didn't I? I didn't know anything except that you became a doctor in Africa. I knew nothing—so, why pick me? Later, when alone, I allowed myself to cry for the first time in years, having experienced a deep emotional breakthrough of some sort. Feeling depleted and empty, I decided to take a nap. In the early evening I went back out to my chair on the porch and wrote more poetry.

Only this time the poetry became more personal. Still in a very emotional state, I wrote a long poem to my father, followed by a poem to my mother. It was as if I suddenly saw them as fellow human beings, instead of just my parents. I forgave them for all the hurts, imagined and real, I had experienced in my childhood. Then I thanked them for doing the best they knew how. It was as if a big load had been lifted from my shoulders. I saw them through new eyes and any resentment I had stored up inside was suddenly gone, as if by magic. I had experienced the power of forgiveness!

Later that evening, my friend came out to talk to me. She asked me about the healing session of that afternoon. I told her briefly what had happened. I almost felt foolish sharing this experience. Who would ever believe me? I asked her if she had experienced something similar. Her answer was, "No, not really."

Listening to her answer added to my confusion and frustration. I decided not to talk about this to anyone, because they would surely think I was crazy. I felt that the only one who would not think I was crazy was the therapist. She approached me the following day as we were ready to leave, giving me a hug and the following advice: "Should you ever find yourself in the position to give interviews, make sure they are *live*, not pre-recorded or edited. In this way your words will not be twisted or misunderstood." I jokingly replied: "You mean live, like radio interviews?" Her answer was, "Yes, that's what I mean." I laughed and shook my head, thinking, 'Now she is crazy too? She obviously did not know about my shyness and stage fright!'

I don't remember being very talkative on our drive back to Florida. I treasured the book of poetry I had written and knew that it was finished. As I looked at the postcard I had used as a bookmark, I decided to call this small book: *"Our minds are like parachutes—they only function when open."* During the drive back to Florida, my mind kept going back to you and my unusual experience—*your visit*—the day before. Every time I closed my eyes, tears welled up under my closed eyelids. I did not understand this sudden burst of emotion.

We were back in Florida the last week of August, which I now realize, is exactly sixteen years ago. How time flies! It seems like yesterday—yet, my dear Dr. Schweitzer, so much has happened to me since then, it often seems like a lifetime ago.

One of the things I occupied myself with on my return, was to type the poems on the electric typewriter at the office. I then photocopied them to form a book. On the cover I proudly pasted the postcard mentioned earlier. I gave a few copies to friends and got absolutely no response. My ego was crushed. You see, no one seemed to see any value in what I had written, except me. I started to wonder if perhaps all these poems were only meant for me. Were these poems personal messages or lessons, meant for my own growth only? I wondered...

This reminds me of an encounter I had a few years later in New York City. I had the opportunity to talk with a woman who wrote children's books. I shyly told her that I was also very interested in writing and that I had written two books of poetry a few years ago. She replied: "Ahh—poetry—that's the *voice of the soul*." I thought about this for a long time, deciding that she could possibly be right. On some level this began to make sense to me.

There was a small mystery connected to my writing. The mystery was—why did this inspired writing of poetry suddenly stop after a total of forty-seven poems? Why did they come so fast and furiously? I had decided early on, that this was not what was often referred to as 'automatic writing'. My pen did not fly off on its own with me looking at the results in awe.

Rather, the thoughts seemed to be coming from my mind and emotions, one thought at a time, based on my personal experiences. I felt an inherent *truth and wisdom,* while I was writing. My first book of poetry was written in two parts. Part one was completed *before* I went to Georgia, and ended with the following poem:

Beginning
With every end—comes a new beginning
A new day
A new chance
A new challenge.

Be open—not trapped
Look at the possibilities
Some things you can change
Others you must simply accept.

Be happy or sad
The choice is yours
Your life is a precious gift
Given to help you—to find your soul.

RzT August 18, 1985

The last poem in part two, *after my experience* was just as bewildering and almost prophetic as I look at it now.

My Purpose
This book was not written
To give you—all the answers.

Those answers will come—on their own,
In due time.

The start—my friend, is in
Asking the questions...

Trust yourself
You will be free—just like me.

Enjoy the journey...
RzT August 26, 1985

The question that kept recurring and would not leave me was: "Why me?" I certainly had no educational qualifications to speak of. As a matter of fact, I was what you might call self-educated. I did not consider myself worthy of the attention from a man of your stature.

This whole thing was an absolute mystery to me at the time. But you know how I react to mysteries, don't you? Is that part of the answer to this puzzle? Some of the possible answers are just beginning to dawn on me right now—in the summer of 2001. You mean it takes that long to grow—to mature? I can feel you smiling, and I can see why. Am I getting ahead of myself again?

Looking at this mystery again, I will only mention here that my writing of poetry started again—very suddenly—in the spring of 1996. Since I had not gotten any response from the small circle of friends and relatives to my first book, I hid the second one in a closet and did not look at it for the longest time. I also found myself quietly wondering whether I should discuss my experience in Georgia with anyone. This was a very touchy subject for me. I know too well what it feels like to be a skeptic. You were on my mind a lot, yet I realized, that perhaps you wanted me to learn something.

Since I had been very interested in the subject of reincarnation, it also occurred to me that my experience with you proved this belief to be real and truthful. I silently labeled your visit as *the most important experience of my life.*

You see, I knew nothing about you at that time, except what my mother had told me—back in 1952—when I was eight years old. One of my teachers may also have mentioned your name at that time. But it was my mother's voice I kept hearing in my mind saying, "this man was a great humanitarian, he gave up his own comfortable life to move to Africa and help people who were less fortunate than himself. He built a hospital in the deepest jungle for people who had been totally neglected by our western civilization, the black Africans." Africa was often referred to back then, as the dark and mysterious continent.

Your selfless mission must have left a deep impression in my mother's heart, resulting in her feelings. It was only after I returned from Georgia that my mother's life and her experiences kept coming back into my mind. I remembered that she had lost both her parents during an influenza epidemic raging through Europe in 1917, when she was only six years old. I began to see my mother in a different light. She had become very bitter after the separation from my father, and tried to find her own answers to life's riddles and challenges. I also remember that she seemed to blame my father for much of her unhappiness. May her soul find peace!

I thank you from the bottom of my heart for having come to visit me that afternoon in Georgia. This visit has changed the direction of my whole life. Of course, I only see this now—in hindsight.
With deep gratitude, I remain your devoted student, *R.*

Bonjour, Professeur Schweitzer,

My trip to Europe is only a few weeks away and I feel that my French will be totally inadequate. Oh well, I'll just have to do my best and wing it. I'll use gestures to communicate. Speaking of communication...

Dear Dr. Schweitzer, how do I communicate the feelings that arose once I came to know you better, and that it took me sixteen years to come to the realization that I may have something to say?

Where do I get the passion, desire and courage to continue my dialogue in these letters? Are you smiling—again?

Every time I get stuck, or feel at a loss for words, I see your face looking at me from the picture I placed on my writing table. You are my inspiration and you give me the courage needed to continue. You make me feel comfortable in speaking freely about what is in my heart and mind.

What happened to me after I came back from Georgia, was not of earthshaking importance, except for a most important incident, which I will mention now.

During the fall of 1985 I had made the decision to return to Toronto. A green card was very difficult to obtain, so a permanent stay was not an option. My friends in Toronto had been urging me to return. "The real estate market is booming, you could make a lot more money here," followed by "Why are you wasting your time sitting on this 'white elephant'?" After careful consideration and looking at my choices, I made the decision to return to Toronto. My children had graduated from High School and were enrolling in college that fall. Both boys knew the value of being self sufficient. Did they understand my need to be independent? I don't know... I had not made much money in Florida, and felt the need to move back to Canada. My talents were wasted in the position I found myself in. Two years of solitude was enough.

Would I have done things differently? Absolutely not, as I would have missed the *experience of my life*. Plus, the reading I did during that period had opened my mind—I had become a *free thinker*. I took it upon myself to educate myself in many areas. That is true, as I remember the numerous books on my night table then and now.

After I announced my decision to leave, a new person was hired. I agreed to stay on until the end of January 1986. The fall of 1985 was a busy time for me in many respects. My doctor friend had returned from Saudi Arabia, and in October announced that he wanted to move back to Canada to start his life over. He was following up on offers to head an Obstetrics department at a hospital. This took him away on several trips. He had proposed marriage, but I had not been clear in my mind or my heart, whether this would be in my future. Although I loved the dream of being a doctor's wife, I felt it was better left as a dream. His depressions had started to annoy me. Every attempt to help him fell on deaf ears and his constant negative emotions, especially the emotion of self-pity, had become a bore.

I began to see that we had very little in common. He was certainly not interested in any of the subjects that were of interest to me at the time, such as meditation, self-discovery, self-improvement and creativity, not to mention the far-out subjects of metaphysics or my esoteric interests!

He considered these ideas to be fancies of my imagination. As a matter of fact I don't remember ever showing him my poetry. What would I be getting myself into, what kind of a life would I be living? These questions plagued me during this time—as I looked at the fork presenting itself in my road—and at the choices I had then. Yes, I had decided to move back to Canada, but not as his wife. The words, 'be true to yourself' kept reverberating in my mind.

Shortly after the festivities of Christmas and New Year I went to the local library one last time. I had spent evenings packing my few belongings. My days were filled with instructing the new person taking over my job.

The important incident I referred to earlier in this letter is this: About a week before my scheduled departure on January 28, 1986, I decided to visit the local library. I spent a few minutes browsing through the shelves, looking for any books written about you. A Reader's Digest condensed book is not where I would normally have thought of looking for a story about you. Yet, there I found an excerpt of your life story, focusing on your years as a doctor in Africa, condensed into thirty pages.

I then discovered a book written by Norman Cousins entitled: "*The Words of Albert Schweitzer.*" I could not believe my luck. This was a newly published book, back then. The copyright date was 1984. I briefly leafed through this book before taking it to the checkout counter. I almost fainted when I saw a particular picture. Before me was a black and white photograph of you sitting at a desk in Africa. *This picture showed the room **exactly** as I had seen it during my session in Georgia.* My experience had not been a hallucination after all.

It took me by complete surprise. As I stared at the photo of you, sitting at your cluttered desk, tears started to form—again. My experience—the experience of a lifetime—had been *real*. All doubt was beginning to leave my consciousness as I clutched this book walking back to my apartment. It was evening, so I just went to bed and started to read your words.

What I realized very early on is that this was not the kind of book one reads in one session. I found myself having to put the book down after each paragraph. Your words were so powerful and so deep; they became a meditation of sorts. Why? Because they evoked my deepest feelings, they made me stop and think, perhaps on a much deeper level than I had ever experienced *thought* before.

I thank Mr. Cousins for this beautiful book, a collection of your words. Words full of wisdom, words of guidance and understanding. Your words came alive for me each time I opened the book. Norman Cousins was so lucky to have known you personally. I felt so lucky to have found this book in the small library on the beach, which was within walking distance of my building. 'What luck—what coincidence', I thought back then. Now I *know* there is no such thing as luck or coincidence. I am deeply moved as I remember the incident in the library. Since this book had to be returned, I promised myself to buy a copy as soon as I returned to Toronto. I knew I needed to study your words at my leisure.

This is a good time to end this letter. I look forward to continuing my dialogue with you tomorrow.

Your devoted pupil, *R.*

Bonjour le Professeur de Mèdicine,

Parlez-vous Allemand? Oui, Madame? I could hardly wait to get to my writing table this morning. I showered faster than normal, drank my coffee faster than normal, even dried my hair faster than normal.

Why do I have this urge to speed things up? I've learned not to question these urges, instead I just go with the flow. On my table lies the open book I mentioned in my last letter. Norman Cousins certainly knew what he was doing. On the front cover is a picture of you sitting in a dugout canoe. Two men standing with long poles, maneuvering this boat, are guiding you through the quiet waters of the Ogawe River. Your silhouette is distinctly visible. The unmistakable pith helmet you wore at all times to protect you from the brutal sun of Africa can be seen against the calm shining water. The photo appears hazy, almost mystical. It appears to be an evening photo and the only light provided is from a full moon.

As I look at the back cover, there is that famous picture of you sitting at your table. The walls are covered with notes—pieces of paper hanging from nails. On the table, right beside you—staring at your writing—is a small kitten. Cats are so curious aren't they? Well, I was curious too!

Since I have never been to Africa, and never had the pleasure of meeting you during your lifetime, let me quote Mr. Cousins impression of you as I read this paragraph in his introductory words:

"The biggest impression of Schweitzer that emerged for me was that of a man who had learned to use himself fully. Much of the ache and brooding unhappiness in modern life is the result of the difficulty people experience in using themselves fully. We perform compartmentalized tasks in a compartmentalized world. We are reined in—physically, socially, and spiritually. Only rarely do we have a sense of fulfilling ourselves through total contact with total challenge. We find it difficult to make real connections even with those who are nearest to us. But we live with vast yearnings demanding air and release. These yearnings have to do with our capacity for moral response. And our potentialities in this direction are deep—potentialities that keep nagging at our inner selves. Schweitzer had never been a stranger to his potentiality.
This is not to say that Schweitzer sought or achieved 'happiness' in pursuit of that potentiality. He was less concerned with happiness than with purpose."[2]

An earlier observation of Mr. Cousins also caught my eye this morning. It reads as follows:

"Despite his dual success he decided to *"make my life my argument."* His ideas in theology and his emphasis on personal commitment were somewhat at variance with the prevailing views. Rather than enter into debate or even dialogue, he decided to test his ideas as living reality."[3] **(My Italics).**

There I had it. Mr. Cousins was able to describe your essence very well. I know words to be a bit limiting when describing certain facets of your being. I am so grateful to Norman Cousins for having made a record of his journeys to Africa, and am so grateful for the books he wrote, including *'The Words of Albert Schweitzer,'* which became my first introduction to your words and your life.

This book had further appeal because the author chose to accompany your words with wonderful photographs. He also had the wisdom to know that it is almost impossible to write an objective and untainted biography of your vast life. He allowed *your words* to dominate my experience of you.

I found this first book back in January of 1986. The question that appeared often in my mind was, "Why me?" Why had you chosen to appear to me in this way? Instead of dwelling on this further right now, I would like to close this letter. The Cousins book has become a constant companion to me. It is on my night table and has given me a lot of inspiration when faced with challenging situations in my life. Are you listening? How does it feel to have someone list your virtues, strengths and accomplishments?

How can I possibly describe your path objectively? I can't! However, I can describe the changes and effects your words and life have had on me. Wasn't this part of your purpose? You educated others and me by being an example, hoping to stir us up—encouraging us to think to contemplate and to reach beyond the ordinary Furthermore, as I read your accomplishments in chronological order I was not only overwhelmed, but also confused. I could see that you were not an ordinary person. You must have experienced what is often referred to as 'illumination.' More about this detective work of mine later. Where did you get your courage and your faith? The following passage gave me the strength and faith to continue. Your words:

"I cannot define what 'faithful' means. The real meaning begins at the point at which verbal explanation is inadequate and ceases to be. Yet, we know in our inner heart what it is trying to say. All the good we may recognize or desire is nothing in itself and leads nowhere, unless it is strengthened in the thought of faithfulness. It is just like the hardening of metal. No one can explain how it happens. First it is weak and pliable, but then it becomes a hundred times as strong as it was before. Nor can we explain how every human virtue only achieves strength and fulfillment after it has been hardened on the anvil of faithfulness."[4]

When I asked myself the question of why the two years of solitude were so necessary in my growth and why I had, subconsciously perhaps, chosen them, I saw the answers forming in my inner being. Your words:

**"It is harder for us today to feel near to God among the streets
and houses of the city than it is for country folk. For them the
harvested fields bathed in the autumn mists speak of God and
his goodness far more vividly than any human lips."5**

Yes, I had experienced that being surrounded by nature did have
a certain healing effect, and helped me in countless other ways. The
only dilemma I found myself facing, after reading your words back
then, was that I was not sure at that time whether I believed in God,
at least not the way most people pictured God to be—a personality—
a wise old man sitting on a throne. I, like you, had become a free
thinker and still had many questions that puzzled me about faith
and the childish vision of baby Jesus and the Almighty Creator. I
was a true skeptic.

What about all the latest discoveries made by our scientists
and physicists? What about the discovery that on the sub-atomic
planes everything is vibration? The discovery that matter is only
the lowest and densest form of vibration. Had you wondered about
all of these facets of nature as well? Where did your path lead you?
What discoveries had you made?

Is a sense of wonder—a sense of reverence—and a sense of
awe, a necessary step in our evolutionary growth and maturity?
Do we all travel a similar path? How come more people have not
asked themselves these questions? I will attempt to do my best to
describe your path in life, the one you chose to travel, and hopefully
this may inspire other souls, who just like me, had started asking
themselves these or other profound questions.

Are we that different or do we all have something very deep and
mystical in common? Is there an interconnectedness to be found in
all of nature, in our entire universe? Does the same energy pervades
and penetrates all? I wondered, as I drove back to Toronto that
sunny day on January 28, 1986.

My son Marc, had kindly offered to drive the moving truck and
around eleven o'clock that morning he pulled into a gas station in
order to watch the launching of the space shuttle, which had been
announced on the car radio earlier that morning.

We were only a few miles west of the space center—affording
us a view that was truly magnificent, or so I thought. Marc and I
stood staring at the backdrop of a perfect blue Florida sky, when we
saw the shuttle explode, then break into two distinct parts falling

back into the Atlantic Ocean. A lump had formed in my throat as I watched this tragedy unfold. Needless to say, the next few hours of our trip were spent in silence...

Experience
I experienced my innocence.
I experienced my fears.
I experienced my helplessness.
I experienced my struggle.
I experienced my sadness.
I experienced my guilt.
I experienced my anger.
I experienced my doubts.
I experienced my frustrations.
I experienced my suffering.
I experienced my darkness.
I experienced my happiness.
I experienced my joy.
I experienced myself.
RzT August 16, 2001

I was struck by the question: "Who is the *Experiencer?*" Could it be the part of me that is searching for wisdom—needing to grow? Could it be my soul?

"By three methods we can learn wisdom. First by reflection— which is noblest. Second by imitation—which is the easiest. And third by experience—which is the bitterest."

Confucius

Yes, I had started to reflect on many things in the universe during the two years I lived alone on the beach. There I had learned to still my restless mind. Until you appeared, I had no one to admire—no ideal to inquire about—no example to inspire me. Who was your ideal? All I had to do was to look at your book titles to find the answer. You had studied the works of many of the great philosophers. You had studied comparative religions. You had not only studied the life of Jesus, but also studied his *mind*. Something tells me that you found something of value, something not easily recognized, unless thought about and contemplated on a deeper level. You were never satisfied with anything less than Truth:

"But what matters is not what is witty but what is true. In this case the simple thing is the truth, the uncomfortable truth with which we have to work."6

A light started to dawn in my inner awareness. What makes us so uncomfortable in facing truth, especially the truth about ourselves? Could it be that we feel comfortable in pointing out the truth about someone else, but live in the comfort of complete denial about ourselves? Suddenly I saw that all emotions create feelings, which have an affect on my state of mind. These feelings either create confusion and separation—or peace and harmony! Who creates these feelings? I do... Thank you so much for helping me to understand this. I truly feel that experience isn't the best teacher, it is the *only* teacher.

In hindsight, I dared to speculate on why you appeared to me. Is it because no particular religious belief systems had been able to indoctrinate me? I was not forced in my early childhood to conform to a certain mode of thinking, so in this respect, I had not been too 'conditioned'? Was I still open to look for new aspects of, and open to find new possibilities in spirituality? Was it because I was so eager to learn? Or did you know that I, like you, loved a mystery and would dig deeper, eventually finding my own truth? All of the above? I really don't profess to know the answers to these questions.

My heart is filled with love and a deeper understanding, as I think of you and your mission of healing. Please send the light of understanding to all of us who are still struggling, resisting an inner Truth which can only be found in the deep recesses of our own hearts. I thank you and remain,

Your devoted and grateful student, *R.*

Sources Chapter 3:

1 P.27-28 *The Light Within Us*, Albert Schweitzer, Philosophical Library Inc., New York, NY.
2 P.9 *The Words of Albert Schweitzer*, Norman Cousins.
3 P.7-8 *The Words of Albert Schweitzer*, Norman Cousins.
4 P.49 *The Words of Albert Schweitzer*, Norman Cousins.
5 P.51 *The Words of Albert Schweitzer*, Norman Cousins.
6 P.1 *The Light Within Us*, Albert Schweitzer, Philosophical Library, Inc., New York, NY.

Part II

The Path

"I intentionally avoid technical philosophical phraseology. My appeal is to thinking men and women whom I wish to provoke to elemental thought about the questions of existence which occur to the mind of every human being."[1]

Albert Schweitzer

"The paths into which God leads mankind are shrouded in darkness for us. There are only two ground rules. They go together, and each taken by itself is enigmatic. The first is that all sin requires atonement. The second is that all progress demands sacrifice, which has to be paid for by the lives of those chosen to be offered up. We sense this more than we understand it."[2]

Albert Schweitzer

4

Choices

Good Morning Dr. Schweitzer,

When it comes to the word sin, I like to think of the analogy of an archer. A metaphysician explained it to me this way: "We, like an archer who is poised and focused on a target, occasionally miss our target. Therefore, the word sin can be seen as missing our target—missing the mark." The target is 'doing the right thing'.

The results of missing the target affect us, and we see that perhaps we can do better next time. The important thing is to try again and not give up. When you are sinning, you work against yourself. I am sinning when I don't listen to my conscience or I don't recognize that I have a conscience. Most of us are doing the best we can at our current level of awareness. In order to do better we must increase our awareness. This in turn will change our conduct. If our thoughts create our level of awareness, I must look at the choices I make on every level—every day, every hour and every minute.

Another way to view sin and atonement is to view it from the eastern perspective, the target being in *harmony* with the Laws of our Universe. We sin, when we are not aligned with these immutable Laws, including the Laws of Nature. This Law is impersonal. This Law governs all that exists. It is the Law of Karma also known as the Law of Cause and Effect. How does this relate to us? We all have to experience the consequences of our own, often self-defeating thoughts and actions. Atonement to me means correcting past actions. Past actions which caused me not only to feel separated from others, but also to feel separated from my true self—my soul. The opposite of separation is *union.* Any corrections I make will help me to move towards AT-ONE-MENT. No one can make these corrections for me. I will talk to you more about these laws at a later time.

Sacrifice, when seen from this point of view makes absolute sense. In order for something new to grow, the old must die. Without this there is no progress. I have to sacrifice, destroy or *let go* of the old in order to make room for something new to come into existence. It means slowing down and stepping off the treadmill. It means taking the time needed to reflect on what is meaningful and satisfying to me on a deeper level. This also includes old belief systems and notions created in my childhood experiences and conditioning, some of which I may still be carrying around in my mind. Common sense tells me that these old beliefs and ideas affect the way I view others and myself. Letting go of childish things comes naturally as I grow up and mature. It is only experienced as a sacrifice when I am *attached* to something. This can be a *physical, mental or emotional* attachment.

It has been my experience that among my circle of friends it was not until we reached the critical age of forty or forty-five that we started to ask ourselves questions such as: "Why is this happening to me?" I found that at this mature time in life, we often wonder if perhaps there is something larger at play here, something that directs our fate, our destiny. This leads us to look and read about eastern philosophies, searching out new avenues for understanding our universe and ourselves. Some of us were drawn to books such as 'The Road Less Traveled' or the Edgar Cayce material.

I've always been intrigued by the saying, 'all paths lead home.' I am instinctively reminded of the Buddhic symbol of the path or journey through life. This ancient symbol is also to be found in the Tarot, which is based on the Kabbalistic Tree of Life. I am referring to the symbol of the wheel, with many spokes leading to the center. The question arises: "Where are we on this wheel of life?" Have we made the conscious decision to follow one of the spokes (paths) leading home? Where is our true home? What is interesting to note, is that all spokes or paths lead to the center. So, there is no wrong path, there is only a different path. The different spokes of the wheel can also be viewed as the different religions, different mysteries and beliefs to be explored on a deeper level. What will we find in the center? The center leads to a single point, which is no thing—or nothing—yet encompasses everything! From this center we are afforded a broader view, in other words, we see that all of the spokes lead to the center point. Is it the home of our true selves—the unmasked self—the undivided self?

Is it absolutely necessary to become aware of the path we have chosen? I feel the answer has to be—yes! Yes, because most of us are on a path already, although perhaps still unaware. As our awareness grows, we wake up to this fact eventually. We have a choice as to when we realize this. This realization is subject to, and dependent on our inner development and the stages we have experienced in our individual present and past incarnations.

There is no wrong way. There is only *the way*. When this circle or wheel is viewed from above, the center dot can also symbolize the apex, or the top of a mountain, because 'the way' is sometimes described as climbing a mountain. We can chose to experience this climb by going around the mountain, ascending slowly but surely, or we can climb the steep path straight up, which is much harder but faster. Our decision as to which path we will chose depends on our previous experiences, and what we have learned and assimilated from those experiences in this and previous lives. The purpose of 'the path', is the process of the evolution of each individual soul, and of mankind, which encompasses all souls. As we grow in understanding, we *sense* the necessity of letting go and realize the true meaning of sacrifice.

Were you better prepared for this climb than most of us? Where did you get the preparation to let go of glamorous, trivial and unimportant things? Was it in your *previous life experiences*?

The belief in reincarnation is increasingly accepted by a larger segment of our Western population. The Eastern philosophies and religions have known about this all along. The ancient Egyptian, Indian and Chinese texts incorporate this belief system into their teachings. They knew about the seven levels of consciousness, the seven levels of existence.

Who in our Western civilization were the forerunners bringing this knowledge to us? Or did we always possess this knowledge, but for some reason decided to cover it up or ignore it? The Bible refers to reincarnation, perhaps a little veiled at times. Later Christianity is the last to recognize this teaching. I say later Christianity, because I have become aware that what you call *early* or *primitive* Christianity knew this all along.

It is clearly demonstrated by one of the Master Teachers, and a man known to us as Jesus. Didn't he try to make us understand that there is another world, another plane of existence to come?

Where do we connect to this other plane, this other Reality? What about our teacher's words, "The Kingdom of God is within?" How do we go inside, and what do we discover about ourselves, once we look there? Who or what is God? What about the ancient Eastern traditions and philosophies that encourage meditation? Again, by reviewing the titles of your books on this subject, I am led to believe that you knew something on this subject matter having studied comparative religion.

You, dear teacher, had chosen the steep way to climb the mountain. Was it an easy climb, without any sacrifices along the way? I read a passage in your book where you describe that you were prepared to make all the necessary sacrifices, but found that this was not necessary. I feel it was your true *intention* to sacrifice that brought about what I call 'a state of grace'. You were prepared to give it all up, even the indulgence of writing and your passion for music. Your words on this subject:

"How wonderful were the experiences of these years! When I first went to Africa I prepared to make three sacrifices: to abandon the organ; to renounce academic teaching activities, to which I had become quite attached; and to lose my financial independence and rely for the rest of my life on the help of my friends. I had begun to make these three sacrifices, and only my intimate friends knew what they cost me. But then it happened to me what happened to Abraham when he prepared to sacrifice his son. Like him I was spared the sacrifice. Thanks to my good health and thanks to the piano with the attached pedals that the Bach Society of Paris had given me as a present, I had been able to maintain my organ technique in the tropical climate. During the many peaceful hours I was

able to spend with Bach during my four and half years in the jungle I had penetrated deeper into the spirit of his works. I returned to Europe, therefore, not as an artist who had become an amateur, but in full possession of my technique."3

The above quotation speaks to me of so many things. Gratitude, humility, purity of motive and renunciation often called surrender or non-attachment. I began to notice that your actions were never motivated or inspired by standards set by society.

You had experienced that to know God it is not necessary to sacrifice oneself, rather it is a surrender of attachments. To know God is to fearlessly *realize* one's *Self*. Unlike some philosophers, your thoughts didn't languish on outer space and the planets' relationship to man alone. Your priorities concerned human beings, and our relationship not only to the universe, which is important, but how we relate to each other. That has to be the starting point, and makes complete sense to me. You may be interested to know that scientists are sending probes to orbit the different planets in order to obtain more information about our universe. However, we are still not investing money or effort into exploring our own true nature. The state of our civilization is at an all time low, considering the animosity and hatred that still exists between nations. In your books *'The Decay and Restoration of Civilization'* and *'Civilization and Ethics'*, you tried to remind us of this indeed 'practical idea'. Then I read what appeared to be a small contradiction:

"One can't expect philosophers to be romantics, but it is important to remember that the philosopher must deal not only with the technique of reason or with matter and space and stars, but with people. After all, it is the relationship of man to the universe, and not solely the relationship of one galaxy to another, or one fact to another, that should occupy such an important part of the philosopher's quest. There is such a thing as being too detached."4

Then I found your wonderful and honest statement:

"Like all human beings, I am a person who is full of contradictions."5

Philosophy is often described as the acquisition of wisdom. What is wisdom? Can it be taught? Isn't wisdom the opposite of ignorance? Isn't un-wisdom a better word for ignorance? Unfortunately the English language does not have a better word to describe un-wisdom. The word ignorance, the way we are familiar with the term and its usage, has a negative or denigrating connotation. I am beginning to equate Wisdom with Truth. The opposite of truth is falsehood. Can ignorance also be viewed as not knowing? I agree that the ultimate secret of the stars and our universe is hidden from us for a reason. Must we first learn and understand human nature and our relationship to each other, before attempting to solve any larger mysteries? You, being a philosopher must have been exposed to the works of Socrates and his student Plato.

I was forty-two years old when I returned to Toronto, and was fortunate to have been directed to an apartment by a dear friend. The apartment was in a convenient mid-town location and affordable, due to rent control laws in effect.

I threw myself into decorating this space and into my work. Whenever one of my children came to Toronto they requested we drive by the home we used to occupy as a family. Marc was no different. I overheard him on the telephone saying to his brother and sister, "I just drove by our old house and it felt so weird—I had forgotten how large this house was."

Over the years, Marc has been such a blessing for me. He was always there to help me, every time I made a change in residence. Saying goodbye in Florida was very hard for me. Little did I know then, I'd be returning nine years later.

Dear teacher, I must confess that I did not rush to the bookstore after my move to order the book I had read in Florida. Although your words were still on my mind, it took me a couple of weeks to make the effort to find this book. I had other priorities.

What was strange, or so I thought at the time, was that this book could not to be found on the shelf of my local bookstore. I had to order a copy and wait for it. Once it arrived, I leafed through the pages again, only reading a paragraph or two. I admit that I became very preoccupied with starting my life over. This meant throwing myself completely into my work and the Toronto social scene. My old job was offered back to me, and my friends welcomed me back with open arms. Soon, it felt as though I had never left.

Real estate can be an all-consuming profession. I operated with a cell phone and pager, being available at all hours of the night and on weekends. Yes, I was back in the rat race. Although I liked to believe that I could set my own schedule, my life revolved around the timetable of others—namely my clients. During free evenings and a few free hours on weekends, I read. Friends could not understand my love for reading or my love for solitude. I often heard them say, "Why are you such a hermit?"

I jumped back on the emotional roller coaster with full gusto, often remembering the peaceful hours spent on the beach in Florida, knowing I had changed somehow. The emotion of fear, quite insidious, seeped into my everyday life again. Fear of failure, fear of not having enough money, fear of spending the rest of my life alone and the hidden fear of not realizing the purpose of life, including the fear of not realizing my potential or more truthfully—if I *had any potential*.

Garage sales had become very popular in our part of the city. On a Saturday morning in the spring of 1986, I went along thinking this could be fun. As I looked through some books displayed on a separate table, among a collection of the usual pulp fiction one book title caught my eye.

I found the book entitled: '*Albert Schweitzer: Man of Mercy*', among several other books discarded as having no more value to the current owner. One man's junk is another man's treasure—yes indeed! I could not contain my excitement and rushed to pay for my lucky find. The price for this, to me a priceless treasure, was fifty cents. The book was authored by Jacqueline Berrill, and was published in 1956. I couldn't believe my eyes.

There's no such thing as coincidence. I knew instantly that I was meant to find this treasure. What I didn't know at the time, was that the book had been out of print for several years!

My friend thought I was crazy to be so happy over the purchase of one old book. She had no clue that I considered this an 'omen', a gift, a *message*. I could hardly wait to curl up with my treasure, and remember making some sort of excuse for wanting to go home. I still value my extraordinary find today and remember this incident very clearly. This book described your life in Africa, your youth, your curiosity and your struggle with concepts that were not quite in line with what was considered the *status quo* of your time. She described your nature and captured your essence perfectly. As I read about you, I discovered a fearless inner nature, strong willed, driven by and dedicated to truth. You stood out because you were idealistic—reaching—achieving your goals. You appeared to be stubborn, yet, were kindhearted and open-minded. I discovered that the qualities of inquisitiveness, intelligence, self-contemplation, creativity and compassion were fundamental character traits and the essence of your inner nature, which led you to your final destiny—*your path*.

I was amazed to read about the choices you had made early in life. You were born into a spiritual environment. By that I mean several things. Not only was your father a pastor, but you also experienced your youth and childhood in the natural rural environment of a small village, which before the turn of the century was even more beautiful than it is today and you had two very devoted and talented parents.

I learned that you were born on January 14, 1875 in the village of Kaysersberg, which is located a few miles south of Strasbourg. Your parents took you to the smaller village of Günsbach when you were only a few months old. Your father had accepted the post of Protestant pastor in this village. There was only one church, and it had been decided among the villagers that both the Catholic and the Protestant clergy would share the only church in the village. Country folks appear to have a lot of common sense and no one seemed to object to this arrangement.

During your early years you were exposed to music. The church organ held a particular fascination for you as a young boy. You taught yourself to improvise and were found to have a definite talent for this complicated and magnificent instrument. Your desire to play and master it must have been very strong. History shows that at the age of nine, you were delighted to be given the opportunity to sit in for the regular organist. Why were you so fascinated with the organ? Was it the tone? Was it the resonance? Was it the vibration? Was it the melodies and hymns composed by J.S. Bach?

You also exhibited a strong fascination with the construction of the organ itself. You heard the difference between an organ constructed with hand crafted pipes, versus the sound produced by an organ constructed with machine made pipes. You were very sensitive. You felt the vibrations clearly. What is vibration? What mental state did the sound of this music produce in you? Did the playing of the organ, the sounds and vibrations it produced, put you in a state of attention and meditation? I had so many questions, about you and your life, and became more and more curious about you.

It was mainly through the book, 'ALBERT SCHWEITZER: Man of Mercy', that I began to get a distinct *feeling* for your inner nature. Among all the books I have since come across, this particular one, written by a homemaker, captured my imagination. I am so grateful to have found this book in the most unlikely place—a garage sale! It was through Jacqueline Berrill's eyes, that I got to see the other side of your character. It was through her vivid descriptions that I learned about your interests in theology, philosophy, science and music. I began to see you as an artist, a scientist and philosopher, not just as a theologian and medical doctor.

Furthermore, I quickly learned that these subjects were not just a passing interest, or a passing indulgence. You had earned your doctorate degrees in these fields of interest, before you chose the next field of study, resulting in your doctorate degree in medicine. I soon discovered that you were an extraordinary human being. What made you so different from the rest of us? I believe it was the choices you made on your path through life. Why did you decide to become a doctor of medicine?

"I wanted to be a doctor that I might be able to work without having to talk. For years I had been giving myself out in words...this new form of activity I could not represent to myself as talking about the religion of love, but only as an actual putting it into practice."6

Where did this deep feeling of love come from? We all face choices on our path through life. They stare us right in the face at crucial times of decisions. When faced with major decisions, do we see them as choices to be made in a fork of our journey? What are our choices based on? Are they not based on our life experiences, our mental attitudes, our perceptions, our character and our emotions? In observing myself I have come to realize that often our choices are based on our attachments, on our values, and at times dominated by our lower desires and fears, creating very limiting options.

I had experienced my own 'adventure in attitude' back in 1978. I discovered then, that our *perceptions,* creating our experiences and our choices, are often colored and tainted by our *false* conceptions of *'who we really are.'*

For me this truth was becoming very real. Did I consciously start acting on this discovery? Which choices had I made in the past? Must I look back in order to understand my journey better? Is there such a thing as a wrong choice? Why do we choose a path that is often so difficult? Why not opt for the easy way? Do we need these experiences of pain and suffering to grow, and therefore, do we subconsciously seek them out? Who is doing the choosing—is it my personality or my soul? What is the difference? What are we all searching for? How come, that the more I discover and learn about myself and about others, the stronger the realization becomes—that I know nothing about this mystery called—my life? I saw myself as so average, so inconsequential and actually experienced being powerless.

Then I discovered the truth behind *'everything happens for a reason'.* There is no such thing as a coincidence or an accident once we understand the process. It all boils down to cause and effect. Taking full and conscious responsibility for the choices we make on our path through life, is the beginning of walking the path toward growth and understanding. I say conscious, because until this realization becomes a reality and we wake up to our role in the unfolding of events, we are mostly *unconscious or asleep,* acting very much like robots set on automatic pilot. We react in very predictable patterns, more often than not, seeming to be blown and tossed around by our turbulent emotions.

We often resist change and dare not even think that perhaps we have the power to choose a new way of looking at ourselves. Seeing our own reactions and actions when faced with choices is very important to the growth we are all seeking. Seeing our role in a new light is the beginning—of walking the path consciously. A gratitude that is born in our hearts and a good dose of common sense is needed along the way.

"Developing a true sense of gratitude involves taking absolutely *nothing* for granted, wherever it be, whatever its source. Rather, we always look for the friendly intention behind the deed and learn to appreciate it. Make a point of measuring at its true value every act of kindness you receive from other

men. Nothing that may happen to you is purely *accidental*. Everything can be traced back to a will for good directed in your favor."[7] (My Italics)

That's what made you so different. You thought about things the correct way. You dug deeper into the well of knowledge. You were curious. I began to see you as an old soul, having gathered more experiences. Is that why you accomplished so much in your life? Where did you get your wisdom? We all have approximately the same number of years in the physical body. I am overwhelmed and in complete awe of what you accomplished in your lifetime. You certainly never wasted a precious moment feeling sorry for yourself. On the contrary!

At every opportunity you were filled with a *deep sense of gratitude*. Your attitude was different. I began to admire your straightforward common sense and had started to respect your views. Why? They were filled with honesty and the result of logical deduction. In philosopher's language it boils down to pure reason.

In the spring of 1986 I was faced with the choice of getting married to my doctor boyfriend. This was my second opportunity to enter into matrimony since leaving my husband in 1976. I chose not to get married. Something about it didn't feel right to me. I was somehow not comfortable with the idea of a very social life as a doctor's wife. Would it have been satisfying and comfortable? I am again reminded of the words of Jane Austin, "It could have all turned out differently—but it didn't."

This letter became a bit longer than normal. I had some extra time this morning, waking earlier than my usual 4 A.M. My beloved teacher, I must leave you for a while, since Saturdays tend to be very busy days at the store, however, something tells me that you'll be in my thoughts and heart today, as usual. Merci mon ami...

Your grateful and devoted student, *R*.

Dear Dr. Schweitzer,

Good Sunday morning to you! This morning, I have so many questions about you and your chosen life path. What gave you the inner strength to continue your quest for knowledge and understanding, resulting in your personal growth? I found your life story deeply fascinating but it was not until just recently, that I made several profound new discoveries about you and began to apply some of my newfound knowledge to my current life situations.

An incident at work today caught my attention. I overheard someone say, "I helped this person on a previous occasion and never even received a 'thank you', so from now on they can ask someone else for help." I sensed anger and resentment in his voice. As I opened Norman Cousins book, *'Words of Albert Schweitzer'* at random this morning, I was awed as your words jumped right off the page:

"Other demands of gratitude, asked by the thoughtless person, must be refused by the ethical person. I mean the silly and superficial expectations we attach as strings to the good we do. When we have done people a good turn, we expect them to speak well of us. If they don't do it loudly enough, we think they are being ungrateful. When you hear the words 'ingratitude is the thanks you get from the world' forming on the tip of your tongue—stop and listen. Perhaps it is the voice of vanity in your heart. If you can still be honest with yourself, you will often find this to be so. Then tell your heart to be quiet, and revise your notions of what gratitude is entitled to expect. Take warning from the realization that thoughtless people generally complain most about ingratitude. Those who think seriously about the ingratitude they encounter do not find it as easy to be indignant."8

Your words helped to me look at my own life, my own vanities— my own expectations—reminding me of several past incidents where I may have harbored similar feelings of resentment. You made me realize that when we *give* with strings attached it is not true giving. I am learning. Thank you so much for the appropriate words of wisdom. Opening a book at random has worked like this for me before. A question that often arises for me at these moments is "What forces are at play here?"

How does all this relate to choices? Who directed you in the choices you made in your life? Life is an enigma. We have to find the answers ourselves, becoming aware of the small and big answers we receive on a daily basis. I am learning to pay attention to my intuition.

As I read the story of your life, presented in the 193 pages written by Jacquelyn Berrill, I began to get a glimpse of the *immensity of your thoughts* which resulted in all of your accomplishments. I had started to think and ask myself, "What are thoughts?"

I discovered that you were not considered to be the brightest in your class back in Middle school. However, as you explained in your autobiography, *'Out of my Thought and Life'*, you had a teacher who took you aside and explained to you how to study. You certainly have heeded this teacher's advice, referring to this incident, looking back with *deep gratitude* as you remembered his advice and tutoring.

You were nine years old when you first started to play the organ in public. Your first public appearance was playing hymns in the small church back in Günsbach. I was nine years old when my mother must have mentioned your name again back in 1953, associated with winning the Nobel Peace Prize for your humanitarian efforts. I assume she heard an announcement on her radio or read this in the newspaper. We did not have a television back then. The news of your winning the Nobel Peace Prize in Oslo quickly spread around the globe.

In 1953 you were seventy-eight years old, full of energy and still fully involved in Africa. Your life was a life fully lived, not a moment was wasted or neglected. What had formed this part of your character? I soon found the answer to my question.

"I listened, in my youth, to conversations between grown-up people through which there breathed a tone of sorrowful regret which oppressed the heart. The speakers looked back at the idealism and capacity for enthusiasm of their youth as something precious to which they ought to have held fast, and yet at the same time they regarded it as almost a law of nature that no one should be able to do so. This woke in me a dread of having ever, even once, to look back on my past with such a feeling; I resolved never to let myself become subject to this tragic domination of mere reason, and what I thus vowed in almost boyish defiance I have tried to carry out."[9]

You never lost your *sense of wonder*, manifesting a youthful innocence, which gave you tremendous energy. As a matter of fact, you could not tear yourself away from your responsibilities and obligations as a physician to accept what society, and humanity in general, would view as a most sought after acknowledgment and reward. There was after all, what some would consider— prestige—involved in being awarded the Nobel Peace Prize. It took you over a year to finally find the time to go to Oslo to accept this prize in person. *Where was your ego? Where was your vanity?* It became very clear to me that you had learned to transcend your small personal ego and had no personal vanities. You didn't value everything according to society's usual standards.

What were the priorities in your life then? Looking back I see that you exhibited a deep ethical concern for others very early in your life. You were different. Is this concern for others still at work, in full force, today?

Yes, you saw the big picture. You saw that the mushroom cloud of a nuclear bomb did not respect borders of countries, that it would affect all of humanity. How come others did not see this then? Isn't it just plain logic? As I observe the news programs of today, I see that nothing has really changed in the general outlook of the masses of humanity. We still consider sectarian religion, nationalism and patriotism as good and healthy, not seeing that it is divisive in nature. You were frustrated with the mentality of ignorance and fear influencing and ruling humanity during the cold war era.

I often wonder what you would say to what is happening in the world today. I am sorry to tell you that nothing much has changed! Has our level of consciousness not changed enough? Nuclear weapons are still being manufactured and held up as the ultimate weapon of defense, along with a new threat—biological warfare.

I am beginning to see that ignorance or lack of wisdom, fear and a lack of education are the only enemy facing us today. Is this only a problem among the masses of poor people living today, or does it reveal itself in our so-called civilized world as well? Why then do we not spend some of the enormous resources now used for weapons of mass destruction and war, on mass education, focusing on peace and on healing and developing instruments for *peace* instead of weapons for hate and destruction?

I recognize that you saw the *big picture* concerning other issues as well. These issues related to the subject of religion. You knew it was meant to be an instrument for teaching us higher values, yet is it used as such today? Or is it used to control and manipulate the masses to a particular mind set? I wonder...

I was very interested to learn what you had *thought* about during your years in the study of theology. You chose to dig further into the mystery of existence, including our Christian view of Jesus. Not being satisfied with the answers, as they are presented to us by the majority of churches, your search led you to see that the fathers or shapers of later Christianity gave Jesus a different meaning. How did all this relate to how you experienced spirituality? I wondered...

Is that why you chose philosophy along with theology as your realm of inquiry? What did you find there? Did this new knowledge lead you to further questions, or did you receive some answers about yourself along the way, allowing these answers to guide you on your path? Whose voice were you listening to? Was it still the 'small inner voice' you had heard as a child? Was it your soul? *Was it your intuition?* Was this intuition becoming stronger, the more you used it? Did you practice what is known as meditation?

You spent a lot of time in contemplation and in nature. Although you led a very busy and active life, you enjoyed being alone, needing time to think and write. I am experiencing that reflection and quiet contemplation are very helpful in order to digest and formulate any form of new insight.

You loved music. How did the music of J.S. Bach affect your emotions? When did you first become aware of the works of Johann Wolfgang von Goethe who lived from 1749 to 1832? Both men are now considered to have been mystics guided by their awakened souls.

What about other men such as, Plato, Pythagoras, Socrates, Moses, Isaiah, Prince Gautama, Jesus, Mohammed, Francis Bacon, Spinoza, Swedenborg, Ghandi and poets like Browning, Emerson, Blake and Whitman? Who were these men now described as possessing a higher knowledge? Today they are all considered to have been mystics.

What about the sages of antiquity such as: Confucius, LaoTse, Zoroaster, Appolonius of Tyana, St. Francis and the ancient wisdom teachers of India? The Bhagavad-Gita, the Upanishad and Vedas originating in India are among the oldest writings known to man. In the Eastern religions they are considered to be the jewels of the ancient wisdom teachings. Where does the myth or legend of Osiris, Isis and Horus fit into the picture? What did they symbolize? Why did the pagans revere nature gods? Could the words *Buddha* and the word *Christ* have been used to describe a higher level of '*being*'?

Perhaps it is best to leave these thoughts for another day. I find myself so absorbed in your world and thoughts that I find it hard to stop asking questions. Today is Sunday and I look forward to having Monday and Tuesday off. Until then, 'Auf Wiedersehen,' Your devoted student, *R.*

Good Morning Dr. Schweitzer,

We are nearing the end of August. The Florida climate is hot and humid during the summer months. As a matter of fact I have grown very accustomed to the heat, having experienced the last five summers in Florida. It is so sweltering that I only venture out on my terrace to water the plants I nurture and treasure. Yes, my terrace is beginning to resemble a jungle. You were very familiar with a jungle atmosphere. I am very tempted to take advantage of this mood and jump ahead to the year 1913, when you embarked on your first journey to Africa. I have this desire to describe your years in Africa—but something tells me to stay on track.

As I mentioned before, the author, Jacquelyn Berrill, did a superb job in capturing your true nature. *Your power to motivate and your power to inspire* jumped out at me between the lines of every page. She described your life, your humanity, your personality and your character.

While reading her book, I started to become curious as to what motivated you to leave behind a life that showed so much promise of being a complete success in the material world. I was fascinated to learn about the years that you spent educating yourself in the various fields of interest. Where did this interest originate? Did your education result in the necessary internal struggle? Don't we all, sooner or later, face the same struggle?

Back in 1986 I saw you as a man with the special capacity for unconditional love and compassion for the less fortunate, the forgotten people of Africa. You were motivated by an unusually strong sense of duty, a palpable sense of responsibility to humanity. You felt a strong need to right the wrongs perpetrated by the white man in Africa. Many of the books you wrote revealed this about you. The other thing I noticed was that you had been a non-conformist! You valued independent thought, and tried to instill the same in us. You *lived* your truth as you saw it. You had the courage and integrity to be true to yourself! Your words began to inspire me! As I allowed your words to have an impact on my consciousness, I began to feel as though you were my father, my older brother, my mentor, my teacher and my friend.

In reviewing some of my activities back in the later part of 1986 and then again in 1987, I see my struggle a bit clearer—in hindsight. I threw myself into my work and soon saw the desired results. My bank account was increasing. I suppose some would equate this with success. However, as I compared myself to my friends who owned nice homes in prestigious areas of the city, I saw myself as poor. I was renting an apartment and decided to spend my money on travel and books. As I yearned to own a place of my own I wondered: 'Why was I always comparing myself to others?' and 'Why was saving money not my strong suit?'

During this time, three of my friends coaxed me to come along to pay a visit to a psychic. Someone had recommended this lady to my friend. Four of us took an afternoon off to drive to a small rural town just outside Toronto. Our career in Real Estate afforded us this luxury.

Being last to see the psychic, and after she had answered the usual queries about money, romance and health, this woman asked if I had any questions. I asked about my children, who were on my mind all the time, especially my daughter Eve. The psychic told me that my daughter would be married soon. She saw a ceremony in a wood paneled room in front of a large fireplace. She saw a man who would not only be her lover, but also be a teacher, mentor and friend. That was certainly not her present boyfriend. My daughter Eve was going through a very difficult time. I felt reassured by her words, that all would end well for her.

She described my youngest son, Steven, *as being born to succeed.* He was still in college at the time, but already showed great promise. I knew what she meant! I had seen his burning desire to succeed and I saw his diligent efforts towards reaching his goals. I saw in him the power of positive thinking. I saw him shaping his own future. In closing, she said that he could fall into a pile of manure but would always come out of these life situations smelling like roses. This brings a smile to my face now...

She also saw my oldest son Marc becoming very successful. It would take him a bit longer—his pace was different. She also said that no matter how successful he would become, in his heart he will always yearn to be in nature. He would strive to own a second home or cottage in the country—perhaps, surrounded by mountains and clear lakes. Just recently, Marc told me of his future dream to build a log cabin in the North Carolina Mountains.

What did she see for me? She saw me moving back to Florida! I said, "No—no, you are seeing something that has already happened", followed by, "I just returned from a two year stay in Florida. That's in my past!" "No", she replied, "I see you settling in the United States permanently—in a few years—down the road." I heard the voice of my dear friend in the background, "I hope this is not true, I am so happy to have my friend back in Toronto!" She had been listening from another corner of the room.

On the way home, we laughingly compared our readings, and I preferred to concentrate on what this psychic had told me about my children. I promptly forgot about her prediction about my own future, thinking she had definitely made a mistake in her predictions for me. Gee, was I wrong—as I look around me now. I had practiced selective believing!

After devouring the book, 'Albert Schweitzer: Man of Mercy' for a second time, I found my curiosity about you growing even stronger. A public library was within walking distance of my apartment and attracted me like a magnet. I often ended my neighborhood walks by resting my tired legs in a comfortable chair at this facility. I checked out books on all kinds of subjects. I explored the difficult subject of physics—quantum physics in particular. I also became interested in esoteric teachings, which means 'inner', vs. exoteric meaning 'outer'.

I continued to be interested in such 'occult' subjects as reincarnation, spiritualism, philosophy and parapsychology. The word 'occult' is often confused with the word 'cult'. I discovered that these two words had absolutely nothing in common.

'Occult' simply means 'hidden', lying beyond our ordinary vision, or our present perception. There are many things hidden from our ordinary vision. For instance, what were the ancient mysteries all about? What were the so-called 'Mystery Schools of the Ages'? Who were, or who are—these lofty beings often referred to as Master Teachers? The word metaphysics, what it means, and how it relates to my existence, had not become part of my awareness or part of my vocabulary back then.

I admit to becoming fascinated with the mystery of the mind and how it operates. How we as human beings, receive and perceive information and process this information. I also read a few true crime stories, becoming intrigued as to why certain people, often intelligent people, became absolute monsters, manifesting what we would term as *evil*. I could not relate to such behaviors, yet, I found some of the details of a murder's path through life, especially the formative childhood years, very interesting. I became interested in psychology and the mysterious workings of the mind.

Before leaving Florida in January of 1986, a friend gave me a book as a farewell gift. It is relatively small and entitled—*'Siddhartha'*. It depicted the life story of Gautama, the Indian prince known later as Buddha. It is the story of Gautama's search for meaning in a life filled with experiences of pain and suffering along the way. He finally—after years of contemplation and meditation—achieved 'enlightenment'. Does enlightenment always follow after a great deal of struggle along the path? Is it always the result of our own efforts—our own seeking—making our own choices—having to live with the often quite painful results of those choices?

Are the qualities of gratitude, devotion and detachment, coupled with a sense of awe and reverence a necessary step in our evolution as human beings? Did all of the great Masters of antiquity posses these qualities? The story of *'Siddhartha'* was written by Hermann Hesse and first published in 1951. A German, writing a story about eastern philosophy—how interesting!

Another book I purchased that had a deep impact on me and is worth mentioning is *'Cosmic Consciousness'*, written by the Canadian psychiatrist Richard Maurice Bucke M. D. in the year 1900. What struck me as odd was the fact that his list of individuals having reached a 'cosmic level of consciousness', consisted mostly of men. Under the heading 'Last Words', however, this question was partially answered by the editor and I quote:

"Many readers, before they have reached this page, will have been struck by the fact that the name of no woman is included in the list of so-called 'great cases'. And the names of only three in that of 'Lesser, Imperfect and Doubtful Instances.'

"Besides these three the editor knows another woman, still living, who is undoubtedly if not a great, still a genuine case. She would not, however, permit the editor to use her experience even without her name, and the case is therefore reluctantly entirely omitted. The only other woman known to the present writer, either in the past or in the present, who is or was, either certainly or almost certainly, a case of Cosmic Consciousness is Madame Guyon, who was, it seems to him, a genuine and great instance, though unfortunately the evidence in her case is not as definite as could be wished."[10]

This section is then followed by a short description of the life of Madame Guyon who was born Jeanne Marie Bouvieres de la Mothe, on April 13th, 1648. It is beginning to dawn on me who the other mysterious woman was that he alluded to. *She was alive in 1885.* Do you know to whom I am referring? Are you smiling at my detective work?

What is the mystery? Am I seeing differently now, able to uncover a larger portion of it? It is more than a hundred years since the above mentioned book was written. Has humanity grown in awareness since then?

One thing came to mind as I put down this particular book. The author, Dr. Richard Maurice Bucke, died very suddenly in a fatal accident on December 8, 1899, at the age of 31. On that cold evening, while going outside to admire a clear and star studded sky, he slipped on a patch of ice on his front porch and died of a head injury. His book was published in 1901.

He was an extraordinary example of a person on a quest for truth. What a brilliant man, having discovered so many things, especially the phenomena of 'cosmic consciousness' and to have written such a profound and well researched book on the subject!

What choices did he make in his short but productive life? I'll look into this and will write to you again tomorrow. I hope I am not boring you with my verbosity...

Your grateful and devoted student, *R.*

Good morning my dear teacher,

I have decided to dedicate this whole letter to telling you about Richard Maurice Bucke, an important teacher in my life. Dr.

Richard M. Bucke's book on cosmic consciousness has become one of my most prized possessions. It is perched on my bookshelf right beside your books.

Last night, before falling asleep, I reviewed certain passages in this book. I couldn't help but stop at certain points of interest again. These passages concerned the life of Gautama, the Buddha and the life of the Apostle Paul. Since you had also plunged into the mystery of the life of St. Paul, I found his discoveries of great value. I also reread the introduction by George Moreby Acklom, which only appeared in the later editions since it was written on February 25th, 1946.

Few people had heard of Richard Maurice Bucke outside of the medical profession and his circle of friends, which included Walt Whitman. His book appeared in 1901, the same year you wrote 'The Mystery of the Kingdom of God". Today thousands of people have read these books, yet both of you, authors and medical doctors, are seldom remembered.

Both of you were on a special quest. Exploring not only the mind but what is behind the mind. You both discovered something we call spirit. Richard Maurice Bucke had very little in the way of early formal education. He was a farm boy, growing up in Creek Farm, a rural setting, outside the small town of London, Ontario. Working on a farm without the convenience of electricity or automobiles must have been hard. When he was twelve, his father had encouraged him to explore the books in his library, which contained thousands of volumes brought over from England. He was told to educate himself. His father was a scholar who spoke seven languages. He taught young Richard Latin.

At seventeen Richard set out to see the world and left home to explore the United States. He wandered from place to place, doing odd jobs such as gardening and becoming a railroad hand in Cincinnati. He ended up as a driver of a wagon train leading 26 wagons west, to what is now known as Nevada. His adventures led him through Indian Territories. He worked in gold mines, being one of about 100 white men in 1600 square miles of Indian Territory. These territories were without laws, courts, churches or schools. During one harsh winter, due to expose to the extremely cold weather, one foot and part of the other foot, needed to be amputated, leaving Richard badly maimed.

At 21 he inherited his late mother's small estate and went back home, using the money to enter medical school. His postgraduate schooling took him to Europe. He returned to Canada to settle down and to raise a family. An ordinary professional man, or so it appears on the surface. Only, just like you, he was anything but *ordinary*. In 1892 he became Professor of Mental and Nervous Diseases at Western University in London, Ontario. In 1898 he was elected President of the Psychological Section of the British Medical Association and became President of the American Psychological Association, introducing many reforms in procedures.

A friend had quoted some verses of Walt Whitman to him. Whitman's words must have had a tremendous effect on him, opening new doors to his mind. The poet and the doctor became close friends. That spring he recalled having *experienced* the most memorable moments in his life. He experienced 'illumination', the account of which is recorded in the 'Proceedings and Transactions of the Royal Society of Canada', and re-quoted by George Moreby Ackholm in his Foreword entitled 'The Man and the Book'. I quote:

"He and two friends had spent the evening reading Wordsworth, Shelley, Keats, Browning and especially Whitman. They parted at midnight and he had a long drive in a hansom. His mind, deeply under the influence of the ideas, images and emotions called up by the reading and talk of the evening, was calm and peaceful. He was in a state of quiet, almost passive enjoyment.
"All at once, without warning of any kind, he found himself wrapped around, as it were, by a flame-colored cloud. For an instant he thought of fire—some sudden conflagration in the great city. The next (instant) *he knew that the light was within himself.*"[11]

This experience was followed by a sense of exultation, immense joy and intellectual illumination impossible to describe, giving him the knowledge and insight described in his book 'Cosmic Consciousness.' He began to ponder the relationship between the mind and man's moral nature. In 1894 he gave lectures before the American Medico-Psychological Association in Philadelphia. He had developed the idea of the *mental evolution of mankind*, and that it would lift all human life to a higher plane.

Dr. Richard M. Bucke did not live long enough to experience the rewards or the success of his own book, yet he has left us his experiences and discoveries as a legacy to ponder. Why did he die so young? Had he completed his mission?

As I read all this I was reminded of another man's journey. I am referring to Gurdjieff's book 'Meetings with Remarkable Men.' These journeys appeared to be *spiritual quests* of some kind. Both men were searching for teachers, sages and seers, who could explain the elusive existence of the human spirit and the mystery of the meaning of life.

Dear Dr. Schweitzer, you must know what these men had experienced and written about, because your life reflects that you were definitely on a quest and had reached a level of understanding way above that of the average human being. You knew about the 'light within', yet you did not talk about your illumination—your enlightenment. Why?

Your book entitled 'The Kingdom of God' was ignored by most scholars of your time. Either they did not understand it, or, if they did understand it, they would have had to admit that their belief system would have to be re-examined. I wonder how many of these scholars have taken the time to really understand what you had discovered. It goes to show me that being educated and intelligent does not make a man wise... Many chose to ignore your book altogether. You were seen as a non-conformist—a rebel. I guess you were in good company!

Jesus was a rebel too, wasn't he? So was the prophet Elijah, so was Gandhi, so were Beethoven, Mozart and Wagner; so was Dr. Martin Luther King and Dr. Richard Maurice Bucke, not to mention Jakob Boehme, Paracelsus, Gallileo, Swedenborg, Krishnamurti, Rudolf Steiner and Helena Petrovna Blavatsky.

The evidence is to be seen in everything you did and said. Your book called 'The Light Within Us', was the third book I purchased. Again, someone had taken your words and put them into a book. Did you choose the title? I wonder...

Dearest teacher, it is getting late and I have many things I must do today. Sometimes I feel as though my life is stuck in the fast-forward position. I will make some time today for play and relaxation—keeping the balance.

A thought just occurred to me. Had you lived during the Inquisition, the pope would have called you a heretic and ordered you killed for being a free thinker and for voicing your thoughts, and they would have done it in the name of Christianity, in the name of Jesus. What a gruesome thought! So much for religion...

Your devoted and grateful student, *R*.

Guten Morgen, Dr. Schweitzer,

This morning I am listening to the famous organ works of J.S. Bach. In my mind I picture you sitting at the organ. Too bad I have to play this music so softly. My neighbors are surely still asleep at this early hour. Tonight I will play it at normal volume. This particular music seems to help my focus and concentration. Is that how it affected you? I am presently searching for a recording of one of your performances. Knowing you are at the organ would enhance my experience of this music tenfold.

Were you able to tap into the power of the *now* moment, pushing away all other thoughts while playing this magnificent instrument? I am currently reflecting on what I wrote you yesterday. I strongly suspect that your name would have found its way to Dr. Richard Bucke's list of famous people with higher than normal consciousness, had he lived long enough to *witness your life path.*

Aren't the men on the list, found on page 81, in the earlier mentioned book, also referred to as mystics? They had experienced a new state of *being*, an illumination, often called 'an awakening' between the age of 29-39. The average age is cited to be around 35. You made the decision to enter medical school at the age of 30, commencing your study of medicine at the University of Strasbourg in 1906, at the age of 31. However, your decision to serve humanity in one way or another was already made at the age of 21. Can all this just be a coincidence or is there more to my assumption?

Dr. Bucke was a contemporary of yours and just like you, he had researched his subject matter with deep integrity and great attention to detail. Just like you, he had dedicated his life to healing others, stressing the importance of a moral and ethical outlook. Attitude and conduct were discovered to be of utmost importance. He chose the field of exploring the mind, the field of psychiatry.

Just like you, he was driven by his curiosity about religion. Like you, he explored the subject of mysticism. He studied the mind, as you studied the mind of Jesus. As a thesis for your medical degree you wrote a paper called *'The Psychiatric Study of Jesus'*, which was published in 1913 by Mohr at Tübingen.

I can see from this that you and Maurice Bucke uncovered very similar facts, and had the courage to voice your findings. What had you learned that was so life altering for you? In your case, there must have been some other revelation besides the later one, which you often referred to as your 'big' revelation, namely *"Reverence for Life"*.

You mentioned that the idea for *'Reverence for Life'* came to you after months and months of struggling with the universal concept of ethics. Reverence for life, became the principal lead thought of your philosophy of life. Why and how it relates to our civilization was a subject matter of great interest to you and resulted in your book *'The Philosophy of Civilization'*. You had found a Truth. The idea for which you had been searching and on which you subsequently built your whole philosophy of life, is the idea, *'that God exists in everything and everyone'*. It is manifested in the will-to-live seen in all of nature. Such a life-view is all encompassing, all-inclusive and truly enlightened.

This truth became very obvious to you, after years and years of delving into different kinds of study, including the study of eastern belief systems and philosophies. You also exhibited and talked a great deal about faith. Are faith and intuition somehow related? Richard Maurice Bucke referred to this phenomenon, as *'the knowing without learning'* and he believed this to be the natural next step in man's evolution. He states:

"The passage from self to cosmic consciousness, considered from the point of view of the intellect, seems to be a phenomenon strictly parallel to the passage from simple to self consciousness.

As in the latter, so in the former, there are two chief elements:

a. Added consciousness;

b. Added faculty.

a. When an organism which possesses simple consciousness only, attains to self consciousness, it becomes aware for the first time that it is a separate creature, or *self* existing in a world which is apart from it. That is, the oncoming of

the new faculty instructs it without any new experiences or
process of learning.
b. It, at the same time, acquires enormously increased powers
of accumulating knowledge and of initiating action.

So when a person who was 'self' conscious only, enters into
cosmic consciousness—
a. He knows without learning (from the mere fact of
illumination) certain things, as, for instance:
1. That the universe is not a dead thing, but a living
presence;
2. That in its essence and tendency it is infinitely good;
3. That individual existence is continuous beyond what is
called death. At the same time:
b. He takes on enormously greater capacity both for learning
and initiating."[12]

There it is. This certainly is true and applies to you, when your
life and your work are examined in hindsight. This book, more
than any other, had opened my eyes to the truth of the existence
of a higher state of consciousness, a truth known, yet—so hard to
describe.

What is initiation? Do the stages of growth include tests to
be passed? Are the mysteries of life only revealed to the Masters
and the mystics? What makes them different? Is it the choices
they make along the way? Do we really have choices? Is there
such a thing as free will? Is our free will hampered by past and
presently created karma? Were these higher beings just like us at
one time, groping and searching in the dark? Were these souls
more evolved, having experienced many more incarnations? Does
our free will expand or widen once a higher level of awareness is
achieved? Is this new awareness coupled with a new and deeper
sense of responsibility?

Do these Masters have compassion for those of us struggling
here on earth? Do they only help those who make an effort to
understand? Do they only help those who are sincerely seeking
and are on a *quest for truth*? What inner qualities must we
possess before this teaching process begins or becomes apparent?
Can these Masters be reached, once we make the conscious choice
towards self-improvement?   Must our character be pure and
exhibit certain *altruistic intentions*? I wondered...

On my bedside table, in 1986 and 1987, were many books. Some, I only glanced through, while others were of great interest and captured my attention—sometimes I read all night. I became a collector of books. I found the subject of reincarnation to be of particular interest. Was it because of *my experience*—your visit?

On a chilly spring day in 1987 I found myself in a second hand bookstore. It was a sunny but crisp Sunday afternoon. I loved walking on days like these and often ended my excursions at this store, hoping to find unusual books.

As I glanced through my copy of your book *'On the Edge of the Primeval Forest'* this morning, I noticed the stamp of the second hand bookstore on the inside flap. The pages have turned yellow with age. This book was first published in 1922 but my copy dates back to the second printing in 1952. Someone had made the astute decision that this book had a new value after you won the Nobel Peace Prize, and fortunately for me, put it back into circulation.

I am so grateful to the person who had the foresight to donate this book—instead of throwing it into a trash can. It's as if it was waiting, just for me. Was this another coincidence? This book has become one of my favorites! Your dedication on the first page reads as follows:

"To all the friends, dead and living, who have helped me in the enterprise of which this book is a part, in deepest gratitude."[13]

In this book you write about your adventures, discovering new territories, new customs and new experiences. It describes your voyage into the *unknown*. I would like to remind you of your first impressions of Africa:

"River and forest...! Who can really describe the first impression they make? We seem to be dreaming! Pictures of antediluvian scenery, which elsewhere had seemed to be merely the creation of fancy, are now seen in real life.
It is impossible to say where the river ends and the land begins, for a mighty network of roots, clothed with bright-flowing creepers, project right into the water. Clumps of palms and palm trees, ordinary trees spreading out widely with green boughs and huge leaves, single trees of the pine family shooting up to a towering height, in between them, wide fields of papyrus clumps as tall as a man, the rotting stems of

dead plants shooting up to heaven... In every gap in the forest a water mirror meets the eye; at every bend in the river a new tributary show itself. A heron flies heavily up and then settles on a dead tree trunk; white birds and blue birds skim over the water and high in the air a pair of ospreys circle. Then—yes, there can be no mistake about it!—from the branch of a palm there hang and swing—two monkey tails! Now the owners of the tails are visible. We are really in Africa!"[14]

You certainly have a talent and magic for words. I devoured this book when I first bought it, and plan to read it again. Your dry sense of humor and stoic disposition jumped out at me from each page. This book, along with 'Out of my Thought and Life' (your autobiography) which I bought much later, gave me a deeper insight into your world of experience. I was smitten, caught like a fish and then reeled in. I was allowed to see a New World. I saw a world of courage and adventure. I could not forget your words. I began to get a feeling of what your life was all about. Thank you so much for sharing your stories about Africa.

Your choices—your renunciation—your sacrifice of a scholarly life in Europe, were not clear to me then, as they are now. You often said that you felt indebted for having had such a good life. You felt you had to repay or give back to humanity because of the early comfort and happiness you experienced in your youth. You had to contribute something to those less fortunate. You felt it was your duty, your responsibility, and you never wavered on this issue.

The questions I asked myself were, "Why so much emphasis on duty and service?", and "Why didn't you reap all the material benefits of your knowledge and studies?" followed by, "What had you discovered about life's purpose—about core values—ethics—growth and the connection of *body, mind, soul and spirit?*"

It became clear that material accumulations, such as accolades and prizes, were not your intended goals in life. You had recognized that this is not our purpose for being on this planet. You were inspired by the life of a man named Jesus, in the same way I am inspired by you. You knew he was a teacher, a messenger, and a signpost along the road. You were one of the few people who truly understood the deeper meaning of his life and his *message*. You recognized that his message went beyond the usual Christian dogma and doctrines, which have for the most part become empty platitudes.

My curiosity drove me to order several of the other books you had written. Your books were not readily available at libraries or displayed in bookstores, back in 1987. I spent a lot of money on books in those days. Thank God for books. I wrote a poem about how I felt about books after moving back to Florida in 1996. I must have asked myself, 'Why do I treasure books?'

Words
There's been a dramatic change
Almost beyond words
While packing my possessions—strange
I noticed, that only my books
Were of value to me—yet, only words.

Those books were my companions
Helped me make sense of it all?
Some—way over my head—and yet
I read them—allowing the chips to fall.

Those books were my teachers
Chosen by my soul? Yet only words
Until I realized the creation
Of thought—pen to paper—my words.

"Who would ever listen—to what I have to say?"
Was my first reaction.
Looking at my journal
Showed no promise—just dissatisfaction!

Whose words do we value?
Who were the 'Inspired Ones'?
Were they just like you and me?
In 'silence'—they correspond—and respond.

As I roll up my Persian rug
Carefully pack my so-called treasures
What have they given me—prestige?
For a while feeling comfort —at ease?

The best experience of my life has been
To discover—these are just things,
Tying me down—draining my energy.
While books—replenish me—those words
Expanding my horizons.
RzT March 1996

Yes—I chose to love books. That seemed to be the only thing
we had in common, or so it appeared to me back then. The
experience of re-writing this poem brings tears of gratitude to
my eyes. I remember the mellow spring evening spent looking
through my books, when the answer to my question poured
into my consciousness. That night I was filled with a feeling of
gratitude for having been led to some extraordinary books, and I
was very grateful to be back in Florida.

The clock tells me that I must close this letter. It's almost 7:30
AM. The time has come for me to dry my hair and get ready to face
another day—out in the jungle!

Your devoted student, R.

Dear Dr. Schweitzer,

Early this morning while pouring my first cup of coffee, the
thought popped into my head, 'What if I don't have anything
to say to you this morning?' No sooner had I experienced the
fear this thought represented, I saw what was happening and
dismissed it from my consciousness. I then stepped into a bubble
bath in order to empty my mind and experience *being*, allowing no
fearful thoughts to enter my mind for a while. This was my special
time for relaxation.

While in this state I began to contemplate the importance
of choices, the subject of these letters, and *knew* that you would
inspire me somehow, as you have inspired me in the past. Was
I experiencing the meaning of faith? Fear is an ugly emotion,
appearing very real while it is experienced, but I chose not to
entertain this emotion this morning. It has done its number on
me long enough. Did you ever experience fear? Did you allow
it to rule your choices and actions in life? I don't believe so.

Reviewing the long list of your accomplishments has answered that question.

At random I opened your book, 'The Light Within Us' for inspiration. Here is what I saw:

"I always think that we live, spiritually, by what others have given us in the significant hours of our life. These significant hours do not announce themselves as coming, but arrive unexpected. Nor do they make a great show of themselves; they pass almost unperceived. Often, indeed, their significance comes home to us first as we look back, just as the beauty of a piece of music or of a landscape often strikes us first in our recollection of it. Much that has become our own in gentleness, modesty, kindness, willingness to forgive, in veracity, loyalty, resignation under suffering, we owe to people in whom we have seen or experienced these virtues at work, sometimes in a great matter, sometimes in a small. A thought which had become an act sprang into us like a spark, and lighted a new flame within us.

"I do not believe that we can put into anyone ideas which are not in him already. As a rule there are in everyone all sorts of good ideas, ready like tinder. But much of this tinder catches fire, or catches it successfully, only when it meets some flame or spark from outside, i.e. from some other person. Often, too, our own light goes out, and is rekindled by some experience we go through with a fellow man. Thus we have each of us cause to think with deep gratitude of those who have lighted the flames within us."[15]

You certainly rekindled my flame, as I allowed your words and the example of your life to have an impact on me. I now remember all the previous teachers in my life—lovers included. Some of the teaching experiences are long forgotten because of the subtlety of their influence. What remains is the feeling of the true goodness of certain people.

Thank you so much for your words. They never fail to inspire me—to light the often, dormant spark in my heart. Here is that feeling again—*gratitude.* I am deeply moved by your honesty, integrity and gratitude—by your values. These values, combined with tolerance, patience and a deep understanding formed your conduct and your character. I know that these three characteristics are essential on the path, and often we don't recognize the subtle changes these values instill in our consciousness!

Now I see why the people in your congregation loved your sermons. You always spoke about your experiences and opened your heart to others, allowing them to relate to what is true, for them as well as for you. Your words are not just that of a preacher, they are seasoned with the knowledge and understanding you assimilated as a human being. You *lived* your philosophy, steeped in wisdom—you lived your truth.

What is philosophy? Is it not our search for the meaning of our existence—our search for wisdom, purpose and the reason we are experiencing this life? This brings me back to the choices I made, and having to live with the consequences of those choices.

During the years from 1986-90 I was only faced with small choices—small forks in my road, or so I believed at the time. Because of my desire for independence I became quite successful in the material sense of the word. This allowed me to travel back to Florida every few months to see my children. This routine had become a joke around my office. Colleagues often asked with a grin, "So, when are you booking your next flight to Florida?"

During the Christmas holidays Eve and I drove the many miles south. My friends thought we were crazy to drive this distance alone. "There are so many dangers, especially for two woman traveling alone, are you out of your mind?" The thought of being afraid never entered my mind, as I replied, "There is nothing to be afraid of. You can't live your life ruled by fear!"

Every Christmas, I went through the same ritual, planning to leave in early December, returning a week after New Year's. I actually enjoyed the long drive, since being alone with my own thoughts had become important to me. Our trunk was always loaded with presents for my children and friends, and I saw this trip as the highlight of my year. Saying goodbye to the boys, after spending a month together was never easy for Eve and me, and it didn't become easier as my boys got older.

My daughter, Eve, was then also living and working in Florida, after having spent the years 1980-1984 living with me in Toronto. Eve, was twenty, Marc was nineteen, and the youngest, Steven was eighteen. All three were young adults finding their own path, making their own decisions.

One other important thing I just remembered. I had started keeping a journal again, but didn't take it too seriously. Although writing down thoughts or experiences seemed therapeutic and soothing to me, my entries as I look back, were sporadic and often trivial. But, that's who I was back then. Back then, I was still very critical of myself, censoring my entries, robbing myself of wisdom by entertaining thoughts such as, 'What if someone should read this one day...?' I was searching in the dark, looking for answers and trying to solve the mystery of—'who am I'?

What does, I AM THAT I AM mean? I had read this phrase and could not quite get a rational handle on its meaning. Why are we not given the answers to our questions right away, only to find the answers later—hidden in some sort of new experience? Is that, what is meant by *occult* teachings? *Hidden* bits and pieces of knowledge revealing themselves at the most unexpected times. Small revelations, one at a time—that's how I experienced my path. It seems that the knowledge is always there, I just fail to see it, or am unaware of it, often walking around in a daze, a dream state—as if asleep. Or, is this knowledge only recognizable when I am ready?

I did not experience illumination, not in the way it was described in the literature that I had read. My *mind* had opened to a new way of thinking—yes, my *heart* became more open—and yes, I knew I was guided—but by whom?

Is there a connection between mind and heart? What are thoughts? Where do they come from? Is the mind the same as the brain? Can't be the brain is only an organ, just like my liver or spleen. What is meant by the word spiritual? To me being spiritual is associated with aspiration, inspiration and overcoming obstacles and hindrances such as fear. It is the beginning of seeing things as they are, no longer seeing through the lens of self-deception. Must I pierce the veil of darkness or ignorance, allowing old beliefs and traditions to fall away? How much of what I experience is tainted by these old beliefs? Spirituality for me, is the quest for truth. It means reaching beyond my comfort zone—extending myself. Spirituality is making the *choice* to be open to receive. I already knew it had very little to do with attending church every Sunday!

I was searching for higher knowledge and had read somewhere that 'when the student is ready the teacher appears'. You had become my teacher without me being *aware* of it. I also discovered that a teacher never gives you the answers. I had discovered that life is the teacher and we are all in the classroom together. Breaking down barriers—beginning to see things as they are—this was my new frontier. My religion consists of searching for truth, keeping an open mind, and searching for meaning in my varied experiences of life. It also meant I had to educate myself, to learn to think on new levels. Then I thought, 'Aren't we all searching for answers? Why are some people just not interested? Do we have to be alone on this path? Is it the lone path we will all eventually travel?' I often chose to be alone, yet, I never felt lonely.

The questions forming in my mind continued. What energy made my heart beat? Where did the inborn intelligence of my body come from? How did my liver *know* its job is to detoxify, and how did the cells in my kidney *know* its job is to act as a filter? These organs did not have to be taught anything—they just *knew*.

Was this a demonstration of the God *Intelligence* at work? Where did this intelligence and innate knowing originate? What made me different from others? On some deeper level, am I really that different from others? Is my individuality a part of my soul? You may have asked yourself some of these questions. How else would you have found the answers? And I *knew* by now, that you had found certain answers. *I knew it in my heart!* You were my messenger. What is your message? I almost feel faint as I look at the poem I wrote in the spring of 1996.

The Messenger
I hear a knock—open the door.
To my mind—who's there?
Recognize you—from before
The message—not quite clear.

All I hear is static and crackle
Wait—until clear—the reception
Which channel must I tune into?
You are kidding—start at conception?

You want me to look—back—not forward?
But...I'm eager...
Do I have to play this tape—again?
To see—the message—to find its meaning?
RzT 1996

The only thing that creates static and crackle are my fear-based thoughts. Could the message be—to look back—reflect on my journey, in order to get to 'know myself'?

I took one European vacation during 1986-1994. My sister, who still lived near Düsseldorf, Germany, closed every letter with, "Please come to visit me again." In my heart I knew that I should go back, and this time without a boyfriend in tow.

Something just occurred to me as I stopped to re-fill my cup of coffee. I was thinking ahead as to what to call my next letters, when I noticed that each heading of my previous letters are actually the titles of poems. Poems I had written so long ago! I had not noticed this before, and honestly had not planned this in any way... Well, I'll be darned! Is that what you meant by saying, 'we only see the significance of events in hindsight?' I'll have to stop for today, as I digest and ponder this strange or synchronized event.

My heart is filled with fond memories and gratitude as I look back on this particular trip to Germany more than ten years ago. Tomorrow I will write about this special journey. Thank you for introducing me to the music of Bach. I have purchased more of his compositions, now on CD's, and use these sounds as background music while I write to you each morning. Knowing you had listened to his music is comforting and inspirational.

Your grateful and devoted student, R.

Dear Dr. Schweitzer,

Upon reviewing yesterday's letter, I realized that I asked a lot of questions back then, and saw some of the answers appear in my poetry. Is this knowledge *hidden* until we start to ask ourselves the questions? I wondered...

I began to think of you and saw that you embraced certain questions very early in life. During your teen years you experienced religious teachings of the formal type for the first time, in your confirmation class. In your book '*Memoirs of Childhood and Youth*', I got a glimpse of your '*free thinking*' spirit.

"I was sent to old pastor Wennagel for confirmation classes. I had great respect for him, but I did not open up to him. I was a diligent confirmation student, but the good pastor never had an inkling of what moved my heart. So many problems that occupied my mind were not solved by his teaching, even

though it was quite solid. How many questions I would have liked to put to him! But one was not allowed to do that. On one point, despite my respect for him my thinking differed markedly from his. He wanted to make us understand that all reasoning had to give way to faith. I, however, was convinced, and still am, that it is precisely through reasoning that the fundamental ideas of Christianity have to be confirmed. Reason, I told myself, has been given to us so that we may grasp through it all thoughts, even the most sublime ones of religion. This certainty filled me with joy."16

As a matter of fact going back even further to when you were only eight, you remembered:

"When I was eight years old, my father gave me, at my request, a New Testament, which I read eagerly. One of the stories that occupied my mind most was that of the Wise Men from the East. What did Jesus' parents do with the gold and precious things they received from these men? I wondered how they could later have been poor again. It was incomprehensible to me that the Wise Men from the East never bothered about the Christ Child later on at all. I was also offended that there is no report about the shepherds of Bethlehem having become disciples of Jesus."17

Reading this passage gave me a glimpse of your curious mind and common sense. Is that why you decided to study the New Testament in more detail later on? Is that why you not only learned Latin, but decided to teach yourself Hebrew and Greek? Is that how you discovered the *esoteric* meaning of the life of the man we remember as Jesus?

I have been pondering on the meaning of numbers. I want you to know that I've become aware that the number seven appears frequently in my life lately.

Adding the date of my birth and reducing it to one number, becomes seven. My home address is 777. My business address is 777. My new home telephone number, which was assigned to me, adds to 7. My cell phone number if added comes to 7. My business phone number has five 7's. Is this a message for me? Is the number seven a special number? I know that I am getting off my current subject, and will address this magical number again, since I have become very interested in numerology. The vibration of each number is beginning to fascinate me.

Each time I review your book '*The Light Within Us*', the enigma of your life becomes a little bit clearer for me. Your life number, your birth date (1/14/1875) adds to nine, the number nine represents completion. It is also the number of great personal effort, encompassing and affecting all of humanity. It is the number of a truth seeker. You were a Capricorn, the sign ruled by earth. You became a natural healer and leader, a Master in your field. Did it also mean that you had to walk the path alone? Loneliness would not apply to you. You faced challenges and obstacles often alone, but you were never lonely!

Did you search for meaning and through self-reflection, inspiration and devotion you found your *Inner Light*? Who rekindled the flame or ignited this light in you? Was it the voice of your teachers, your ideals?

A person needs to be alone while reading, studying and while writing. Every person needs some solitude to contemplate and meditate upon the immensity of the universe and the miraculous world of nature in order to discover how it relates to oneself. Do Beethoven's nine symphonies depict his journey on the path? The *ninth* is certainly one filled with joy, expressing the feeling and recognition of the oneness of the brotherhood of man. This insight inspired his last triumphant composition, creating his new vision, resulting in a sense of release and peace at the end of his life. As mentioned earlier he called it the 'Ode to Joy', after Schiller's poem. It became clear to me that you also discovered the oneness or brotherhood of man.

Are there sacred principles hidden in numbers? What is sacred geometry? What is the significance of the triangle—and the number three? What do the two interlaced triangles in the Star of David represent? There goes my curiosity again, running ahead of itself. Sorry for this slight diversion... I will now go back to your knowledge of languages.

This knowledge allowed you to go back to some of the original writings, allowing you to see passages and parables, originally written in Aramaic, the language of Jesus, then translated into Hebrew, Greek and Latin. How much is lost during translations? Had you discovered that some of the original metaphysical meanings were misinterpreted and therefore, misunderstood? Since Jesus did not leave us anything written by him and he spoke in Aramaic, everything we know is only a translation. Not only that, it has been suggested that the New Testament was not written until 40-100 years after his death.

I began to wonder what you had discovered, and eagerly ordered your books *'The Quest for the Historical Jesus'* and *'The Mysticism of Paul the Apostle'*.

I found these two books to be well researched, and written in a most scholarly fashion. Since I was not a scholar I found them heavy going. It became clear to me that you wanted to appeal to the world of religious scholars and teachers. So, every statement you made was backed up by the irrefutable facts, as you uncovered them during your research. What had you discovered? What was of such importance, that you dedicated many years to this sort of religious analysis and writing? Your writing continued while you were working as a doctor in Africa. As a matter of fact, you spent most of your leisure moments writing. Quite often, because of the shortage of paper in Africa, you wrote on envelopes and made use of every scrap of paper you could lay your hands on. You even used the backs of letters that were sent to you by friends and colleagues in Europe. You never wasted even the smallest scrap of paper! You re-cycled everything!

You certainly had your hands full with the enormous task of being a doctor in the jungle and your days were never long enough. Yet, you accomplished so much more than the average human being! You were different. This enigma stimulated my mind and heart over and over again.

Then it slowly began to dawn on me. You had concerned yourself with and researched the subject of spirit and spirituality all your life. Never being satisfied with someone's theory alone, you not only investigated the meaning of spirit and the soul, you tried to show us how this spirit made itself known—how it manifested in our lives and in the process you realized your full potential!

Was it your mission to be an example for the rest of us? An example of what it means be a highly *evolved* human being? Your life became a perfect example of the evolution of a man— mentioned in the book *'Cosmic Consciousness'*. You lived your life in accordance with certain universal principles, as you understood them. That's why you said, **"I made my life my argument"** and constantly admonished the rest of us to become free and independent thinkers. Were you hoping this would result in us forming our own inner conviction, replacing the notion of *blind* belief with faith?

This reminds me of an incident reported in the life of Gandhi. As Gandhi was boarding a train, several reporters were scrambling after him shouting, "Gandhij, can you say a few words to us?" Gandhi entered the train and as the train started pulling away he wrote something on a piece of brown paper torn from a bag, and handed it through the open window. As the train started to roll, the anxiously waiting crowd had gathered around asking, "What did he write on this scrap of paper?" The crowd became silent as they heard Gandhi's words being read, "My life is my message."

The word Mahatma was often used to describe Gandhi. Mahatma means great soul or a part of spirit. Atma is used to describe spirit in its unified or unmanifested form, as in the number zero. Gandhi's life, not unlike yours, exemplified the power inherent in the human spirit. He never used violence to accomplish his reform. He used the power of truth and passive resistance based on justice and integrity. Is that where the future evolution of human consciousness will be leading us? This new understanding has to be fully lived in whatever expression is best suited for our current life and natural talents.

These ideas are finally beginning to sink into my consciousness. I see you as a great doctor, (the natives often called you a shaman, witch doctor, and miracle doctor) who had chosen to help the less fortunate people in Africa, but I see much more than that, experiencing you now as a world teacher or a physician of the soul.

Norman Cousins, was the editor in chief for the '*Saturday Review*', when he visited you in Africa back in 1957. He saw the same thing. He was so impressed by your spirit and your philosophy that he became motivated to write several books about you and your mission in life. He saw that your mission and the message of your life, went way beyond being a medical doctor in the tropical jungle of Equatorial Africa. He found your writings to be of such importance, that he visited you again, in order to rescue your latest manuscript. The hungry mouths of ants and antelopes threatened to devour the precious papers filled with your words of Wisdom and Light. This manuscript turned into your revised edition of '*The Kingdom of God —The Secret of Jesus' Messiahship and Passion*'.

Didn't you write this story as early as 1914? It was translated from the original German title, *"Das Abendmahl. Das Messianitäts und Leidengeheimnis. Eine Skizze des Lebens Jesu."* The proper translation is as follows: "The Evening Meal (referring to the Last Supper)." "The Secret of The Messiahship and Suffering. A Sketch of the Life of Jesus."

Just by reviewing these titles, I began to get an idea of what secret you were referring to. And, because I am an archaeologist by nature, I needed to dig deeper! The last question on my mind this morning is, 'Who or what led me to the choices I made in my life?'

Just now I begin to realize that the choices I had made, whether the choice of parent or husband, where absolutely perfect for my growth. My husband broke my heart but not my spirit. This experience forced me to look at myself for all the answers. It took many years of searching and self-examination to be able to heal myself, and to put the pieces back together. I now see this as the greatest benefit to my growth and the fountain of my current strength and courage. Do I owe my ex-husband a thank you letter? Would he understand, or would he be offended? I better keep this new insight to myself for a little while longer. Wow... is that how it works?

This morning's letter turned out differently than I had expected. I had looked forward to telling you about my trip to Germany back in 1987. This warrants a new set of letters, doesn't it?

My dear friend and teacher, I will have to continue this one sided dialogue tomorrow as I recall my journey across the Atlantic, revisiting my childhood environment and the unexpected train ride. Until then, I remain

Your devoted and grateful student, *R.*

Sources Chapter 4:

1   P.1 *The Light Within Us*, Albert Schweitzer, Philosophical Library, NewYork,NY.
2   P. 53 *The Words of Albert Schweitzer*, Norman Cousins.
3   P.199 *Out of my Life and Thought*, Albert Schweitzer.
4   P.17 *The Words of Albert Schweitzer*, Norman Cousins.
5   P.21 *The Words of Albert Schweitzer*, Norman Cousins.
6   P.17 *The Words of Albert Schweitzer*, Norman Cousins.
7   P.20 *The Words of Albert Schweitzer*, Norman Cousins.
8   P.21 *The Words of Albert Schweitzer*, Norman Cousins.
9   P.22 *The Words of Albert Schweitzer*, Norman Cousins.
10 P.364 *Cosmic Consciousness,* Richard Maurice Bucke MD, 1923 E. P.Dutton & Company, New York, NY.
11 PP. 159-196   Proceedings and Transactions of the Royal Society of Canada.
12 P.75-76 *Cosmic Consciousness*, Richard Maurice Bucke MD.
13 P.ix *On The Edge of the Primeval Forest*, Albert Schweitzer, Fontana Books, First published 1922, A & C Black Limited, London, England.
14 P.23 *On The Edge of the Primeval Forest*, Albert Schweitzer.
15 P.16-17 *The Light Withis Us*, Albert Schweitzer.
16 P. 53 *Memoirs of Childhood and Youth*, Albert Schweitzer, 199 Syracuse University Press, Syracuse, NY.
17 P.22 *Memoirs of Childhood and Youth*, Albert Schweitzer.

"The older we grow the more we realize that true power and happiness come to us only from those who spiritually mean something to us. Whether they are near or far, still alive or dead, we need them if we are to find our way through life. The good we bear within us can be turned into life and action only when they are near to us in spirit."[1]

Albert Schweitzer

5

The Train

Bonjour, Docteur Schweitzer,

The heat in Florida is continuing. As I begin this letter, I must tell you that I am planning a trip for two weeks from today. Yes, I am going back to the old country on September 7th to spend some time with my sister and to experience the ambiance of the North Sea in early fall. The old country is what we call Europe. America is so new compared to the history and culture of the Asian and European countries. This morning I am feeling a bit ambivalent about my upcoming journey, but don't know why. Could it be that this trip may not live up to the experiences I had during my trip to Germany and France in 1987? I now allow my thoughts to drift back to these memories.

Back in the late summer of 1987 I bought a ticket for a direct flight Toronto-Düsseldorf. It was to be a two-week vacation. My sister was very happy to see me. Describing her nature as kind is an understatement. She greeted me with a bouquet of fresh flowers at the airport. After a few days of visiting cousins and much sightseeing, I became restless. She had planned trips through the beautiful rural countryside, including an excursion to the Cologne Cathedral. During a shopping spree in Holland, she sensed that my mind was elsewhere and asked, "Is there anything you'd like to do?" "Yes", I replied, "if you wouldn't mind, I would like to find a bookstore."

The following day she took me to the 'old town' of Düsseldorf, where I soon found an appropriate establishment. I inquired if perhaps, they had any books written by you. "No", replied the clerk, "these books are not in stock, however, I can order them for you, it will take a few days." I ordered your books *The Quest for the Historical Jesus*' and *'The Mysticism of Paul the Apostle'* wanting to take this opportunity to read your words in German, your mother tongue. After relaxing in a café with cake and coffee, we went home. I remember the puzzled look on my sister's face when she heard the title of the books I ordered. "Since when are you interested in religion?" she asked. I honestly do not remember my reply to her question.

Near the end of my stay, knowing I only had a few days left, I had the sudden urge to be alone. Much to my sister's surprise, she was puzzled at my impulsive decision to want to travel alone, I decided from one moment to the next to visit the place of your birth and perhaps end up in Günsbach, the village of your home away from Africa.

The thought of visiting Africa had occurred to me, but that was out of the question at the time because of my limited financial resources. I rationalized that boarding a train and going south to where you grew up and used to live, was the next best thing.

After having made the decision, I became excited. Early the next day my sister dropped me off at the main train station in Düsseldorf and I relaxed into my seat, knowing I would arrive in Strasbourg, Alsace, later that afternoon, although Günsbach was my planned final destination.

I found it hard to concentrate on the beautiful scenery as the train route took me along the Rhine, past Cologne, Koblenz, and Mainz. This part of the Rhine Valley is very picturesque. Medieval castles are perched on rocks and mountains, lit by the morning sun and visible on both banks of the river. I thought of the history that surrounded this part of Europe. Many battles were won and lost in this valley. The victor or conqueror of these battles knew the river Rhine would be a huge asset used for navigation, commerce and progress. Many of the hillsides are now utilized for the cultivation of grapes, producing several varieties of local wines. Arriving in Baden-Baden, the train turned west towards Strasbourg. I was in France.

There was a change of crew, and the atmosphere changed. By this time it was Saturday afternoon and most of the people boarding the train in Strasbourg were locals. Because of the bags they carried, they appeared to be returning home to their respective village after spending a day at the market in Strasbourg.

The din increased to a different pitch as the train rolled south through the pretty countryside. The province of Alsace, now French, used to be part of Germany before World War I, and everyone spoke German in the year of your birth in 1875. All is different now, and it was at times like this that I regretted not speaking French. I only caught bits and pieces of conversations, so it was easy for me to retreat back into my own thoughts—in silence.

My first stop was Kaysersberg, the place of your birth on January 14, 1875. Here I decided to stop to rest, wanting to arrive in Günsbach, which was still a few miles south, renewed and refreshed the next day

It was early evening when I disembarked from the train I had boarded in Düsseldorf earlier that morning. Looking around I scouted this village for a place to spend the night. Everything was within walking distance in this almost medieval looking hamlet. I found it storybook beautiful in every conceivable way.

Every home or establishment had window boxes filled with a colorful display of flowers clinging to its exterior. Most windows had contrasting shutters. The roads were very narrow and paved with ancient cobblestones. A small bubbling stream dissected the small central area, which was reserved for pedestrians only.

Kaysersberg is nestled in a valley at the foot of the Vosges mountain range and there wasn't a high-rise in sight anywhere. In the distance I saw a tower, which appeared to be the remains of an old castle or fortress. In town, one house caught my attention because it had, what appeared to be a church steeple projecting from its roof. How strange I thought...

Making an inquiry as to where to stay, I found myself walking up a hill to a charming home. It was a bed and breakfast establishment, run by a local couple who only spoke French.

After stowing away the few items of clothing I had brought I decided to walk this village at sundown, hoping to find a café for a light dinner and a glass of the famous Alsatian wine, which

Kaysersberg was famous for producing. The strange name, '*Gewürztraminer*', reminded me of an occasion a long time ago.

In the spring of 1979 I was sitting on a hotel terrace overlooking a magnificent sunset in Vancouver. My boyfriend at the time, who was older and more sophisticated than I, had ordered this wine explaining that it was produced in Alsace, followed by the words, "This wine reminds me of the time I was stationed in Belgium during the Second World War." Isn't it strange, how the name of a wine can evoke these memories? All this seems to have happened a lifetime ago.

In Kaysersberg I absorbed the scenery like a sponge, feeling very much at home. These charming surroundings felt as comfortable as an old shoe. Most structures were '*Fachwerk*' which is what we would call 'Tudor' in appearance, yet different. Most were finished in white or ochre colored stucco. Old rustic beams were a prominent feature of construction dating back to 1600-1800. Some doors were large and arched leading to an inner courtyard. In short, everything appeared very ancient—frozen in time.

Finding a quaint looking restaurant ended my search for a quiet place to eat. It was getting dark as I went inside and found a corner table empty—just waiting for me. I ordered from a menu of home cooked cuisine. Sitting at the next table, was a group of older men, deep in animated conversation. I detected a German dialect. Feeling their eyes upon me, I thought, 'They are probably wondering what I am doing here? To them I am just another curious tourist sitting there all by myself.'

I was still very shy back then, so for me to strike up a conversation was quite out of character, but I did! I couldn't resist... Was it because of hearing them speak German, or was it because I started to think that perhaps this group was old enough to have known you? I believe it was both. I considered this pure luck, and could not resist this opportunity to ask them all sorts of questions. I struck up a conversation, telling them about my journey to Germany, and about my desire to see this part of the world. They in turn had many questions about America and Canada.

As I looked into their faces it dawned on me, that these men were definitely old enough to have some memories of a certain personality, namely you, Dr. Schweitzer. Again, I became aware of my good fortune and was filled with the thought: 'This is my lucky day!'

The evening passed quickly, as we became involved in a most stimulating conversation, revolving mostly around you and your life. They were thrilled to speak to someone from another country, someone who had come all the way to this remote village, inquiring about their most famous citizen. I sensed a certain awe and reverence in their voices as they talked about you. They told me that the house of your birth was now a museum and that I must stop there in the morning, before traveling on to Günsbach. They also informed me that your former home in Günsbach was now open to the public, having become a museum as well. I became excited and ordered another round of wine for my new friends.

I discovered that these gentlemen, all four of them, were born before the turn of the century. This made them range in age from 89-94, able to remember the time before the car became our form of transportation, certainly before jet travel became common. Their youth was spent here, before the invention of computers and space travel; before the major discoveries in physics, and science were made, leading to the atom bomb and the cold war of the fifties. They told me about your father, who had been a pastor in the small church I planned to visit the next day. The word *pastor*, stems from Latin: meaning herdsman, relating to a flock. Yet, we often use the synonym *preacher* in English. This seems the wrong way to describe a learned theologian.

I thought about the lives of my dinner companions, spent mostly in the surroundings of this village. It was not uncommon then to live in one locality all your life. You, of course, were the exception to this, weren't you? My ability to converse in German was a bit hampered by the fact that I had lived in Canada and the US for most of my life. However, after a few hours, and the consumption of a few glasses of the local wine, I even surprised myself at becoming quite fluent again. Their local dialect was not easy to understand. The days spent with my sister had brought the German language back into my consciousness. I found myself using words I had long forgotten I knew. They said they loved my enthusiasm!

Since none of this trip was initially planned, I was so grateful for this special experience and thought about what the next day may have in store for me, as I slowly walked back to my room in the *pension*. Smiling at my good fortune I silently said: "Thank you God", turning out the light that evening, wishing it was morning. 'Was I led to these experiences?', and 'Who was guiding me?', were thoughts that at these times had entered my mind.

My dear Dr. Schweitzer, you had a great effect on so many people. It is now 2001 and I know these men are probably not with us any more. My heart is filled with gratitude this Saturday morning, as I remember the kindness and hospitality shown to me, a lone tourist, by these four individuals. They had so much to share, on that special Saturday night in Kaysersberg, back in the summer of 1987—fourteen years ago! I will close with the thought of remembering the rest of my journey for you tomorrow, as I plan to again go back to your part of the world.

Your devoted student, *R.*

Good Sunday, le Grand Docteur,

As I stepped out of my hot shower this morning I couldn't help but be reminded of all the conveniences I take for granted. There were no hot showers in Africa for you. I am constantly reminded of the sacrifices you made! For me, not having a hot shower would be a sacrifice. It's all relative?

Today is Sunday. On Sunday mornings I have two extra hours to devote to this journal. Although I work in the afternoons, the fact that Monday and Tuesday are my weekend ahead, I already begin to relax on Sundays. I find myself relaxing three out of the seven days of each week. Will I be able to create this feeling of complete relaxation for each day and stay at my current job? What a challenge! Pachebel's Canon in D major is softly playing as in my mind I go back to another Sunday morning fourteen years ago.

You chose to be a doctor in this lifetime, so you never experienced a day off, did you? While in Africa, you were on call seven days a week—twenty-four hours a day—and used the quiet hours of evenings to play your music and to write. I am definitely, a morning person, often rising at 4 AM. My energy level is at its highest in the early hours of morning. This morning I find the exercise of going back in time, re-living my visit to Günsbach—very pleasant, indeed.

Back in 1987, upon waking that morning in Kaysersberg, I heard church bells in the distance, reminding me that it was Sunday. While traveling I often lost track of what day it was. I could hardly wait to get up and dressed quickly with the anticipation of walking the streets of this village again. As I stepped outside, an early morning mist seemed to veil everything. The scene was almost mystical as I walked up onto a hill, absorbing the view from above before walking down to the village. Except for one or two pedestrians and a lone cyclist, I appeared to be alone in this heavenly environment. One house in particular caught my attention again! It was the one I had seen the night before—the house with the steeple protruding from its roof. As I came closer, I could see the inscription on one wall: 'CENTRE CULTUREL' and underneath 'DOCTEUR SCHWEITZER'.

I had missed this inscription the night before. The sun had already set and it was too dark to see everything. I tried the door, but found it to be locked. Then I realized it was too early in the day and returned to my pension for a continental breakfast. Again I heard church bells ring, as if calling a flock, while I savored the crusty rolls, cheese and home made preserves. I packed my belongings hoping the *Centre Culturel* would be open by the time I was ready to go back to the train station and continue my journey south to Günsbach.

I headed straight for the house, which looked like a church, and found the door open. The house of your birth is a museum now, displaying a lot of the artifacts and tools you used in Africa, including a large number of photographs. This was the church of your father's congregation! Entering the building through an ancient arched courtyard, I was immediately struck by the simplicity of the interior and its altar. Yet, I sensed a spirituality that is often lacking in modern churches. I sensed a presence, if you will, that stayed with me long after leaving these premises. I said a silent prayer in the still empty church and thanked the universe—and whoever was directing me to this experience! Then I experienced a deep sadness at having to leave this place. Life felt so real to me there. Being surrounded by nature, and by people who enjoyed the simple things in life, felt very comforting. It was *gemütlich*.

Consoled by the words of my companions the night before, and remembering that your home in Günsbach had become an archive museum, I slowly made my way to the train station.

The train took me south and I arrived at the Günsbach train station early afternoon. Seeing that this was a much smaller village, I immediately ventured out on foot and explored my new surroundings. After asking a fellow pedestrian for directions to your former home, I saw her point to a stucco structure, up on a slight hill ahead to my left. The afternoon sun bathed the white shutters. Your house was partially covered in ivy. From this viewpoint, I noticed the garden behind your home, sloping down a gentle hill.

I could feel my heart beating faster as I walked along the road, approaching the intersection where I would have to turn left. A sense of shyness, mixed with a strange excitement, seemed to envelop me. I actually passed by your home several times, working on gathering the courage to knock on the door, remembering your words: *"This is the house that Goethe built."* My mind drifts back, to the years before this house was built.

You had been a prisoner of war during the later part of World War I, having been kept in confinement because you were still a German national. After being released by the French you returned to this area, this village in particular, and described your impressions:

"Since Günsbach was within the sphere of military operations, many office visits and papers were needed to obtain permission to find my father. Trains still ran as far as Colmar, but the ten miles from there towards the Vosges had to be covered on foot. "So this was the peaceful valley that I had left on Good Friday, 1913. There were dull roars from guns in the mountains. On the roads one walked between lines of wire netting packed with straw, as between high walls. These were intended to hide the traffic in the valley from the enemy batteries on the crest of the Vosges.

"Everywhere there were concrete emplacements for machine guns. Houses ruined by gunfire. Hills that I had remembered as covered with woods now stood bare. The shellfire had left only a few stumps here and there. In the villages orders were posted that everyone must carry a gas mask with him at all times.

"Günsbach was the last inhabited village before the trenches. Hidden by the surrounding mountains, it had not been destroyed by the artillery fire on the heights of the Vosges. Among crowds of soldiers and between lines of battered houses the inhabitants went about their business as if there were no war going on. That they could not bring the second hay crop home from the meadows by day seemed as natural to them as rushing to the cellars whenever the alarm sounded, or the fact that they might at any moment receive an order to evacuate the village on short notice if an attack was imminent, forcing them to leave all their possessions behind.

My father had become so indifferent to danger that he remained
in his study during the bombardments, when most people went
to their cellars. He could hardly remember a time when he had
not shared the vicarage with officers and soldiers."2

You described the state of mind of the villagers who depended
on the harvest for survival, and I quote your words again:

"Anxiety about the harvest, however, weighed heavily on people
who had otherwise become indifferent to the war. A terrible
drought prevailed. The grain was drying up; the potatoes
were ruined; on many meadows the grass crop was so thin
that it was not worth mowing; from the stables resounded the
bellows of hungry cattle. Even if a storm cloud rose above the
horizon it brought not rain but wind, which robbed the soil of
its remaining moisture, and clouds of dust adumbrating the
specter of starvation."3

This must have been a hard time for you, having spent the
previous years in Africa building a hospital facility for the ailing
natives, then returning to your previous home, a village completely
devastated by the ravages of World War I. It was during this time
that you felt a deep exhaustion.

"I hoped in vain that among my native hills I should rid myself
of the fatigue and the now slight, now severe attacks of the
fever from which I had suffered since the last weeks at St.
Rémy. From day to day I felt worse until, toward the end of
August, a high-fever attack followed by violent pains made
me realize that these were the aftereffects of the dysentery I
had contracted at Bordeaux and that an immediate operation
was necessary. Accompanied by my wife, I dragged myself six
kilometers toward Colmar before we could find a vehicle of any
sort. On September 1 I was operated on by Professor Stolz in
Strasbourg."4

As a result of the war, Strasbourg was now the new border
of Germany. Many of your friends and former teachers found
themselves displaced and destitute. Your kind and loyal nature
must have seemed *heaven sent* to those who suddenly found
themselves hungry and homeless. Cosima Wagner was among the
displaced. This is how you described meeting her again:

"During the armistice period and the following two years I was a familiar figure to the customs officials at the Rhine Bridge because I frequently went over to Kehl with a knapsack full of provisions for starving friends in Germany. I made a special point of helping in this way Frau Cosima Wagner and the aged painter Hans Thomas, together with his sister Agatha."[5]

Cosima, Richard Wagner's widow was at that time eighty-one years old. You never forgot your friends, did you? Your nature was always giving! How time flies, I must get ready for work... Tomorrow I will describe my impressions of your home in Günsbach in more detail. Until then,
I remain your devoted student, *R.*

Dear Dr. Schweitzer,

This morning I decided to start writing a little bit later so I could listen to *J.S. Bach's Toccata & Fugue in D Minor*, at full volume. This particular recording features as organist E. Power Briggs on the Flentrop organ in the Busch-Reisinger Museum, at Harvard University. During the early part of this morning I re-read several chapters of your book '*Out of my Life and Thought'*.

It is my hope, that with these letters I may rekindle the flame you lit so long ago and to allow others to be inspired by your wisdom and vision. To learn more about you, your life mission and your philosophy, seems to be most appropriate for a new generation. The message your life represents is as relevant and fresh today, as it was when you were alive. Now I'll allow my mind to drift back to my visit to Günsbach.

At the time of my visit in 1987 I felt this strong desire to *see* a part of your world—the world of your childhood and youth. At that time I had already gained some insight into what comprised your inner life. Having immersed myself into your world of thoughts and values, I had recognized the importance of your ideas. I wondered where this inner yearning to see your physical surroundings came from. Would it further validate what I was beginning to sense on a deeper level of my being?

After gathering the courage to knock on the door of 8 Rue de Munster, I remembered that this was not the home you grew up in. You had this residence built after being awarded the Goethe Prize in 1928, which was quite a substantial sum of money back then. However, before you allowed this money to be used for this personal purpose, you spent the next few years giving concert tours throughout Europe earning an equal amount to be used for the new facilities you had envisioned in Lamberéné, Africa. You never forgot your priorities.

It was not until 1936 that you had this house built, making it the headquarters for your activities in Africa, sharing these premises with all the volunteers who needed a place to rest after having spent time with you in Africa. In this respect you never referred or thought of this structure as *your* home. The home in which you had spent your childhood and youth with your father Louis and your mother Adele Schweitzer, was known as the pastor's residence, a very prominent house, located up a small hill behind the local church.

When I rang the bell at 8 Rue Munster, I was actually surprised at receiving a response. On Sundays most European establishments were usually closed. To my delight and surprise, a fit and elegant elderly woman opened the door. Was she your former secretary Ali Silver? I can't remember if I asked her this question. The state of shy nervous excitement had narrowed my state of awareness, so this fact had slipped my mind completely.

The first thing that caught my attention in your former headquarters was the number of books lining several shelves along the walls! They were your books! Volumes and volumes you had read during your lifetime. They were as important to you, as food is to the average person. I can relate to that! Walking through your home was an experience I will never forget!

The second observation that left me a bit speechless, was the fact that this residence had an atmosphere of complete simplicity, bordering on austerity. I reflected on you and your personality. This place reflected the fact that you only needed the essentials in life to be content. I was struck by the thoughts, 'This is the home of one of the most famous people of the Twentieth Century, a man who could well have lived in the lap of material luxury.' 'A man who certainly deserved everything a material world was prepared to offer and throw at his feet.' 'Here lived a man who was revered and adored by millions of people—a man who inspired and changed the lives of so many.'

You clearly knew that material possessions bring only momentary pleasure. The lasting peace of mind, that the material objects promise, are an illusion of the mind. You knew that peace of mind will only be experienced when leading a meaningful life.

In Günsbach you rested, away from the responsibilities of running the hospital in Africa. History shows that you only spent a few years here, using it mostly to write and to prepare for your European concert tours. I saw many of the articles and objects you had utilized during your life, including your writing desk, a narrow bed, which looked more like a cot than a bed, and the beaten up traveling bag you used, which was given to you by your grandfather.

On a side table was a replica of the head of a black man, a reminder of your experience during a visit to Colmar during your youth, where you first saw this statue in the town-square and were moved by this man's expression. Your words rang through my head as I remembered:

"My interest in missions goes back to the afternoon services in Günsbach. On the first Sunday of every month, my father conducted a service dedicated to missions in which he spoke about the life and work of missionaries. On a series of Sundays, he once read to us the memoirs of Casalis, the missionary to the Basutos, which he had translated, from French for this purpose. They left a deep impression on me.
"Next to Casalis, it was the sculptor Bartholdi from Colmar, the creator of the Statue of Liberty at the entrance to New York Harbor, which directed my young thoughts to faraway countries. On his monument of Admiral Bruat on the Champ-de-mars at Colmar there is the sculpture of a Negro, carved in stone, no doubt one of the most impressive works his chisel created. It is a Herculean figure with a thoughtful, sad expression. This Negro gave me a great deal to think about. Whenever we went to Colmar, I sought an opportunity to look at him. His face told me about the misery of the Dark Continent. To this day, I make a pilgrimage to see him when I am in that town."6

In the living room, a room with a view of the garden stood your mother's upholstered chair. In front of your famous pedal piano stood the back-less small stool that you had used for writing at your desk in Africa, and while playing the piano. Your writing desk was stacked high with the many books you had written, including the world-renowned books on Johann Sebastian Bach.

Over your piano hung an oil portrait of you, sitting at the organ with an open music book. It was a great painting—revealing your energy and vitality. Your youthful face was captured in a thoughtful, dream like expression. Your dark hair was already unruly then. Your famous mane and mustache, which later became gray, turned completely white during your 52 years in Africa.

I lingered a few extra moments and received a few brochures about your life's work and all the organizations that had been established bearing your name over the last few decades. All are dedicated to the continuation of your work—having been inspired by the example of your spirit.

After saying goodbye, and expressing my gratitude to this gentle woman so dedicated to her job, I left your former home, remembering your humble expression, '*This is the house that Goethe built*'. Completely uplifted by my experience, I almost floated back to the train station.

As I sat on an ancient looking bench waiting for the next train north, I had time to reflect on the many times you must have embarked and disembarked at this exact spot during your travels. I found myself inspired by my serene surroundings that Sunday afternoon, and could understand your fondness for this place in the countryside. I looked at the beauty of everything, including the building of this train station with its closed shutters and peeling paint. After glancing back at your home one last time, I spotted a flat stone lying in the gravel. I picked this stone up and slid it into my pocket. Sentimental? Perhaps, but it certainly describes the mood I was in, and this stone has served me well as a talisman over the last few years. As a matter of fact I now use it as a paperweight and it has the power to transport me back in time, back to this particular journey.

Reflecting on the train ride back to my sister's home, I remember that my heart was filled with a strange emotion. I suddenly felt that I needed to know more about you. A wave of passion washed over me. Your life, its purpose and its deeper meaning must have eluded me somehow. There must be something I hadn't grasped as yet! The spectacular passing scenery did not seem as important as what I was experiencing—on the *inside* of my being.

I experienced a sense of love for you as a human being, a feeling so different from the feelings of what is often called—romantic love. My heart seemed to become more open, more receptive to everything and everyone around me. Tears started to well up as the train slowly wound its way north, traveling faster once we crossed the border back into Germany. I cried that day enveloped by a strange feeling of deep sadness while contemplating the meaning of your life. I seemed to be releasing a dam of pent-up emotions. What was this feeling? The shedding of tears, especially in a public place came as a complete and utter surprise to me, yet I allowed the tears to flow.

Had you felt this emotion as love for humanity? Had you sensed our suffering? Had this love turned into full-blown compassion over the many years of your studies? Is this what is meant by real Love—Divine Love, unconditional Love? I started to ask myself the questions. 'What is the matter with the rest of us?' and 'Why are we so indifferent and complacent, involved mainly in pursuing material things, knowing full well that they do not give the promised happiness and satisfaction?' 'Why are we constantly rushing, running and hurrying—to get where?' 'How come we have our priorities so mixed up?' 'Do we suffer from the symptoms of fallacious thinking?' 'What made your thinking so different?'

These questions must have deepened my concentration, and before I knew it the train had arrived in Düsseldorf. I felt elated about this experience as I reminded myself of the saying, "The best things in life—are not things!"

Another insight I had forgotten and just remembered, is that I had written a poem after my second journey back to Florida, in which I compared my life to a train ride. Do you know what I mean? Something tells me you do!

The Train
'Silence is golden'
An adage, the author
Has been long forgotten.
Are we to him beholden?

My life has been a train
With many twists, turns and bends.
My baggage always closely watched
The stops—I hated—sitting still.

Once new passengers boarded
I was involved again.
Talking—laughing—comparing?
Thinking: "Thank God, this isn't boring…"

Until the next stop—on this line.
All got off—alone again,
Thinking… 'This is a crime.'
A pause—a time to think—how I strain!

I closed my eyes—became aware
Heard the distant whistle—blare.
Then felt the steel wheels—rumble
And smelled the distant sea—in the air.

Aware of clamoring and chatter
People saying their good-byes
I continued my daydream
Beginning to see —with closed eyes.

Became aware—this silence
Feels nice
I've tried it again—once or twice
And found true relaxation—in silence!
RzT 1996

The train ride from Günsbach is forever etched into my mind.
The quiet hours alone gave me the time to reflect on your words: 'I
made my life my argument."

Dear Dr. Schweitzer, I'll be back tomorrow. Some of my chores
have to be attended to. The mundane duties in my life, such as
doing my laundry and shopping for my upcoming trip, are calling
me.

Before I leave you for today, I must tell you something funny
that just happened. My sister called while I was writing this letter,
to inform me, that she had purchased train tickets for me, and
would send them today, in order to save me time at the airport.
I again asked her if I could bring her something from the United
States? After a long pause she replied, "Perhaps you could find a CD

for me, one that would help me to appreciate the music of Richard Wagner?" This was music to my ears. She then hastily added, "But, please don't make it too heavy—highlights only, please!"

Life is full of small miracles, isn't it? I will go to the mall and find a recording of 'Wagner's Greatest Hits'. Any start—is a good start!

With a deep sense of gratitude I remain,
Your devoted student, *R.*

Dear Dr. Schweitzer,

It feels so strange to remember my trip to Germany and France in these letters, knowing I will be leaving for that part of the world in a few days. What experiences are waiting for me this time? Something tells me this trip will not even come close to the experiences I had back in 1987. Why do I want to compare? Why can't I just go with the flow? Why do I feel so strange and up tight about this trip? I bought the requested CD's, along with Beethoven's 9th and a few J. S. Bach concertos.

I just lit a fresh candle in front of your picture to bring me back to the time fourteen years ago and the train ride back down the river Rhein. Upon my return my sister had many questions which I was not in the mood to answer. The following afternoon we went back to the old part of town to pick up the books I had ordered. We again strolled leisurely through the narrow cobblestone streets and my eyes looked up as my sister pointed to a particular historic house. "This is the birth place of the German poet, Heinrich Heine", she announced. Were you familiar with his writings? He was also a non-conformist, wasn't he? I decided to learn more about him.

My encyclopedia revealed that Heine was born in Düsseldorf on December 13, 1797. He is now remembered as a prolific writer of poetry and prose; he was a satirist, possessing a wit of exceptional skill; often using his talents as a writer for political and social commentary in opposition to the oppression of his time.

Today, these writings form the base for a new evaluation of his life and work. Heinrich Heine gained international fame, to a large extent with his *'Buch der Lieder'* (1827; The Book of Songs), the poems of which have been carried, in Heine's own phrase, "on wings of song" throughout the world by the more than 2,000

Lieder settings of Robert Schumann, Franz Schubert and several other composers of his time. But he became more than the usual 'love poet' of the 19th Century. His love poems, though they employ romantic materials, are at the same time suspicious of love as we know it, and of the feeling love purportedly represents. The poems are bittersweet and self-ironic.

He took a walking tour through the Harz Mountains and wrote a series of stories about his experiences, fictionalizing his modest adventure and weaving into it the elements, both of his poetic imagination and his sharp-eyed social commentary. 'Die Harzreise' (The Harz Journey) became the first piece of what were to be four volumes of 'Reiseblätter' (Pictures of Travel) written 1826-31.

Some of the pieces were drawn from a journey to England Heine made in 1827, and a trip to Italy in 1828. But the finest words of wisdom are found in, 'Ideen. Das Buch Le Grand' (1827); ('Ideas. The book Le Grand'). Being blessed with a keen sense of observation, he ventured on a journey into the self. It became a wittily woven fabric of childhood memory, enthusiasm for Napolcon, ironic sorrow at unhappy love, and political allusion.

Heine's power to annoy was as great as his power to charm and move, and rarely had a great poet been so controversial in his own country. Many of his poems expose the 'human condition'. Heine died on February 17, 1856, and was buried in Montmartc Cemetery.

Many of his works are very philosophical; he was interested in travel, politics, or as he described it, the folly of politics. He was very interested in the theater and the 'arts' in general. My encyclopedia lists a whole column of his works, and another column of biographies of his life, written by others after his death. Heine was quite a character wasn't he? What had he discovered about the emotion we call 'love'? I wonder...

My sister and I strolled through these ancient streets, which now have been reserved for pedestrians. Some little passageways were very narrow.

Fortified by pastries and coffee, we walked through the historic section at our leisure. Suddenly, I saw an advertisement posted on an old church. The public advertisement announced a free organ recital to be given that afternoon, starting in less than five minutes. I looked at my sister and asked if she wanted to go inside. I assumed from her facial expression that she was not too thrilled with the idea. However, I was her guest and would be leaving the next day, so she slowly followed me inside.

The music was J.S. Bach! As I looked around I observed the church filling to standing room only. We had gotten the last seats. 'How wonderful', I thought as the vibrations of this great organ began to fill the church. This was a great ending to my vacation! The air vibrating through the huge pipes created magical music. The music seemed not only to fill the space outside of myself but somehow also began to vibrate my inner being.

Leaving the church, we were both very quiet. I was wondering whether my sister had enjoyed the same feeling this music had invoked in me, when she turned to me and said, "Thank you, I am so glad you had the idea to go inside."

The next day on the airplane high over the Atlantic, my thoughts drifted back to you and your life of service; a life spent giving to humanity. I thought about the modern conveniences of today, conveniences we take for granted, and you had to do without. The mode of transportation when you were a boy was the bicycle and horse and buggy! I looked forward to reading the two books I had stowed in my luggage, along with German coffee and chocolates for my children and friends in Canada. I thought about my sister's kindness and generosity, which was part of her whole nature.

In hindsight I saw that this journey had been a pilgrimage, as I remembered all of the events of the previous days, especially the emotional train-ride from Günsbach. I remembered that you had written a book called 'The Pilgrimage to Humanity'. Falling asleep exhausted from the many walking tours I woke up as we landed. It is now nearing the end of August 2001. I will be boarding a direct flight from Miami to Düsseldorf in twelve days. Until tomorrow, I remain your devoted student and admirer, R.

Sources Chapter 5:

1   P.65 *The Words of Albert Schweitzer,* Norman Cousins.
2   P.178-179 *Out of my Life and Thought,* Albert Schweitzer.
3   P.179 *Out of my Life and Thought,* Albert Schweitzer.
4   P.180 *Out of my Life and Thought,* Albert Schweitzer.
5   P.181 *Out of my Life and Thought,* Albert Schweitzer.
6   P.57-58 *Memoirs of Childhood and Youth,* Albert Schweitzer

"The main point about Schweitzer is that he brought the kind of spirit to Africa that black persons hardly knew existed in the white man. Before Schweitzer, white skin meant beatings, gunpoint rule, and the imposition of slavery on human flesh. If Schweitzer had done nothing in his life other than to accept the pain of these people as his own, he would have achieved moral eminence."[1]

Norman Cousins

6

Courage

Dear Dr. Schweitzer,

Courage is a subject you must know something about. I will tell you now that I attempted to write a book about your life, but felt too ill equipped and under-educated to even attempt to be a chronicler of all of your unusual accomplishments and interests. I lacked the courage and the stamina. I had wanted to capture your spirit on paper and had actually written a biography of your life two years ago, which is now sitting in my closet. How did this come about? Well, I will tell you what happened!

My career of selling real estate in Toronto during the years of 1988-1994 became less and less important to me. Yes, I was successful, yes I fulfilled my duties and did what was expected of me, but I was yearning for something else! I found myself restless and often experienced a deep feeling of discontent, without knowing its source.

During those years I suffered from depression. I felt listless and very unmotivated. Yes, I dragged myself to the usual parties, and also gave a few, but my feelings of downright lethargy persisted. A dear friend, whom I had met in 1974 when I first entered the world of Real Estate, had been a rock of support over the years. Not only did she become like a sister to me, we even shared the same first name. In the office we were known as 'Renate 1 and Renate 2'. She has a fabulous sense of humor. In her company my feelings of discontent and restlessness momentarily subsided. In retrospect I see that laughter is good medicine, releasing a lot of inner and outer tension.

There was one major difference in our make-up. She was quite adventurous in some ways however, in other ways she was quite fearful. This showed as she admonished me not to travel alone in the car or while entering Manhattan one evening, she hastily locked all the car doors as we came out of the Lincoln Tunnel. She became scared to death as a man approached our car window with a squeegee, starting to clean our windshield. I always had to calm her down. 'Relax', was a word I often heard myself use. It became my admonition for her when we were faced with unusual situations during our travels together. We always ended up laughing about these and many of her other fears, but at the time she was often quite frantic.

I, on the other hand, experienced a different kind of fear. The fear of not having responded to your words adequately. Yes, I read many of your books, now what? Only in hindsight do I now admit and begin to understand the causes of these fears. I wondered, 'Was I living up to my potential?' Along with, 'What's the purpose of my quest—my life?' and especially, 'What was your message really about?'

At times I felt as though I was carrying the whole world on my shoulders. I was still carrying lots of guilt around as well. This guilt goes back to leaving my husband, leaving my children, and believing myself to be selfish for having had the courage to escape. Yes, I had lots of issues in my life that I had not dealt with, emotionally, mentally and spiritually.

Knowing today, that I did the best I could, under the circumstances and the awareness I had *then*, frees me of guilt about any past actions. All I can do is my best not to repeat past mistakes. I learned that the emotions of guilt and regret are very powerful in keeping me stuck in the past and draining my energy. I see that I had already started to think that way back in 1985.

Stuck
Your job can be a pleasure
Or a bore—it's all up to you.
It is a mirror of where you are
In your personal growth.

What makes you unsatisfied?
Can you change it?
Can you accept—that you are
The master planner of your life?

Become aware of the reality
That where you are right NOW
Is what you are committed to,
Otherwise, you would not be there.

A change of commitment
Will change your life...
RzT August 1985

Writing this, before my experience in Georgia, I knew it was time to make changes in my heart and soul, but found it hard to act. It was fear that held me back. Fear of change and the fear of letting go of things I had become accustomed to, although I knew I had outgrown them. To some extent the same is still true for me today, right now for instance. Am I truly satisfied with my present job, or is it the present *comfort zone* that keeps me stuck? Why is it so hard for me to let go of this comfort zone, change my commitment and move on? Where is the sense of confidence, the sense of destiny I experienced while writing you my first letter? Was I arrogant or egotistical for having these feelings? Where does my vacillation come from? Is the yearning for change first felt in my heart, and then it takes my mind time to surrender and follow its advice? Is there a mind-heart connection?

In the early 1990's my children were grown and my daughter had settled in New York with the new man in her life. This gave me new opportunities to travel, not only to Florida, but also to my favorite city, New York! My fondest memories include a lunch on top of the World Trade Center, a boat ride around the island of Manhattan, and the night view of the skyline on a cold December day before Christmas, while dining with friends at the River Café.

I especially loved the atmosphere of the older sections of the city and often walked the streets of lower Manhattan, gazing up at the ornate architecture, admiring the facades found on many buildings around Gramercy Park and Soho. My friends marveled at my courage saying, "You are so brave to walk the streets of New York alone" followed by, "You are so brave to drive to Florida alone." The idea of being afraid of *that* never even entered my mind. Fear of this kind was just not a part of my nature and I could never understand or identify with it.

I had been extremely shy growing up, yet I had chosen a career that involved dealing with the public. I was shy around lots of people and never felt very comfortable on a stage or at large parties. At social gatherings, for instance, I often found myself retreating to a solitary place. Some people would consider me a bit of a loner.

I was and still am, quite content to be alone with a good book or two, for days—even weeks at a time. So, what brought me back to Florida in 1995? I will leave the details of that story for tomorrow as I now realize I would like to visit my grandson today.

Little Marco has been in Toronto for a whole week, where the family attended a wedding. I miss him and look forward to seeing him soon. The rest of my adventure with fear can wait until tomorrow.

Your longwinded, but devoted student, *R.*

Dear Dr. Schweitzer,

Good morning to you! This morning I have a very special heavenly treat for you. It is 4 A.M. and I am playing a CD entitled '*Wings*'. I found this recording in 1996 and use it often. It has become a tool I use to relax and to focus my mind, while reading, writing or during meditation.

I describe this music as heavenly, because it is so lofty and ethereal. When I purchased this CD in 1996 the title had appealed to me since I had already entitled my second book of poetry '*WINGS*'. Each individual piece, as I now discover while looking at the inside jacket cover of the CD, has its own title. I had never closely inspected the cover insert before this morning. The experience gives me the chills!

Let me tell you what these composition are called. They are: 'Once in Ancient Greece', 'A Year and A Day', 'The Sands of Crete', 'Icarus', 'Athens Memories', 'The Tower of Minos', 'Wings', 'Feathers', and 'The Temple of Apollo'. This particular CD has become one of my favorites and I now introduce you to these serene and meditative sounds—the sounds of the heavenly spheres. I quote the words of the president of the Music Company from the jacket of the CD.

"Within each of us is a loving, magical, powerful being... a Real Self. Music, friend that it is, cocoons us from our worries, enabling that hidden self to emerge."

Terence Yailop.

Is that how music impacted you? I wonder... Turning the page I see another inspiring message·

"With eyes closed we can find a place of safety... a secret room, a magic cave, somewhere in nature. That place has its own resonance—which in turn has its own music. This CD comprises music to discover your own realm in which to be creative, renewed or to just quiet the spirit—whenever you choose to listen."

Dear Doctor, I hope you like the sounds. No wonder it has had such positive effects on my psyche.

My years from 1992-95 can be compared to living in a form of cocoon. During this episode, my reading material became more eclectic and more esoteric. For instance I became very interested in the healing power of crystals and minerals in general. I loved incense and the aroma of certain natural oils. Did I hope to find the key to some of the secret knowledge hidden in these books?

I found solace in reading about philosophers such as Plato and the *'Meditations'* of the Roman emperor Marcus Aurelius. I kept wondering, 'What did the ancient men of wisdom know about life and suffering?', because I was suffering. Outwardly this manifested in weight gain and depression. I was appeasing my emotions with food. I also experienced the emotion of fear welling up—again.

Without fear there can be no courage? Did I heed the wisdom of my own advice? This poem describes how I felt at times—lost!

Fear
Be strong and hold on
This too shall pass
This test—no nest to build upon?
This restlessness can't last.

Things will be better
That's the advice I hear
Family, friends—a letter
All help to subdue this fear.

This time—this place will
Remind me—once I look back
Hope and change—don't sit still
They come back—once I attack.

Fight for your life—don't wallow
In things past, gone—and done.
Hold up your head—take a big swallow
Face things and problems—head on.

Relax in the knowledge
Help is at hand
Reach out—build a bridge
Not a dam.

The flow will return
A soothing kindly word
Will heal all—even the burn.
From fear comes courage—the cure.
RzT 1996

Yes, I had my times of doubt, especially when I found myself longing to move back to the US.

My daughter, Eve, and her boyfriend and protector, Steve, had decided to buy a house in the country. The stress of living and working in New York was not to their liking anymore. They found a charming home in what is known as 'horse country'. She must be very serious about this relationship, I thought, as I drove to visit them in the spring of 1993. The setting was beautiful. I could understand why they chose this place to settle down. The next St. Valentine's Day I received the news that they had decided to get married. The wedding would be early September.

In the fall of 1994 we all gathered to attend the beautiful outdoor ceremony. It was a glorious early September evening as we gathered to watch a spectacular sunset of orange and pink. Deer roamed in the meadow below us, while we enjoyed appetizers. I took a picture of Eve sitting on the stone steps gracing the rear terrace of this establishment. Her face was illuminated by a golden orange sunset. She looked serene and radiantly happy.

The reception room was very elegant. Wood paneling graced the formal dining room. As I prepared to sit down at my table, I saw a large fireplace on my right side. Had the psychic back in 1986 been right? She had seen Eve getting married in front of a large stone fireplace! After a wonderful evening of dining and lots of dancing, the happy couple left for their honeymoon in Italy.

I was very happy for my daughter, but felt totally down and deflated driving back to Canada. I began to feel a strong desire to move back to the United States permanently. What was I doing in Toronto? I could not discuss my deepest desire or my feelings of discontent with my friends, because I knew they would try to discourage these inner yearnings.

A few years before this happy occasion I took my sons Marc and Steven on an Hawaiian vacation. We explored the island of Oahu, driving to the north shore, walking through sugar cane fields. Pineapple fields bordered the roads on both sides for miles and miles. We stopped at a Macadamia nut plantation and admired many exotic plants, including flowers I had never seen before! At times it was hard to look past the commercialization of this beautiful place. It reminded me of what 'paradise' may have been like! Getting away from the crowded beaches of Honolulu gave us a glimpse of what this island must have looked like hundreds or thousands of years ago.

The highlight of our trip was a short flight to the island of Hawaii. We drove to a large, now inactive—volcano. The power of nature and its fury was very evident, especially on this particular island. The tour bus took us along roads that were still covered in hardened black lava. We saw hillsides that had completely recovered from previous eruptions. These hillsides were now thriving coffee plantations. The earth was fertile, now covered with such rich soil that it was hard to believe that tons of molten lava once flowed down this lusciously green mountain.

We were intrigued and puzzled by the natural phenomena—the earth erupting with such force and violence. While visiting the top of an old crater, which was about a mile in diameter, we were warned not to take any lava rocks home. "They bring bad luck", we were told by the tour guide. I must admit it was very tempting to keep a piece of lava as a very unusual souvenir, but we heeded the advice given by the local people of Hawaii. They seemed to know what they were talking about. It felt a bit eerie. The local people described the bad fortune, which seemed to haunt the people who did not follow their advice.

Was it true that this group of islands is all that remaines of the mystical continent of Mu? Was this what remained of Lemuria— quite often referred to in esoteric literature? A continent, that had preceded the stories and mysteries of Atlantis? Lemuria was supposedly destroyed by fire. Volcanoes are the evidence that this could very well have been the case? I wondered...

All in all this was an educational holiday. The trip was a belated present to my boys, for having graduated from college, and having become all-around wonderful young men. It wasn't just me who felt their positive energy. All of my friends, including people I barely knew, commented on their disposition and practical common sense. Parents of their friends often told me, "You are so lucky to have such great and smart children."

Yes, I realized quite early that I was blessed in that respect! Both had their hearts set on becoming independent early in life and chose careers to speed this along. I did not have to worry about them anymore. Since when did worry ever solve anything anyway? Isn't it a total waste of emotion?

Early in 1995, I started to look into the possibility of moving back to the US permanently. My son was applying for his US citizenship and would then be able to sponsor me. I yearned for a more creative way to earn my living. Real estate had become a rat race. We all had cell phones and pagers. Although we could make our own schedules and appointments, the pressure of always being available, plus the fact that you had to be *aggressive* to succeed in a materialistic sense, did not appeal to me any more. I had lost interest in living only for the almighty dollar. Worshipping or saving money had never been my strong suit.

Again I was faced with the questions of friends, who meant this kindly, "Aren't you scared to make this move again?" "Haven't you learned from your previous experience?" and "Do you know how hard it is to earn a decent living, especially since you do not want to continue selling real estate?" This was followed by, "The wages in Florida are very low, because everyone wants to live in a warmer climate!" I know some of these words were meant to warn and perhaps to protect me. "Protect me from what?" I thought. The idea of moving, at first a small glimmer, had grown into a flame. I decided not to be discouraged by their remarks and suggestions!

In the spring of 1995 I found myself on the road to Florida. Once again my son Marc had offered to drive the truck. I had sold practically everything, only taking a few pieces of furniture and of course my beloved books. This made the transition easier. I had already decided not to place too much value on things. Once I had a proper job, I could always acquire new *things*

After an enthusiastic, but physically exhausting false start, which drained me completely financially, I started to look for a job. I had attempted to open my own business with the little money I had been able to save, but soon recognized that I was creating new stress. I looked around for a more peaceful way to earn my livelihood.

In late 1996 my papers were finally in order and I received my green card. I finally settled down and looked for the right position. Did you ever experience the kind of fear and insecurity I am talking about? Did your friends and family try to dissuade you from making a major decision, namely giving it all up and starting in a new direction? Did you have fear before you entered medical school? Did you have fear before you embarked into the unknown territory of Africa? Or had your spiritual background and the knowledge of philosophy given you emotional stability? Did the years of studying this subject give you the courage to find your own way? What is the lesson in embracing insecurity and change? Your record shows that fear was not one of the motivating factors of your personality. I found this emotion to be so strong, so devastating, so debilitating, that I would like to read you another poem I wrote back then.

Prisoner
Alone—a prisoner of my thoughts
A fear so overwhelming
Frozen like a statue
Not responding.

No motivation—no self love.
Where is my spirit—my light?
Where are the friendly faces—above?
What does it mean—do I now fight?

Fight those dark moments
Despair—depression—destitution
The inner voice, my spokesman
Comes to rescue—a solution?

Those thoughts always hidden before
Now threaten to envelop
My being—my body—my core.
My soul—it needs to develop?

My character needs shaping?
How wise and introspect
The chasm—tears—no escaping
A time to heal—and reflect?
RzT 1996

That's when I became interested in the question, "What are thoughts?" "Where do they come from?" "Isn't my brain just an organ, a bunch of cells like my liver, only a bit different in its purpose?" "Are the mind and the brain the same thing?" "Who puts thoughts into my mind?" Was I experiencing 'the dark night of the soul'?

On that note, I will leave you for today. I express my deep gratitude and devotion to you, my mentor and teacher.
Your happy student, *R.*

My dear friend,

I hope you don't mind my addressing you in this informal fashion. Knowing you are constantly there to inspire me, as you have inspired millions of people in the past, has brought about this familiarity. I see you as an older brother who is trying to teach me the meaning of life and its ultimate purpose. I see you as a 'thinking' person's friend.

It's only lately, while writing to you, that I have actually looked at and reviewed some of the poetry I wrote back in 1996. It helps me to remember and look at the emotions I experienced back then.

Back in 1985 in Georgia, during a meditation session someone had compared me to a rose. Am I like a rose that is slowly starting to open? Is the force of nature at work here? When I observe nature, I see that it unfolds naturally. Am I like a flower, already programmed to blossom or like a tree that is programmed to bear fruit? Do I have a choice in the matter? What is this Law of Nature? Are we all subject to this Law? What about the Law of Cause and Effect?

As I review my life, I can honestly say that I remained a skeptic. The word God, is a word I could not really relate to. It seemed to be connected with so much tradition and dogma. The real meaning of this *creative force*, can never be completely comprehended with our limited human understanding. I can only relate to this energy by seeing it as the Unknown or *the Source*.

The Source of all Creation—The Source of all Intelligence—The Source of all Consciousness—The Source of Light. Seen in this light, are the creator or creators and the Source the same? I found it very arrogant to try to explain something we knew absolutely nothing about. This did not stop me from being curious, so I kept wondering...

I asked myself so many questions. What does the triangle represent in sacred geometry? Is it a symbol of creation? This symbol, the triangle or trinity, is to be found in all ancient teachings and religions.

Is everything taught in these symbols? Is all of mythology a series of symbols? Is the kernel of truth hidden in stories, legends, allegories and myths? Is Wagner's hero, Siegfried, on a quest, trying to find his real self, his true self, his soul—his spiritual Self? What does the dragon of mythology symbolize?

What is gained by this knowledge? A paradox presents itself. The more I learn—the more I realize—that I know nothing! Does this paradox present itself to every philosopher and every student of physics and metaphysics? If everything is cause and effect, how does this relate to my life?

I found myself searching! Is that what you were doing during all your years of study? Is that what we all end up doing, sooner or later, as long as we are alive?

How come some people will look at the stars and never even wonder? Yet, I look at the stars at night and I find myself filled with this sense of wonder, this sense of awe and reverence for creation and nature and the immensity of it all. Where did I get the courage to start my life over at the ripe age of fifty-one? Is it sometimes necessary to leave everything behind and start anew? Do material possessions weigh us down—keep us stuck—chasing for more and more? Was the time right for me to get off this treadmill?

Looking back, the only criteria in my mind while I searched for work once back in Florida, was that I needed a job that allowed me some free time to think about subjects that were of interest to me. This ruled out real estate, the profession I had been trained for.

I went on several interviews that looked promising, but somehow *knew* when the position offered did not feel right. I began to heed my intuition, the small inner voice, and *knew* that something better would come along. I began to trust that I would be guided to the right job. Who was guiding me through these moments of making these decisions? I became calm and did not panic, trusting some force inside of myself to guide me. Who was instilling me with this new sense of confidence and courage? Is there such a thing as a guardian angel?

As I looked at my finished book of poetry, which I had named 'WINGS', I recall feeling that it was somewhat symbolic of getting *my* wings back. Oddly enough, I did not show this book to anyone, knowing that it was meant for my own growth! If there was such a thing as guardian angels, were they guiding me? Where did the word 'Angel' originate from?

As I opened my dictionary I found that the word angel—stems from the Greek word '*ANGELOS*'—meaning messenger. Then I remembered that the majority of figures in Greek Mythology had wings. Most ancient murals depicted beings with wings. Who were these heavenly creatures? Where these angels, or godlike beings, a representation of a force of nature, depicting divine attributes?

Were they forces of energy, part of the almighty Source?   Were these *beings*, seen and unseen reflections of this Source?   What treasures of knowledge did they possess?

Treasures
Where is my search leading—home?
A new town—different surroundings.
Will I join a team—or work alone?
At my leisure—discover the treasure?

This journey is long and hard—a labyrinth—a maze
I've come through—maturing—more serious.
Clearing new paths—in the haze.
Finding Zeus, Apollo, Hermes and Horus—mysterious?

These Gods of legends and myths
What remains of their glory?
Were they just like you and me?
Were their secret powers real—let's hear their story.

What can we learn from their conquests?
Baptism by fire—chariots—wings—fancy helmets
Angels—magicians— Anubis and Isis
Where are they now—incarnate?

What are their secrets and treasures?
Guarded, sealed—not revealed.
Are we not ready—according to their measure?
To be released—and healed?

Their themes have been set to music—Drum rolls
Thunder and lightning—wrath—severe betrayals
Lorelei—a mermaid or vixen?
Paracelcus—alchemy—what did his magic tell?

Were these beings with power real?
Or just some folklore stories
Like sylphs, gnomes and fairies—they appeal
To the hero in us—Merlin?
RzT 1996

Why this quest for knowledge? Where was it leading me? Just around Christmas, after my son Steven's wedding, I started looking through the newspapers again, continuing my job search.

I experienced a short bout of depression and the emotion of fear was not far behind. The roller coaster of pain and pleasure was being felt again. However, the valleys were not as deep this time around, since I knew that the downs don't last and eventually lead to the slow climb up.

Not only was I completely broke, due to having borrowed some money for my entrepreneurial venture, I found myself in debt. My son Steven had offered to lend me the money for my first month's rent, which I accepted only after I found a proper job and knew I could pay him back.

While going through these uncertain experiences I noticed a certain change in my perception. I had begun to trust my intuition, the 'small inner voice' that told me that everything would be all right. On my job hunt one ad intrigued me. It was obviously a retail position, but the company's name rang a bell. I had not considered a job in retail, because this had not been a part of my professional experience.

That's when I suddenly remembered my daughter and I strolling through the streets of New York City in 1992. I remembered the name of this particular retailer as the one that my daughter and I came to enjoy. Why did we both like this store? Because if was different! It was eclectic and the merchandising was innovative, appealing to the individualist in us. I remembered our trip to this establishment fondly, because we ended up walking the short distance back to her apartment, carrying an Oriental rug on our shoulders.

A few days later I received a call. Yes they wanted me to be a part of the Oriental rug sales team. They liked my enthusiasm about the product and felt I would be a good addition to the sales team, although they knew I had never sold retail before. I considered rugs to be works of art, and soon realized that I was very good at sharing my love and enthusiasm with potential buyers. Not only that, I had two full days off. They were never weekend days, which in hindsight was perfect. I needed my days off to be quiet, so I could perhaps start to write again.

Instead of using my two days off to run around and socialize, I found myself relaxing with a book, going to the beach, on most occasions—alone. The financial rewards at work seemed to come all by themselves. I remember telling my sons, "All I have to do is show up, the rest seems to take care of itself. This job is great. I get to use my creative ability and my innate sense of color and design."

I obviously had this inner creative ability, because I was soon making very good money. This job, just like my job in Real Estate, was strictly commission based. During that time I found a rental apartment and I put my energy into paying off my debts. Walking one evening, I spotted a particular condominium complex. I figured with some effort and fortitude I would be able to save enough money for a down payment. I needed to create a nest of some sort, a place that was truly comfortable and nice.

In the meantime, I thoroughly enjoyed learning about the art of area rugs. I became intrigued with the heritage and culture of the remarkable people who created these rugs. I especially enjoyed the visits of our company president who regaled us with tales of the Silk Road and the Khyber Pass. He had visited what I considered to be exotic places, such as India, Pakistan, Turkey, China and Nepal, on a regular basis. His enthusiasm was transmitted to me as he recalled his travels to the Orient.

Oddly enough, I never worried too much about not being able to make a sale. I just concentrated on finding the right rug! For the first time in my life, or so I thought at the time, I took on a position that allowed me a certain amount of creative freedom. I found myself enjoying this new challenge!

What happened to my desire to write again? For a while nothing. I did not own a computer, and kept putting this expense off, buying furniture and other necessities first. Why was I afraid to purchase a computer? Did it mean I would have to make use of it? I silently said to myself, "If the universe wants me to write, a computer will surely appear, as a message—from somewhere!" Until then, I will just enjoy my new life and relax.

During the latter part of 1996 we received the news that my daughter was pregnant, and the baby would be due some time in May. I was delighted and thrilled to become a grandmother. Time was certainly not standing still. I was now fifty-three.

That year I became aware of an apartment for sale in the park-like setting I had been admiring from afar. Since I did not have the necessary down payment, it remained a dream for a while. My goal to finally put down some roots, made me work harder. Both sons reminded me that I needed to think of my old age.

Going back to the year 1997, I must mention three particular incidents that were out of the ordinary. By accepting the position as a commissioned salesperson I had unknowingly entered into another competitive atmosphere. The business opened in February and became a success right away. Everyone I worked with on the selling floor had previous retail experience. I was the new kid on the block, and I had to learn this field quickly! I kept my eyes and ears wide open, focusing on the customer and the product. I drifted back into a competitive whirlwind with a different level of stress and anxiety, without being aware of it at the time. I also started to accumulate things, new furnishings, along with necessities such as a new car.

During this time, among the junk mail that we all have to contend with, was a letter that somehow looked different. The letter arrived around April, before the birth of my granddaughter. The reason I did not discard this letter immediately with the other advertisements that fill my mailbox on a daily basis is not quite clear. Perhaps it was because my name on the envelope was handwriting instead of the usual pre-printed label. I certainly did not recognize the return label.

To my surprise it was an invitation to higher learning. The booklet cover was graced with the symbol of the Egyptian Ankh, which I recognized as representing Eternal Life. 'Astara' called itself a modern day Mystery School. I was puzzled and intrigued as I started to read the accompanying booklet. The words: "IF YOU ARE A SEEKER..." seemed to jump off the page at me. I read every word very carefully and realized right away that this was not just another moneymaking scam. The words—seeker—mystery school—teachings of ancient wisdom—appealed to me instantly. I was invited to send away for lessons called degrees, which would *not* be sent unless I requested them. Also, what appealed to me was the announcement that no one would call me, that I would be studying these lessons at my own pace. This was a non-profit, educational publisher of mystical teachings embracing all religions and philosophies. The idea of joining any organization or religion repelled me then, as it still does today. Organizations have the tendency to promote their way of thinking, which is contrary to what I call '*free*' thinking.

The lessons were titled *'Astara's Book of Life'*. I read that:

"The principal mission of Astara is to help you obtain a thorough knowledge of life and its purpose—why you are here, how to live in harmony with the universal laws in operation all around you, to help you find and travel your personal path to wisdom, offering Self-realization, to real and lasting spiritual, emotional, mental and physical attainments. 'Astara' is a rebirth of one such school and in its current form has been serving humankind in a non-profit capacity since 1951."

There were no annual dues and no meetings to attend. I could study these lessons at home. They also mentioned words such as intuition—light—transformation—healing—science and philosophy. These were all subjects I had been interested in for quite some time. Needless to say, I sent away for my first lessons. I had unknowingly taken the first step towards returning to my Self.

Return
We are so busy—running to and from.
Paying 'past due' bills—acquiring new things.
Catching up on the news—calling old clients.
Checking the computer
What's for dinner—will I be thinner?
Tuning in on what—we think is important.
Will that lamp shade match?
What's the latest bug called—will I catch it
Is it contagious—you bet!
It is spreading like a vicious virus
Us—wanting to forget...
Staying in this mode a little longer
It gets more hectic—and yet...
There is this enigma—the faster we run,
The further we get away—from ourselves.
Isn't it time—to return?
RzT 1996

On the early morning of May 18th, 1997, I received the long awaited call. My granddaughter Alexandra was born. I was flooded with tremendous feelings of love and immediately arranged to take a few days off, booking a flight to New York. I needed to be with my daughter and hold the new addition to the family in my arms. It would be springtime in the country, my favorite time of year. The thought of a new baby made me quite euphoric.

As I prepared for the flight to New York I remembered to pack a few books to read on the plane. Guess which books I chose? Yes, I took along books written by you. Oh, oh it is almost 7:45 A.M., and this is a workday for me. I will tell you about my experiences on the plane and the feelings that the birth of my new granddaughter evoked, tomorrow. Until then,
I remain your grateful student, *R*.

Dear Dr. Schweitzer,

I remember the week spent in the country fondly. My daughter had decorated the baby's room in a teddy bear motif. Soothing pastel colors surrounded me as I sat in a rocking chair and watched the baby sleep. I find it hard to express the feeling of love expanding my heart as I observed this new life, my tiny little granddaughter nestled in her big crib. I also remember the look of love on my daughter's face as she nursed her little one. In the photos we took, I am smiling from ear to ear. Outside, as if to help in the celebration of a new life, everything was in bloom.

The peonies had opened, the rhododendrons were in full bloom, the lilacs had opened overnight, and the perfume of lily of the valley, which were shyly hiding under the growth of ground cover, was permeating the spring air. It was a week I will always remember!

The flight home was bittersweet. While waiting for my return flight to depart, I was filled with that incredible emotion again, not unlike the emotion I had felt after leaving your home in Günsbach. The feelings I experienced on the train ride were love, gratitude and compassion.

I felt my heart opening again, brought on by the unconditional love I experienced for my granddaughter. This love created a deep connection. I thought about the reality, that she would be twenty-one when I was seventy-four, should I live that long!

While browsing through a bookstore at La Guardia Airport I saw a particularly attractive journal. A thought occurred to me. I would like to record the feelings I am presently experiencing in this book, and save it for her until she is older. I would like her to feel this connection of love. I wanted to tell her about my previous visits to New York City, and how different they were from this special visit.

Needless to say, I bought this journal. On the flight home I thought only about what I would write in this journal. My mind was filled with memories she may be glad to know about—the experiences of her grandmother's path. Thinking ahead, in my mind's eye, I saw her grow up in a country setting, surrounded by nature and animals. I thought about the parents she had chosen! I thought about how nice it would have been for me to have a little book, written by my own grandmother, in which she had recorded certain experiences, not only of her youth, but about her fears, challenges or the trials she may have experienced later in her life. I never even knew my grandmother! How would my grandmother, had she lived, have felt about me?

A few days after returning home, I sat down early one morning, silently talking to Alexandra in my mind. This small book was filled in no time, and I put it on a shelf hoping that after I am gone someone will give it to her. The experience of writing felt wonderful. It reminded me of the evenings I had spent writing poetry.

That summer I studied the lessons arriving in the mail from 'Astara'. Around the Thanksgiving Holiday I was preparing a special package of Christmas presents for my daughter and her family. I looked at the forlorn figure of a Teddy Bear propped up on my dining room sideboard. I had purchased this bear for little Alexandra. The bear, wearing a knitted dress and sporting a red and white scarf, appeared to be watching me make all the preparations. This incident stirred my desire to a write a story for Alexandra.

Before leaving for work the next morning, I wrote the book 'The Red and White Scarf' in less than thirty minutes. The theme of the story is a very simple one. It's a Teddy Bear's search for love, in her heart longing to find a happy home. As soon as I started my writing again, I felt as though I too was returning home! I was returning—by turning inward—to my real Self.

I used my son Steven's computer to create a small book, which was the last present I placed into the Christmas parcel. Since my drawing talents are very limited, I used my camera to create the necessary illustrations. Everyone I showed this book to, including friends and relatives, loved it! I was very happy with the thought that I had actually created something. I had re-discovered that I could write. Yes, in hindsight I see that it was another step towards getting to know myself. Writing had become my tool of choice.

I thought about you last night, and wondered how much of the credit for this newfound courage and inspiration belongs to you. I had started walking on a different path. Without my actually being consciously aware at the time, everything started to change. My internal change started to manifest itself in the outer world as creativity.

Dear Dr. Schweitzer, I want to let you know that your words were starting to have an effect on my thinking, on my feelings and my *knowing*. The results became noticeable in small increments at first. I was beginning to feel freer—less encumbered by desires for material possessions. In quiet moments, moments filled with deep gratitude, I experienced a feeling of peace and contentment.

I began to *know* what you felt when you talked about *gratitude*! This is only a word, yet when it is experienced... Thank you! Until tomorrow, I remain,
Your devoted student, *R.*

Dear Dr. Schweitzer,

This is my last Sunday morning with you before my trip to Europe. Will my letters continue? I honestly don't know. I do not own a laptop computer, so I will have to resort to writing in longhand or take a short respite.

Yesterday's letter brought back the memory of another trip. While waiting at the airport the following year, in the spring of 1998, I was again loaded down with presents for my two girls. Eve and Alexandra both had their birthdays in May. Sitting in the West Palm Beach departure lounge, waiting for my plane to depart for New York City, I had a chance to be still—and to reflect.

It was only 6:30 in the morning, yet I observed businessmen on cell phones, engaged in animated conversations, giving last minute instructions to fellow colleagues, or perhaps saying goodbye to loved ones. I was struck with all the modern conveniences I had just used. For instance, the toilets in the rest rooms actually flushed automatically.

Even though I was surrounded by the noise created by the revving up of jet engines, and the usual chatter of fellow passengers,

I became less and less aware of them. I started to reflect on my relationship with my children, seeing for the first time how all three had become my teachers. Suddenly, my whole being was again flooded with this sense of gratitude.

My oldest child, Eve, and her husband had taught me a new respect for nature and animals. I remember her desire to become a veterinarian when she first started to ride at the age of nine. Eve did not like school very much, so this desire did not materialize. Back then, we did not know too much about dyslexia, and I had no clue that Eve had a mild form of this condition. She loved her animals unconditionally and loved to help creatures that could not speak for themselves. She was able to communicate to them the love in her heart. She used a special tone of voice, a tone she knew the animals would respond to. She, like my mother before her, could always identify with the underdog.

Eve had also inherited my mother's talent for painting, except Eve's subject was more often than not an animal, usually the horse. She has her own style, which is becoming even more pronounced now that she is a mother. She takes great pride in being aware of little Alexandra's need for creativity and love. Eve has a natural affinity for creatures that can't speak for themselves, this includes babies. She has on occasion shared her good fortune with underprivileged children who would not normally be accepted as students in a horse facility. Will she continue in this vein of sharing and giving of herself? As her mother, I can see this in her future.

Her choice of life companion was definitely part of her destiny. Steve, her husband, is quietly tolerant, very forgiving and very generous. His emotions run deep and he is wise beyond his years. He became the teacher and protector she had been searching for. Eve and Steve both enjoy the countryside. Finding this rural house was a real blessing. Every time I drove the short distance from the train station to their home, I felt a serenity wash over me. I saw trees, clear lakes and rushing brooks. Deer were often seen at sundown. In the spring there was often a mother deer, with her little ones following close behind. I loved the stone walls gracing the roads, and learned that the original settlers made use of these rocks while clearing the land. All this helped in creating this enchanting atmosphere.

My daughter's home is often a beehive of activity. In the backyard is a barn with three horses. A dog named 'Sugar' and a cat named 'Baby Girl' complete this menagerie. Eve expressed her creative talents by turning this house into an inviting home. It is not only charming but very comfortable. Eve often said, "Mom, I know I am really lucky to live in such a wonderful place!" Was it really luck? Or do we create our own luck by attracting things and conditions with our emotions, desires and thoughts? I wondered...

My relationship with Eve has not always been an easy one. We have had our ups and downs, and are only now reaching a new level of communication. Eve is one of the most generous women I know. She feels there is so much to share—the beautiful surroundings and the animals. I am convinced there will be other talents emerging as she grows and discovers more about the true source of her creative nature and generous heart. I am reminded of the poem I wrote in 1985, inspired by Eve. Thank you Eve, thank you Steve!

Woman
Who is this beguiling
Woman?
A real treat to the eye
A willow—sensuous and stunning.

She has feelings so deep
For all of God's creatures
Stray cats, dogs—you ask,
"Does she include me"?

At times she is wild and crazy
Disturbing the peace
Causing tempers to flare—at times
She is homey and lazy...

She knows who she is
That's her attraction
When she gives—it is all
No small fractions.

Men are attracted
Puzzled and charmed.
She's got something...
I'll be darned!

To top it all off
She uses her intuition, has a sixth sense
She is aware—lives in the here and now
Not—in the past tense.

Who is this lovely creature?
So soft, curvy and bright?
Surprise—it's Eve...
What a delight!
RzT 1985

On that early morning I also thought about my son Marc. He taught me the value of patience, the value of saving money and made me very aware of the need to be grateful for all I have. He also possesses a great sense of style, and has a talent for harmony in color and design. Marc taught me tolerance and his presence brings happy moments of laughter to my often hectic life. His laughter is very infectious, and I can't help but smile as I am writing this, thinking back to all the times that he has helped me move. Marc's most endearing features are an inborn kindness, patience, a good heart and a clear mind. He thinks things through before he acts.

At the end of January in 1999, Marc married a very noble, aristocratic woman from Colombia, named Giovanna. Aristocratic in the sense that she has the quality of discernment. She knows who she is. Giovanna is very kind and thoughtful, always wanting to help those who have not been blessed with her good fortune. When first encountering her energy, the words *ethereal* and *child-like innocence* seemed like the appropriate words to describe her. Giovanna, like her mother, is an artist. The medium, through which she has chosen to express herself, is bronze sculptures. In both I see a kindness and a sense of generosity of spirit. I have since discovered that hidden underneath her delicate and beautiful exterior is strength of character and a fearless, yet kind soul. If, 'like and like attracts'—it is certainly true in the union of Marc and Giovanna.

Marc often shared his deepest feelings and concerns with me. I remember his feelings of elation after reaching what he referred to as a mile marker on his road to independence. He had become financially secure and bought his first luxury car. He called to share his feelings, as he drove out of the car dealership. This poem was inspired by his words.

Cloud 9
There was a blond boy—with big dreams
Started small—struggled to swim
Weathered all rough times—took chances it seems.
It must have been hard for him—but he wanted to win.

He has a Guardian Angel—who hears
His pleas—his dreams—brushing away
Doubts and fears.
Putting him on a cloud—you say?

He feels he has earned his good luck
He survived those moments of doubt.
Although a rough road—he didn't get stuck
Always retreating to his cloud.

Guess what just happened? He bought a new car.

Expensive leather—fine motor—he likes it a lot
Proudly he said: "That's my new Jaguar…"
Strangely, his first words in the seat were: "Thank you God!"
Then he drove off the lot.

This is not strange once examined—of course.
He is fully aware of his contribution.
But does not forget—the Source
Of this good fortune—therefore—the salutation!

Is that his secret? Perhaps so…
He doesn't appear preachy
Just discovering—he's in the know
From now on—things will be peachy?
RzT 1996

Marc has the gift of gratitude I so admire. I see why his marriage is working. Both partners respect each other's independence and freedom and both have a deep inner strength. On weekends, Marc can be found tending his luscious garden filled with exotic tropical fruit trees and plants and Giovanna enjoys sorting and placing the photos of their latest trip into a 'memory album'. In her garage I always find a bag in which she collects clothes and items to be given away to the less fortunate. Thank you Marc, thank you Giovanna!

My youngest son, Steven, on the other hand, has taught me to focus my attention and energy. He has the ability to focus his attention on goals with laser like precision. He is single minded in this respect, charting his own path in a very short time. He is ambitious and in a great hurry to succeed. He could easily have written the book, 'How to Make Friends And Influence People'. This ability came very natural to him. He has a thirst for knowledge and is able to study a subject, absorbing new material like a sponge, in essence learning things very quickly. Steven is what I would consider 'an Idea man', coming up with ideas and innovative solutions to problems. His nature is analytical. He too is creative and likes to get his hands dirty. Renovation projects are an ongoing theme. Steven and his wife Yvonne came together quite unexpectedly. They had known each other since childhood but had lost touch over the ten years following high school

"This relationship, like all relationships, is karmic," I thought when they announced their engagement after only two months of courtship. They were married at the end of December in 1996. My second grandchild, Marco, was born almost two years later, and he is one of the great joys in my life.

Yvonne is a natural beauty of Italian descent with an intensity and ambition of her own. She is very open to new ideas when it comes to child development, doing her best in her focus on their child. Watching her son play elicits one of her prominent features— her radiant smile. Is it true that the new generation, the generation of my grandchildren, is much smarter and wiser at an earlier age than we were? I must learn to learn to understand his drive, his uniqueness and his need to remain an individualist. It is part of 'who' he is. Like his brother, he is generous and has a wonderful sense of humor.

Thank you Steven, thank you Yvonne!

As I walked to the plane that spring morning, I was filled with a sense of deep appreciation, and felt a lump in my throat as I recognized that we had come full circle. I saw how they had become my teachers, valuable contributors to my past, present and future. Thank you for all the wonderful memories, making my present life so rich and colorful, thank you—my three children. This reminds me of the Goethe phrase: "Whether king or peasant, he is happiest who finds peace in his home."

Although all of our experiences are different, I feel we are all treading a path. Is life the classroom? Are we the pupils, constantly learning from each other? Was I beginning to see the miracle of it all?

The Circle
Our children become our teachers
When does this role reversal happen?
A slow process—yet very sudden.

We guide them—love them.
They scream—shout and kick
Through adolescence.

When grown—we find it hard
To accept—to let go
They are now men and women—coming back.

Guiding me through the fire
I rely on their wisdom and advice
We've come full circle—a surprise?
RzT 1996

Yes, dear doctor, letting go at certain times is painful. By still wanting to guide them once they become adults, aren't we robbing them of the joy and the necessary pain of their own experiences?

Dr. Schweitzer, are you wondering why I am telling you all this, or do you already know what I am feeling? What I started to experience, was that instead of trying to make in impact on my environment, I was beginning to allow my environment—people and nature itself— to have an impact on me. Is this how we slowly awaken and grow in awareness? This was a definite mile marker in my development and growth on the path. Your words never fail to astound me. To remind me I read:

"When I look back on my early days I am stirred by the thought of the number of people whom I have to thank for what they gave me or for what they were to me. At the same time I am haunted by an oppressive consciousness of the little gratitude

I really showed them while I was young. How many of them have said farewell to life without my having made clear to them what it meant to me to receive from them so much kindness or so much care! Many a time have I, with a feeling of shame, said quietly to myself over a grave the words which my mouth ought to have spoken to the departed, while he was still in the flesh."[2]

My sentiments exactly... I have to run to work, but I promise to tell you more about this particular trip to visit my granddaughter tomorrow.

Your grateful student, *R.*

Dear Dr. Schweitzer,

Today is my last day off, before leaving for my vacation this Friday, but I will continue to write until I actually get on the plane. This brings me back to the trip to New York, early 1998.

I remember feeling quite relaxed as I found my seat. I chose your book *'Out of my Childhood and Youth'* as my traveling companion. My eyes found the phone in the rear of the seat in front of me, inviting me to make a call or check my e-mail. I was not that computer literate, as a matter of fact I still did not own a computer back then.

Staring into space through the oval window, I thought about how technology has advanced, even during the last ten years. My mind drifted back to the time when you were a small boy. In your youth you did not have cars, air-conditioning, jet-planes, telephones, computers or space shuttles.

Once in the air, I watched the city of West Palm Beach becoming smaller and smaller as I leaned back into my seat holding your book on my chest. Soon, all I could see were the puffy clouds surrounding our plane. I again started to think about all the conveniences you had lived without. I started to feel your courage, your strength, your quest for Truth, your devotion to ethics and strong moral principles, knowing they shaped your character and therefore your life!

I thought back to the years you spent in the jungle, creating a hospital where nothing but a chicken coop had existed at your first arrival. Where, until you were awarded the Peace Prize in 1952, you lived and worked without attracting the attention of the public.

Were you disappointed? What gave you hope during those years, what sustained you? What and where was the fountain of your strength, courage and wisdom to be found?

At times you were criticized. This criticism originated mostly from journalists, who in the 1950's and early 1960's were chasing a 'good story'. Their criticism exhibited their mediocre minds, taking a self-righteous pose while reporting on your work as a doctor in the jungle. This showed me that they had absolutely no clue as to the life path you had chosen, and its meaning. They had no clue about the struggles and hardships that you endured. They knew nothing about your ideals and the energy you drew on along the way. They had no idea about the determination, courage and physical labor needed to bring this hospital into existence. They had no clue about the medical needs of the neglected African people. They had no clue about the tribal customs and tribal traditions of the native people. They had not experienced living in sweltering heat; they had not experienced life without electricity; they had not experienced life without indoor plumbing and without running water; they had not experienced operating on a critically ill patient for hours during the sweltering summer heat without air conditioning; they had not experienced life without radio, telephone and TV. They had no clue, about the sacrifices you had made on your path. Perhaps they didn't *resonate* with your altruistic nature? Perhaps they were on a different vibration or wavelength? Are you smiling?

You had little patience for their lack of understanding, their lack of knowledge and wisdom, nonetheless, you tolerated their presence. Their ignorance showed when a simple thing such as wearing a hat, which is an absolute necessity in the equatorial sun, was ignored. You had to constantly keep reminding them of this and yet, your advice was often not heeded. This ignorance led to many visitors ending up as patients in your hospital suffering from severe sunstroke, creating an extra load for your already overworked staff. This made you angry, because you did not 'suffer fools gladly'!

Or perhaps you stirred up a sea of emotions, bringing them face to face with their own *mediocre* thoughts and existence, allowing them to see themselves, and their lives of quiet desperation? Whatever their ultimate motives were, I don't profess to know. Did some of your critics, journalists and reporters, expect to find a perfect little clinic with white sheets and perfect antiseptic conditions found in our Western hospitals? Furthermore, they knew absolutely nothing about the African people, their culture, their beliefs, their customs, their superstitions and their way of life. I am again reminded of Einstein's words: *"Great spirits will always encounter violent opposition from mediocre minds."*

As I closed my eyes that morning on the plane, some of the answers came to me. My investigation into your *'true being'* seemed to be rewarded at last. It began to dawn on me who you really were—a teacher—a doctor not only of the body, but like Jesus, a healer of the spirit—a physician of the soul.

As I thought about your character, and how you had made monumental courageous decisions that are now part of history, your path became clearer in my mind. I thought about how you must have felt leaving the comforts of Europe, the comforts of an assured future in the arts or a career in philosophy, music, theology and writing. I thought about your motivation to become a doctor of medicine. I thought about your ability to be remain silent, living your truth without fanfare. I reflected on the deeper meaning of 'Reverence for Life' and life's diverse manifestations. I thought about your love and consideration for animals. I thought about your dedication to Truth. A dedication so genuine and pure, you never looked for rewards of any kind. I believe this to be one of the characteristics that made you stand out from the rest of us.

This same dedication was evident in the lives of the men you admired and loved. There was the poet Goethe. There were the composer Bach and Jesus. All three became your inspiration and an *ideal* of what one single man is capable of creating in one solitary life. You never admitted to being a mystic and stressed being a man of reason, at times describing yourself as a Stoic. The men you admired had a strong intuitive or mystic nature. All were of strong character driven by a search for truth, purpose and meaning. Like you, they exhibited pure motives and ethics. They knew who they were.

All of you had the ability to inspire, to lead by example. Your motives were to be admired and aspired to, because you gave with the purest intentions. That's real giving!

The best way I can describe the unfolding or maturing process as I witnessed it in you is by using the analogy found in nature. A fruit tree is already programmed to bear fruit. The tree gives his fruit to all, never expecting a reward or a thank you. A tree never judges or decides who deserves the fruit or who does not. Similarly, our sun provides energy and shines on all equally. It shines on the so-called evil and the so-called good in the same measure. That's what I have come to recognize as pure or impersonal love.

I recognize you as one of the world's great teachers a Master. A Master first masters himself. One of the ways a Master can be recognized is by asking the question: "Does he have *disciples*?" You inspired many people who worked long hours by your side, people who admired and respected you, people who never expected material rewards for their service. The picture in my mind became very clear, as if a fog had been lifted from my eyes. You were a hero whose courage, love, compassion and integrity inspired others to perform heroic acts. Am I becoming one of those disciples?

That's when the thought first entered my mind, 'Perhaps I could write a story—your story.' It was as though I had been struck by lightning. Yes, of course, I did have something to say about your life. I had studied your words for the last sixteen years, resulting in the insight just revealed to me. The more I thought about this back then, the more compelling the idea became. Where did I get the courage to even entertain such a thought?

This courage came to me as a result of getting to know who you were, and what your life was all about! I also found courage in the fact that you had endeavored to reach the *'average'* thinking man and woman. I recognized this desire in several passages of your books. You had stressed the importance of remaining a free thinker and becoming your own authority. You had stressed the importance of keeping an open mind. In that respect my skepticism had helped me. Although I had read a great deal about many different subjects, I did not accept everything I read. I used my *inner* sense of discrimination, remaining open and curious. I now recognize that my previous shyness was fear. Fear of rejection and fear of being a non-conformist. The mystery of *who* I am, needs to be solved, because I intuitively *know*, that once I discover who I am, any remaining fear will be dissolved. The archaeologist in me needs to dig deeper!

Yes, I had grown and learned a lot. My inquiries about subjects of interest gave me a wider perspective into human nature and nature in general. But, I also knew that at that time only a small fraction of the mystery had been revealed to me and that I didn't have all the answers to life's mysteries, and certainly do not profess to have them now.

Admittedly, this frame of mind or *attitude* helps me to remain open and flexible. It creates a space, allowing room for future potential and different possibilities. I started to think outside of the box, growing and shedding old outdated belief systems that did not fit anymore. I found that 'opinions' are often based on perceptions that keep changing, and are therefore not truth. In this respect a lot of our current science is based only on opinions. Once a new fact is discovered, scientists change their minds and the accompanying opinions get revised. True knowledge, on the other hand, knowledge that is based on the truth of pure reason, is quite different. It is timeless and eternal. At times I felt that I was being guided to certain truths. I did not know by whom...

For example, I felt intuitively, that if the universe wanted me to write, I would be presented with a computer. I had experienced serendipity of this sort before. Life had provided me with the necessary tools, just at the right time. Everything in my life had started to go this way, so I began to *trust the process*. I somehow *knew* on some subconscious level that when I was ready a computer, the tool, would appear.

This happened the following spring. My benefactor was my daughter in-law Giovanna. Her mother was in the process of upgrading to a faster system, and she asked me if I wanted her old computer. She had seen the book I wrote for Alexandra, and thought it was a good time for me to join the computer age. How thrilled I was to finally have this gadget, this wizard of the new age. At the same time, I felt a new sense of responsibility. Did this mean that I must now take my writing to a new level?

All the courage I had professed earlier seemed to fly out the window. I was gripped with a fear so great, I did not even touch this new acquisition for weeks. Was I ready for this new challenge? Could I really write? What could I possibly have to say? How can I do justice to what you have meant to me? Would I be able to write and describe how you inspired me?

It was not until I returned from my 1999 New York trip, while looking at the photos of Alexandra, that the idea presented itself again. As I gazed at this small girl sitting on a white horse in her purple birthday dress, I found myself reliving the moments. I had watched Alexandra play with her Teddy Bears and remembered the morning we planted seeds and flowers in the garden. That's when the idea of a second children's book popped into my mind.

Again, I allowed the Teddy to be the narrator, and found myself writing the story in long hand. I then attempted to use my computer for the first time, learning the mechanics of this machine through trial and error. I used the photos I had taken that spring as illustrations and planned to make this book a Christmas present for little Alex. The exercise of writing the children's book '*Springtime in the Country*', helped me in getting my courage back.

As I reflect on the story line for the books I write for children, they appear to reflect my own inner journey. In the first book, I allowed the Teddy Bear named *Zandi,* to be the narrator. Zandi was searching to go home, finding love after an unexpected long journey. Wasn't this my journey—my search—as well? In the second book Alexandra teaches *Zandi* the meaning of planting seeds and taking good care of them. Seeds will not grow unless watered and tended to. They also needed the right conditions, including sunshine and fertile soil. This book illustrates the cycles of nature resulting in renewal each spring. Was I in the process of planting seeds, the seeds being *thoughts*, which if properly cared for would one day grow into manifestation? Why do I only see this in hindsight? I wonder...

I would be amiss if I failed to mention another great influence during those spring months of 1999. The lessons I had faithfully ordered and studied at my leisure were of tremendous value in finding my way back to writing. The skeptic in me found some of the things I was learning hard to fathom at first. However, the more I learned about the authors, Earlyne Chaney and her husband, Dr. Robert Chaney, the more I valued the teachings. Everything I had experienced, and am still experiencing right at this present moment, started to become clearer to me.

Was my mind expanding? Was I experiencing a new awareness, a new state of mind difficult to describe in words? I found the teachings to be of great value as I began to look *inside* for my life direction. I had started to meditate, although not on a regular basis. Yet, I felt something was happening to me as a result of these meditations and self-reflections.

I was becoming more at peace with the world and with myself. I wanted to share this new feeling with others, and must have said something at work about my experiences, when one day, out of the blue, a colleague asked me to hold a meditation class. I responded by saying, "I'll have to think about this." They were obviously curious, but was I ready to take on the role of teacher? After all, I was just a beginner myself.

The idea of teaching is very appealing to me. Did I have the qualifications? Before I would commit to anything of this sort, I started to use my computer to write a few pages of what I considered to be useful guidelines for these meditation sessions. I ended up writing several pages of dialogue to be used as an introduction, followed by a meditation. The words seemed to fly into my mind as if by magic.

Before I knew what had happened, what appeared to be a first session was ready. I knew this was not enough, and started to formulate a plan. This would become a four-week study session, each ending in a meditation. I knew I had something of value to share with others, and finally invited a group of seven to come to my home once a week for the next four weeks. I asked for a commitment for the full four sessions, instinctively knowing there would be little benefit in coming just once.

I asked these friends to come on the same day each week, selecting a day when I myself was off. This allowed me to prepare myself. I knew I needed to be relaxed and in a quiet frame of mind. As I now look back at the response I received from each individual, I knew it was a success. Some of the people who attended have left the company for other jobs, but some are still working with me. They still talk about the quiet evening hours we shared together in June of 1999, and at times I get asked to repeat this experience. What had I done? All I really did was to put them in touch with themselves, their inner 'true' self! Not only that, I discovered that the teacher is also the student, as I learned more about myself in the process.

In hindsight, this was a very good exercise in concentration and discipline for me. Why did I not repeat this exercise? I had become interested in writing another story. I had gathered some ideas to be used in a book. This book was to be about you!

Several things had become clearer to me over the last few years, as I read your words. Suddenly, I reached a deeper level of understanding and saw another meaning in what your life was about. I felt that your attempt to reach the average human being had not been in vain. You had gotten the world's attention with your huge contribution as a human being, by doing what you felt you had to do. However, how many people had read your books? This would have revealed to many, that there was another level of learning for all of us.

Was a new dawn approaching, revealing new insights about human nature? Can we and are we ready to reach beyond religion in order to touch the true essence of spirituality? Would I have to start living and expressing my truth in my everyday life, just as you had done? This reminds me of the words of another philosopher, namely Ludwig Wittgenstein, a man of reason who, nearing the end of his life said: *"If you want to know whether a man is religious, don't ask him, observe him."*3

You had discovered many things about the human condition, and you tried to the best of your ability to pass this information on to us. You, like Wittgenstein had studied the philosophy of Immanuel Kant.

This led me to the question, 'Can philosophy be taught?' The way I see it, philosophy is the inquiry into the origins of the cosmos and man's *relationship* to this grand scene. Philosophy does not give the student all the answers. On the contrary, philosophy is the quest or journey of man towards knowing himself and towards *thinking freely*. It becomes the *process of questioning*, and must be combined with some knowledge of history, archaeology, biology, the sciences of physics and astronomy, the science of mathematics, and last but not least, *religion*. It must include spirituality and the *examination* of our belief systems. Philosophy is the acquisition of wisdom, through understanding the Laws of Nature, followed by *experiencing being*, which in turn taps into a higher level of consciousness or a higher state of awareness. In other words *we become aware of our awareness.*

The answers lie hidden from us and are only found by discovering our essence—our soul—infused by spirit. Discovering who we really are, beyond our old conditioning, our old beliefs and traditions, becomes the quest of the soul of man and humanity as a whole. We are first and foremost, *spiritual* beings having a physical or personal experience steeped in layers of matter. Jesus was the ultimate philosopher when viewed from this perspective, becoming an example for us of what is possible to be achieved, once we fully understand this premise. I began to see that Jesus, our older brother, was trying to teach us how to revise our thought processes in how we view ourselves. He used parables, which is still the best way to transmit this teaching, in order to get through to our limited thinking.

Your thinking was not limited, as you have demonstrated in your writings and actions. Your book 'The Mystery of the Kingdom of God' is profound, revealing a crucial part of a deep mystery. It was your inquisitive mind that led to your discovery of the eschatological viewpoint of Jesus. It seems that Jesus knew that our true home, the home of the soul and spirit is not to be found in this material world. Jesus tried to teach us the real meaning of pain and suffering and the transcendental quality of love. He had reached, what metaphysicians call, the lofty state of 'Christ', or 'Cosmic Consciousness'

In this respect 'Christ' is a level of consciousness and not a person. You saw that Jesus had come to teach us about the higher levels, and that he was the forerunner, an example of what is still to come. He tried to show us a new way of thinking, allowing a larger perspective to emerge. Is that what is meant by *being* in Christ, a state that lies beyond our average level of awareness?

Like most scholarly books, your volumes were mostly read by philosophers or fellow theologians, scholars who were not too interested in making your words public. Why?

Had they understood your message, they would have had to re-examine the values of their dogmatic belief system. Christianity is often very confusing not only as it was taught then, but also as it is still being preached today. There must have been some who understood what you were trying to tell us, but they too ignored your metaphysical insights, preferring the comfort of an old outdated system based on punishment and reward. Why did your discoveries and ideas based on a new insight threaten them? Perhaps they did not understand? They did not *resonate* with it? How could that be the case? How come I understand your message and they didn't? Some profess to be searching for truth and when the truth uncovered is uncomfortable, they ignore it or deny it.

What is the message you gave to us? A message you spent your life researching, resulting in your pronouncement of the Religion of Love. Your most profound statements regarding your discovery of the life and meaning of Jesus are to be found in the summary of your book, *'The Quest of the Historical Jesus.'* In the last chapter, entitled *'Results'*, I found your observations, which resulted in a deep revelation for me.

What you found in your research and so eloquently described for us, is that the *historical* Jesus, may never have existed. However, the fact remains that Jesus, as described in the gospels, had perfected himself to the extent that he was able to tune into a higher vibration, and be overshadowed by a highly evolved being, thereby *becoming a clear channel for a higher power.* His words are still as vibrant and as powerful as when he spoke them two-thousand years ago, once we understand his true message. His words were, and still are steeped in Truth! He became a channel for what we now refer to as the 'Christ Consciousness', which embodies the Universal principle of LOVE. He not only invited us, but he admonished us to look inside and 'get to *know* who we really are'!

I had to read your words several times, in order to completely understand, what you were trying to tell us back in 1901:

"The Jesus of Nazareth who came forward publicly as the Messiah, who preached the ethics of the Kingdom of God, who founded the Kingdom of Heaven upon earth, and died to give His work its final consecration, never had any existence. He is a figure designed by rationalism, endowed with life by liberalism, and clothed by modern theology in an historical garb.
"This image has not been destroyed from without, it has fallen into pieces, cleft and disintegrated by the concrete historical problems which came to the surface one after another, and in spite of all the artifice, art, artificiality, and violence which was supplied by them, refused to be planed down to fit the *design on which the Jesus of the theology* of the last hundred and thirty years had been constructed, and were no sooner covered over than they appeared again in a new form."4 (My Italics)

Further down the same page I read:

"Whatever the ultimate solution may be, the historical Jesus of whom the criticism of the future, taking as its starting-point the problems which have been recognized and admitted, will draw the portrait, can never render modern theology the services which it claimed from its own half-historical, half-modern, Jesus. He will be a Jesus, who was Messiah, and lived as such, *either on the ground of a literary fiction* of the earliest Evangelist, *or on the ground of a purely eschatological Messianic conception.*
"In either case, He will not be a Jesus Christ to whom the religion of the present can ascribe, according to its long-cherished custom, its own thoughts and ideas, as it did with the Jesus of its own making. Nor will he be a figure which can be made by a popular historical treatment so sympathetic and universally intelligible to the multitudes. The historical Jesus will be to our time a stranger and an enigma."5 (My Italics)

On the next page I read:

"The historical foundation of Christianity as built up by rationalistic, by liberal, and by modern theology no longer exists; but that does not mean that Christianity has lost its historical foundation. The work which historical theology thought itself to carry out, and which fell to pieces just as it was nearing completion, was only the brick facing of the real immovable historical foundation which is independent of any historical confirmation or justification.

'Jesus means something to our world because *a mighty spiritual force streams forth from Him and flows through our time also.* This fact can neither be shaken nor confirmed by any historical discovery. It is the solid foundation of Christianity."6 (My Italics)

You describe Jesus as *a spiritual power in the present.*

"And yet the time of doubt was bound to come. We modern theologians are too proud of our historical method, too proud of our historical Jesus, too confident in our belief in the spiritual gains which our historical theology can bring into the world. The thought that we could build up by the increase of historical knowledge a new and vigorous Christianity and set free new spiritual forces, *rules us like a fixed idea* and prevents us from seeing that the task which we have grappled with and in some measure discharged is only one of the intellectual preliminaries of the great religious task. We thought that it was for us to lead our time by a roundabout way through the historical Jesus, as we understood Him in order to bring it to the *Jesus who is a spiritual power in the present.* This roundabout way has now been closed by genuine history.

"There was a danger of our thrusting ourselves between men and the Gospels, and refusing to leave the individual man alone with the (words) sayings of Jesus."

"There was a danger that we (theologians) should offer them a Jesus who was too small, because we had forced Him into conformity with our *human standards and human psychology.*"7 (My Italics.)

Down the same page you continued:

"Many of the greatest sayings are found lying in a corner like *explosive shells* from which the charges have been removed."

"In the process we ourselves have been *enfeebled,* and have robbed our own thoughts of their vigour in order to project them back into history and make them speak to us out of the past. It is nothing less than a misfortune for modern theology that it mixes history with everything and ends by being proud of the skill with which it finds its own thoughts—even to its beggarly pseudo-metaphysic with which it has banished *genuine* speculative metaphysics from the sphere of religion—in Jesus, and represents Him as expressing them."8 (My Italics.)

On the next page I read:

"The abiding and *eternal* in Jesus is absolutely *independent* of historical knowledge and can only be understood by contact with His spirit which is *still* at work in the world. In proportion as we have the Spirit of Jesus we have the true knowledge of Jesus."

"But in reality that which is eternal in the words of Jesus is due to the very fact that they are based on an *eschatological worldview*, and contain the expression of a *mind* for which the contemporary world with its historical and social circumstances no longer had any existence.

"They (Jesus' words) are appropriate, therefore, to any world, for in every world they *raise man who dares to meet their challenge,* and does not turn and twist them into meaninglessness, above his world and his time, making him inwardly free, so fitted to be, in his own world and in his own time, a simple channel of the power of Jesus."9 (My Italics)

"But the truth is, it is not Jesus as historically known, but Jesus as *spiritually arisen within men*, who is significant for our time and can help it. Not the Historical Jesus, but the spirit which goes forth from Him and in the spirits of men strives for *new influence and rule*, is that which *overcomes the world*."10 (My Italics)

It looks to me as if you also were a channel for this kind of spiritual energy! And finally you closed this last chapter with your words to us:

"The names in which men expressed their recognition of Him as such, Messiah, Son of Man, Son of God, have become for us historical parables. We can find no designation which expresses what He is for us."

"He comes to us as One unknown, without a name, as of old, by the lake-side, He came to those men who knew Him not. He speaks to us the same word: "Follow thou me!" and sets us to the tasks, which he has to fulfill for our time. He commands. And to those who obey Him, whether they be wise or simple, he will reveal Himself in the *toils*, the *conflicts*, the *sufferings* which they shall pass through in his fellowship, and, as an ineffable mystery, they shall learn in their *own experience* Who He is."11 (My Italics)

You not only exhibited strength and a strong will, you showed us what the word 'courage' truly means. You voiced your findings, knowing that certain scholars, some being your contemporaries, would see you as a heretic. You had recognized that Buddha or *Buddhi* is a state of consciousness, just as '*Christ*' is a state of consciousness. When Buddha was asked by one of his students: "What is the difference between you and me?" The Buddha answered: "I am awake!"

Gautama's life, like the life of Jesus, represents a Divine principle or process, which is the state of awakening, a state in which a higher form of *being* can be experienced. Once we recognize that we are all *equipped* to experience the latent power hidden inside of us on some level, the question becomes, 'How willing are we to understand that this world isn't all there is, that this world is the school or training ground for the soul?' Our existence on this planet is steeped in lessons, often experienced as pain and suffering, which are meant to challenge us and to help us to grow—'awakening' in the process. This and other paradoxes we will eventually be forced to look at and begin to understand. The lesson of the evolution of man must be understood as a constant evolving or *growing*. The process of *growing* is an internal one. Jesus' message, just like yours, reveals itself in our constant struggles, conflicts, in our pain and suffering. It behooves us to look at this aspect of our nature with a new attitude and an open mind.

You not only studied the life of Jesus, but you took it one step further. You studied the mind of the man—based on the sayings attributed to this enigmatic person. You had recognized that he had *earned* this lofty state we now begin to see as 'cosmic consciousness'. He saw beyond the duality of our current existence, becoming your example of what a *perfected human* being will be like in the future, once the four levels, the physical, emotional, mental and spiritual vehicles are perfected and work in perfect alignment.

Scholars preferred to ignore your findings about the truer meaning of the life of Jesus, and the truths he represented, if we begin to see him as a great Master of an *internal* metaphysical process. This being so, this process is still alive and in full force 2000 years later.

You had studied the New Testament, even learning to read Greek and Hebrew in order to search for certain answers to the riddle of his life, his teachings and the deep significance of his subsequent crucifixion. You questioned everything! Just like me, you felt that the teachings as relayed to us in the Bible are not truly comprehended. There are many contradictions and misinterpretations found in the Bible, not to mention serious omissions. Our modern Bible was edited and revised several times and cannot be read as a perfect chronological history book. Not only that, it is not the only book that reveals the journey of our soul. For instance, the missing Gospels found in the desert of Egypt in the upper Nile region in December of 1945, and now referred to as the *Nag Hammadi Library*, were never included in the New Testament or 'official' version of the Bible. Why?

These writings have now surfaced as *'The Gnostic Gospels'*13 by Elaine Pagels. Pagels is the winner of the National Book Award for this groundbreaking work and has written several books on the re-discovered gospels of the early Christians, also known as the Gnostics. The word **'gnosis'** means *'direct knowing'*.

One other observation that is very important for me to grasp is that you described yourself as a Stoic after having studied theology, philosophy and many of the earliest biblical writings in their original language, namely Greek and Hebrew.

You studied comparative religions, which I had done in a much more limited fashion. You studied Hinduism, Bhakti Mysticism, Brahmanic Mysticism (the union with pure being) and various forms of Buddhism. You had studied the Bhagavad-Gita, the Upanishads and other ancient Vedic verses, which without the principle of reincarnation don't make much sense. These teachings are now part of the Ageless Wisdom teachings. Being the most ancient texts in existence, they predate Christianity by thousands of years. These teachings all reveal us to be souls—souls on a journey—who through evolution, growth and assimilation reach for liberation; and that we will attain perfection eventually.

Your book *'Indian Thought and It's Development'* shows me the depth of your independent research. You did all this before becoming a medical doctor. Anyone who just glances at the titles of your books will understand that you were on a mission. What was that mission? Is a great part of the lesson found in overcoming or transcending our small ego, creating a new attitude, seeing and reaching beyond our lower nature?

You declared yourself to be a Stoic. It stands to reason that you also studied the words of Zeno, the life and words of Plato and the writings (*The Meditations)* of the Roman emperor Marcus Aurelius, who like you, became a Stoic. I see that your mission was to educate us, leading us to the truth of 'who' we really are—souls evolving, growing in awareness. You showed us where the tools are hidden. You encouraged us to go *beyond* thinking in order to *experience* our true being. For me you were, and still are, a sign-post along my journey through life.

Your life is now becoming an example for me of what a fully awakened spiritual human being is capable of. What keeps us asleep, while you were fully awake?

You understood and voiced the fact, that even if Jesus had never existed, the message of what his life represents is still valid today! Where do I start to apply this new knowledge? If I understand your message correctly, then this secret, and the Mystery of the Kingdom, must be hidden inside each and every one of us. I must have the courage to take a deep look at myself!

Thank you from the bottom of my heart, as I ponder this idea and digest all I have recently discovered. I remain,
Your devoted student, *R.*

Dear Dr. Schweitzer,

Has the time arrived for us to remove the blinders and cut the chains that hold us to our outdated beliefs? Has the time arrived for us to take a closer look at the conditioning we have been exposed to by the beliefs of our parents, our teachers and society as a whole?

Your volumes on this subject reveal just how many of these questions were on your mind. I began to understand that by studying the lives of the awakened Masters in depth, Masters such as Jesus, Saul of Tarsus (St. Paul), Krishna, Gautama, Pythagoras, Socrates, Plato, J.S. Bach, Kant, and Goethe, you became wiser than most people. You became a Master teacher yourself. I see these

men as great teachers, men who had looked higher or deeper into
their own nature and their souls.

Did you find a new Reality—a Reality underlying our usual limited
vision? I see you as joining ranks with other great teachers such
as: Moses, Abraham, Zoroaster, John the Baptist, Elijha, Gautama,
Mohammed, Lao Tse, Confucius, Francis of Assisi, Francis Bacon,
Dante, Mozart, Geothe, Beethoven, Schiller, Paracelsus, Boehme,
H. P. B., Maurice Bucke, Gurdjieff, Krishnamurti, Ralph Waldo
Emerson, Rudolf Steiner, Walt Whitman, Gandhi, only to mention
a few. And yes, let us not forget to mention your friend, Dr. Albert
Einstein.

All of the above exhibited a higher level of consciousness, a
higher awareness, practicing a new discipline, in *varying* degrees.
Had they experienced transcending the lower self, the *separate
personality*? I believe this to be true. What had they experienced
and found? The above mentioned accepted the idea of reincarnation
as fundamental knowledge, as can be seen by examining their
words. They knew about the learning experiences of the soul. Did
they reincarnate, to become our teachers? Most were dedicated
to *serving* humanity in one form or another, all were creators
of their own destiny in one way or another. They, just like you,
were dedicated to showing us the Laws of Nature, the principles of
Brotherhood and Love. They were what we would call, *deeper* than
normal thinkers, each in their own way must have on some level,
not only discovered, but *experienced* the Universal Laws, which
govern all of existence. When seen from this viewpoint, your life
became the perfect argument!

They tuned into their intuition, heard the small inner voice,
the *voice of the silence*, as it is often called. It appears to me that
they discovered another Reality underlying our perceived three-
dimensional world, the world dominated by our senses, our linear
world of time and space. A Reality that can only be occasionally
glimpsed at and on rare occasions is felt. What ancient wisdom
existed before? If you remove the Buddha from Buddhism,
remove Krishna from Hinduism, remove Abraham and Moses
from Judaism, remove Mohammed from the Islamic religion, and
remove Jesus from Christianity what is left? What did they all
experience? Was each of these teachers depicting a stage towards
the eventual evolution of man? I wonder...

Don't they all point to the origin of the Wisdom of the Ages?
What is *the source* of the teachings of the ancient mystery schools,

including the teachings of Hermes Trismegistus, going back thousands and thousands of years? Isn't that what all religions are based on, including Christianity? They are all a different rendition of the same tune. You were a doctor and must have known that the symbol of the caduceus dates back to hermetic origins.

The afternoon lecture on Pythagorean teachings was another eye opener for me. I got a glimpse of the values of his discoveries and teachings back in 500 BC. His philosophy and knowledge was only dispensed to a select group of serious disciples at his Academy at Krotona. He was a mathematician, astronomer, astrologer, philosopher, scientist, psychologist, a metaphysician and a mystic. Where did his knowledge and wisdom come from?

Since you studied philosophy, you must be familiar with some of these ancient teachings. What does the study of philosophy lead to? I decided to look in my dictionary and under 'philosophy' found:

PHILOSOPHY: Greek words *philos* – **loving**; and *sophos* – **wise**. Philosophy therefore means loving wisdom, or the love or pursuit of wisdom. It is the study or science of truth or universal principles underlying all knowledge. It is also known as a *detached-calm-study* based on rules of practical wisdom.

Sophia means wisdom. Can wisdom be taught? Can love be taught? I dare ask these questions because in order to understand wisdom and love we must understand its meaning and purpose on our path. I see wisdom as a series of revelations and the recognition of certain fundamental Truths, recognized at certain stages in our life. Love and wisdom are the *outcome* or **result** of certain independent realizations. These two attributes reveal themselves naturally, after a certain amount of energy and effort is put into self-examination. I can only describe it as the Aha.. factor.

Gautama, the forerunner of Jesus, taught us to use our mind or intelligence to find truth. Jesus taught us to open our heart, using the love aspect of our nature. Both are needed in a perfect balance for us to rise to the level of our full potential.

I see wisdom as the mind (Intelligence) lovingly applied, or our heart (Love) applied intelligently. This leads us to understand the true value of our experiences.

Slowly we begin to recognize the value of our experience of pain and suffering. Will it lead us to look at ourselves and to ask the questions, 'Who am I?' 'What does it mean to be human?'

What do the words I AM mean, or I AM THAT I AM? Love will be experienced as a power existing inside each and every one of us. I became curious about your study of theology and looked this word up as well:

THEOLOGY: Greek words *Theos* – God; and *logos* – **word**. It is described as a branch of Christian systematics dealing with man's state as a creature. The historical analysis of the doctrines and beliefs of a religion.

Just above this word I found the word:

THEOCRACY: Greek word *theokratia; Theo* – God; and *krotos* – power. The government of state claimed to be by the immediate direction of God; or other deity. Government by priests.

Does humanity need this kind of *human* authority or government? Doesn't all government involve politics? Yes, some of today's religions are more concerned with ego or human power, with politics and with corruption, than with true Spiritual power. Does it not behoove us to take another look, instead of accepting everything at face value? Do we need this kind of government imposing human rules and regulations as a mediator of our own experiences? An authority created my men who don't have all the answers? How about becoming our own authority? Are we paying the price for our own lethargy and laziness? Can we afford this price? Where is our courage? Whatever happened to *independent* thinking? All great men and women were and *are independent* thinkers. All great men and women were and are individualists! They dared to think outside of the self limiting, self-imposed box... Only this state of mind will lead us to new discoveries. Only this will lead to the eventual awakening of our true nature—our soul— linking us back to our Spirit.

I thank you so much for having been instrumental in opening my mind and heart on this path of self-discovery. Going *behind* the theory of a teaching, and living a truth that once discovered, is very hard to ignore, is the true challenge. This has been a long and heavy letter I admit, but I needed to express my feelings about this matter before I go on my vacation, and remain as always,
Your very grateful student, *R*.

Dear Dr. Schweitzer,

I would like to briefly recall what happened to me in the summer of 1999. I became more and more aware of the meaning of your life, and intrigued with the *power* of your thoughts. I found myself making more regular entries into my journal. That summer I became aware that I had changed—and continue to change—still today. Not so much externally—but, internally. I started to get up earlier in the morning, finally beginning to feel good about myself. What happened that summer brings a smile to my face.

At work, I had been promoted to assistant manger of our department and started to shed some of the extra weight I had carried around for years. At home, I started to write on a daily basis. At first it was painful, I still felt very intimidated by my lack of education. I found articles and books, written about you and your exceptional life, and saw that most of the authors were scholars, intellectuals, successful and learned men and women except one. I am of course referring to Jacquelyn Berrill, the Connecticut housewife who loved gardening. The reason her book had so much appeal for me is undoubtedly, because it was the first and only biography of your life I read, but it also awakened a deep emotion. It touched my heart on a new level. Her inspiration and talent gave me the extra courage and the reassurance I felt I needed.

I still needed more discipline to get started. This became my pet project. During the hot and humid summer months of the year 2000 I began to write again. It became my project of love. The word love just reminded me that I also wrote another children's book back then entitled, '*The Story of Ben*'. It is a love story between a woman and a previously abused horse. This is the true story of how my daughter Eve came to adopt her third horse, a former racehorse named Ben.

No one knew what I was doing, friends and family seemed to accept that I was always very busy. At work, no one knew that by the time I arrived at 9:30, I had already been up long before dawn, spending the early hours of each morning on my new computer. If ever the subject of writing came up, I allowed them to believe that I was only writing children's books, not in the mood to be questioned about the subject matter of my writing and research.

Since this was to be a biography of your life, I needed to research all facts and make sure all the quotes utilized were absolutely correct. As I researched and re-read your life story I soon saw that you were a man of extraordinary will, discipline and courage. I started to form new habits and created a new pattern for myself. During the spring and summer of 1999 I allowed myself more time for reading and study. I used every free moment, right into the month of November to work on my pet project. Most social activities were put on a back burner. Loving every moment of my new activity, it was around Thanksgiving the next year, that I patted myself on the back thinking: "This is as far as I can go with this material, I am finished!" I chose the title: 'Remembering ALBERT SCHWEITZER. An extraordinary life of LOVE AND COMPASSION'.

After rereading all chapters several times in my computer, and making the many needed corrections, I happily handed the disc to an expert in the computer department at my local print shop with the request that they print and bind this manuscript, creating a book.

Nothing seemed to go right from that moment on. Every time they called me in to inspect their work and give my final approval for layout and paging etc. something seemed to go wrong. I should have recognized the signs that something else was at work, but I didn't.

My enthusiasm and small ego were at an all time high, preventing me from paying attention to the glitches, signs that I would instantly recognize today as red flags. Was the universe actually trying to tell me something? Why was it not meant to be? I had no idea what was going on. After several weeks of frustrations and hassle the ten copies I had ordered were ready to be picked up. They must have been so glad to get rid of me. I had become a real pest!

"How could they mess up my hard labor, what is it that they don't understand?" "Why are they not trained to do a good job? Does no one care except me?" I had taken several photographs of a typical Florida sunrise during the month of October, and had decided to use this as the front cover of the book. It looked quite good, quite professional.

At Christmas 2000, I handed a total of five copies to my friends and children as a present, the rest I stuck into a box in my closet. That's where they remain to this day! The book was O.K. I felt I had already seen beyond your life as a doctor in the jungle, however, something about it bothered me. I couldn't quite get a handle on what it was. Yes, I knew it needed to be polished, professionally edited and parts rewritten. But, that wasn't it!

Ignoring the book for the whole winter months that followed, seemed the right thing to do. I somehow sensed that there needed to be more of a change in me internally. My character needed shaping. I needed to *let go* of more stuff, before I was ready to fully absorb your higher teaching. What is it about asking myself questions that is so magical? I found that when I asked myself deep questions, with sincerity and the right intention, the answers *always* appeared. Not always instantly, but they did appear. Who was leading me to the answers I received? Was I giving them to myself?

I had discovered something about Universal Laws. I discovered that they do not change. Did my personal life reflect or align itself with the Divine principles reflected in the Laws of Nature and with values such as:

Compassion
Tolerance
Selflessness
Charity
Unconditional Love
Peace
Honesty
Courage
Appreciation
Goodness
Humility
Forgiveness
Unity

I thought I was true to myself, but when I asked myself honestly if every part of me was aligned with these values, I saw that I still had a long way to go. You called these values 'ethics'. I hadn't transcended my lower self, which is dominated by vanities of the ego and my outer personality. Was I still at war with myself? Granted the battles weren't as huge any more. They were more like small skirmishes, therefore easier to tolerate and easier to overlook. If I still struggled with the deeper meaning of courage, tolerance, forgiveness and fearlessness, and reacted in my usual fashion, was I really honest with myself? Is this what you meant by the *uncomfortable* truth? I wonder...

During the month of March, I received my usual lessons from *Astara* along with the news that they would be holding a spiritual retreat at the beginning of June.

They had advertised these retreats the previous two years, however, I had made the choice back then, that I could not afford to take time off from work. Now, I felt quite differently. I remembered my special week spent in Georgia, back in 1985 and felt I needed some time for myself. Perhaps I would gain some new insight into my self and why I felt so confused and blocked. I also looked forward to spending a week with like-minded people. People, who like me, were searching for something greater than material possessions. People, to whom I could perhaps communicate my deepest feelings.

Once I made the choice to go I could hardly wait to pick up the phone and make my reservation for the first week in June. During the weeks that followed I felt great, having something special to look forward to. Another 'coincidence' occurred shortly after I had decided to go for a week of spiritual renewal.

During the month of April, on April 14th, which happened to be Good Friday, I had experienced a stressful day at work. On my drive home I knew I needed to relax and try to connect somehow to the *feeling* of Good Friday and the *symbolic* meaning of the teaching, the suffering and the struggle of the life and death of Jesus. Instead of taking the highway home, I drove along US I, which is the main north/south artery in Boca Raton. Since I don't usually attend church services, I decided that if a church would appeal to me on the way, no matter what denomination, I would stop and go inside. I purposely drove slower to allow a feeling or *intuitive sense* to guide me, showing me where I should spend this Good Friday evening. This had worked for me in the past and I trusted this process.

I was disappointed to find that nothing appealed to me by the time I needed to make a right turn towards my home. That's when I remembered the Yoga Center located in the small plaza along this turn. I parked my car and decided to take a Yoga lesson instead. This appealed to me at that moment. The relaxation of Yoga and meditation is just what I needed, or so I thought. As I walked towards the Yoga Center I noticed a sign right next door 'Quest Books', followed by 'The Theosophical Society'. I glanced at the notice on the door as I passed and went into the Yoga Center. As it turned out, I was too late for the 7 P.M. class, which had just started. I chastised myself for driving slower than usual and left taking some literature.

On the way back to my car I stopped to read the schedule of events posted on the glass door of the Theosophical Society next door, when a woman spoke to me. She was perched on the bench in front, and asked me: "Are you here for tonight's class?" I answered: "No, I did not know there was a class tonight." I was still reading the schedule for Monday nights and my eyes had not yet come to the Friday evening sessions. I became very interested in what I was reading. She continued the conversation with, "Tonight's teacher is one of the most amazing men I have ever met and I highly recommend that you stay and find out what he has to say", followed by, "His esoteric knowledge and wisdom are very profound." Without answering her my eyes drifted to the Friday evening session and I read, "A teacher of metaphysics, is exploring the science of esoteric knowledge by reading and discussing the book 'White Magic' the Ageless Wisdom Teachings of Alice Bailey. All are welcome."

It was as if a light went on in my head. I had purchased this book around 1989 and found it too hard to understand back then. At that time I couldn't get past the first few pages. I guess I wasn't ready. It was still on my shelf somewhere, collecting dust. "That's very interesting", I thought. I looked at the woman waiting and heard her say, "The others should be arriving shortly, the class starts at 7:30," followed by, "It's free of charge." Something inside me told me to stay, and I waited with the anticipation of meeting this teacher.

He arrived soon after, followed by a loyal group of students searching for a higher wisdom. I can only tell you that my *intuition* had guided me correctly. I later learned that among this diverse group of seekers was a medical doctor, a nurse, a retired school teacher, a geologist, a physicist, an architect, a retired professor of philosophy, a psychoanalyst and a massage therapist. They appeared to be highly intelligent individuals. What an evening! I was in a state of complete joy, feeling uplifted by the topic of discussion. By the way, I found out since that 'White Magic' is the inherent light and power of the soul. In hindsight, this became the perfect way for me to *honor the feelings* I had experienced that 'Good Friday' evening. Needless to say, I have not missed a Friday night group discussion unless I am away on a trip. That's how I met the metaphysician, Mr. Fisichella. On the way home I reflected on the sentence he had used, *"When the student is ready the teacher appears."*

I took some literature in the form of pamphlets. As I went to bed that evening, I read about the Theosophical Society's three objectives:

- To form a nucleus of the universal brotherhood of humanity, without distinction of race, creed, sex, caste, or color.
- To encourage the comparative study of religion, philosophy, and science.
- To investigate the unexplained laws of nature and the powers latent in humanity.

These objectives appealed to me instantly and I intuitively knew that I could learn something. I also felt that these objectives were right on the mark as I thought about what you had been doing all your life. Their motto is: "There is no religion higher than Truth." It was as if you were speaking to me. All the titles of your books reveal the same purpose. Before I fell asleep that night I thought about you and how you devoted your life to this purpose. I thought about your words: **"My religion is the religion of LOVE."**

I couldn't help but wonder—who had led me to this group and this new experience, including this teacher? I reflected on what had happened, because that evening I not only took the metaphoric 'road less traveled', but I also literally took a different route home, guided by an inner yearning or impulse. All the people in attendance that evening, just like me, sought a deeper understanding and a higher level of learning.

Another feature that instantly appealed to me was that Theosophy is not a religion. It is tolerant of all religions, since it recognizes that the root of all these different paths is the same, once these paths are looked at from a wider or deeper perspective. Theosophists are tolerant and compassionate, allowing everyone to experience spirituality in the way best suited to the individual's natural inclination. It does not matter whether you are a Buddhist, a Jew, a Hindu, a Muslim or a Christian. Their main objective is to educate and to point out the *unity* underlying all religions by encouraging the study of comparative religion, philosophy and science. They stress that a certain *insight* is gained by being open minded. Insight is the sight I use to see below or beyond the surface, so that I can fully appreciate the *context* and meaning of everything.

Becoming a member of this society was not necessary in order to participate in the discussion groups or classes. They were open to everyone. Incidentally, remaining an independent free thinker is very much encouraged. Also, no one recruits or tries to persuade another and they don't solicit. Madame Helena Blavatsky, a courageous, charismatic and adventurous woman of Russian nobility, a free thinker who dared to ask questions, founded this society in 1875. She is often simply referred to as H.P.B.

What is most extraordinary about my experience that Good Friday evening, is that I have not seen the woman on the bench since. She was not a regular at these weekly group discussions and has not been seen again. I tried to find out if someone could give me her name, but no one knew her, and she has not attended a meeting since. Before long it was June, the time had arrived for me to prepare for my flight for a week of spiritual renewal at the chosen retreat. One thing I will mention now before closing. The book I wrote last summer, the biography of your life, is still lying in my closet.

I have had no desire to re-read it, number one because I already knew the content, and number two, I instinctively, perhaps the word *intuitively* is more appropriate, began to know that the story, if any develops, had to be different. It must be about, what knowing you has done for me along the path and where this road is still leading me today. That's all I can honestly know and write about.

For me the great challenge ahead is to *align* my personal values with the larger eternal values or principles. I began to understand that the two must be synchronized and in balance in order to create peace and harmony in myself. Most of us can't accept the fact that the universe is inexplicable—therefore, we look outside of ourselves, searching 'out there' somewhere for answers and direction, failing to see the miracle of creation in 'ourselves'. Once we examine the mystery hidden inside each and everyone of us, including the mystery of our physical body, we come closer to the Source of Consciousness (Q or Quelle, in German)—which some call God. The Mystery of the Kingdom of God will be revealed to those who make the honest effort to seek Truth and understanding, including finding the needed courage and determination to explore new ways of seeing people and the world we live in.

You understood the power of values, telling us over and over again that 'ethics' and goodness are the foundation blocks of any culture and civilization. Is ethics the light on the path?

The word 'path' itself can be somewhat deceiving simply because it is a 'pathless path'. As I start exploring this, I see that it is a journey where you don't have to 'go' anywhere—because it is a path leading me to discover or uncover my core, my true self. My intuition understood this process; my mind was not as cooperative at first.

The mind is limited by language, and words are very confining when attempting to describe certain insights experienced. What led me to these insights? Was it my heart or my intuition? Could they be connected? Yes, *intuition* is a better way for me to recognize this wisdom, shining a light on what has been there all along, lying in wait for me. The re-discovery or the 'remembering' of certain principles will in turn lead to new and different, perhaps even *mystical* experiences.

I found that these experiences are essential in order for me to understand any spiritual philosophy, including that of Helena Petrova Blavatsky, a mystic who lived before the turn of the century. She had described 'Theosophy' as the *synthesis* of science, philosophy and religion. You had educated yourself in all three of these categories, resulting in the expansion of your consciousness. Blavatsky, like many of her students, was self-taught, self-motivated and self-sufficient. I learned that she was guided and had become a channel for some of the Wisdom Teachers and would like to read you a quote:

THERE IS A ROAD

"There is a road, steep and thorny, beset with perils of every kind, but yet a road, and it leads to the very heart of the Universe: I can tell you how to find those who will show you the secret gateway that opens inward only, and closes fast behind the neophyte for ever-more. There is no danger that dauntless courage cannot conquer; there is no trial that spotless purity cannot pass through; there is no difficulty that strong intellect cannot surmount. For those who win onwards there is reward past all telling—the power to bless and save humanity; for those who fail, there are other lives in which success may come." H.P.B.14

Are you one of those teachers who opened the door for me? Where is that door which leads inward? Or did you only lead me to the door, a door I had to have the courage to open myself, you pointing only in the general direction, towards my own heart? I started writing again a month and a half after I returned from the retreat, on July 22nd, to be exact. That Sunday morning I wrote you my first letter, 43 days ago.

I now recognize that we *do* have something in common. Namely our love of books, our desire to know Truth, the desire to share and help others, and the desire to learn and grow, emotionally and mentally, as well as spiritually. Where is this quest leading me? I honestly don't know, but I trust that I will find out as soon as I am *ready* for the next challenge. This journey, including the 'looking back' has been very helpful in bringing me back to myself. Thank you, my dear friend and teacher. I am filled with a new confidence, and see a new vision ahead.

I hope we'll meet again soon, here in my closet, as time will permit in the future. Your photo is looking at me and I see something new in your beautiful face. Something has changed in me. I feel I understand your struggle, I understand your concern and compassion for humanity on a deeper level. Yes, I have matured as I now take full responsibility for 'who' I AM. A soul growing and searching to re-link with my spiritual home.

Was your appearance to me a response, an act of compassion for another being in distress? You had come to my rescue, and through you I found the way back to myself. And yes, your level of thinking has inspired me, to look beyond the ordinary reality—recognizing that transformation is possible and becoming a part of my new Reality.

Thank you for coming to my rescue that special August day in Georgia. I have since discovered that you were not an ordinary man. If it is true that we must find an ideal, a hero we can look up to and emulate, I had found one. You were a man who had the right priorities. You became the light on my path. You cared about humanity. Where will knowing this lead me?

Recently, someone told me that although I am a Libra, the sign of balance and relationships, my rising sign is Cancer, the sign of the crab. Libra is also Air and ruled by the planet Venus, while Cancer is Water and influenced by the Moon. My moon is also in Libra, what does that mean? Do I have to come out of my shell and stick my neck out for what I believe to be true? Do I have the required courage? Does it have to happen in this lifetime? I wonder...

All I know is that I am, like you, searching out the 'road less traveled'. A road now leading me to new and almost miraculous discoveries about myself as I close with your profound question:

"Will we be able again to entertain and exercise ideals which transform reality? This is the question before us today."[15]

I see this as the question facing every man and woman today. I feel quite melancholy about going on this trip.

I am filled with deep gratitude and a love in my heart that is getting stronger every day. Today I reflect and remember that on this day in 1965, you passed over to the other side. Please know that I am very grateful for everything you have taught me, and that I will remain,

Your student forever, *R.*

September 4th, 2001

Sources Chapter 6:

1   P.10 *The Words of Albert Schweitzer*, Norman Cousins.
2   P.20 *The Words of Albert Schweitzer*, Norman Cousins.
3   P.11 *Wittgenstein's Poker*, David Edmonds and John Eidinow, published in Great Britain as 'Wittgenstein's Poker: The Story of a Ten-Minute Argument Between Two Great Philosophers by Faber and Faber, 2001, Harper Collins Publishers Inc., New York, NY.
4   P.398 *The Quest for the Historical Jesus*, Albert Schweitzer, A Critical Study of Its Progress from Reimarus to Wrede, 1998, The Johns Hopkins Press, Baltimore and London.
5   P.398 *The Quest for the Historical Jesus*, Albert Schweitzer.
6   P.399 *The Quest for the Historical Jesus*, Albert Schweitzer.
7   P.400 *The Quest for the Historical Jesus*, Albert Schweitzer.
8   P.400 *The Quest for the Historical Jesus*, Albert Schweitzer.
9   P.402 *The Quest for the Historical Jesus*, Albert Schweitzer.
10 P.401 *The Quest for the Historical Jesus*, Albert Schweitzer.
11 P.403 *The Quest for the Historical Jesus*, Albert Schweitzer
12 *The Secret Teachings of Jesus*, Four Gnostic Gospels, The Secret Book of James, The Gospel of Thomas, The Book of Thomas, The secret Book of John. Translated by Marvin W. Meyer, 1986, Vintage Books (Random House Inc.) New York, NY
13 *The Gnostic Gospels*, Elaine Pagels, 1989, Vintage Books (Random House Inc.) New York, NY.
14 *Collected Writings*, Helena P. Blavatsky, Quest Books, Wheaton, Il.
15 P.6 *Pilgrimage to Humanity*, 1961, Philosophical Library Inc., New York, NY.

Part III

Know Thyself

"The beginning of all spiritual life is fearless belief in truth and its open confession."[1]

Albert Schweitzer

"The greatness of Schweitzer rests not just on what he has done but on what others have done because of him. What has come out of his life and thought is the kind of inspiration that can animate an age."[2]

Norman Cousins

7

Recognition

Dear Dr. Schweitzer,

Today is January 14, 2002, the date of your birth 127 years ago. Happy Birthday! Today is the first time I felt a desire to sit at my computer and write to you since last September 4th. That was four months ago. My trip to Europe started on September 7th and I was very busy on the days leading up to my departure.

The date of 9/11/01 will forever be imprinted on our minds. Did it take me four months to digest the fact that our world has changed? This change came suddenly and was a complete surprise, as wake-up calls often are.

I was with my sister that fateful afternoon of September 11, 2001, when the world as we knew it, seemed to go up in smoke. It was just before 3 P.M. local time in Germany, (9 A.M. in New York) when I heard my sister turn on the kitchen radio. It was her custom to listen to the news while preparing our afternoon tea. I was in the living room, when I heard the word New York mentioned during a German radio newscast. She closed the kitchen door, which was usually open. Becoming curious, I opened the door pretending to see how the tea was coming along. She looked at me with a worried expression and said, "I wanted to spare you this unpleasant news until after we have had our tea." I asked: "What news?" She had shut the radio off as I entered. "What's wrong?" I asked, surprised at her curious pallor and behavior.

"Something terrible has happened in New York", she said. I immediately walked to the television and tuned the TV to CNN, which is also broadcast in Europe. The local time in New York was shortly after 9 A.M. I was in Germany that fateful day as I watched the twin towers of the Trade Center collapse on live television, in complete shock at what had just happened. Needless to say I did not participate in the afternoon tea ritual that day. Instead, I stayed glued to the television, much to my sister's dismay. She of course felt my sadness and horror. However, not living in the United States, and never having seen this monument to capitalism herself, she may have felt a bit more removed from the horror of the situation emotionally. The initial disbelief turned into a silent shock.

I tried to reach my daughter Eve, but all the phone circuits to the US were tied up. I picked up the phone every few minutes, but always got the same busy signal, followed by a recording. I experienced a deep grief and a lot of tension in my body, but strangely no tears. Had this happened a few years ago, I would have collapsed in tears. Had I changed?

Finally, the next day I was able to reach my daughter. Knowing they were all right was a huge relief, and the tears formed in my eyes as she told me the news that two of the fathers of my granddaughter's Kindergarten class did not return home that night.

The deep ache inside continued throughout the rest of my vacation. Everyone seemed to digests this event differently. This became very evident as we went about our daily sightseeing trips and I encountered different reactions to the events in New York. Reactions to an event, that is now simply referred to as—9/11. I have not re-read my journal entries from that evening. Perhaps I will look at these entries later tonight.

The days that followed are still a blur to me. I do remember my sister's opinion that there must be a deep-seated hatred among some people in this world against the gluttonous and blatant capitalism of America. I felt offended by her remarks, understanding on some level that these observations were probably true, yet, I was too confused, filled with mixed emotions of loyalty and nationalism. I did not feel like getting into an argument and kept silent.

This in no way stopped my internal dialogue. My first instinctive reaction was to catch the next flight home, but all the US air traffic had come to a complete halt. I forced myself to spend the next two days taking day trips, one of which, was to the shore of the North Sea. The long walk we took along the wind blown shoreline felt soothing to my aching heart. I watched the tide recede, exposing a huge expanse of previously hidden gray sand. On this windy fall day I thought about how different this shoreline is from the sunny expanse of beaches in Florida. As soon as we returned from these excursions, I was again glued to the television set long after my hosts had gone to bed.

Since there was no way to get home, I decided to continue to plan the second part of my trip. My sister tried to keep me at her home for the next week, with the admonition that at a time like this it is better not to travel alone in a foreign country. Little did she know that I was not ruled by this kind of fear. After saying a sad goodbye, and giving thanks for their kind hospitality I hugged my sister and brother in-law. In order to pick up the car I had previously reserved at the airport, I boarded the train to Düsseldorf to continue on the second part of my vacation. I knew that she felt that this could be my last visit to Germany. I saw sadness in her eyes. She also knew that her little sister had grown up and was independent.

The weather during the time I was in Germany was often rainy and windy, enhancing the strange mood I was in. After a short drive through the neighborhood of my youth, and walking through my old school yard, I strolled past our old home, allowing my mind to go back in time to the simpler days of my carefree childhood so long ago. Everything seemed so much smaller than I had remembered it. I was glad to see the same large tree still standing in front of our old home. To my surprise, the streetcars where still in operation on the same track and routes, as I had experienced them fifty-one years ago. Walking the path I took as a child from my former home to my old school brought back dreamlike memories. It was around noon and I saw mothers picking up their children in cars, maneuvering U turns in the narrow street.

While in this melancholy mood I thought about some of my childhood friends and what may have become of them. I regret not having kept in touch with some of them. The same is true for my teachers of course. While walking the familiar streets I thought about how many of them would still be alive today. They would be around ninety years old, if still alive. I would have loved to sit down and talk to them, about their lives, and what motivated them to become teachers. This would have given me the opportunity to thank them for their patience and guidance so long ago.

Filled with these thoughts I lit a cigarette and went back to my rental car. All my good intentions about not smoking again went by the wayside—out the window. What excuse did I use this time? Ah, yes stress! The afternoon traffic was heavy as I entered the Autobahn heading towards Cologne. After Cologne I picked a route that hugged the shoreline of the Rhein, but found it congested and slow going. The winding roads were single lane traffic. I wanted to get to a hotel before sundown, since I could feel a slight headache coming on. I was not used to the European signs and had to pay strict attention to the highway exits, trying to follow the route I had highlighted on the crumpled map beside me. Most exits came up suddenly, and this kind of concentration did nothing to alleviate the pounding in my head not to mention the guilt trip I was giving myself about smoking again.

Soon I saw a sign ahead that read 'Bad Kreuznach' and remembered this town as a health resort my parents had sent me to when I was around six years old. I had been sickly and my parents thought the fresh country air would help me get my strength back. I stayed with friends of my parents for a whole month hating every minute of it. I remember being very homesick, unable to appreciate the beauty of the surrounding mountains. Taking this exit, I looked for a hotel to spend the night, hoping to sleep off this dull ache in my head.

Since all the rooms were taken near the spa area of this village, known for its healing waters, I drove back towards the highway. That's when I spotted a sign leading up the mountain to a hotel located above town. While driving up this mountain I passed a sign, which read 'Römer Museum'. I realized that I was in a very old part of the world, and looked forward to exploring these ancient ruins left by the Romans, over two thousand years ago.

On checking in, I was surprised that the rates were not as astronomical as I had expected. This hotel, at first glance appeared to be out of my category of budget hotels. At this point I was so sick, and knew from experience that vomiting would be the next stage of this migraine. I also realized that I was in Germany where all the stores, including pharmacies, close early. It was after 5 P.M., and I hoped that the hotel receptionist would have a couple of Aspirin to spare. I was in luck.

After opening the door to a charming room with gabled windows, I fell fast asleep, too ill to appreciate my nice surroundings. I woke during the night and promptly turned on the television. It was evening in the U.S. so all the newscasts were 'live'. The horror in New York was still unfolding before my eyes.

My headache was gone the next morning, but the dull ache in my heart continued. After breakfast and a short walk through the adjoining gardens, I felt refreshed enough to continue my journey. The view from the hotel was breathtaking. The sun came out briefly bathing the hills and valleys surrounding the town below in a warm fall light.

I stopped to explore the 'Römer Museum' on the way back to town. This site had been excavated to expose the ruins of Roman palaces and homesteads. Marvelous art and mosaics had graced the floors of these ancient homes. I saw columns and remnants of architecture that were totally out of place in this German village. Had the Romans known about the healing springs of this area, and therefore, had built the opulent baths I saw? The archaeologist in me was satisfied, and I was glad to have stopped.

The sun appeared briefly as I headed back to the main Autobahn running parallel to the scenic river road. I realized that this was the road to Bingen, which is a port on the Rhein. It is the main port from which several sightseeing boats commence a scenic tour of this historic part of the river. I had never taken this particular boat journey, which is the best way to view the castles hugging the mountains on both sides, and decided to experience this adventure on my way back. My destination on that day, was Strasbourg. However, once I got close to making my turn towards this city it was raining heavily. My idea to walk the small center of this old city to visit the University and the parish of St. Thomas, had to be shelved. Instead, I drove straight through to Kaysersberg, the village of your birth.

During those quiet hours driving towards Baden-Baden I had had a chance to reflect. All the sights and sounds around me seemed to disappear when I got into one of these moods. The deliberate destruction of life in New York was felt as a deep ache in my heart, yet, I thought of all the other countries where citizens are constantly coping with famine, lack of medical care, hunger and death on a daily basis. I thought about India, Africa and Somalia. What makes our suffering so special? Ah yes, terrorism...

Isn't it also a form of terrorism to allow babies to die of malnutrition, by the thousands on a daily basis? Oh, that's a different continent, so this does not affect us? Oh, *but* they have a different religion and pray to a different God. Oh, but they have a different government and don't understand democracy. Are they less important as humans, because they don't speak English, because their skin is of a different shade and they don't have a nice house and two cars in the driveway? They have not yet understood the great value of progress shrouded in blind and gluttonous materialism? What kind of an example have we been? What kind of an example is our kind of philosophy? What is our current philosophy? Where is our modern life filled with stress, anxiety, tension and our insatiable appetite for material possessions leading us?

Is our obsession with technology, power, glamour, greed, and unbridled ambition a good example? Where is our wisdom? Where is our love? Where is our goodness? Has materialism completely obscured and blinded us to our spiritual nature? Has it clouded our minds and hearts to the extent that we forget who we really are?

I am certainly not condemning the people of the Islamic religion, since most people of this faith are peaceful and law abiding citizens—not fanatics. Do they really believe that God or Allah is on their side? How can God be on either side of a war, when energy is impersonal? God is what I see as being *beyond* good and evil and can only be experienced in the comfort and peace that lie *beyond* these two opposites. I see hope, providing we, humanity as a whole—take a look at what we collectively have created and take responsibility for our creations. In other words, recognize the *cause* and change it, since everything in our universe is governed by cause and effect.

The thoughts occurred to me, "Since when does responding to hate with hate, solve anything? Since when does creating a new wound heal the wound? Where is the age of enlightenment? Where is my enlightenment?"

Isn't the act of war contradictory to the idea of the peace we often proclaim to want? Isn't war the exact opposite of peace? Yet, we keep thinking that one will lead to the other. Has our motive been peace and truth, or has it been power and greed? Is our motive hate, revenge, control, intolerance and resentment or—is it peace? If hate and resentment are the cause of the terror in New York, how can our response, if also fueled by resentment and hate resolve this problem?

"Peace cannot be achieved through violence, it can only be attained through understanding."

Albert Einstein

What have we learned during the last two thousand years? Has the gap between the 'have' and the 'have-nots' not grown larger? Was the event in New York a wake-up call, a warning to all of us to take a good look at our core values, our ethics, our humanity and our lifestyle? It is not so much death that frightens me, because death is inevitable for all of us. To me death is only a transition from one state of awareness to another. Consciousness is part of spirit energy and energy does not die, it can only be exchanged or transformed into another.

It is the violence in the minds of the living and breathing human beings that concerns and stirs me. What kind of an example are we to *our* children? What are we teaching *our* children? If our western civilization is so advanced then where is our *understanding*? What are we collectively creating? Can we create more tolerance by being *intolerant*? Is *homeland security* really the answer? Can it really address the issue of hate in someone who is willing to put his life on the line for what he believes?

Once death is fully faced and examined I am left with a deeper appreciation for the meaning of life. As I write these words I am reminded of how you expressed your feelings on this subject:

"We must all become familiar with the thought of death if we want to grow into really good people. We need not think of it every day or every hour. But when the path of life leads us to some vantage point where the scene around us fades away and we contemplate the distant view right to the end, let us not close our eyes. Let us pause for a moment, look at the distant view, and then carry on.
"Thinking about death in this way produces true love for life. When we are familiar with death, we accept each week, each

day, as a gift. Only if we are able thus to accept life—bit by bit—does it become precious."
"How can death be overcome? By regarding, in moments of deepest concentration, our lives and those who are part of our lives as though we already had lost them in death, only to receive them back for a little while."3

Thank you. Your words of wisdom always inspire me to see things from a larger perspective. My heart goes out to all the relatives of the people who died during this disaster.

Why is it so hard for me to accept 'what is'? I am filled with all these idealistic thoughts, yet what am I doing about it? Am I not just as self-absorbed as all the rest of humanity? What makes me that way? Have I changed at all during the last sixteen years of educating myself, learning about meditation, love and enlightenment? I seek truth and honesty, yet do I have the courage to look at my self?

Are we collectively heading towards spiritual bankruptcy? When will we begin to see that we are not alone, we are all in this together and must find a cure for the disease of our world together? Knowing, is step one. However, knowing is simply not enough. To make a contribution, is step two. Enlightened beings like you have *demonstrated* to us that it is possible!

How come I wasn't enlightened instantly, like some of the people I have read about? Why am I still struggling? What sense of false self am I still clinging to? What is it that I don't understand?

Reading about anything does not make me an expert. Just like reading a book on yoga or gymnastics does not make me more flexible; and reading a book about love does not make me more loving! The key must be found in my heart leading to deeper understanding. I have to first *understand* what I learn and relate this knowledge to myself, know and experience the process on a deeper level. How can I apply this in my life? Apply it I must, otherwise, it is just a bunch of information! I thank God for brave souls like you, who showed us the way—being an example—not only of discipline, but an example of what it means to have humility, a sense of responsibility, showing us the meaning of love, compassion, peace and faith.

What has this random act of violence and destruction taught us? Will it bring all the leaders of our world closer together, or drive us further apart? I often think about all the people who have sacrificed their lives during this historic event. What are we to learn from this? How would you view this turning point in history? We are at war, fighting the 'enemy' in Afghanistan. Nuclear bombs are being discussed. Chemical warfare is feared. I see that fear is running rampant and out of control. Does that remind you of a previous time? What are our values now in the year of 2002? Are we changing and growing? Is this process so slow that it can't be observed within the span of a hundred years? Or is it speeding up? Are we evolving through this kind of conflict? Is it all unfolding as part of a cosmic plan? Is the earth able to cleanse itself of this kind of fear, negativity and darkness?

What is our true intention, our true motive for war? Is it to heal a wound or to create more wounds? Are we being honest with ourselves? Are our motives selfless or selfish? Are our motives true peace and true harmony, or are they fueled by corruption, power, control and more intolerance?

You were on my mind a lot today, your earthly birthday. After 9/11 I felt lost, perhaps I wasn't the only one. Humanity appears to me to be without any inner direction. However, your star is still burning brightly, and in the mist and fog that surround me it is showing me the way. For that I thank you! I send you my greetings and love and remain,
Your grateful and devoted student, *R.*

Dear Dr. Schweitzer,

It is now the middle of March. I have not written for the last two months. My reason became clear as I now sit at the keyboard. I needed to process my experiences and look at the changes that have taken place—externally, as well as internally.

I've been thinking about death and how it is part of the natural rhythm and cycle found in all of nature including our human life experience. The cycle is seen in the four seasons, as the cycle of spring (birth/renewal), summer (growth/preservation), fall (harvest), and winter (death/destruction), repeat themselves. We experience this cycle every year in nature without paying too much attention. Yet, our own death is hard for the 'mind' to accept. We often dance around this issue, hiding our true feelings by not allowing our thoughts to dwell on death. We cling to our material existence and possessions, due to our lack of understanding of 'who' we really are, robbing ourselves of joy and of the gift of life in the process. Having reached the age of 58 I am fully aware that I am in the fall of my life. Fall is the season of harvest and thanksgiving. As I look at your words I feel a chill run down my spine.

"Only familiarity with the thought of death creates true, inward freedom from material things. The ambition, greed, and love of power that we keep in our hearts, that shackle us to this life in chains of bondage, cannot in the long run deceive the man who looks death in the face. Rather, by contemplating his end, he eventually feels purified and delivered from his baser self, from material things, and from other men, as well as from fear and hatred of his fellow men."4

Yes, we have the ability to reason. Yes, death shows me that I don't really own anything. I can just borrow and use certain things, for a while be the custodian. Nothing in the material world belongs to me, in that I can't take it with me when I die.

We all possess the ability to contemplate higher values. However, the *desire* to do so is different in every man. The average man seems to be content with deceiving himself not recognizing the illusion. I spent the last two months reviewing some of the changes I am experiencing and embracing. I changed my outlook, putting my mind on a diet of more positive thoughts. This time of year seems to be appropriate to put myself on another kind of diet. I put my emotions on a diet as well, as I refrain from watching any kind of news on television. Today's journalists seek sensational stories and give them their interpretation, their opinion—their spin. I've learned that opinions are not truth, therefore why listen to them? An opinion is simply someone's point of view. It is nothing more, nothing less! This diet is serving me well. It allows me to focus on the positive and creative aspect of writing and learning about myself. Here is what you had to say about some parts of modern journalism:

"I am worried about present-day journalism. The emphasis on negative happenings is much too strong. Not infrequently,

news about events marking great progress is overlooked or minimized. It tends to make for a negative and discouraging atmosphere. There is a danger that people may lose faith in the forward direction of humanity if they feel that very little happens to support that faith. And real progress is related to the belief that it is possible."5

Are belief and faith the same thing? I am experiencing a deep sense of *'knowing'* during meditation, when I allow my usual thoughts to simply melt away. During the last few months I watched very little television.

How did this come about? On the flight home from my spiritual retreat, back in June, I recognized that I would have more time to read and more time to spend on creative efforts, such as writing, if I just stopped watching television altogether. I knew a diet of negative reporting was not good for my general well being. I knew the often negative and fearful thoughts of others influence my thought process. I intuitively knew that my inner being was not strong enough, not to be influenced on some level. Not yet! The wound of previous conditioning has not been completely healed.

Not to mention that there is very little of interest on television. Except for PBS, the History and Discovery channels, television is set up to entertain the mindless masses. If it is a reflection of what society wants—God help us all! Even the cable channels that I have to pay for are filled with talking heads and advertising. They should be paying me to watch this... For the time being, I disconnected my cable TV and don't miss it.

You had recognized that our civilization is undergoing a severe crisis. Is our spiritual nature being diminished and thwarted by unbridled materialism in the name of scientific progress? Have we have fed into the herd mentality and have we lost our true identity in the process? While opening a book of your words, *'The Spiritual Life'* selected writings of Albert Schweitzer, I found your words:

"The modern man is lost in the mass in a way which is without precedent in history, and this is perhaps the most characteristic trait in him. His diminished concern about his own nature makes him as it were susceptible, to an extent that is almost pathological, to the views which society and its organs of expression have put, ready made, into circulation. Since over and above this, society, with its well-constructed organization,

has become a power of as yet unknown strength in the spiritual life, man's want of independence in the face of it has become so serious that he is almost ceasing to claim a spiritual existence of his own. He is like a rubber ball which has lost its elasticity, and preserves indefinitely every impression that is made upon it. He is under the thumb of the mass, and he draws from it the opinions on which he lives, whether the question at issue is national or political or one of his own belief or unbelief."6

The thought just occurred to me, "When was the first time I asked myself 'Who am I'?" I know that reading 'Handbook to Higher Consciousness' awoke certain feelings in me, opening chambers in my mind and heart, chambers, which had previously been closed. More than anything else it made sense to me. But it also raised new and profound questions for me, since it never mentioned the word God. The year was 1985 and I was about to turn forty-one. The questions I had started to ask myself: "Am I—my body? Am I—my brain? Am I—my emotions? Am I—my thoughts? Am I—my mind?" resulted in this poem eleven years later...

My Self
Who am I—who made me?
My parents?
I wonder and ponder
This question...

You see me—and through your eyes
I see myself—a reflection
Of my creation—No?
Then who—is myself?

You know me—you think.
Do I know myself?
Who chose the role I am playing?
With such zest—this time around.

Are what you see and I see
The same? The same me?
Or is it all a game
The inventor smiles—satisfied?
RzT 1996

During the past years I often wondered what made you so different from the rest of us. Your early school years do not indicate that you were more 'intelligent'. You struggled with school lessons just like the rest of us. Were you more privileged? Perhaps, but only in the sense that you grew up surrounded by nature and music. Your family saw you as a dreamer, a person happy to be alone with his own thoughts. Your family was at times concerned with not having money, since your father was living on a meager stipend allotted to the local pastors. This did not allow for many of the luxuries or comforts we seek and pine for, in today's world.

As I re-read some of the books you wrote, I feel that I've gotten to know you a lot better. I purposely avoided any biographies, except *'Albert Schweitzer: Man of Mercy'*, the book mentioned in the beginning of my letters, in order for me to concentrate on your words only, unfiltered and unedited by the views and opinions of other people.

The following questions nagged at me: "Did you know you were different? Did you know that your mind worked on a higher level even as a youth? Who inspired you? Your mind appeared to be occupied with searching for truth, pure reason, the subjects of thoughts, and the process of thinking. Your thoughts were different. Your focus was different. "What are thoughts?"

Medical science is catching up to what the ancient philosophers and mystics knew long ago. We now know that the brain is just an organ, like any other organ in our body, although it can correctly be compared to a computer. It *follows and reacts* to the instructions given by thoughts, which are generated in the mind, often relying on old information and old programming, buried in the subconscious mind.

The mind, therefore, is not a physical organ. The brain can be compared to a receiving station, much like a television set receives pictures and images over airwaves. The mystery of the mind still baffles modern science today. Scientist, so far are able to discover and categorize the mind into the conscious mind, the subconscious mind and the super conscious mind.

The subconscious mind can be compared to the hard-drive in a computer. Our memories, experiences of pain and pleasure are stored and relived on a moment to moment basis on our journey through life. It stands to reason, therefore, that in order for our lives to change we have to recognize the power of the subconscious, which acts like a *robot or computer*. We have to learn to reprogram our minds, delete the old in order to become more efficient in accepting fresh and new ideas about ourselves, and the world we live in.

I found Darwin's theory of evolution to be only partly correct. The animal mind is not self-conscious, not able to reason and not able to reflect, therefore, man has evolved to a higher level of response-ability. We are *aware* that we are aware, so man is an evolved being, able to contemplate his/her own nature. His theory of evolution does not explain, to my level of satisfaction, why animals are still animals, thousands and even millions of years later, while man has evolved to a higher level of *'being'*. Man is self-conscious and through reasoning, self-observation, self-reflection and self-understanding is able to reach a higher level of creativity.

So, to me that theory is only a step, the *biological aspect* of our evolution, and therefore incomplete and unsatisfactory. What makes us humans different? What is the spark that generates thoughts in our minds? Is it our soul, our connection to *spirit*? This brings me to the next mystery.

We are not just physical beings. We are also mental, emotional and spiritual beings. What is beyond the mind, if not spirit? Having studied many books on philosophy prompts me to agree with you while contemplating Descartes' famous statement: "I think, therefore I AM." You wrote the following:

"One would think that Descartes lived just to emit a line of staggering profundity: 'I think, therefore I am'... I find it difficult to be impressed by 'I think, therefore I am.' One might as well say, 'I have a toothache, therefore I exist.' These catchwords are tricky things. I don't think they serve the cause of creative thought in philosophy."[7]

Yet, Descartes was often called the father of modern philosophy, taking a very *mechanical* view of man and the universe. Most of us don't realize that we are *not* what we *think* we are. His statement only creates more confusion. In order to fully comprehend, 'who' we are, we must *transcend* thoughts, and experience *being,* thereby gaining a deeper understanding of our complex constitution and reality. Our body and personality, including our emotions and our rational mind, are the vehicles used by our soul.

'I AM THAT I AM', means something quite different. How many people take the time to think deeply about who we really are? I discovered that I am so much more than just my ordinary, often stressed out mind thinks, and therefore *believes*. I recognize that stress often creates a distorted perception. What do we do to cope with stress? Do we know its true purpose?

Most of us are caught in a web of just coping with the stress of everyday living, preferring to go home at the end of the day, turn on the television and allow someone else's thoughts to entertain us. Are we afraid to be alone with our own thoughts? You have become my teacher. Your words kept reminding me to *think freely* and deeply. Therefore, I began to explore and nurture the other side of my being. I began to educate myself about myself.

As I reviewed your life, and the discipline you exhibited in every area of your life, I became motivated to act. During the last few months, I spent more time gazing at the stars, often rising early to catch a magnificent sunrise and to spend more time in meditation. I spent more time reading and reflecting in general. I call it the *assimilation* of what I was learning. My behavior, towards myself, and towards others is changing as well. I now see myself in others, and don't feel the need to judge and criticize as often. For instance, it now becomes very obvious to me when someone else is suffering from faulty thinking. I recognize the results of a faulty attitude by being a witness of the chaos this attitude is creating in our lives and our civilization. Do we always see it first in others?

I see all *others* as teachers, as I observe my internal reactions to 'what is'. This is now becoming an opportunity, the instrument I use to always look at myself, becoming more accepting of *what is*, yet, seeing each incident as confirmation that change is needed if I am to grow and evolve into a more forgiving and more complete human being.

Quite often, late at night as I review my day, I see having automatically reacted in a certain way or said something that may have hurt someone. That's when I see that the attitude I embraced needs an adjustment. I try to think of a better way to handle certain situations next time. There is no guilt. Only by putting my *awareness* on my attitude and reactions can I change them.

Not being perfect, I do the best I can at every given moment. That is all I can do at the present stage of my development. I stopped blaming others a long time ago, because my attitude or state of mind has nothing to do with them. It is just about me! That's all I ever have any control over!

It seems to me that my learning is speeding up. Some teachings are finally sinking in, creating this change within, while other teachings are admittedly still above my head. I make it my practice to live more in the *now* moment and have experienced a deep sense of peace, a deep sense of appreciation and gratitude, coupled with a new sense of freedom.

Before leaving you this morning I would like to tell you a story I found retold in 'Handbook to Higher Consciousness'. It is a Buddhist parable that gave me the insight to understand the *now* moment better than anything I had ever read since:

"The meaning of here and now is beautifully illustrated by a Zen story of a monk who was being chased by two tigers. He came to the edge of a cliff. He looked back—the tigers were almost upon him. Noticing a vine leading over the cliff, he quickly crawled over the edge and began to let himself down by the vine. Then as he checked below, he saw two tigers waiting for him at the bottom of the cliff. He looked up and observed that two mice were gnawing away at the vine. Just then, he saw a beautiful strawberry within arms reach. He picked it and enjoyed the best tasting strawberry in his whole life!
"Although only minutes from death, the monk could enjoy the here and now. Our life continually sends us "tigers"— and it continually sends us "strawberries." But do we let ourselves enjoy the strawberries? Or do we use our valuable consciousness worrying about the tigers?"[8]

Yes, life presents us with both strawberries and tigers. Are we only focused on and aware of the tigers? Or do we in moments of silence acknowledge and give thanks for the strawberries and their solace and beauty. I thought about this truth for a long time, and found myself becoming a more grateful individual. If there is something I can do intelligently to alleviate the tigers (modern worries) I must do it now. If there is nothing more I can do in this present moment, I must learn to let go of the tigers, for they are robbing me of my moment to moment experience. They are robbing me of energy needed to focus on the present moment, which is all I really have. I am learning to relax and see the truth of this more clearly.

I will describe what I am clearly recognizing, as not only letting go, but as *growing up*, at a later time. Now the time has come for me to jump into the shower, as I look forward to seeing the strawberries in my life, right now— today. Until later,
Your devoted and grateful student, *R.*

Dear Dr. Schweitzer,

I have some tremendous news! Since I have become more competent in using my computer, I joined the Internet. So far, I had only used this tool very much as a typewriter. Yesterday evening, while browsing through the Internet, looking for books you wrote, books I may have missed, I found a set of CDs. These discs are audio recordings made of *you* playing the organ. I was so thrilled I almost fell off my chair. My son showed me how to use the Internet and my order should arrive in a few days. Until then, I want you to know that I am listening to Bach this morning.

To actually know you are the artist sitting at the organ, performing the music of this great composer is the next best thing to attending one of your concerts. I am thrilled and delighted. What a great moment, like finding a ripe strawberry... Thank you for taking the time out of your busy schedule and allowing these concerts to be recorded. This morning I would like to look back at my experiences in France and Germany last September.

I arrived in Günsbach on Saturday afternoon, September 16th, 2001. The rain had not stopped. I found a hotel room in the charming village of Munster, a few miles down the scenic road from Günsbach. I drove around looking for the road leading to the old train station. I couldn't find it and instead I saw a large football field and a few new homes.

I rose early the next day. It was Sunday and I had planned to attend a service in the church where your father had given his sermons during your youth, and where you first played the organ. It was a damp and somewhat chilly morning. I was the first one to arrive and parked my car on the incline just to the south side of the church. Being the fist one to arrive, I found a seat in the empty church and looked at the simple altar. My mind was trying to imagine the scene of over a hundred years ago, when you were a small boy, looking forward to the Sunday sermons given by your father.

You were on my mind during the whole service, which was performed in French. Although I did not understand every word, I understood the general message. It concerned the events of the previous Tuesday in New York City, a place so far removed from the idyllic village of Günsbach—yet so close! During the emotional sermon the pastor could hardly contain his tears. I noticed the sun, as it began to stream through the stained glass windows to my right. The event was still on every one's mind and for the next few moments I felt tears running down my cheeks. It felt like a dam had been released and I allowed myself to grieve, not just for the people who had been killed, but for myself and for all of us who are alive today. While the pastor was talking in French, your words: *"It is my philosophy for which I want to be remembered"*, kept reverberating in my mind. You stressed that it was necessary to adopt a *life-view* instead of a *world-view*. A life-view is spiritual and expanding, while a world-view is material, and is therefore very limiting in its scope. A life-view encompasses every living creature and everything that exists, including what is hidden or beyond our normal level of perception.

A deep sadness about the state of current world affairs washed over me. What are we thinking? What dark and fearful forces are we feeding into, giving them power? By *we* I mean all of the world's citizens, not just Americans or fearful terrorists. Is killing in war, the same as murder? In what way is it different? I wondered...

I talked to the minister briefly before leaving, and he admonished me for not telling him that I don't speak French. He would have gladly given the service in German, had he known. In this small church the service is performed in both languages on alternating Sundays. His kind gesture reminded me of what life is like among *real* people. By that I mean people with a lot of common sense.

Climbing the staircase up to where the organ is located, I briefly chatted with the organist. She told me that this organ is not the same instrument you had practiced on. This new organ was built to your specifications and installed around 1965. Unfortunately you never heard or played on this one. I estimated the age of the organist to be beyond 85. She was old enough to remember you.

Upon leaving I noticed a small booklet with the German words meaning '*The Messenger*' jumping off the page at me. Knowing that you had tried to reach us with your words and humanity, this somehow seemed to be the appropriate description of you. You, like many enlightened beings who lived before your time, had spent your life trying to give us a message.

Before leaving the village of your youth and childhood I walked the narrow streets behind the church, going up a small incline, examining each old structure and taking in the natural beauty of this quiet hillside where you had spent many days, months and years dreaming and contemplating your future. I asked a fellow pedestrian, "Is there a cemetery in this village?" "Yes, about a half mile down the road," she replied. Before leaving I stopped along a road surrounded by open fields and found the final resting-place of several of your relatives, among them your parents and your brother. I knew that the final resting-place of your and your wife's physical body was in Africa. Everything else about you is still alive today!

My thoughts drifted back to an earlier time. The time of your youth and the years you spent as a student of theology, music and philosophy, which were then followed by years spent as a medical student in Strasbourg. You were on a quest; you were searching for Truth.

I reflected on the discipline you exercised in each one of these fields. I marveled at your ability to focus and concentrate on each task at hand. Around 1905 you were an accomplished organist and an expert on the musical genius of Bach. You became a true master of this magnificent instrument and audiences in Europe packed the concert halls at every one of your performances. You not only studied his music; you studied the life of this extraordinary man. You often referred to Bach as a painter of music. I quote your words:

"Before all else he aims at rendering the pictorial in lines of sound. He is even more tone painter than he is tone poet. Bach has, in fact, his own language of sound. There are in his music constantly recurring rhythmical motives expressing peaceful bliss, lively joy, intense pain, or sorrow sublimely borne."

"The impulse to express poetic and pictorial concepts is the essence of music. It addresses itself to the listener's creative imagination and seeks to kindle in him the feelings and visions with which the music was composed. But this it can do only if the person who uses the language of sound *possesses the mysterious faculty* of rendering *thoughts with a superior clarity* and precision. In this respect Bach is the greatest of the great."9 **(My Italics)**

We know, through scientific research, that all sound is vibration and frequency, therefore, it becomes clear to me that you must have felt these sounds, these higher vibrations, and allowed them to penetrate your physical, emotional and mental bodies.

I feel that Bach's greatness is due to his recognition that we exist in a world of opposites. He saw that our world consists of light and dark, divine joy and deep sorrow, up and down, front and back, noise and silence, heaven and earth and good and evil. Bach was able to express this duality in his compositions painting us a musical picture, not only of nature but also of man's constitution. Who inspired Bach?

After entering medical school in 1905 you said that the study of natural sciences was of great interest to you because you were now able to gain the additional knowledge to put your philosophy of 'life affirmation' to good use. Through the intellectual pursuit of studying science and medicine you could finally make a contribution as a complete human *being*. I quote your words:

"Intoxicated as I was with the delight of dealing with realities that could be determined with exactitude, I was far from any inclination to undervalue the humanities, as others in a similar position often did. On the contrary. Through my study of chemistry, physics, zoology, botany and physiology, I became aware more than ever of the extent to *the truth* established by facts. No doubt something subjective clings to the knowledge that results from the creative mind. But at the same time such knowledge is on a *higher plane* than the knowledge based on facts alone."
"The knowledge that results from the observation of diverse manifestations of being, will always remain incomplete and unsatisfactory because we cannot give a definite answer to the main question of what we are in the universe and to what purpose we exist in it."

"We can find our place in the existence that envelops us *only if we experience* in our individual lives *the universal life that wills and rules* within it. I can understand the nature of the living being outside of myself only through the living being *within me*."
"It is to this reflective knowledge of the universal being and of the *relation* to it of the individual human being, that the humanities are devoted. The conclusions at which they arrive are determined by the sense of reality with the *creative mind*. Knowledge of reality must pass through a phase of thinking (*meditating*) about the *nature of being*."[10] (My Italics)

If you had never said another thing in your life, this would have been enough for me to see that you were an Adept in tapping into the knowledge that *lies beyond* our normal field of vision. You saw and understood the importance of the spiritual aspect of our nature. Is the key to freedom and power found in taming our restless monkey mind, making it our *servant*, instead of being ruled by it?

You, like Einstein, had recognized that our lower mind couldn't be trusted to give us new and creative ways of dealing with problems and finding solutions. Only when we are able to tap into the higher mind, some call it entering into a transcendental state can we tap into our *intuitive* or *creative mind*. However, a struggle arises, because our (lower case) ego wants to keep things the way they are. Our lower self finds comfort in sameness and mediocrity.

Or mind, often called the concrete mind, has been *conditioned* since infancy with experiences based on information and perceptions assimilated during our childhood. This lower mind creates our view of life. We have further been conditioned by our parents, our society, our surroundings and our early environment, instilling us with belief systems, often based on our parents' belief systems, creating perceptions that are different for each and every one of us. Since all our thoughts in the mind are based on *past* experiences and our interpretations of these experiences, *including* perhaps the assimilation of experiences of past lives, it can only act and think about things already known, already experienced. How can there be room for any new and creative thoughts to emerge? Since thoughts have energy and power, doesn't it behoove us to review the process of thinking?

Thoughts, generated in the mind seem to jump from subject to subject, with lightening speed, seemingly without any justification, creating havoc, fear and dissatisfaction, leaving very little room for creativity and love. In Zen Buddhism a solution is found in the art of detachment, beginning with the discipline of *self-observation,* a practice outlined in '*Handbook to Higher Consciousness*'. Who is the observer? Could it be our real self, our Higher Self? This would show us that there are two selves. This often creates much confusion for beginners, and new students of metaphysics. In contrast to the small ego, we also possess another, a higher Ego— our soul—trying to show us our purpose for being here. I see your argument and the need for sacrifice perfectly explained in the following passage.

I had found myself puzzled by your reference to the eastern philosophy of life-negation vs. your philosophy of life-affirmation, until I read your words:

"In the profoundest form of world- and life-affirmation, in which man lives his life on the loftiest spiritual and ethical plane, he attains to inner freedom from the world and becomes capable of sacrificing his life to some end. This profoundest world- and life-affirmation can assume the *appearance* of world- and life-negation. But that does not make it world- and life-negation: it remains what it is—the loftiest form of world- and life-affirmation. He who sacrifices his life to achieve any purpose for an individual or for humanity is practicing life-affirmation. He is taking an interest in the things of this world and by offering his own life wants to bring about in the world something which he regards as necessary. The sacrifice of life for a purpose is not life-negation, but the profoundest form of life-affirmation placing itself at the service of world-affirmation. World- and life-negation is only present when man takes no interest whatever in any realizable purpose nor in the improvement of conditions in this world. As soon as he in any way withdraws from this standpoint, whether he admits it to himself or not, he is already under the influence of world- and life-affirmation."[11]

Non-attachment to the world is not the same as life-negation. Non-attachment is therefore not to be confused with indifference. Indifference creates slaves. Indifference keeps us ignorant. Indifference and complacency creates lethargy and stagnation, which is the opposite of purpose, action, life, growth and creation.

Life on this physical plane must be understood for what it really is. It is *soul growth*. It is the assimilation of all our experiences, which gives us the opportunity to see through and lessen our attachment to the worldly and awaken us to our *true* nature, which is spiritual, not material. Our material existence is very necessary and must be honored because it is our tool. We must honor this vehicle and respect our body. Yet, it is only *one aspect* of our nature, without which there is no vehicle for growth.

In contrast, non-attachment becomes an integral part of the inner realization that there comes a time when we will be able to transcend our material existence, which is temporary, and focus on the eternal one, the home of our true nature. Non-attachment seen from a higher level can't be confused with not caring. On the contrary, it allows us to see and find a higher purpose and to understand the need of caring enough, to want to contribute towards improving world conditions. Seen from above our earth has no borders. Seen from above, nations that are fighting each other are seen as ludicrous. Humanity collectively seems to have a very microscopic view and attitude. It's as if we have lost our connection to who we really are. I understand your argument!

Everything is spiritual and conscious on different levels, therefore, all is filled with the life essence, a will-to-live, resulting in the beauty and logic of having reverence for all life. We can create more harmony in ourselves by tuning into the harmony of nature itself.

There are many stories about you, told by people, who were lucky enough to have known you personally. Once you were convinced of the truth about something, you became as stubborn as an ox. Your sense of humor is legendary as well. Tomorrow I will continue to tell you what I found so fascinating about your character and personality and how this relates to the disciplines as they manifested in your life, and what this discipline is teaching me right now, this day. Without these strong character traits, and a sense of non-attachment, which you called the renunciation of the superficial things and trimmings in life, it is very doubtful that you could have accomplished all the marvelous and extraordinary feats in your life. Renunciation is no more than the *recognition* that something or other does not serve me any more, therefore I *voluntarily* let it go.

You lived an impersonal life, disregarding your personal comfort, making the *conscious choice* to give to this planet all of yourself, knowing that true happiness can only be found in the harmony of the human with the divine, and that deep compassion, the joy of contribution, sharing and giving, are right actions and are the natural outcome of this Higher state of mind.

You had transcended your *lower self*, the personality and the small ego, in the process allowing your Higher power, your true individuality and uniqueness to fully emerge. In the process you experienced a higher Reality and found yourself living this higher Reality based on the immutable Laws of the Universe. These immutable Laws became your Truth. Furthermore, you had aligned your whole being with the deeper *understanding* of these Universal principles and *lived* these principles, becoming a natural channel for its spiritual energy and expression.

The paradox presents itself, that although seeking fame was the least of your motives, you became famous for just being you. You had made the ultimate sacrifice. You had dedicated your *self* to our planet. You considered all of humanity your family, and knew that to heal one is the beginning to healing all. Your love and compassion are the expression of your *impersonal* self—your Higher Self—your soul—which you had recognized and allowed to guide and inspire you. You had *transcended* the *personality self*. You had a higher vision of Truth. You acted from a higher plane of being and understanding. Did it involve sacrifice and pain? My emotions are aroused because I find it difficult at the moment to comprehend this kind of sacrifice, this kind of love, but I am beginning to recognize what it is. You understood the deeper meaning of the paradox hidden in the words: "He who shall lose his life will find it!"

Your innate curiosity led you to study philosophy, including the transcendental nature of being, allowing you to experience an awakening. Did this complement or resonate with your deepest feelings, allowing you to understand the human condition? Were you able to see our suffering?

Observed from a higher viewpoint, your path was not a sacrifice anymore. *You had fully realized yourself.* Everything else that happened in your life was the outcome of this profound realization. In this way you became immortal, if I may call it that. Your words and thoughts are still alive!

I must close and get ready to perform my duties at work. This letter will be continued later this evening, because, today there is much more on my mind than usual.

Your devoted and grateful student, *R.*

Dear Dr. Schweitzer,

In order not to lose track of the thoughts aroused earlier, here I am at my desk again late this evening. Earlier, I reviewed some of the material I had studied during the last few years. The subject of thoughts and their importance, as it relates to the energy field that surrounds us, is coming back to me.

One aspect of our nature, the one I have never talked to you about, are the seven energy centers in our life/energy body, known as the etheric double. The word chakra is an ancient Sanskrit word meaning wheel or vortex of energy. How can I begin to describe these energy fields in order to make them understandable?

Scientists call this energy the magnetic field that surrounds the body. A mystic sees it as an aura. They are the same.

Science has caught up with mysticism in that it is now believed that the universe consists of sound and light—both are vibrations. It consists of atomic and sub-atomic particles such as electrons, protons and neutrons, which all vibrate to a certain frequency.

The ancient mathematician, mystic and philosopher Pythagoras, taught that it also includes *sacred geometry* such as the triangle, which represents the trinity of creation. Out of the Absolute, the unknowable ONE come the TWO or the duality of existence in our manifested physical world. I learned that each number has a different vibration. I also learned that each color and each sound have a different vibration. Goethe wrote a book entitled '*Theory of Colors*' which I bought but have not as yet had time to study.

The field of energy that surrounds us is alive and pulsating, according to the state of our consciousness, our *being*, reflecting and influencing our physical, emotional and mental state. In other words, according to *our thoughts*. Later I will talk to you about the Law of attraction, which is based on the Law of Correspondence.

In describing the chakras I must understand that there are seven unseen, energy fields surrounding and *penetrating* our physical body. Let me clarify this statement. This field is not seen by our ordinary vision, yet a sensitive person or a clairvoyant can see this field of color and vibration, forming the human aura and the energy body which penetrates and radiates from the physical body.

All numbers are sacred but I don't want to get into the subject of numerology per se. However, the number seven has always been a prominent influence in my life, therefore, I took the time to examine this number and its meaning in depth. The number seven consists of the number three, representing spirit, symbolized by the triangle, and the number four which represents matter, and is symbolized by the square. Is it a coincidence that the number seven has so many representations in our daily lives, seen and unseen? Here is what else I discovered:

There are 7 sacred planets.

There are 7 notes in the musical scale.

There are 7 colors in the rainbow, known as rays.

There are 7 days in a week.

There are said to be 7 Archangels or spirits before the throne.

There are 7 days in each phase of the moon.

There were 7 loaves.

There were 7 golden candlesticks.

There are 7 cycles in the life of a person, each period subdivided into 7 years.

There were 7 gods of Egypt.

Seven was the holy and mystical number of the Hebrews.

There are 7 creative Hierarchies manifesting through the emanations of the 7 rays, each represented by a different color, a different sound and a different vibration.

If 'as it is above, so it is below' is true, it is not surprising that we humans have seven major energy centers, known as the major chakras. The word 'chakra' stems from ancient Sanskrit and means wheels of light. Each chakra or wheel vibrates to a different frequency and to a different color. I am reminded that pure white light consists of all of the seven colors. A rainbow for instance, is the refraction of the one white light.

Ancient Eastern medicine has been aware that the chakras in our energy body are connected to seven different hormone glands in the human physical body. These seven centers are connected to our emotional and mental bodies and reflect the magnetic energy produced by these bodies.

1. The first or root chakra is located at the base of the spine. It is perceived as red. It represents our physical connection to the earth plane. It is the seat of our security, our *fight and flight* center, relating to self-preservation. In our endocrine system it externalizes as the *adrenal glands*, connected to the male prostate and the female uterus, the kidneys and the spinal column. It governs our understanding of the physical dimension. It gives us our physical energy and it keeps us grounded.

2. The second chakra is also called the sacral chakra. It is located just below the navel. It is perceived as orange. It governs our attitude towards relationships and reproduction. It is also sometimes called the *spleenic* chakra, because it extends some of its roots into the spleen. It represents our emotions and sensation, including our relationship to food and sex. It also represents the sex organs and is very much part of our creative center.

3. The third chakra is located just above the navel. Its color is seen as yellow. It is known as the *solar plexus*. It externalizes as the pancreas, governs the action of the liver, and aspects of our nervous system. It is the clearing-house for emotional sensitivities and issues of personal power. It is also said to be the seat of our *small ego*, seeing itself as a *separate* individual. It is probably the most sensitive of all chakras, because we feel it as the personal ego. This gut feeling, or instinct, is not to be confused with intuition or love. It is the seat of our personal power, desires and attachments often erroneously thought of as love.

4. The fourth chakra is located near the heart area. It is called the *heart* chakra and observed as being green, at times of true feelings of love turning pink or gold. It connects to the *thymus* gland. This center governs the heart, the blood, the circulatory system and the *endocrine immune* system. It is the center through which we *feel and experience love*. It is also now recognized as **our healing center**, because it is located midway, between the three lower and the three higher chakras. Higher or lower not referring to level of importance. It is the center of awakening or the center of *transformation*.

5. The fifth center is located near the throat area. Its color is blue. It connects to the *thyroid* gland, and governs the lungs, vocal chords, the bronchial area and our metabolism. It is also the center of speech, represented by the power of the **Word**, our center of higher creative expression, communication and discernment.

6. The sixth chakra is located between the eyes, in the middle of the forehead. It is located behind what is often referred to as the *third eye* or Ajna Center. It connects and externalizes as the *pituitary* gland. It governs the lower brain and nervous system, and the left eye. Through this center we consider our spiritual nature and use the awakened intuition. It is seen as the color indigo. A combination of red and blue.

7. The seventh chakra is located at the top of the head and is called the *crown* chakra. It externalizes as the *pineal* gland and governs the upper brain and the right eye. It is seen as violet or white light, which is the combination of all colors. It radiates upward and outward to cover the whole head.

The relationship between the pituitary and pineal gland seems to be a process we are just beginning to understand. Could it be referring to the union of male and female, the harmonizing of opposites or dual energies? This knowledge has existed for thousands of years, yet it has only recently been accepted and acknowledged in our Western philosophy. Sanskrit is the ancient Hindu literary language. It describes these centers as *wheels of energy* or *vortices of power*. This is appropriate, because when seen from the front, they resemble a wheel in constant motion. Seen from the side they look more like two trumpets, one facing towards the back, and the other facing the front of the body. Our vital energy is in constant motion up and down the central channel in the middle. In the center of this wheel are rays of energy, streams of radiation also described as spokes in a wheel or petals of a flower, increasing in number as follows:

The first or root chakra, is seen as having four petals or spokes.

The second or sacral, is seen as having six beams or petals.

The third, the solar plexus is seen as having ten.

The fourth or heart center has twelve.

The fifth or throat center has sixteen. .
The sixth or brow center has ninety-six petals. .
The crown center has close to one thousand.

As we can see, the two higher centers the sixth and the seventh are subtler or finer and therefore vibrate at a much higher speed or frequency.

The colors of each of these centers also change according to the vibrations of energy or the state of awareness of the individual, and can be seen as a mixture of varying hues, depending on the state of spiritual, mental and emotional development of the individual person. For instance, because human emotions fluctuate and are predominantly animalistic in nature and in our expression of life, the root chakra emits the varying shades of red. When carnal love is transmuted into the sublime emotion of divine or unconditional love, the dark red changes to a more clear, pink red.

The color of the heart chakra also varies. It can become pink, green, or a bright golden color, when the heart is uplifted spiritually. It is the midway point, between the three lower and the three upper centers.

In the throat center the colors also change and become weaving rainbow shades, almost like a river of light. It is blue, but it can also become silvery blue.

It is in the heart and throat center that the awareness of a *seeker of Truth* initially resides. The heart being the center of compassion, and the throat being the dominant center of creativity, discernment, expression and communication.

The brow chakra is different in that it seems to be divided in the middle by a powerful current from above, causing it to appear as two huge petals, with forty-eight smaller petals in each half, totaling ninety-six. Some people call this the left and right brain function. I see that both are needed in proper balance, because it is the seat of reason (left brain) and the seat of higher creativity, higher knowledge, inner wisdom (right brain). The current of power which divides this bow chakra, rises straight up through the top of the head to connect us with the spiritual aspect of our nature by what is often described as a silver cord.

The crown chakra, often referred to as the thousand-petal lotus, not only lies on the top of the head but rises to connect with our higher Self. It's color can only be described as 'Pure White

Light', changing to the dazzling radiance of blinding sunlight. I like to compare it to a lotus with a multitude of petals.

Now I understand why the saints—*Initiates*—as I prefer to call them, including the Master Jesus, are pictured with a halo around their head.

This knowledge is often taught in parables or picture form. The Buddhic comparison of a soul to a lotus flower is quite appropriate, as I think of how a lotus grows. Its roots are in the bottom of a dark and muddy lake, then expressing and unfolding its full beauty, floating on top of the water absorbing the light of the sun as it unfolds into a magnificent white flower. The element of water is symbolic of our ever changing emotions. When words don't suffice, the ancient knowledge is often presented in symbols and parables, as well as myths and dramas. The early or primitive Christians used the rose to symbolize this awakening process.

It is through these whirling vortices of power that the life-force or prana, is distributed into the bloodstream. I picture this as a silver cord with seven strands, each connected to a different chakra.

Intuitive or sensitive persons, including mystics and healers, can see this life energy. It is called by so many different names that it can be confusing. Some call it pranic energy, some call it chi or life energy. Others call it our spirit energy, our connection to the Universal Mind or God. This animating creative life force, the will-to-live, is present in all of us and in *everything* that exists.

Mystics of the Indian and Tibetan traditions have been aware of the electrochemical properties of the corresponding endocrine centers for ages. The root chakra at the base of the spine is connected to the adrenal glands. The sacral chakra is connected to the spleen. The solar plexus is connected to the pancreas. The heart chakra is connected to the thymus. The throat chakra is connected to the thyroid. The brow chakra is connected to the pituitary and the crown chakra is connected to the pineal gland.

While reading books or any material containing these higher wisdom teachings, I became aware of the different terminology used, all however, mean the same thing. Our breath for instance, distributes this *prana*, or life-energy into our blood stream as oxygen, that is why breathing is a very essential factor of meditation and relaxation. We all draw this energy in all the time, otherwise we would not be alive. However, when the energy is blocked, the flow, and its corresponding chakra become inefficient. In order to clear, balance and increase the flow of this energy, we must first become aware of it. The key to a healthy and productive life is to keep our channel open and in complete harmony or balance. The practice of deep abdominal breathing is recommended in most spiritual teachings.

The thread of energy which connects us to our Higher self, at death is disconnected completely from the physical being, and the soul, our connection to spirit, is freed enabling its return to the eternal home or the One energy. It is this energy connection which we want to strengthen with our conscious effort. How? I found that through meditation or quiet contemplation I became more aware of its calming and healing effect, its power and its purpose.

The benefits of quieting the conscious rational mind, thereby stopping the constant, often *negative chatter*, became more and more obvious to me. It became apparent, that it is necessary to move beyond thinking, by that I mean relaxing the analytical mind moments at a time at first. This is essential in order for anything *now* to appear. To stop thinking does not mean we lose control and stop being. It means the opposite. When we move beyond thinking, or enter the space between thoughts, we will become *aware* of our awareness and *experience pure being.*

All of the centers are important. It is only the imbalance or blockage of these energy vortexes, an imbalance caused by our fear based thinking, which creates a corresponding attitude, which then translate into negative and hurtful emotions throwing us into stress, conflict, disease and depression, which is the opposite of harmony. How this energy coming through is modified, either creates a clear channel for spirit, or a distorted and fractured one. In this respect all depends on our own *thoughts* and *emotions*, which *create* the corresponding vibration. It stands to reason that any change in the external energy vibration must come from the *inside.*

I was taught that it is not necessary to concentrate or to dwell on these centers. These centers become naturally increasingly active and more balanced as the student progresses in spiritual awareness or awakening. Once a student is serious, and ready to embark on a spiritual path, the path of self-mastery and the path of purification, nature itself helps to clear and balance these energy channels.

As we approach this knowledge, the meaning of the 'inner light' becomes clearer. This light is trapped in all of us, located in our heart center waiting to be released, or better put, to re-connect—or to re-link with its source.

Some people see this light as a dimly burning light bulb, which needs to be polished and cleansed, to allow more light to shine through. These types of allegories are sometimes necessary to transmit information that is esoteric and so hard at first to comprehend and put into words, since all language often gets caught up in semantics. Our transformation occurs when we experience a change of heart and we *make the effort* to clean this bulb, starting with the recognition that it is our own, often limiting negative thought forms that cloud the bulb, dimming the light available. It is our responsibility to increase this light, not someone else's. This means becoming aware of being completely *responsible* for all we imagine, *think* and do.

I found some of the metaphysical concepts hard to grasp when I first read them. The same must be true for other people. The light of recognition does not always dawn instantly. I had to digest everything slowly as the truth about—'who' I really am—has revealed itself to me through experience. I am again seeing the wisdom of Einstein's words: *"Knowledge leading to wisdom is found in experience—everything else is just information."*

Our schools and universities give us only re-cycled information, but do they really educate? The word educate comes from the Latin—to draw out—not put in. This means, to teach children not **what** to think but **how** to think and in the process able to draw their own conclusions. Aren't we doing the opposite by focusing all of our attention on just cramming or putting information in?

The physical body is also a replica of the symbolic Tree of Life, once esoterically examined. Is all this knowledge shrouded in symbolism and veiled in mystery until we evolve enough to truly understand the significance of each stage of development and evolution?

Finally, the necessity of the soul needing to reincarnate over and over again in order to gather and assimilate new experiences, over many lifetimes in different circumstances, becomes clearer. Astrology, an ancient science taught by the mystics is beginning to make sense. The learning and growing process, in each incarnation experiencing the different astrological planetary influences, is beginning to dawn on my reasoning mind. Growth is obtained through the recognition of all the fractured and different aspects of human existence and human experience. Growth is the process of letting go of certain lower influences and moving towards our ultimate state, the state of perfection. Is that what you meant? Is that our purpose—therefore the struggle?

The world has given us many teachers who's sole mission it is to help us to understand this. I see you as being the perfect example for me. On that note I must leave you for today and remain,
Your grateful student, R.

Dear Dr. Schweitzer,

Earlier today, while reading a book the thought occurred to me, "Where you a mystic?" If so, I see that mystics can also be very practical and action orientated. You didn't hide in a cave and contemplate your navel... Here I am this evening, feeling the need to talk to you before falling asleep. The lessons from *Astara's Book of Life* have helped me to recognize that:

1. A scientist sees a human being composed of fluids, gases, bones, muscles, nerves and glands ONLY. They can't explain the mind, because it is not part of the brain.
A mystic knows we are spiritual beings, endowed with mental powers and the potential for God realization.
2. A scientist limits our life on earth to a certain number of years, and that's it.
A mystic declares that the mortal you becomes immortal, and shows us the way towards immortality of the soul.
3. A scientist believes you are capable of controlling your destiny in this world.
A mystic shows us the potential of controlling the destiny of our universe.
4. Science and most theologians tell us that this earthly existence is our only opportunity.
The mystic knows that our present earthly existence, our birth into it and our exit from it, is only an incident in our eternal destiny. It is only a simple mile marker on our long journey from clod to God.

5. Science is trying to tell us that the brain is the greatest instrument we possess, encompassing all our thinking mechanism.

A mystic knows that the brain is only a mass of cells acting as an *instrument or receiving station* for your mind, which is in fact the agent for the invisible and individual soul.

6. The mystic also knows that the soul is an extension of the spirit, sent down into this earthly existence, to gain and grow through the assimilation of experiences and upon graduation into its ultimate divinity, to unite again with spirit.

7. The mystic knows that the physical is just as necessary as the soul or spiritual. Ignoring the physical is like ignoring the vehicles that gets you where you need to go. Finding a proper and healthy *balance*, therefore, seems to be what we can strive for.12

Is that what is meant by the Buddha's advice: 'Find the middle road or the middle path?' The gap between the scientist and the mystic appears to be getting smaller. Science is finally catching up to what the mystics have known, experienced and written about throughout history.

According to the secret Ancient Wisdom Teachings, pleasure and pain are necessary phases in the process of evolution. Often that, which brings momentary pleasure, is the cause of later pain, such as a hangover after excessive drinking. Pain as such, serves a great purpose, because it forces us to look at ourselves, reaching for understanding of what we might have done to cause the pain, and what *we* can do to heal it. Deep sorrow or deep discontent, resulting from this pain and suffering, is our greatest teacher and is our first step towards self-realization if properly recognized.

Knowing this, I recognize that mental and emotional pain, are the necessary catalysts in our awakening process. Were it not for the warnings of these wise teachers, we would keep on violating Nature's Laws until we destroy our physical bodies. Pain gives us power, when properly understood, interpreted, used and *transmuted*.

Once I recognized and understood that my brain is not my mind, I started to wonder: "What controls my actions and behavior?" *My thoughts* of course! What controls my attitude? *My thoughts*. What controlled my moods? *My thoughts*. I then realized that **all** thoughts create. Since all thoughts are qualified or filtered through the lower or concrete mind, is my concrete or lower mind my enemy or my friend? Is it my servant or am I its slave?

If my thoughts create, then who am I? That's when the truth of my full potential hit me. *I am a creator*. I am a creator to the extent that I recognize this power. I create what I give my attention to.

This truth made me wake up and take a second look at my thoughts. Since *all thoughts create* and eventually manifest in the physical world I recognized that fearful thoughts only create negative or imperfect manifestations. By now I also knew that 'Like, attracts like'. For example, people of like-mind seem to attract each other. The saying: "Show me who your friends are, and I will know who you are", is a truism. It is the irrefutable Law of Nature, the magnetic Law of Attraction in manifestation, also known as the Law of Correspondence.

Our thoughts create our reality and our perception. Who controls my thoughts? My mind does. If thoughts create feelings, who creates these feelings? My mind does. If thoughts create disease, who creates my illness? My mind does. If thoughts create everything, what then, is responsible for all the conditions presently manifesting in my life? My mind is. In this respect I now see that my *untamed mind* is my only enemy, in that it is the **cause** of unhappiness and suffering. If that is true, then how do I recognize what I need to change my mind about?

My individual mind is a spark of the ONE mind, the Universal Mind. In a physical manifestation it is expressed or emanates as a duality, yet the ONE mind resides beyond the duality.

That's when the recognition dawned: *Is my lower mind controlling me—instead of me controlling my lower mind?* Has the time come for me to put this knowledge to use and start to change my mind about certain things? Where do I start, if not by observing my mind, my thoughts and myself? Have I only allowed the hardened concrete mind, the lower mind, to be the driver of my vehicle, instead of my higher mind, the *wiser* knowing, the *intuitive* aspect of my soul? My body is a vehicle, a vessel or instrument my soul uses to grow. My soul is the vehicle or instrument of the Spirit.

For me, the first step towards growth in consciousness and understanding is the realization that taking responsibility for *all* that happens to me is essential. I've been blessed with a certain amount of free will, the free will to choose.

Instead of cursing the darkness, I must now choose to light a candle or turn on the light switch. This is meant symbolically of course! I must make the effort to come out of the darkness of ignorance into the light of understanding and recognition. I came across this poem the other day:

Recognition
Many of us lose confidence in prayer,
because we do not recognize the answer.

We ask for strength—
    God gives us difficulties
    Through which to make us strong.
We pray for wisdom and understanding—
    God sends us problems to solve.
We plead for prosperity—
    God gives us brain and brawn
    With which to think and work.
We plead for courage—
    God gives us dangers to overcome.
We ask for favors—
    God gives us opportunities.
We ask for abundance—
    God gives us talents.
             —*Author unknown*

The word *recognize* according to my dictionary means: 'to know again; to see again, to know as existing or true; to acknowledge or treat as valid; to realize something, to acknowledge something as formally existing.'

Does the word responsibility literally mean—to respond to—my inner ability? I think about the difference of responding to something, instead of re-acting... It also means that I have only to look at myself for all the answers. Looking at myself is often painful, yet avoiding it causes even more pain and suffering. Since I recognize the inherent value and see that it is essential for my growth, I might as well get on with it!

This led me to further investigate where my thoughts were most of the day. If I am constantly thinking about what happened yesterday, which does not exist anymore, am I really present? If my thoughts are mostly focused only on the future, which is imaginary and does not exist as yet, am I really present? Am **I** out of my lower and analytical mind enough?

Why must my mind become empty in order for any insight to manifest? I see that the analytical mind certainly has its place in time and space and can't be completely discarded. However, has it become so rigid that it rejects anything new? I guess it is called the concrete mind for a reason.

Where is the 'I', I am referring to and identify with, most of the time? If my mind is not completely focused on every present *now* moment in my life, the **I**, the spiritual part of my nature, the real me, the creative part of my nature is definitely not present. Since nothing can be created in the past, because it is dead, and nothing can be created in the future, because it is imaginary, how can I create anything?

That's when I recognized that I must consciously become more *aware* and attempt to live in the now moment in order to create. What does that mean? It means that I will choose to *observe* or *witness* the workings of my lower/concrete mind, the mind that presently creates the constant chatter of my thoughts, fear and emotions—and just allow myself to be. I prefer to call it harnessing my mind, because the real me—the OBSERVER—the spiritual me—my impersonal Higher Self—which guides me through my intuition, now becomes the driver of my vehicles, instead of the other way around. Meditation is a good tool for silencing the lower mind. This new *open* state of mind allows me to become more flexible, more adaptable in recognizing the priorities of what needs to be done in every one of these *now* moments. So this is what the mystics call *transcending* the ordinary mind—a process necessary on the road to self-mastery!

The first time I started practicing sitting still for five minutes—doing absolutely nothing—I felt I was wasting time. We are so used to always doing something, thinking something, that we are afraid to be still and do nothing. It felt almost scary... I couldn't understand the value of doing nothing. Then slowly, upon entering the NOW moment of my life, I discovered a sense of comfort and peace that is hard to describe. As a matter of fact, this feeling can't be described—it must be *experienced*. It is not a *forceful* controlling of thoughts that creates this feeling, because the more you force your thoughts to be still, the more thoughts you create. I can only describe it as a gentle process of—*letting go*—surrendering—transcending the personal self often called the personality. That's when I experienced a surge of peace and energy that is hard to describe in words. Yes, words are at best an honest lie...

Dear Dr. Schweitzer, this has become a long letter and I must leave you for today. In closing I must admit, that I am gaining this recognition—the desire to know myself— very slowly, understanding it in segments, or in stages only, exploring its validity by practicing it. I began to see it as a process that is universal in nature. Also, no one served this knowledge to me on a silver platter. On the contrary, I, like you, had to search diligently for the answers to many of these questions on my own—turning inward—shining a light on my thoughts, although I give you all the credit for igniting the light in my heart. So—that's how it works? Through self-observation I eventually become my own teacher? I opened your book at random and found this:

"But what matters is not what is witty but what is true. In this case the simple thing is the truth, the uncomfortable truth with which we have to work."13

Thank you for the reminder. The beginning of all growth and understanding of truth is to start contemplating some of my deeper questions on my own. Then I watch the answers appear as the process unfolds quite naturally. Goodnight my dearest friend and teacher. Thanks to you, my eyes, my mind and heart are being opened in a fascinating new way. I am becoming more receptive to a new way of thinking and being.

It is almost midnight and time to blow out the candle I had lit in front of your picture in order to keep my attention in the now moment this evening. I wish I had more time. This is my wish, yet I have learned that wishing alone does not create more time, or more freedom, or more love and more peace. The liberation I am referring to takes recognition, understanding, courage, and a strong will. By taking full responsibility for my thoughts and actions, I found a new level of self-respect, leading me to hope and faith. Every time I live in the now moment, time seems to stand still and I experience eternity. Thank you from the bottom of my heart. I remain,

Your very grateful and devoted student, *R.*

Dear Dr. Schweitzer,

It is nearing the end of April and I have been spending a lot of my time this month in study, contemplating what I have learned and making meditation a more regular practice. I also attend the regular Friday discussion group.

H. P. Blavastsky refers to the ancient Indian Vedic scriptures and the Hermetic Laws. How did Blavatsky get all this information? She started out as a courageous seeker of higher Truth and understanding, a rebel, who just like you, dared to think for herself.

This remarkable and extraordinary woman extensively traveled the world before the turn of the century. Before coming to New York in the early 1870's she had traveled to England, France, Italy, North Africa, India, Turkey, Egypt and Tibet. In Tibet she found and read texts of ancient secret knowledge, a body of knowledge that had been hidden from the people in the West. Yes, her story is most remarkable, even heroic, considering the travel conditions at that time. She wrote and received the Ancient Wisdom Teachings from mystical spiritual Masters. Included in her vast collection of writings are books titled 'The Secret Doctrine', 'Isis Unveiled' and the book 'The Voice of the Silence'.

I started paying attention to my intuition some time ago, and the paradox of 'the voice in the silence' does not escape me. However, it has only been during the last few months, that I fully realize the positive impact this has had on my life. I started to wonder whether the 'Voice of the Silence' is my soul, my inner teacher, or the voice of Spirit. Is our intuition our direct line to the soul, guiding us through our earthly experiences? Do we become still enough to hear it? Do we listen? Is it the 'small inner voice' you often heard—even as a child? Many books have been written about this type of guidance.

As a result of the growth of my inner life, I spend more time alone. I enjoy my own company and find it very relaxing to read and to listen to good music while I learn more about these ancient mysteries. I have recognized that looking for happiness and fulfillment outside of myself is unwise and foolish.

Happiness
Is there such a thing—we all ask,
Where does it hide?
Is it in the future,
Or hidden in the past?

We search, reach and pursue—is it all in vain?
What gives us the drive,
To keep looking and looking?
Yet, finding pain, sorrow and emptiness.

For one brief moment—we almost had it.
And on and on it goes.
Like in a treadmill—the faster we run
The further it gets away.

Stand still and look around you,
There was a time—when the comforts and riches
You have now—seemed to be the answer
Is enough—ever enough?

Stop searching—and accept what IS.
Let your soul be your true guide
Trust it to help you to
Wake up!
RzT August 14, 1985

What I see, as self-focus and self-motivation, may be interpreted by some people as selfish and self-indulgent. I stopped paying attention to what other people think about me! I now know that this is not important. What is important, is that I take the time necessary to educate myself and to grow using my own volition, my own will. I now take full responsibility for the consequences of everything I create.

Pointing fingers at other people, looking at others in general, is looking in the wrong direction. No one can help me when it comes to facing myself. If that does not suit anyone else, that is not my problem. They don't have to live my life. It is not my intention to hurt anyone, but I must honor my truth, on whatever level I am experiencing this truth now.

During this time of self-discovery I stopped going to parties and social gatherings. I stopped listening to gossip and refrained from such behavior to the best of my ability, correcting myself gently but firmly. Gossip is in all cases more hurtful to the person who is engaged in gossiping, than to the person gossiped about. Yet, it is often the topic of conversation at gatherings or parties. So, I politely excuse myself from attending. As I grow stronger mentally and emotionally my circle of friends has become smaller. They tend to be people who are also interested in the journey of self-mastery and learning. They tend to be people who, like me, are searching for truth, looking to improve the quality of their lives. I even re-examine my desire for knowledge. What drives my curiosity? Where does my deep passion for knowledge and truth come from? Where is it leading me, back to myself? I must have already asked myself this question eight years ago, as part of the answer seemed to come through in this poem.

Desire
This quest for knowledge
Where does it lead?
Does it lift the—veil
Of eternity? I ponder—I read.

The Wisdom comes in stages
Not all at once
The world—my reality
Is my classroom—me—scholar or dunce?

That is my decision—I guess.
Sorting—sifting—deciding what is true
What's right, what fits—let some notions go.
My evolution—my growth—my desire to know.

Is knowing really the answer
To happiness and bliss,
Or is it the journey—the game
I've chosen not to miss—who knows?
RzT 1996

Dear Dr. Schweitzer, is the observer the same as the knower? Is it my soul? I see that the timing for this recognition is different for each and every one of us, and I have to accept that we are all evolving at a different pace. Each one of us is doing the best we can, depending on our level of growth in awareness. And yes, it is only a game where there are no winners or losers, because the experience and growth benefit both.

Why is the search for Truth at times so uncomfortable? Is it because as a truth is uncovered, we may find aspects of ourselves that we didn't expect to find, or that we are attached to a certain outcome, or have certain expectations that must now be abandoned or revised? Does truth change if we live in denial or try to twist and manipulate the outcome?

Why is it so important to have courage? Because the opposite of courage is fear and fear on any level imprisons me and limits my choices. Fear is the emotion I must confront head on, or walk through, if I ever want to experience freedom.

One day more of us will come to recognize the Reality that our present life is part of the ONE life, of which this incarnation and others to follow are only a fragment. Thank you for being my ideal and my inspiration.

Your grateful and devoted student, *R.*

Sources Chapter 7:

1   P.1 *The Light Within Us*, Albert Schweitzer
2   P.11 *The Words of Albert Schweitzer*,
     Introduction by Norman Cousins.
3   P.67 *The Words of Albert Schweitzer*, Norman Cousins.
4   P.68 *The Words of Albert Schweitzer*, Norman Cousins.
5.   P.87 *The Words of Albert Schweitzer*, Norman Cousins.
6.   P.199 *The Spiritual Life, selected writings of Albert
     Schweitzer, edited by Charles R. Joy.*
7.   P.16 The *Words of Albert Schweitzer*, Norman Cousins.
8.   P.27 Handbook to Higher Consciusness. Ken Keyes Jr.
9.   P.66-67 *Out of my Life and Thought*, Albert Schweitzer.
10. P.103 *Out of my Life and Thought*, Albert Schweitzer.
11.   P.6-7 *Indian thought and Its Development,* Albert
     Schweitzer.
12. Astara's Book of Life, Earlyne Chaney.
13. P.1 *The Light Within Us*, Albert Schweitzer.

"The purpose of existence is that we human beings, all nations and the whole of humanity, should constantly progress toward perfection. We must search for these conditions and hold fast to these ideals. If we do this, our finite spirit will be in harmony with the infinite."[1]

Albert Schweitzer

8

Growth

Dear Dr. Schweitzer,

The recordings have arrived! I listened to them yesterday and became filled with a peace that is hard to describe. I pictured you sitting at the organ and felt your energy more than at any other time. Your music is playing in the background this morning. Thank you so much!

The above quotation of your words appears at first very idealistic, yet in my heart I know it to be true. The key word jumping off the page for me is *harmony.* I see harmony in most of nature. Yet, I see disharmony and imperfection in other conditions and beings around me in the world. I see injustice. I see war. I see discontentment and disillusion. I see hunger, suffering and homelessness. You mean to say I can't look at it this way? You mean to say that the only thing that matters is that I strive to harmonize and perfect myself? That's a pretty tall order! Yet, in my heart I know this to be true. I can create change only by changing myself. I can change my mind, review my choices, and I can change my reactions to people and events. In this respect, I can begin to heal myself.

I see that you knew that it's all about me, and that the purpose of my life is to grow through my own experiences and through trial and error, through pain and suffering, which are the most powerful catalysts. Will I gain a deeper understanding of myself and eventually progress to a higher state of awareness?

It is now almost May. While collecting my thoughts this morning in order to focus my energy, I found new meaning in your words, and I quote:

"What does the word 'soul' mean? No one can give a definition of the soul. But we know what it feels like. The soul is the sense of something higher than ourselves, something that stirs in us thoughts, hopes, and aspirations which go out to the world of goodness, truth and beauty. The soul is a burning desire to breathe in this world of light and never to lose it—to remain children of light."2

Yes, we know what the soul *feels* like! This brings a smile to my face as I realize you sound just like my other teacher who is a metaphysician. You were a philosopher who studied the great minds of history. You had studied Plato, among others. Plato like you, was an inclusive thinker.

"The Platonic philosophy may be regarded as a summary of the best and noblest in Greek thought, but it should not be accepted as a mere compilation. Everywhere throughout his writings is evidence of a master intellect digesting, assimilating, and arranging, so that all ideas become part of one idea, and all knowledge becomes part of one magnificent summary. Plato was an inclusive thinker, the finest type of mind the race has yet produced. He synthesized the arts, science, philosophies, and religions, uniting them all and forming from their compound the enlightened man's philosophy of life."3

Your soul was indeed a bright light, a much needed light guiding me through life's many challenges and pitfalls. I've recognized by now, that you were what we now call a Master, a man who had many disciples. Some of your disciples got together and founded *'The Fellowship of all who are suffering'*, a fellowship which is still functioning in your name today. Your life reflects that you personified the meaning of the words 'goodness, charity, truth and beauty'.

You were a man who had learned to harmonize the physical with the spiritual or the human with the divine. In other words, you *mastered yourself*. Knowing now that this is my biggest challenge ahead, I feel inspired to do my best and follow your example by growing as much as I can in this lifetime.

In this respect I want you to know that I am a Hindu, Buddhist, Moslem, Jew and a Christian. I know that this will sound strange to some, but my religion is the religion of growth, the religion of Love and of Truth, which can be found in any one of the above teachings, once we look deep enough. And yet, I am not associated with any of the religious organizations founded based on the lives of higher beings such as Krishna, Gautama, Mohammed, Abraham or Jesus. Organizations and institutions seem to take on a life of their own. They often obliterate or loose track of their original purpose. What could that purpose be? I see that the original experience of a prophet can and must be experienced by each and everyone. It surely won't be exactly the same experience, because each of us is so different in our constitution and each of us is on a different level of awareness.

Each of the teachings, once deeply examined and used for contemplation, will lead us to an inner transformation. To me that is the true meaning of religion. Sadly many people today have lost track of its true purpose and the full extent of its meaning.

If any one of the earlier mentioned organized religions preach that they are right and all others are wrong, they are not for me. If they are trying to recruit me to their way of thinking, they are not for me. If they instill fear and separation, they are not for me. If they threaten hellfire and brimstone they are not for me. Those religious organizations are not telling the truth and are therefore not going to serve my needs. I feel I've been indoctrinated long enough and need to stand up for myself and think for myself. I must search out and test for myself what is right and true for me. I have chosen the eclectic route, exposing myself to many different teachings, analyzing and digesting ideas of value and letting the rest go.

Languishing in the belief that religious leaders, or theologians, have all the answers already and are therefore exclusively 'right' makes no sense to me. That is too much like the blind leading the blind.

It is the height of arrogance and ignorance to think that God resides only in temples or churches, calling these edifices 'Houses of God'. What people call God is in everyone and in everything. The

Creative Source or First Cause we call God is nothing, meaning NO THING or the UNKNOWN

The God as described in the Old Testament is vengeful, judgmental, envious and full of other human qualities. Therefore, he is not the Power I am referring to. Taking the Bible too literally can be most confusing. The Bible is part history and part metaphysics and will only make sense once we recognize that it describes a process—namely the process of first recognizing, then harmonizing our lower nature. That certainly is the message I see in the New Testament, as it describes the struggle of the soul.

In this sense I see God is not a being. I see God as BEING. God is neither male nor female, but the perfect harmony of both. It is an energy, a will-to-live that is all-inclusive. It wants everything that exists, to grow up and flourish. The nature of God can be seen in a tree, in the miracle of a flower, in a sunrise or a sunset, in the rhythm of the ocean, in the sand on the shore and in the birds. It is seen in the beauty that surrounds us, in the mountains, rivers and plains. I can see it in my grandchildren's eyes! It is seen in our will to live, and is therefore in all that exists in all of life. Therefore your 'Reverence of Life' expresses the unity I feel at the present moment. Isn't that what Plato's philosophy reveals as well? Plato was born in 428 B. C. and died in 347 B. C.

"Plato's philosophy surrounds the principle of unity. To him the concept of unity was all-pervading, everywhere present and evident. Division was illusion. To accept a philosophy of division was ignorance. Unity was reality and the doctrine of unity was truth. Ignorance sees many separate things in the world; wisdom sees only the many parts of one thing. God, man, and the universe are related fragments of a common unity. This concept is true monotheism, for monotheism is more than admitting the existence of one life of which all things are part. All learning, then, is the study of relationships. It is not the analysis of isolated natures but rather the coming to understand the part that each plays in the drama of the whole. "Plato's concept of God is moral rather than physical. To him God is truth, the fact or the reality which sustains the universe. Unity, or oneness, is the evidence of truth, even as law is the evidence of intelligence. Whatever truth does must be unity or oneness, for truth cannot be parent of diversity. What we call diversity is merely an infinite process in unity which we do not understand."[4]

Yes, I am a rebel when it comes to organized religion! Trying to confine this essence and reducing it to a personality and to a form of idol worship makes no sense to me. It seems to encourage the belief, that God is something outside myself. If this makes me an iconoclast, so be it!

If the earlier mentioned houses of worship instill a sense of deep reverence, in other words, *re-link* humanity with its true nature—its soul—and help all people to be self-reliant, it will serve them. However, if it becomes pure indoctrination and idol worship, I can't see the value. Each religion appears to teach the *'exoteric'* wisdom only, giving us an overview and in the process gets *enchanted* with its own dogma, tradition or belief system. The *esoteric* meaning and its essence is discovered by those who seek, those who want to discover. It seems to be reserved for those individuals who have developed mentally and emotionally enough to be able to use and apply this higher knowledge, having recognized the unity of all and applying the wisdom gained for the good and growth of all.

Underlying every religion can be found a deeper truth, revealing the meaning and purpose for being on this planet. Our purpose seems to be to discover that we can harmonize or unite with the divine. If God is the Cause of creation, then we are all co-creators of life.

We also create, all the time, without being consciously aware of it. Every one of our thoughts creates our reality. Is it our mission to recognize that we can evolve? Could it be that we must become the agents of our own transformation?

Throughout history, many different teachers have told us this over and over again. For me Gautama and Jesus are true examples of this teaching. You were one of the souls who understood and responded to their profound and timely message. It is the message that we must heal ourselves; the message of transformation through purification of thought energy; thus becoming able to see unity beyond the manifested duality, teaching us the harmony of all that exists. I see you, Gautama and Jesus as the healers of humanity's psyche or physicians of the soul. Both were once human and accomplished a most difficult feat. Jesus in his life demonstrated the struggle of the soul and He, like you, came to show us what is possible.

He also taught that our mental, emotional and spiritual evolution is our responsibility. It must occur through our own volition. Didn't Jesus often remind us of the transitory nature of this material world?

Seen in this light all experiences are important. They are only labeled as good or bad by us, due to a lack of perception, when in reality they are our tools for learning and growing. It is only through *struggle* that we grow. These experiences can't be labeled good or bad. After all it is only through experience that we awaken our *feelings*, allowing us to look at our physical, emotional and mental states. Who said, "There is no good or bad—only thinking makes it so?"

Jesus' mission was to awaken the ***feeling*** of love. He encouraged us to look at ourselves differently. Is this the first step? Only then, can we feel for others and help others? I can only share what I've learned, by being an example, which is all a teacher can do.

The thought of becoming a teacher is frightening to me, I prefer to call it becoming a facilitator, yet at the same time I couldn't think of anything more rewarding, anything I would rather do, knowing and *feeling* the suffering that exists in the world today. How will this lofty goal of mine be accomplished? I have no idea at the present moment. I go to work each day, until the universe and circumstances show me that I am ready and prepared to branch out into something new and different. Until then I must walk the path, create more inner harmony or balance and heal myself.

I have a question... As I grow in awareness will I eventually transcend my shyness, which is nothing but fear of rejection and fear of disapproval? Will I eventually understand that what I have to share may be more important than my shyness? Will it simply disappear? How many souls out there are ready to understand the creative power inherent in all of us and how many are prepared to express their creative ability in this lifetime? Haven't we all been blessed with this precious gift? All I now ask for is guidance. I deepen my faith knowing that the answers will appear as soon as I am ready for my next challenge.

Doing the best I know how to do each day, each moment without judging, comparing or condemning myself for not having gained more knowledge and awareness, is my present focus. I accept that 'my best' will change from day to day, depending on my level of energy. I find that as soon as I accept myself completely, the way I am today, my awareness grows.

The process of growth and maturing can't be forced or rushed. Shining a light on my weaknesses and tendencies, and exposing them, has helped me a lot. Only by becoming aware of them can I hope to change anything. I now see others differently as well, in that they are just like me—searching. Every time I start to criticize the splinter in someone's eye, I immediately see the log in my own. I can forgive others, who are just like me suffering from the same sense of separation and fear—to the degree that I forgive myself. Once I am gentle with myself it is much easier to be gentle with others.

Everything around me is in a constant state of change. As I observe nature, I see that a flower can't grow without changing. Furthermore, nothing in nature can grow without light! This brings me to examine your study of the German poet, Goethe. You greatly admired this man and his work. He left a body of work behind that is filled with personal insight and wisdom. His art was a child of his phosophy.

Goethe was not only a great writer and poet, but also a scientist. He, like Waldo Emerson, was a man who found enlightenment by studying nature. What did he find, and what does it have to do with our human nature and growth? Can we see ourselves reflected in nature? Since the same universal principles must apply to everything, in order to be true, I dare to examine this theory. In 'Conversations of Goethe' he talks about the conditions required for an oak to grow to its fullest potential:

"Thus, the oak may be very beautiful; but how many favorable circumstances must occur before Nature can succeed in producing one truly beautiful! If an oak grow in the midst of a forest, encompassed by large neighboring trunks, its tendency will always be upwards, towards free air and light; only small weak branches will grow on its sides, and these will in the course of a century decay and fall off. But if it has at last succeeded in reaching the free air with its summit, it will then rest in its upward tendency, and begin to spread itself from its sides, and form a crown. But it is by this time already past its middle age; its many years of upward striving have consumed its freshest powers, and its present endeavor to put forth its strength by increasing in breadth will not now have its proper results. When full grown, it will be high, strong, and slender stemmed, but still without such a proportion between its crown and its stem as would render it beautiful."

"Again, if the oak grow in a moist marshy place, and the earth is too nourishing, it will, with proper space, prematurely shoot forth many branches and twigs on all sides: but it will still want the opposing, retarding influences; it will not show itself gnarled, stubborn, and indented; and, seen from a distance, it will appear a weak tree of the lime species; it will not be beautiful—at least, not as an oak."

"If, lastly, it grow upon a mountainous slope, upon poor stony soil, it will become excessively gnarled and knotty; but it will lack free development: it will become prematurely stunted, and will never attain such perfection that one can say of it, 'There is an oak something that creates astonishment'."

"A sandy soil, or one mixed with sand," continued Goethe, "where the oak is able to spread its strong roots in every direction, appears to be most favorable; and then it needs a situation with the necessary space to feel the effects on all sides of light, sun, rain and wind. *If it grows up snugly sheltered from wind and weather, it becomes nothing; but a century's struggle with the elements makes it strong and powerful, so that, at its full growth, its presence inspires us with astonishment and admiration.*"5 (My Italics)

After contemplating the above, I see that you fall into the category of *strong and powerful*, having been able to spread your roots by growing up in a most suitable home environment. And further that this environment was *self-created* from the age of twenty-one, although you were a *free* thinker long before that age. You indeed became the beautiful oak!

Can the same also be applied to all human beings, considering the conditions of our early environment or circumstances? Can I identify myself with a tree? Didn't I compare myself earlier to a plant that was root bound? As a matter of fact I did and used this analogy, writing a poem in 1996 in which I compare myself to a tree. Something for me to reflect on!

The potential in each acorn is the same. However, depending on the circumstances and environment in which it is placed, each tree, in its struggle to survive will show different results. Growth, in this respect, means years and years of the right conditions, which in human affairs is not always possible. Is that where our will comes in? Is that why we humans often don't start to grow until we have reached middle age or a certain age of maturity? Do we, like the tree in nature, grow stronger by having weathered many storms?

You exhibited a very strong will at an early age. Not all of us have our will this strongly developed during the early years. When you *knew* something, and it felt right to you, you did not budge from your position. That's why I often refer to you as an old or great soul.

I see growth as an assimilation of learning in stages, whereby we grow through struggles and opposition, becoming stronger and wiser gives us the opportunity to recognize not only our talents, but use the struggles as an opportunity to grow into more ethical, more harmless human beings. This kind of growth gives us the courage and the endurance needed to evolve.

Growth is not becoming more of something, it is becoming aware of our hidden potential, followed by *acting* on the passions arising out of our deepest nature. Could our life's purpose be to reach our fullest potential? Is a divine plan already in place?

Our uniqueness, our individuality and our talents are often hidden or covered up. Just like the seed of a flower, or the acorn, we must allow the protective covering to fall away naturally in order for our powerful potential to sprout. Just like the oak we must spread our roots deep and nurture them. All young roots are fragile, but already contain the *will-to-live,* the will to survive. This phenomenon can be seen in all of nature once we taker a closer look. You and Goethe, have given me a new appreciation and a new view of nature as a whole.

Nature, in order to grow needs soil, light, air and water. Seeds will only grow in the right conditions. The same is true for animals and for humans. However, we are one step ahead of the domestic animal in our evolution in that we have developed *self-consciousness*, the power to reason, the power of discernment and the power to choose.

What else is necessary for growth? Why were we born with a mind that is connected to a higher level? How do we use this mind?

Self-inquiry and quiet contemplation seem to be a necessary ingredient. Shedding light on the nature of our consciousness—our being will lead us to questions such as, 'What is truth? What is Light? What is consciousness?'

"To see the world in a grain of sand, and heaven in a wild flower, hold infinity in the palm of your hand and eternity in an hour."
William Blake

Writing to you has been helpful in that my own words lead me to a deeper understanding and a new way of seeing.

Admittedly, I have experienced only a small part of this wisdom and know that I have a long way to walk on the path. I also see the path ahead as becoming a bit narrower and steeper. Along the way, I find that striving for materialistic values and the glamour often associated with outside appearances, have lost its attraction for me. They have become a burden on my path. Is that what is meant by 'letting go' along the way? What is meant by renunciation? Isn't it simply outgrowing something that does not serve me anymore? The 'way', is becoming clearer to me each day. I am reminded of the ancient teaching: "The student grows in daily increments—'The Way' is found by daily loss." In other words the way is found by letting go of more and more fears and attachments, or a false sense of security, on every level of our being, physical, emotional and mental.

At first this appears paradoxical. Yet, it is steeped in truth—the truth that once the light of understanding reaches a certain level of intensity, the process increases. Just like the paradox: 'In order to find yourself, you first have to loose yourself' or, 'The more you give away—the more you receive.' What I am learning is very reminiscent of what you called renunciation. You became less and less attached to the material world, and did not value social standing the way we do. Contribution and sharing, in the way of love, compassion, clear thought and understanding, education and service were the priorities in your life. None of these values can be categorized as material ones.

I found myself attracted to this greeting card the other day:

"To study the way is to study the self. To study the self is to forget the self. To forget the self is to be awakened with all thing."

Dogan

Right now I see this as transcending the personal self, laying aside the mask of the personality, and thereby experiencing *pure being*. It reminds me of a statement attributed to Jesus: "Those who loose their life will find it." Your work shows that you had experienced this state. This transcendental state was studied and explored by Plato, Kant, Spinoza, Leibniz, Fichte, Nietzsche and Schopenhauer. They were philosophers whose work you had studied. You sought and found your own philosophy and Truth by adopting a more encompassing view, the all-inclusive philosophy of '*Reverence for Life*'.

Who else inspired you during your student years? The knowledge and wisdom of transcendence had been around and taught in the East for many centuries before we acknowledged it in the West. J. Krishnamurti was a contemporary teacher who fully understood this wisdom and spent his life trying to help us open our hearts and minds. So, we are only re-discovering the thread that binds East and West together. It has always existed as part of the Ageless Wisdom Teaching in India, China, Tibet, Egypt and in the philosophy of ancient Greece. It was known then as:

"Know thyself...and you will know God."

Pythagoras

On that note I will stop for today as I contemplate the deeper meaning of this wisdom. I remain as always,
Your devoted and grateful student, K.

Dear Doctor Schweitzer,

Something rather extraordinary happened to me during this last week, and I feel the need to tell you about this incident. It started this way...

The other day at work, I noticed a sign over the computer in the receiving area for our rugs. As I glanced up I saw this crudely hand written sign.

GREAT minds...   discuss IDEAS.
AVERAGE minds... discuss EVENTS.
SMALL minds...   discuss PEOPLE.

I immediately thought about you, Dr. Schweitzer, and about your friends. People like Einstein, and the great minds throughout history such as Pythagoras, Socrates, Plato, Goethe, Emerson, Blake, Ghandi and Blavastky.

I promptly asked someone: "Who wrote this sign?" followed by: "How long has this sign been here?" No one knew the answer to my question, but all agreed it has been there ever since the store opened. In other words, this sign has been there for the last five years. Yet, I had never noticed it before this day.

What happened next is even more extraordinary! I received an invitation to a typical house party, an invitation I would normally politely decline. I am not blessed with the gift of making idle conversation nor do I have the talent for empty chit-chat. As a matter of fact, I often found myself cutting these conversations very short. I don't feel very comfortable at large gatherings, where the general topic more often than not revolves around furnishings, what the neighbor's house sold for, clothing styles, food, gossip and the weather. This time however, I decided it was too much trouble to think up an excuse, knowing intuitively I would hurt the feelings of our friend, the hostess. The party was last Sunday night. In order for you to understand the complete picture and circumstance, in which I found myself, I will give you a little history about a mutual acquaintance.

I had been avoiding a relationship with this particular person, because of her strange, jealous, envious and manipulative behavior towards others, including the harassment of a beautiful and kind coworker. I had already understood that her problems were rooted in deep emotional disturbances not obvious or detectable at first glance. On several occasions I found myself advising others to ignore her comments and behavior. This person's inner disturbance had manifested as a disease we call bulimia.

A week or so ago she announced her engagement to a former boyfriend, whom she had left standing at the altar a year or so ago. She had described him in very unflattering terms, such as boring and stingy. Now, this is a woman with a strong need to be the *center of attention,* As a matter of fact, someone had labeled her a 'materialistic drama queen', because she was so deeply impressed by social standing, glamour and pined for all the outer trappings of material wealth. A few weeks ago she announced that she would be getting married to her old boyfriend, the one she had left at the altar. She proudly returned to work displaying a huge diamond on her finger.

Guess who became the center of our attention and gossip at the party I attended? As we were gossiping I was reminded of the sign I had read two days before. I started to think and focus on how this discussion could be turned into an idea—a learning process— instead of hurtful negative gossip.

When I expressed my feelings of compassion for her a whole new topic of conversation was introduced. I drew attention to the fact that her kind of behavior is a sickness caused by deep insecurities, manifesting as mental and emotional disturbances. This sickness is based on fear, lack of self-esteem, lack of self-respect, lack of self-reliance and lack of self-love. Instead of looking at her, I suggested we look at ourselves. Are we any better or any different? Aren't we all more or less avoiding the issue of self-reliance? Are we looking for a husband to provide it all and do it all for us? Aren't we all looking outside of ourselves for happiness? Aren't we all trying to fill the empty void inside with material things? I saw from the group's reaction, that I had hit the nail on the head. Some in this group started to have compassion for her and her condition.

As you can imagine, this turned into a very interesting evening after all, and I was glad I had attended the party. My intuition had told me not to cancel, and I didn't know why at the time. Is this how everyday experiences are used as tools for our awakening? The person in question became my catalyst, helping me to see the symptoms of our general dis-ease more clearly.

In order to grapple with the idea of perfection, I am using my analytical mind to solve this problem. In such situations, either problem solving or growth, I like to use the analogy of getting from A to B. **A** being the lower mind and **B** being the Higher Mind. How is that accomplished?

Let's say I have identified **A** as *fear* and *ignorance* resulting in disease and lack of wisdom, and **B** is its opposite, which is *love and wisdom* resulting in health, energy, and growth, how do I get from **A** to **B**? Reason tells me that I must first *identify* **A**. I must take a look at it or shine the light of my awareness on it. What are the emotions or vibrations of **A**?

The next morning, I got up and wrote down a list of the symptoms of the disease, as we had discussed it that evening. Here is a partial list of what I have labeled as 'the symptoms of **A**', (the problem). I thought you might be interested, since you were a medical doctor.

Fear	Ignorance
Blame	Pride
Self-pity	Prejudice
Anger	Ingratitude
Jealousy	Competition

Manipulation	Self-righteousness
Greed	Possessiveness
Arrogance	Cruelty
Gossip	Control
Envy	Violence

As I look at this list, I see it as clearly representing the emotions of our lower self, driven by instinct, fear, comparison, competition and survival only. This low vibration is often called our animal nature.

I feel that all of the above symptoms can be summed up under the first two words on my list—*ignorance and fear*. None of the above mentioned states of mind correspond with a state we call **Love**. Yet, we expect others to be different. We are all suffering from the same symptoms.

All of the above vibrations or emotions are created by the lower or untamed mind, and all create the feeling of separation and conflict, which is the opposite of wisdom and harmony. These feelings in turn create the illusion of being alone and frightened in the world. They create the 'me vs. them' perception or fight and flight mentality. It is a state of mind or attitude born of fear. This fear is not real, yet we give it power and hold on to it, allowing it to feed our many false perceptions. This false notion is encouraged and fueled by our lower ego and results in our erroneous sense of identity. We are robbing ourselves of wisdom and power in the process.

An example of early conditioning by an unaware parent can be observed as soon as a child starts to think. By putting competitive thoughts into a child's head we force and encourage him or her to evaluate or judge something that does not need to be judged or evaluated. The other day I witnessed an incident that illustrates what I mean by early conditioning.

On the 2nd day of pre-Kindergarten a parent, while just making 'harmless' conversation asks a four year old girl: "Which teacher do you like better, Miss Smith or Miss Brown?" We choose our words carelessly and instill thoughts of comparison that are very unjust, not based on truth, thus conditioning the child at an early age to compare others. Even more harmful, the child will learn to compare him or herself to others. The question arises, 'Is this kind of comparison creating competition healthy?'

Dear Dr. Schweitzer, is this how the sins (ignorance) of the father or mother can get transposed to the innocent child? Is this how our fallacious thinking creates and perpetuates wrong beliefs? Therefore, such a comparison is unhealthy, creating an unhealthy attitude towards others where none had existed before. It is always something in us that makes us dislike or like another. It is never **them.** We might as well teach children early, even if **our** parents failed to do so. Two wrongs don't make it right!

This is just a small example of how 'harmless' conversation turns into subtle conditioning forming the *future beliefs* of a child. We put thoughts into a small child's mind, thoughts they would not have entertained on their own. But how can a parent know this, if he or she is unaware, thriving on and nurturing a deeply competitive nature in him or herself? As you can see I am very passionate about the subject of conditioning, also when it concerns religious conditioning. We listen to opinions as if they were truth. While in fact they are just opinions, based on our parent's opinions and their parent's opinions. Until people become wise and increase their own awareness, allowing them to break these insidious habits of fallacious thinking, nothing will change in this world.

While on the subject of erroneous thinking, I must tell you that we are paying athletes millions of dollars, while teachers, who are so instrumental in forming the minds and thoughts of our young children—the future generation—are being paid a pittance. Isn't it a reflection of how much we collectively value education, since we *are* society? It looks like we have that backwards too! My question is this: 'Is it appropriate to voice my feelings in situations like this?' When is it appropriate to speak and when is it appropriate to be silent? Is it loving to speak out, or is it unkind? Thank God, I have you to talk to!

What I learned from this evening is that we always recognize the faults and flaws in others first, not knowing that they exist in us in equal measure. Only by becoming aware of this fact do we have the ability to change ourselves. On that note I will close my conversation with you today. I have a lot of new insight to digest and look forward to writing to you tomorrow.

Your devoted and grateful student, *R.*

Dear Dr. Schweitzer,

It's been a week that I will remember. Everywhere I found tests of my small ego. I observed how strong and courageous I have to be in order to talk, as I risk being ridiculed for my new attitude. It is best to speak only when it is appropriate or when asked. There is no such thing as constructive criticism. To embarrass someone is not my intent. This does not make me feel superior, on the contrary I am beginning to feel compassion for people who are on a train, and don't know where they are going! I got off that train some time ago. So did you.

Sorry to let my frustrations enter a good conversation... Talking about trains, I remember that you always insisted on traveling 3rd class on a train. And when asked why, you answered, "Because there is no 4th class on this train". I now understand why and would have enjoyed the pleasure of your company, riding in 4th class together! Knowing this has freed me of any frustration or ego related imagined hurts I may have entertained for a while. The need to be right is slowly dissipating, furthermore I can't change others, but I can change myself.

Where was I? Oh yes, I remember—I talked about the symptoms of our collective dis-ease. It is a dis-ease our small ego likes to hold on to, because it seems to be so much easier than to *struggle against the tide* of commonly held opinions.

Our small ego—the false sense of **I**—is in full control of our mind, therefore, it stands to reason that it controls our emotion and our physical body as well. Since the mind influences the physical body to a larger extent than we currently admit, what results do we expect? What results manifest in our physical and emotional body? How do we unchain ourselves from these self-defeating influences? I have discovered that by silently observing my own thoughts I increase my awareness. It's as if a flashlight has been used illuminating a situation. For some this can be painful at first, but slowly a transformation occurs, as we begin to see with our inner eye.

Our intuition begins to tell us to take full responsibility for our hurtful and separating thoughts—which are the chains—of our own creation! That's when we realize we have the inner potential to set ourselves free, by becoming detached from the outcome of our addictive struggling. We can still prefer one outcome to another, but we are not addicted or attached to the results of our labors. By letting go of all manipulations, we allow others to be, without losing our own integrity. There comes a time when agreeing to disagree seems to be the only solution.

We begin to be guided by an inner expanded awareness that everything is exactly the way it is supposed to be for our maximum learning. That's when we become aware of the wisdom of letting go! We begin to relax, seeing the beauty and perfection of it all.

The offices of psychiatrists and psychologists are filled with people who have spent their whole life blaming someone else or something outside of themselves for the challenges they are faced with in this life. They have relinquished their power by not realizing that their individual strength can only be found by examining themselves. Why are some people so scared to look at themselves? It is painful? Yes, in this respect truth is painful, or as you put it—uncomfortable... However, what is pain and discomfort, if not a wake-up call?

If the above vibrations are self-created and represent our lower nature steeped in ignorance and fear, what then are the corresponding opposite vibrations of our Higher nature, the ethical virtues seen as **B**, our soul vibrations?

Upon reviewing this list I actually sat down and wrote all the opposite emotions, indicative of a higher state of mind, or a higher vibration, a state we often equate with *love*. I like to call them the divine attributes. The most prominent ones are: Love, Humility, Joy, Courage, Gratitude, Justice, Charity, Generosity, Non-attachment, Respect, Sharing, Integrity, Truthfulness, Self-respect, Tolerance, Patience, Understanding, Appreciation, Serenity, Compassion, Peace of mind and the desire to serve.

Some will say these are unrealistic ideals, yet in my heart I know that we **all** already possess these qualities, in varying degrees. However, we spend a great deal of time dwelling on the opposite and giving it our energy. The first step, the way I see it, must be to recognize and *expose* **A**.

Will shining a light on and becoming aware of the destructive and hurtful symptoms create a change in my state of mind, in my heart, and in my consciousness? Will it eventually result in different reactions, followed by different actions? I see now that *I am presented with a choice.*

I see my **soul vibration** as one of *wisdom, unselfishness and love.* While feeding into the fear based vibrations we have to honestly acknowledge being in a competitive rat race where there are no winners, and admit to being a part of, and contributing to the general problem. Instead of becoming part of the solution, we keep on supplying thoughts with energy that have created the problem, *exhibiting* not knowing who we really are. In Einstein's words: "Applying the same solutions to problems and expecting a different result is insanity."

Our soul *responds* to and *resonates* to a higher level of vibration. It stands to reason then, that we have to tune in to this higher vibration in order to create harmony, first in our own lives, and then in our world.

How can we expect love, gratitude, freedom, consideration and respect if we don't value and nurture these qualities in ourselves first and then give them freely?

As I awaken to this truth, I recognize the limiting nature of false beliefs. Negative emotions are created nowhere else but in our own mind. Our old thought patterns and conditioning have forged habits that are hard to break. As I grow-up and reach the stage of maturity, I must take full responsibility for my thoughts, feelings and emotions, because I now recognize them as my own creation and the product of false thinking, often based on the limited perception of my mind. Many of my intellectual pursuits give me information and make me smart, but they don't make me wise.

I now see that gossip, for instance, does not only hurt the person gossiped about, it is more damaging to the person who gossips. That's what I mean by *reverse* or *fallacious* thinking. Do we have everything else backward as well?

It's not about how many people like me, the question must be, how do I like myself? It is not about how many people are devoted to me—what it boils down to is—do I have self-devotion? It's not about seeking the approval of others—it's about having self-approval. It's not about seeking the respect of others—it's about gaining and nurturing self-respect. It's not about how many people love me—the question becomes—do I love and appreciate myself? Do I love myself enough to pay attention to what I think and how I feel at all times? That's when a revelation took place! How can I love my neighbor, if I don't love myself? How can I give something I don't possess? Do I have a choice?

The choice only presents itself, once I have the *awareness* that I am creating my own suffering. Until then I do not have a choice! All I am able to do is run on my previous pattern of old thoughts and programming, based on old superstitions and old beliefs, showing that I do not know who I truly am.

At times I get a glimpse of the self-created prison we are in. A prison that has been created by our beliefs and conditioning. Not only are we in a prison, but we have become our own prison wardens, because no one keeps us there but our lower self. In order to be able to free myself, I must first become aware of the fact that I am *not* free.

Plato in his '*Republic*', in chapter 7, uses a myth to instruct his students. He described our state as being chained to a chair in a dark cave with the light coming from behind. We sit and stare at the wall watching the shadows that the light has created. That's all we know, therefore we make no effort to remove the chains, turn around and see what is really going on in the light. We are not aware that there is another way, having gotten so used to our state of bondage. Thus we begin to see that we are chained by our own fears and ignorance. I love these myths and see that they are teaching tools he used to explain Universal Principles. That's the beauty of myth. Are there Cosmic Myths and human myths?

Although we can be prompted from the outside, in the final analysis, the desire and impetus to change can only occur from within. Therefore, any help offered must be in response to a request for help, otherwise the effort of the teacher or helper is seen as interference and it becomes counterproductive.

If you had done nothing else for me other than to lead me to the recognition that we, individually and collectively are suffering from *wrong or fallacious thinking*, reminding me that a new attitude, a shift in thinking is needed, this would have been enough. You have given me *one* of the keys to unlock the door to one of the greatest secrets, a key that partially unlocks the mystery of our existence and being. This key unlocks the door leading to freedom from outgrown sentimental attachments, suffering and sorrow. We do have a choice. Freedom is a choice. Self-reliance is a choice. Love is a choice.

As a victim, I allow other people and society as a whole to control me. As a victim I surrender my own power. In this sense there are no victims there are only volunteers. Who was it that said: "I looked for the enemy and found it was me?"

My freedom and independence can only become possible if I make the *effort* to know and understand myself. As I seek wisdom and growth through self-knowledge and self-observation I begin to recognize that this power is inherent in all of us. True inner freedom, and true power is found in the recognition of this basic and fundamental Truth. The questions then become: 'How can I align myself with the higher vibration of my true or higher Self—my soul—and thereby connect to my Higher Power, the spiritual aspect of my nature?' 'How can I create a healthy balance between my lower ego and my Higher Ego?'

Suffering
Pain—how we avoid it
Not knowing its true purpose.
How crucial and necessary
The suffering is for our growth.

Let go—the desire to control
Expecting complete devotion.
A cloudy mind—the pain,
Caused by untamed emotion?

Get into the suffering—don't run...
Feel the sensation
It will have been worth it
Your opportunity—at last—has come!

Revelations? Yes, indeed...
Take the moment and try—try to be still
Listen—what is the lesson
Your Karma?

The world is not perfect
Neither are you—accept what is!
Use this opportunity—to gain understanding
Flow with the winds of change.

Pain—oh, how it can misguide you
Trying to justify selfish satisfaction
Don't blame—don't run—use it
To set yourself free—that's what I've done!
RzT Aug 1985

What about the mental, emotional pain we all experience? Your books on philosophy bear witness to the fact, that you had examined the subject of consciousness. What had you learned by studying the mind of Jesus? For your doctoral thesis you presented the faculty of your university with a paper called, *'The Psychiatric Study Of Jesus'*. You explored the mind of this teacher of mankind by studying the words attributed to him. Was he sane or was he crazy? Did he suffer from hallucinations, paranoia and schizophrenic delusions? You had explored the idea of Jesus' sanity and proved to yourself that he was sane. *We* are the ones who still suffer from the delusion and illusion of being separate! We are the creators of our own misery... and he tried to show us the way out! The great Master teacher kept reminding us that the Kingdom of God is not to be found in the material world it is only found inside! I guess we weren't listening or decided to look in the wrong direction. How can we 'listen' when we are so busy talking and trying to be right all the time? Ah, yes our ego! I can't find God through the intellect or by performing mental gymnastics. I can't find God through my emotions or through religious ceremonies. I can only find God by entering the silence within!

All suffering stops, once we *think correctly,* or better yet transcend thinking and see situations as they *really* are, seeing beyond the illusion and waking up to the experience of a deeper and more profound Reality. All suffering stops once we 'let go' of false beliefs, stop making assumptions, ask questions and take responsibility for our own thoughts, perhaps for the first time in our lives. Why are we running through life constantly re-acting in a knee jerk fashion, instead of responding calmly and appropriately, if a response is required, that is... Controlling our reactions is not easy, but it is very essential that we do it. Do we insist on being right all the time? Are our 'opinions' worth more than the 'opinions' of others? By trying to be right all the time aren't we creating more suffering for others and ourselves? You have shown me that opinions are not Truth. Why? Because they change from moment to moment and from day to day! Truth does not change...

As a perfect example of what happens when I compare myself to someone else I must look back to the early 1990's. By then I had read some of your books, and I remember going through a phase of feeling depressed and helpless as I compared myself to you. You see what the mind is capable of creating when allowed to run unchecked? I tell you this now, because I only recognized this phenomena in hindsight. Instead of focusing on being grateful for what I was learning, seeing that there is hope for me, at times I chose to focus on all the things I lacked, such as a formal education, musical talents, money etc. etc. During these times of depression I focused on what I didn't have, falling pray to fear and the victim mentality. What did it do for me? It kept me stuck and I felt numb for a long time. Was this phase necessary? Yes, seen in a new light, it was all absolutely necessary. Depression is often our great wake-up call. Instead of giving up, I continued studying your life and rereading your words. I started to get a glimmer of hope for myself and the rest of humanity. I saw that you seemed to know what I was experiencing and I began to feel that you were speaking to me with love and compassion. Your words led me to ask myself many questions about myself.

The judge and critic inside each of us is powerful, governed and controlled by our small ego—our lower fearful self, justifying every manipulative and destructive thought. We constantly compare ourselves to others, not realizing that this creates unhappiness and suffering. Do we stop to think deeply about this phenomenon and that this state of unhappiness is self-induced?

People who suffer from the symptoms strongly enough will sooner or later end up in the care of a physician or psychiatrist. Unable to face this truth and unwilling to find the answers on our own through self-observation, we willingly accept a prescription of pills, often sedative in nature. Most psychological disorders arise when a patient finds himself alienated and isolated, caused by the *me vs. them* attitude. This disorder is based on fear and is often the cause of depression. The end result is the manifestation of disease, since every cell in our body responds to our mind and our thoughts.

Children, who have lived through the divorce of their parents, feel a sense of abandonment. While they are in the dependent stage of development, they don't understand as yet that both parents love them, and that a split of partnership has nothing to do with them. Some will become stronger out of this kind of experience and some will spend the rest of their lives blaming their parents for their attitude and outlook. This kind of co-dependency stems from living in the past and a deep neediness, which is often then transferred to their children and partner. And so the cycle of blame continues...

Furthermore, does labeling this thought pattern as dysfunctional allows us continue to blame our parents or some other authority figure in our lives for our problems? Blaming someone else is looking in the wrong direction! No one is responsible for my thoughts but me. This blame game has to stop, because it does not help anyone. It is shifting the responsibility to another party, when it is basically our own creation.

Another example of *fallacious thinking* is the excuse some people who are suffering often employ. It's the excuse of blaming their parents, saying, "I didn't choose to be born, you brought me into this world—I am your responsibility." When in truth, it is our soul's need to grow which attracts us to be born to the parents, the location, and the circumstances that will afford our soul the maximum learning experiences. Our parents did the best they could under the circumstances and based on their level of awareness. Constantly looking back is only rearranging the dust. It accomplishes nothing. Some things we just have to learn to accept. Any change in attitude can only occur in the present. First we must realize that we have the power to change.

This view shifts the responsibility, shifts our thinking, followed by a better understanding of how the *Law of Nature works*. I learned that nature's impersonal response, the law of cause and effect, spares no one. It is the impersonal law of action and re-action we often call karma (deed).

In the more advanced stage these symptoms will eventually manifest in physical diseases, created by our own thought process. It seems as though our Higher nature, represented by the values of **B**, is present in each of us lying dormant like a sleeping giant.

Our soul, having an earthly experience, is working on *freeing* itself. Like a butterfly leaving its cocoon, it will eventually reflect the image of the Higher Self. Slowly outgrowing my old thought patterns by allowing them to become the catalyst is my first step towards a higher awareness and my first step towards freedom. This transformation is best seen in nature by observing the metamorphosis of a butterfly. A caterpillar can't be a caterpillar and a butterfly at the same time. However, the caterpillar already has the spark of 'butterflyness' inside his being. He is already programmed to fly, but doesn't know it while he is still a caterpillar. I guess the butterfly, just like us, is in a state of ignorance at a certain point in its development. I will review and study, perhaps meditate on this process in nature known as 'metempsychosis' during the next few days.

What a revelation for me! Would I have had this revelation, had I not attended the party? I don't know... Perhaps the opportunity to learn the same lesson would have come on another occasion.

It could be said that a shock or a tragedy in our lives, leads us to reevaluate everything that has meaning for us and brings us to the full realization that there is more to life than meets the ordinary eye. Often it becomes our wake-up call in this lifetime.

I thank you for listening to me this morning. Knowing you, and studying your life path has certainly led me into new and exciting territory. It is the territory of my own mind and my own thoughts. How can I ever repay the favor? I feel blessed and need to express my deep gratitude to you and all the teachers who have tried to teach us this throughout history. Now, I must run in order not to be late for work. Until tomorrow, I remain,
Your grateful student, *R.*

Dear Dr. Schweitzer,

I woke a bit later than usual this morning, so this will be a shorter letter. I did not get up right away, preferring to linger in bed, trying to remember the dream I had. I only have a vague recollection. From now on I will place a notepad on my night table so I can jot this down as soon as I wake up. I found myself doodling during the slow part of yesterday, while waiting for customers. I drew strange and unfamiliar patterns. I drew interconnecting spirals and triangles. Are we being taught in our sleep? I must pay more attention to this phenomenon in the future! Now, back to what I learned yesterday.

As I discover, or better put, as I *remember* that I am not that different from anyone else, I experience a deeper feeling of compassion. Compassion arises once I recognize that we are all on the same journey. When viewing someone else's behavior and life, I see that I have either already been there, or when—viewing your life path—that I still have a lot to learn on my path in order to experience a still higher Truth. I will start by listening more often, instead of talking. Plus, we all have something very fundamental in common, we all die. This thought alone brings with it a lot of compassion. I also know that the only thing I will be taking with me as a soul, is the growth in awareness I experienced. That's it! Nothing else is really mine. My possessions are not mine. My children are not mine. All my accumulated material worth is not mine. I take nothing along with me when I die. That's the harsh reality of the transitory nature of life. Any kindness or goodwill I bestow on someone else will be my only reward. The only thing I will take along is the Karma I have created and the strength and growth of my soul.

While I admit that I am still suffering from some of the symptoms, I now use them as my tools for awakening, as challenges to be faced head on, rather than obstacles to be avoided. I also realize that the act of accepting myself unconditionally, exactly as I am at this moment, allows me to accept others. Why? Because I am not perfect! If I were perfect I would not need to be here any more. I would not need teachers like you... The work needs to be done. Denial, avoidance or procrastination only prolongs the agony of the struggle.

The struggle is part of the growth process and can't be avoided. Only by gaining more awareness can this struggle be *transcended*. The pain and disturbances caused by low and negative emotions have now become my wake-up call, a call we sooner or later get in life. I can only let go of the struggle once I fully understand the dynamics involved. The tools are given to us with which to transcend and grow, and heal the mind, the emotions and the body. I now have the power to create a balance. Through contemplation and meditation I experience that I am so much more than my body, so much more than I *think* I am. The true I AM is my soul, connected or fueled by spirit, the life force or my will-to-live, the **I AM THAT I AM.**

As I reviewed the list, I noticed that the symptoms I listed yesterday, that result in a low frequency or low vibration did not manifest themselves in you, or in your ideal of what a human being can 'aspire' to. I am not talking about ordinary everyday human frailties such as moodiness or frustration. Your teachers, your *ideals*, were all persons who had achieved a higher level of consciousness, such as Bach, Goethe, Kant and Jesus.

Jesus is symbolic of a man who had perfected his physical, emotional and mental bodies through the purification of thought energies, enabling him to connect to a vibration of a Higher nature. This higher Power or less dense vibration was able to work through Jesus. This is the law of magnetism in manifestation. Like attracts like... In this sense it does not matter whether Jesus really existed or not. The process his life depicts is still true. He had surrendered his own will to a higher force, as in, "Thy will be done..."

The same purification process appears to apply to all the great world teachers who have appeared to us from time to time throughout history.   Many teachers, who revealed the Ageless Wisdom Teachings, are often referred to as mystics. Jesus is the man, whereas 'Christ' is the achieved higher level of Love. Gautama or Siddartha was the man, while Buddhi or 'Buddha' is the achieved higher level of Mind. Both taught us to look inside for the keys to what we call the 'Kingdom of Heaven' or the 'Kingdom of God', 'Nirvana', 'Devachan' or 'Paradise'. Could this Kingdom be found at a higher level of consciousness, resulting in a larger all-inclusive perception, seeing the unity of all?

Many different religions have been created on these teachings, and the inherent ethical values they represent.   Our level of comprehending these teachings depends on our level of soul growth. We may choose different paths, but it seems to be true that all roads lead the soul back home to the center, even though at times we appear to be going in circles.

For instance, I know that you found the Universe, the macrocosm, by studying yourself, the microcosm. Albert Einstein found the atom, the microcosm, by studying the universe, the macrocosm. A perfect example of the Law: 'As above—so below', approached from two opposite angles. Just as all planets revolve round the sun, so do the electrons, neutrons and protons revolve around the nucleus of an atom. Man is the microcosm, a reflection of the macrocosm, directed by an unseen intelligence. Every cell in our body is alive with this intelligence.

Some of our most remarkable teachers, like you and Albert Einstein have passed on this body of knowledge, each in your own way. Had you and others of like mind, reached a higher level of evolution, a heightened state of awareness, and are able to guide and teach us from the other side? Does a teacher feel compelled to help us, to educate us, showing us the meaning of *compassion* and *unconditional* or *divine* love? Is that how we can recognize Masters, by the extraordinary and self-less qualities they manifest? They all in varying degrees manifest having transcended the lower aspect of self, the 'lower case' ego and the temporary personality. Is that what is still ahead for all of us on this journey? Is that the process that the life of Jesus symbolizes?

Is it the *process* of the evolution of our consciousness that it is important for us to understand? The role our soul plays in this drama will be recognized along the way. Isn't our soul searching for truth and freedom?

You had freed yourself and have tried to show us how we can do it as well. Was that your purpose? You constantly stressed the fact that we must remain free thinkers, independent of tradition and dogma. You showed me how I can use my own experiences and through deep contemplation detach myself from limiting thoughts. Is striving or aspiring towards perfection the deep desire of the soul? Let me see if I understand the concept of growth correctly.

Growth is a quality—not a quantity.
Growth is acknowledging a truth.
Growth is recognition.
Growth is inspiration.
Growth is aspiration.
Growth is change.
Growth is the unfolding of latent potential.
Growth is expansion through assimilation.
Growth is seeing new possibilities.

Before leaving you today, I would like to share another experience with you. The other day I found myself waiting for a local Arts and Crafts store to open. I wanted to frame a picture for a friend. Since I don't wear a watch I must have been a few minutes early, and decided to pass the time examining the window displays. Suddenly, I saw a framed painting of differently shaped leaves. That's when I saw the words:

"Change is 'letting go' of who you are—in order to become who you could be!"

Each one of us will need to recognize the work that needs to be done on the inner level of our being. It is a very impersonal process, yet it touches each and every one of us in a very personal way. We can't begin to know another until we know ourselves. And sadly, we may feel compassion for another, but we can't do the work for another human being, as it would be robbing them of the necessary experiences of growth. All we can do is change ourselves, thereby making a difference to the whole.

I see messages all around me now, how extraordinary! Thank you from the bottom of my heart for this very valuable lesson in *listening*. I remain,
Your grateful and devoted student, *R*.

Good morning Dr. Schweitzer,

Do we suffer from a case of false identity? It's been a week filled with great opportunities to look at myself. Does it mean it was painful? Yes, but my focus is now on first identifying the symptoms, becoming aware they exist, and recognizing that each one is based on fear or ignorance and on false reasoning. I practice first recognizing, then *letting go* of each limiting thought—one at a time—thereby taking away its energy, replacing it with one that is truthful and therefore more potent. The difficulty is clearly in making the choice and deciding to want to change. Each lesson leads to transformation and self-mastery. As I recognize that these thoughts will not serve me, each lesson—even if painful—leads to transcending fear, self-reliance and eventual liberation.

I also see that old habits have formed a deep groove or rut. A certain amount of ego-resistance is experienced and must be expected. My will must be trained in a new direction, forming a new groove or pattern leading to new habits

The idea dawned on me that all our negative thoughts are caused by the values we have established—intellectually—in our mind based on the past. We are constantly judging objects, projecting ourselves on to other people and situations.

I experimented with this idea and allowed myself to go through a day without *judging*, without *comparing*, without *criticizing* and without *evaluating* or *assuming* anything! I observed my thought patterns and found that all my negative thoughts, were created by my own judgments and my past conditioning. I was giving them value. Who created this value system? My mind did! I further recognized that the value system I had created kept me from living in the present moment. My thoughts kept jumping back or ahead. I found that by observing myself in the present moment, without judging myself, I became more aware of my BEING. I continued this interesting observation all day.

By simply observing my thoughts without evaluating or judging them, I saw what I had been doing to myself. I had to constantly bring myself back to the present moment. We take everything personally, when in fact, what *others* do and say has nothing to do with us. Others are just expressing 'who' *they* are, running off their own programming. I am not responsible for others, but I am responsible for myself.

Since I had just learned that all thoughts create, I made it my mission to let go of unnecessary thoughts, in order to fully experience living in the *present* moment. I accepted 'what is' without putting a label on it in any way. What happened is almost magical. I felt free and light all day. Instead of forcefully pushing thoughts away, I allowed them to dissipate naturally. I experienced *transcending* the dictates of my lower mind and my (lower case) ego. It was as though a large chain had been removed, or a burden had been lifted off my shoulders. I experienced a new flow of energy and felt free as a bird. To transcend means to go *beyond*.

I see now that the value system I had established, including desires for material possessions, ambition and competition have lost their glamour and sophistication for me. I see how we operate often like robots, thinking and performing our duties almost mechanically. It's as if we are asleep. Our power trips and ambitions driven by low or blind desires and emotions, if allowed to be the driver of our vehicle, lead nowhere and leave us unfulfilled and empty. We become critical, fearful and distrustful. Acting and behaving from a sense of lack, creates even more lack and a lot of stress. Negative thoughts crowd out our creative thoughts, the ones we most desire, because we can't have two thoughts at the same time!

What is creating this condition? How does the Law of Karma fit into this picture, the Law of Cause and Effect? Why does the feeling of freedom and inner peace I experience in moments of quiet contemplation not last? Why is it so elusive and difficult to maintain? Must I stop seeking, and allow everything just to be? Accept everything the way it is? Because—like and like attract—the feeling of resistance, therefore, creates or causes more resistance? **Only by complete acceptance of a current condition can that condition be changed.** There it is again, a seeming paradox.

Pure reason leads me to take another look at these Universal Laws, the immutable laws of nature, also known as 'The Laws of

Life', and see how they function and affect me. Pure reason leads me to recognize that I 'sin' each time I ignore these laws. In other words I work against myself by ignoring the currents of nature. The Laws of Karma are unavoidable once the cycle of growth is examined. I must face the consequences of all my previously created thoughts and actions, in other words, face myself, providing I want to grow, that is. I do have a choice!

Only then, will I have the strength and awareness not to create the repercussions of more karma and practice harmlessness in thought and action. Is the time right and am I ready to wake up? Am I ready to take responsibility? Am I willing to understand, that perhaps, I (the spiritual **I**) have lived before, and perhaps will live again and again, each time adopting a new personality and a new physical body, before I will fully comprehend these ***impersonal but just*** Laws and begin to harmonize with them? Karma is the Law of balance, a natural Law in Nature. Karma has nothing to do with judgment since it is self-imposed. I must take responsibility for all that I have created. This seems very logical to me. Are all previously created actions carried forward into the next life experience? This truth is making itself known in every aspect of my being.

In order for me to grow spiritually I must become aware of the Universal Laws, one of which is the Law of Karma. In other words I must recognize that every cause has an effect. Along with the Law of Change, this one if understood, helps me to purify my mental, emotional and physical body. Why? Because everything I think, feel and do, is a cause and will manifest in the corresponding effects. The repercussions of what I create are then my fate, my karma and my responsibility. It applies to the negative as well as the positive.

As seen in nature and the four seasons, nothing stays the same, everything is constantly in a state of motion. The energy fields surrounding the physical body are no exception. In order for my energy field to change I must change my thoughts, my feelings and my actions, and further I must take full responsibility for everything I create.

The more I purify my bodies, the finer/higher my vibrations will become. This is a process I am becoming aware of on my spiritual journey. Hidden therein lies my potential for my freedom and my power to change. My willingness to do so is my choice. Nobody can ever force this upon me. I must do this willingly and out of my own recognition of how our universe functions.

The transformer is located in my heart chakra. It transforms the lower-self energies into the higher. I pondered on this for a long time and have come to these conclusions. In order to express unconditional love and compassion for others my heart must be activated and be open to receive these higher energies, not blocked by fear, ingratitude and confusion.

One of the ways that helps to open this heart energy is to develop a sense of reverence for all life, and a genuine sense of gratitude. Using the spoken word is another very powerful tool. This is known as the power of a spoken mantra, a sentence that will vibrate and register deep in our psyche.

Our inner state depends on our intention. If our intention is selfish, more of the same will return to us. If we express lack more of the same will return. Likened to a circle, what goes around comes around.

Another important Law to understand is the Law of Forgiveness. In order to be forgiven, I must forgive. Being phony holy about it doesn't work either. True forgiveness, truly experienced in my heart is what is needed in order for this Law to work as expressed in the words, "Forgive us all our trespasses, as we forgive those who trespass against us." It is a two way street or a two-way channel of communication, never static but in constant motion. When studied further, all of the Universal Laws work in harmony. It therefore become very helpful to study these laws and see how they relate to our everyday lives. By study, I mean not just read them, but contemplate and meditate on them allowing a higher understanding to enter. In this way old habits and old patterns of thinking and feeling are broken, which affect the quality of our everyday life.

Along with that, I must be very aware that my intentions, no matter how well meaning, do not interfere with the free will of another person. They must be for the good of all concerned. In other words, I must practice harmlessness. Understanding and practicing any one of the Laws creates a domino effect since it leads us to understanding all the others.

Give money or inspiration to someone and notice how it increases the flow. As I remember the words of Browning, I see that some wise men had already known this, yet the impact of this Higher Truth is only now beginning to hit its target. What is truth?

The Christian church actually believed and taught that according to Genesis, our earth is only 4500 years old. Since science has now proven otherwise, they had to reluctantly revise their belief. That's why I feel our beliefs must be looked at with an open mind. We must not relinquish our right to think and reason for ourselves. We must defend our right of freedom of speech in the same way and not allow censorship of information. Just because we hide truth and deny it, does not mean it doesn't exist. It helps to admit how little we know about ourselves, and our universe. This attitude keeps us open to learning.

"Truth successively takes shape, one grade above its last presentment."

Robert Browning

In other words the truth does not change, but as I change more truth will reveal itself. As I change my focus, I realize that the symptoms of dis-ease are slowly becoming weaker and weaker on their own. Why? Because I don't give them my *attention*, I don't give them my *energy*. A feeling of utter and complete gratitude seems to envelop me at moments like this—for instance—right now. I think about you, and how often I've seen gratitude expressed in your writings. All the time!

Sooner or later we have to look into the mirror and honestly confront ourselves. Where are we on the ladder of soul growth? This kind of growth is not to be confused with more or less, rather with a change of awareness coming from within. It becomes the *natural outgrowing* of old habits and patters. Leaving old beliefs and prejudices behind seems natural and right as I transform my thinking. It becomes an inner transformation, a form of transmutation. Is this the philosopher's stone? The recognition of *who* we are and acting on this knowing, becomes the fire of transformation. Only by becoming conscious of our lower nature can we transform it. We can't plead ignorance any more. We can't deny it anymore. It is a part of us, just like the Higher spiritual nature is a part of us. Could it be that a part of our purpose here on earth is to undergo a period of purification?

We must embrace both parts of ourselves, our weakness and our strength. In this way we won't be alienated or create a split personality. All we need to do is balance one with the other, as one cancels the other or transforms it, a third energy is revealed. It is the energy of love, the energy of allowing ourselves to BE. 'Being' is an experience. Slowly, as we see that we can change, we begin to see and focus on the beautiful creature we already are inside, waiting to be released, waiting to shine. This growth happens in stages. That's when I recognized that growth—is love—that I am that love.

It is only now that I understand that the real *ashram* or mystery school is not to be found outside of myself. It is inside each and every one of us. I now see that life itself, and the experiences I encounter are the real teacher. The lessons are found in every relationship I am involved in. In other words, everyone becomes my teacher. In others I see my hidden opportunity to see myself. I will have to remain open and **allow the world to have an impact on me**, allowing myself to be taught, instead of having an impact on the world. The moment I think I know everything I close myself off to further learning. In other words I have eyes that do not 'see' and ears that do not 'hear'.

There it is dear doctor. My prescription for good physical and mental health is taking a deep look at my own thoughts and my own creations. Since I had picked up on this truth several years ago, yet never fully understood it—the way I know it now—shows that I have grown. Yes, the growing process has not been without pain and uncertainty. However, change is in the air and I must remain flexible. I am beginning to pay attention. I trust and *know* that I'll be guided to the next experience in order to work through further fears. And I owe it all to you and your love for your fellow traveler:

"God's love speaks to us in our hearts and tries to work through us in the world. We must listen to it as to a pure and distant melody that comes across the noise of the world's doings. Some say 'When we are grown up, we would rather think of other things.' But the voice of Love with which God speaks to us in the secret places of the heart, speaks to us when we are young so that we may become the children of God. Happy are those who listen."[7]

You *knew* that the secret of transformation is found in the chamber of the heart. This Love center, once activated, will help us to see others and ourselves as One. On that higher level of vibration we are all connected or children of the unfathomable ONE. Only through self-devotion can I experience God-devotion. Does it mean I have to start loving myself—my Higher Self—my soul?

During a discussion group, the topic of belief vs. knowing was mentioned. Someone referred to it this way:

> "He who knows not, and knows not, that he knows not,
>   is a fool, shun him.
> He who knows not, and knows that he knows not,
>   is a student, teach him.
> He who knows and knows not that he knows,
>   is asleep, awaken him.
> He who knows and knows that he knows,
>   is wise, follow him."
>   —*Author unknown*

You *know* and are a wise soul Dr. Schweitzer. I say *are*, instead of *were*, because your spirit and the wisdom of your teachings are still alive today. In this respect you have reached immortality. Your thoughts and words live on through every one of your students. Your book *'The Light Within Us'* has a whole new meaning for me now. I now recognize that the 'inner light' is my soul. That's why we are all light beings. It's almost as though someone had turned on a light switch.

The quote I used at the beginning of this chapter reminds me of another person's view of the process and the sacrifices we willingly eventually make, as we reach towards perfection. H. P. Blavatsky said it this way:

The Golden Stairs

"A clean life; an open mind; a pure heart; an eager intellect; an unveiled spiritual perception; a brotherliness for all; a readiness to give advice and instruction; a courageous endurance of personal injustice; a brave declaration of principles; a valiant defense of those who are unjustly attacked; and a constant eye to the ideal of human progression and perfection which the sacred science depicts; these are the Golden Stairs, up the steps which the learner must climb to the temple of Divine Wisdom."8

Yes, all great minds think alike. You could just as well have written these words. Thank you so much for all the wisdom you have shared with all of us over the years. Thank you for showing me how an awakened human being thinks and acts! You didn't just believe in the goodness of man, you *knew* that the virtue of Love and Compassion, is a higher level of vibration, a higher level of being; you *knew* that this higher frequency can be accessed or tuned into because the receptors already exist in all of us. You *knew* that we are all on this climb together. You *knew* and exhibited compassion and love for all. In this respect we are still infants compared to your level of maturity.

You also knew what temptations lie in wait for all of us. Yet, you had drawn on your inner power and strength to resist. You understood something that we at the present time do not fully grasp. You, like Goethe, who spent sixty years writing *Faust*, tried to make us understand that there is more to life than meets the eye. Thank you for being my guide and the physician of my soul, thank you for coming to my rescue. Einstein described you correctly when he called you a 'Giant' among ordinary men.

With love in my heart I give thanks for my current healing. Your devoted and grateful student, N.

Sources Chapter 8.

1. P.63 *The Words of Albert Schweitzer*, Norman Cousins.
2. P.63 *The Words of Albert Schweitzer*, Norman Cousins.
3. P.151 *Twelve World Teachers,* Manly P. Hall, 1965, Philosophical Research Society, Los Angeles, CA.
4. P.152-153 *Twelve World Teachers,* Manly P. Hall, 1965, Philosophical Research Society, Los Angeles, CA.
5. P.192-193 *Conversations with Goethe,* Johann Peter Eckermann, 1998 Da Capo Press, Inc., New York, NY.
6. P. 53 *The Twelve Laws of Karma,* Helion Publishing, PO Box 52836, Tulsa, OK.
7. P.54 *The Words of Albert Schweitzer,* Norman Cousins.
8. The collected writings of H.P.B.

"Love cannot be put under a system of rules and regulations. It issues absolute commands. Each of us must decide for himself how far he can go towards carrying out the boundless commandment of love without surrendering his own existence and must decide, as well, how much of his life and happiness he must sacrifice to the life and happiness of others."[1]

Albert Schweitzer

9

Love

Dear Dr. Schweitzer,

As I review my understanding of growth I realize that we grow in stages. The natural stages are as follows: complete dependency during childhood; codependency in youth and adolescence; independence or self-reliance during adult-hood, and inter-dependency as we grow into full maturity and wisdom. Unity and inter-dependency are only recognized once we have mastered the previous stages. How many of us get stuck in the codependency stage? Is each stage absolutely necessary and is the struggle for freedom and independence a prelude for experiencing the magic and healing power of Love?

It is spring, a season for weddings and the celebration of love. What is this magnetic power we call love—the magnetic attraction—between two people? How many of us understand what love is? How many marriages will end up in divorce court this season? What expectations do we have of our partner? Will he or she make me happy? Where are we looking for happiness? When do we realize that no one can make us happy, that it is our responsibility? Happiness is the *result* and by-product of right and harmonious thought and action.

I read your words in the above quotation in the booklet I took to the beach today. I now call it serendipity, or being guided to the right words at the right time. My mind is reeling with new thoughts about you and the message you have for all of us today, as we face this crucial moment in history. I call it crucial because the time is quickly approaching when we will come to the full realization as to *who* we really are. How else can anything change for us in the world? In order for man to understand the world and the universe, man must first and foremost examine and understand *himself*.

As I think about the word forgiveness, I first and foremost will be presented with the challenge of forgiving myself. I must forgive my own infantile ignorance of the Truth of these matters. Then, I can forgive anyone, who I *wrongly* thought has done anything to me that was hurtful, no matter how awful the deed appears to have been. I will then find it in my heart to forgive them. This forgiveness releases me! How I interpret the deed that may have hurt me is crucial. An action or deed perpetrated by someone else shows how ignorant they are, as *they* will have to experience the consequences or karma of their deed. Not forgetting the *cause*, I will have to look at what in *me* attracted this deed.

If ignorance and fear are our problem, the solution therefore must rest in education, acquiring the necessary insight, and making the necessary changes in our lives. These changes will lead to *understanding, patience, humility, tolerance, courage, faith and love*. This kind of wealth far exceeds material wealth.

I have learned that truth is very relative, as I let go of my old perceptions and beliefs. So, I can only tell you about what appears as truth to me now. I have further realized that this truth will eventually be replaced by a still higher or deeper understanding, leading to more truth. Therefore it is important that I stay flexible, embrace uncertainty and flow with life situations from one moment to the next. Words are often limiting in the recognition of new concepts. I feel somehow hemmed in and limited by language and words. The Truth I am referring to *transcends* words, becoming an *experience* that is not really describable in words. Yet at the present time, there is no other way of communicating. Or is there?

We know from the science of physics that everything that exists is energy and vibration. Energy can't be destroyed—it can only be changed. By changing my thoughts I change my vibrations—my energy. Why would I want to do this? My vibrations and energy attract vibrations of the same kind. In order to get in touch with the real me, the Spirit part of me, the creative part of me, the God spark of me—an energy that vibrates at a higher level, I *have* to change my vibration or energy patterns and align myself with this higher energy. I have to make the conscious choice to reach out with pure intention, energized by a pure motive and unconditional Love in my heart.

Another immutable Law of Creation is that everything has consciousness. At first I found it hard to comprehend that a rock or stone could be conscious, however, if this law is correct, and I now know that it is, then everything in our universe is alive and conscious. Granted, a rock, a plant, or an animal, do not have the same level of consciousness, they are not self-conscious and they don't possess the power of reason, therefore they don't have an ego. For instance, experiments have shown that plants respond to music. Plants are sentient. This is part of scientific discovery. We already knew that to be true about animals. Furthermore, everything in our universe responds to love, because Love is a vibration.

I am not referring to our normal notions of love, such as romantic love. I am talking about Divine Love, unconditional Love resulting in self-less Love, without which a relationship with another person is usually based only on need, dependency and codependency. Out of self-appreciation, and soul appreciation, comes selflessness or the desire to want to give back. I don't mean this to sound selfish—it is quite the opposite. Another paradox! Therefore, everything I do to heal, help and release another, without *expectation of rewards*, benefits my soul. Everything you did in your life to help others—rewarded you—it resulted in the expansion of your soul. By not looking for a reward you were rewarded. It is the soul that benefits, because unconditional Love is a soul quality.

Romantic love, the way we often see it, is not what I am referring to. Isn't it too often conditional upon the object of our affection behaving and being what we had envisioned and expected them to be? Isn't it often based on our illusions and expectations of perfection of someone or something outside of our self? A result of this kind of love is constant disappointment, because it is based on our neediness, our selfishness, our projection, our expectations and fear. We must never have any expectations of another, it is only from ourselves we must strive to expect a lot.

For instance how can I give love, if I don't have love and don't understand what it is? How can I give something I don't have? Love must be the gift I give myself first. Before love can flow freely, I must be so filled with it, knowing that I am enough, that I have enough, become content and filled with a deep and genuine gratitude.

I am referring to the magnetism that is love. Just as a battery needs both poles to be effective, and is the result of the connection or polarization of both, so it is with love. Love is the magnetic stuff of cohesion of our universe and all of creation. It is Love that creates the attraction between two people seeking union. Therefore, the sayings that 'like attracts like' and 'opposites attract' are both true. Another paradox!

Is there not a Divine Intelligence that animates everything that exists? Isn't Divine Love part of that Intelligence? In Buddhism for instance, the word God is rarely mentioned. Buddhism is a mind set or psychology meant to awaken the Power of the Source within each person, becoming manifest through non-attachment to outer senses and appearances. It becomes a philosophy or another way of looking at life. Buddhism awakens the intuition and brings the person back to himself. Some will see Buddha as an atheist. Buddha believed it better to have no notion of God, rather than a false notion. He rightly felt that it would give people the sense that God is something outside of oneself. Having and clinging to a false notion of 'God', more often than not, keeps us from taking responsibility for the experiences we encounter on our journey through life. Divinity, the Universal Mind, Pure Reason or Oneness as you referred to this quality, appears all by itself, as the Life Force/Consciousness is discovered in everything.

God is not a being, God is BEING. God is nothing, yet it is all encompassing. It is ALL. The ancient Hebrew mystics called this force, the God with no name, represented by sacred vowels or letters only. It is often called the Logos (Greek meaning 'word') or sound of creation. In our futile attempt to understand the mystery, we label something that can't be labeled. God is in everyone and in everything that exists; in every atom; it is in the energy of every breath we take. That is why deep breathing is so important, stressed in every relaxation exercise, and in every spiritual practice including meditation and yoga (union).

Our immediate connection to this life giving energy is our soul. What is needed is that we become aware of our soul—tune in—become quiet and begin to listen.

"It is better to have no opinion of God at all, than such a one as is unworthy of Him; for the one is only belief—the other, contempt."

Plutarch

Now I begin to understand that your philosophy of *'Reverence for Life'* was not just based on opinion. You knew about our connection to ALL on the Spiritual level. Coupled with Einstein's theory of relativity, it means that everything is connected even if on a different level of consciousness, a different level of vibration, and everything is relative to our perception, our level of comprehension or awareness. The next question that arose for me was this: "How can I increase my level of perception?"

One of the ways that works best for me is stillness and observation, listening in silence and in meditation turn within. For the body, a practice of yoga is very stimulating and calming at the same time, since it increases the flow of energy in the body. The word yoga means *union,* the union of the physical with the Spiritual, the human with the Divine, presently symbolized by the two interlaced triangles. One triangle pointing down and one pointing up, is not only the symbol of the lower and Higher self seeking union, it also represent involution and evolution. The Star of David, adopted by the Hebrews is only one example.

Reading worthwhile and interesting literature is also important, since all enlightening stories come from the same Source. All creativity has the same author! This is a good time for me to give thanks to all the authors, including you, who have taken the time to write about their experiences, passing on their wisdom. Through each book I read, contemplate and understand, my level of recognition of certain basic principles deepens. Thank you all!

Another way that promotes a deep sense of connection, instilling me with awe and reverence, is being out in nature—preferably alone. As I stare at the miracle of a sunrise on a warm Florida morning, or watch the forever changing, rolling motion of the incoming tide, I am never disappointed by the spectacular show, always returning home glad to have made the effort to go to the beach. The sun represents Divine Love to me. It shines on everyone equally.

The sun does not discriminate, it does not judge or evaluate who deserves its energy or not.

Sometimes I say a prayer of thanksgiving, being overwhelmed with gratitude. At times I just experience the wind and stare at the soft clouds in the sky. Sometimes I drift into meditation, allowing all thoughts and emotions to flow into the sand below me, as I enter the space between thoughts. I return home refreshed and energized. Lighting a candle while I sit down to write in my journal, has always helped me to focus my attention on observing what is going on inside of me. At these moments, time appears not to exist as I enter the *now* moment, the *creative* moment in my life.

Releasing thoughts and emotions on paper has been very therapeutic for me over the last few years. My poems sprang seemingly out of nowhere, in this fashion. This kind of meditation has been my greatest learning tool. I've heard it said that poetry speaks to the heart. I like Robert Frost's definition: 'Poetry starts with delight and ends in wisdom."

Meditation
Awakening slowly on a warm spring day
Like a bud—slowly reaching
The light, the sun, caressing—me, feeling my way.
Many chores lie in waiting—sorting—learning
The cycle all over again.

A new time for decisions
What will I be?
A shy Lily of the Valley, so sweet...yet hidden
A Daffodil, Primrose or—maybe
A tall straight Iris—looking around—at what is forbidden.

The most appealing to me now
Is bold, bright and showy
Ablaze with color—so proud
Fragrance so strong—it is heady.
A feast to the senses, "Peonies" I say loud.

Maybe, just maybe—is there a chance?
Can I be so forward and wait
Be patient, head in the sun
Take on the notion
Of being a rose—a love potion?

Only seduction—won't last
What else can I be?
My eyes look up—there—I behold
Majestic and free
That's it...! I'd like to be a tree.

Strong and enduring
Dependable to give
Cover to the restless—to those who swelter
Give clean air, so others can live.
Branches long—strong—a good shelter.

Deep roots—growing stronger in time
Yes, that's my spring wish
Filling me...
With a feeling...
Oh, so sublime.

It's time to get up and get going
Sow seeds
Wait for the rain.
And in a wink of a moment
Gee, I hope I won't miss the train.

A fleeting meditation—or a dream?
Comparing myself to nature
Being a part—feeling whole
Looking into a stream
Seeing my own reflection?
RzT 1996

Yes, I would consider meditation to be a tool for my personal growth. This particular tool has allowed me to focus and to *listen,* not only to what is going on externally, picked up by my senses, but to look inside. While my outer mind is quiet I awaken to what is happening inside, reaching *beyond* my five senses. Meditation has taught me be true to my inner yearnings to follow that inner voice and to honor myself. Instead of focusing on external influences or circumstances only, and re-acting in my usual mode, I now step back and ask myself: "What is this situation trying to teach me?

What is the correct response?" In retrospect I can see more clearly
that it is all a part of the process of growth, a process that is fueled
by a strong curiosity or interest and an open mind. As I let go of
more and more in my life I am reminded of the lyrics of the Beatles
song '*LET IT BE*'. A poem with the same title was inspired one
afternoon a long time ago while listening with my eyes closed.

Let it be
A certain peace washes over me
As I stop and listen to the lyrics
Of a song called *Let it be*...

Can I go with the flow?
Relax—let things happen
Instead of running to and fro?

Is there someone—who really cares?
About my pain and struggle...
A God—Angels—Beings who've been there?

Beings who already know the choices
Saying: 'Let it be, let it be... let it be...
Are these beings my inner voices?

Sending me this tune as solace—peace
To heal my heart—awaken my soul
A message to be heeded—my release?

Stop this silly struggle and learn to trust
Things come from above—just pray—give thanks
New doors will open—be still—don't thrust.

Trust the voice—it is your soul!
Your light in the dark—bringing words of wisdom
Trying to help you—not just console.
RzT 1996

One of my biggest challenges at the present time is to create
a better balance in my life by recognizing where and how I
must change. This change is an internal one. Feeling the inner
transformation gives me the courage to make the necessary changes

in the outer, when appropriate. Is it a struggle? The answer is a big and definite—YES. I see what I need to learn, every time I open my mouth inappropriately or judge and critique another, even if in thought only. I constantly remind myself that it is not about another, it is only about me. As I consciously 'let go' the struggle ceases to exist.

As I review your life of service I am filled with a desire to help others. Spending so many solitary hours alone, sitting here writing to you has created an inner need for me to take action and make a contribution. How can I honor this inner feeling this new deep desire to help? Is my motivation pure, or am I still ego driven?

Thanks for being on my mind this morning as I salute you for your courage and your devotion to your truth. I am getting a bigger picture of 'who' you are and what your mission is all about. You see—I am beginning to understand your argument. Why is it so important? Because, my real self, my *higher* Self is Love, and real Love transcends the personal and the temporary personality, allowing a complete surrender of what is *not* real.

The personality and my body are the tools I have at my disposal All I can possibly have my dominion over is—me. Do I now have the courage to be different, as I embark on the lone road—'the road less traveled'?

In closing I read your words on making a difference to remind myself to please be here now.

"The great enemy of morality has always been indifference. As children, as far as our awareness of things went, we had an elementary capacity for compassion. But our capacity did not develop over the years in proportion to the growth of our understanding. This was uncomfortable and bewildering. We noticed so many people who no longer had compassion or empathy. Then we too, suppressed our sensitivity so as to be like everyone else. We did not want to be different from them, and we did not know what to do. Thus many people become like houses in which one story after another has been vacated, a lifeless structure in which all windows look empty and strange, deserted."[2]

How many people lead lives of quiet desperation, spending night after night in front of the TV, allowing someone else's thoughts to dominate and condition their minds, yet are yearning and seeking for something new to come along—waiting for a miracle? All miracles are the manifestation of cause and effect! Where is the dream they had as children? What are we teaching our children? What happened to reading, what happened to hobbies or creativity for instance? The word educate means to draw forth, it does *not* mean to put in. How many are waiting for something or someone to rescue them, someone to bring a change to their life situation, not realizing that all they have to do is look at themselves *honestly*, and all the answers will appear. The higher wisdom is all round us, all we have to do is open our heart and mind to ourselves—pay attention—and wake ourselves up!

Growth becomes the process of the recognition of our complacency. As the process is unfolding, uncovering my innermost center, seeing anew, something which has always been there, namely the force underlying all of creation and discovering the magnetism and healing power hidden in my heart, I become renewed and see a higher Reality. All the experiences I have encountered, all the pain and suffering I have experienced, existed for one purpose only, and that is for me to become aware of my 'Source' and my 'Power'—which is LOVE.

As I bring this power into my life, allowing it to dominate, using it to purify and transform my lower nature, my course will be guided, and new vistas will dawn. Opening my heart to this powerful Love energy is bringing the Divine into the human. Thank you for explaining this process to me.

I am preparing for a visit with my grandson, so I will leave you for now. This little boy is so bright and is teaching me so much. I cherish every moment spent in the presence of this child's innocent and curious nature. He is certainly teaching me to live in the *now* moment, the moment of discovery and creation. With Love in my heart and a feeling of deepest gratitude I remain,
Your devoted pupil, *R*.

Dear Doctor Schweitzer,

Summer is slowly approaching. The humidity of Florida is becoming more pronounced each day. I hear my air conditioner flipping on more often. I received an unexpected gift, an extra day off. Here I am writing to you on a Friday morning. I will use this extra time by continuing my conversation with you. What's on my mind today is the subject of reincarnation and the life of the soul. I don't like using the word God, and have used it sparingly for a reason. This essence some call Universal Mind or pure Spirit since it is the Source of all that exists. The Source that encompasses all living matter can't be comprehended by our limited understanding. It's like explaining the meaning of space.

Yet in the past artists have tried. Even Michelangelo, commissioned by the Church of Rome, painted 'It' as a man, a father figure. Is it not man's feeble attempt to understand to picture the incomprehensible? This father figure has been adopted by numerous generations. I now understand this essence to be Impersonal, pure BEING or vibrations of Light and Love. This essence is the Life Force pulsating in and through everything that IS. In this respect its essence is in everything and in every body.

Since everything in the universe is cyclical, there is a cycle in nature observed as the cycle of birth, preservation and death or regeneration, clearly seen in the four seasons. I recognized that reincarnation is part of the cycle of the evolution of our soul—our expansion in consciousness. I not only believe in reincarnation, for me this has a fact, your appearance that day in Georgia is not the only point of reference. It is referred to in many ancient texts including our Bible, a book I now see as part metaphysical and part historical. The Bible can be read on many levels of recognition. What does the word recognition mean? To cognize, is to see. Recognize means to see again, perhaps discover new meaning leading to a deeper understanding of a concept or an idea. As I look at nature for example, I see how a caterpillar transforms himself becoming a butterfly! So, the butterfly becomes a symbol of transformation.

The forerunners, teachers and prophets like Gautama and Jesus, often taught through symbols and parables. Parables and allegories are so effective because they portray the Truth in an undeniable fashion, allowing it to be understood by the multitudes. Allowing us to 'get it' on whatever level we are ready to 'get it'. Parables are often shrouded or veiled in psychological terms allowing a deeper insight to penetrate our hearts and minds. Often they expose our fallacious thinking. They appeal to the lowest and the highest aspect of our mind.

It has been said that several of the original texts of the old and the New Testament were tampered with during the ecumenical council of Constantine of 325 C. E., and again in 525 C. E. Why, must be left to our imagination. The 'name of the game' back then, was power through control and fear. Not too different from today I see. It was part of the mass consciousness. I can see why the reference to reincarnation was brushed aside and partially deleted. Were they making the decision that we would not understand the underlying meaning of reincarnation or the journey of the soul?

True spirituality represents the search for Truth. There is nothing that is higher. Religion, the way we know it, has largely become what I call 'Churchianity', steeped in man-made dogma and tradition. Religion often demands we worship the experience of a Prophet or Saint, without questioning the Universal Process underlying these experiences. Instead of guiding us to find our own experience and truth, we are led to *idolizing* and *worshipping* a Saint's or Prophet's experience.

Theology, science and philosophy each take us only so far. However, when they are combined a larger picture emerges. Only then does spirituality make sense to me. Somewhere along the line the true meaning of the word 'religion' has been lost. The word *religion* means to re-link. To re-link us with our own Divinity—our Source—seems to be its true purpose.

When considering the Law of Karma, it makes sense that we are all suffering to some degree. We must experience the consequences of our previous deeds or actions from this life and our previous lives. We reap what we sow.

The lower our consciousness, the lower our vibration, the slower is the growth, and the more we must compensate in the next cycle. A master returning as slave so that the oppressor must experience being oppressed and the thief must have the experience being robbed. A person filled with hate and bigotry must return as the recipient of the same in equal measure. Most of us have been different personalities, from kings to paupers. Most of us have experienced killing and being killed. Most of us have been Saints and sinners. How else can we experience both sides of the coin? This is justice, the *impersonal* Law of Compensation.

The sooner we recognize that what goes around—comes around—the faster we can begin to clean up our own house, our temple, namely our physical, emotional and mental vehicles, and begin to experience our true nature—which is spiritual. The cycle must continue as cause and effect as the soul continues its upward movement. By correcting or burning up existing karma it enters the realm of Self-mastery. The fire is our awareness. When the soul comes under the guidance and influence of the Higher Self or the 'Christ Consciousness', as it is referred to in esoteric terms, we become more alive and start to direct more of our thoughts and actions outwards and towards the rest of humanity. We are awakened to a feeling of compassion for all still suffering. That's when we realize that we all have something very basic in common. Our physical bodies will eventually die and return to dust. This alone is a very powerful common denominator.

You, dear doctor, had realized that real Love is a spiritual quality. It is not simply being open to experiencing the anguish of another person's suffering. We must be willing to allow the person to make the necessary choices and sacrifices along the way. Your life was spent in educating yourself, followed by trying to educate the rest of us. You felt the physical suffering and injustice of this world more acutely than most. Why did you not dwell on and try to explain reincarnation to us?

Could it be that you had recognized that we must make our best efforts while in the present body, perfecting our present vehicle? That's it? Our opportunity is right here—right now? Is that what you meant by striving for perfection? Did you see that perfecting ourselves on all three levels—mentally, emotionally and physically, is an absolute necessity, and that this purification process is most efficiently accomplished while we are still in the physical body?

Each incarnation brings us closer to the realization that we are inter-dependent and are all a part of, or One with a Universal Soul, or as Emerson puts it the 'Oversoul', Universal Mind or God. All the great teachers who have walked the path knew this to be our destiny. We suddenly understand that all the suffering on this earth has been created by the *minds of imperfect men,* and that all the wars are created by imperfect people. There is no such thing as a vengeful God. There are only people enveloped in darkness and fear—people asleep—people disconnected from Spirit—their Source.

Sharing
The hurt is all gone now
Replaced with pure love
And a desire for sharing.

How can I reach you?
You—who are still looking
If not through my sharing—my caring?

I have no hidden motive
My aim is to help—although it may hurt,
To guide you gently—with my words.

Once I have stirred you,
Sit back and reflect
What are you hiding—'who' are you trying to protect?

The REAL you is love
Just like me
Your guides are there—ready and waiting.

Where are you?
RzT Aug.22, 1985

Not knowing our true nature, not knowing who we really are, has caused much bloodshed and confusion throughout the history of our planet. Was it necessary? Seen as a growing process, yes, it was all perfectly right for our evolution, considering the masses were, and still are, filled with thoughts of fear and survival. Why? Most of us have not as yet recognized that we are one global family, sharing a planetary home. We have not yet grown up enough, to learn the art of cooperation. Is there hope for us, will this wave of humanity survive the onslaught of such negativity, fueled by our ignorance and fear? Are we ready to wake up and recognize our inter-dependency? As I write this I almost hear your words echoing in my inner mind:

"Don't let your hearts grow numb. Stay alert. It is your soul which matters."[3]

Since all thoughts create, I am struck by the notion of what we could be capable of creating, if we would utilize the thought power at our disposal correctly. I see my brain as the receiving station for my mind and thoughts. How can I create when this instrument is still so limited? Scientists have told us that we are only using a fraction of the brain cells available. By using my *will power* to correct fallacious thinking, based on fear not faith, and by entering the eternal NOW moment, I increase my ability to connect and receive

What is meant in the Lord's Prayer: "Thy will be done..?" How do I get to know this Higher Will? If my will and the Creator's Will are in conflict, how can I possibly reach my potential? What does it have in store for me? Can I align with it? I found your advice coming to my rescue:

"The ultimate questions of our life transcend knowledge. One riddle after another surrounds us. But the final question of our being has but one concern, and it decides our fate. Again and again we are thrown back to it. What will become of our own will? How does it find itself in the will of God? The highest insight man can attain is the yearning for peace, for the union of his will with the infinite will, his human will with God's will. Such a will does not cut itself off and live in isolation like a puddle that is bound to dry up when the heat of summer comes. No, it is like a mountain stream, relentlessly splashing its way to the river, there to be swept on to the limitless ocean."

Do you mean that once I align my will with the infinite will all separation ceases? You mean a drop of ocean water contains the same inherent characteristics as the complete ocean? If God is the ocean, I am the drop? Just like the complete blueprint of my being is contained in just one cell? Am I a mini-god?

Before I can attempt the journey to Self-Mastery I have to embark on the path of Self-discovery. It is a very personal journey, this journey home, returning to my own essence—my soul. You continuously admonished us to seek Truth. I saw these words framed and have decided to frame them for my wall as well:

THE THREE TRUTHS
"The soul of man is immortal, and its
future is the future of a thing whose
growth and splendor has no limit."

"The principle which gives life dwells in
us, and without us, is undying and
beneficent, is not heard or seen, or
smelt, but is perceived by the
man who desires perception."

"Each man is his own absolute lawgiver,
the dispenser of glory or gloom to
himself; the decreer of his life, his
reward, his punishment."

"These truths, which are as great as is
life itself, are as simple as
the simplest mind of man. Feed the
hungry with them..."
                    The Idyll of the White Lotus

Yes, we are all hungry for Truth. Yes, we are all creators, creating our own destiny. In order for the flow of Love and the flow of Wisdom of the soul to continue I will practice *listening*! I must listen to the small inner voice—the voice of the silence—my intuition—my inner teacher. It has never guided me wrong—*ever*. I have experienced pain and suffering on many occasions by not heeding its advice on many occasions. I had previously ignored many of the hunches and obvious signs, often appearing as choices on my journey. Materialism is a very dangerous trap. It is the big *illusion* that promises fulfillment and happiness—yet it never delivers. It keeps us stuck like a monkey with his hand in the cookie jar. Have you heard this story?

A monkey sees a jar of cookies and puts his hand in to take the cookies out. His hand turns into a fist and he can't remove his hand. The question now becomes: "Does the monkey have the cookies, or do the cookies have the monkey?"

Has the time for maturity arrived? Has the time arrived where I fully recognize the consequences of all my previous thoughts and actions? Am I afraid? Only fear itself must be feared, nothing else! Fear is false evidence that *appears* real, to the lower mind only! The Higher mind can and will transcend this emotion, replacing it with the healing emotion of Love. Accepting Unconditional Love and surrendering to its Power, I first fill myself with its healing energy and then pass it on to others. Paradoxically, the more I use and give out this energy, the more I receive or increase the flow. I see this as an important key! It is the key that unlocks the door to my heart.

Our heart center, once activated becomes a tremendous transformer. It transforms fear into Love. The answers we are looking for are already inside of us, hidden from us until we are ready to understand. So there is nowhere to go, but *inside*. 'Know Thyself'—has a whole new meaning for me now.

As I view my journey in retrospect, I see that there are no mistakes. Everything happened for a reason. Everything I created has led me to this point in my evolution, this level of consciousness. Everything and everyone has been my teacher. Blame, is not part of my game plan anymore, because of it's limiting nature. All was perfectly necessary to happen the way it happened. As I begin to understand this, I experience a sense of peace and gratitude that is indescribable.

As I work *consciously* on observing and *illuminating* my mind and thoughts, I find it easier to let go of old thought patterns, patterns which create the symptoms of dis-ease. There are no mistakes, only learning experiences. When I find myself surrendering to my higher Ego, my soul is actually helping me to burn away the vestiges of my small ego, eliminating a lot of pain and suffering. This to me is true liberation.

This opens the door for me to be more compassionate and loving to all other beings around me, including animals, because we are all still suffering together. No man is an island. The recognition that I can make a difference, no matter how small, is the first step I must take towards healing myself. The thought that occurs over and over is: "What can I do?" I must start by taking control of my mind and my lower animal nature, which is a part of my emotional or astral body, often referred to as the animal soul. In order for me to progress, my four bodies, the spiritual, mental, emotional and physical, have to be in synthesis for me to perform at maximum level.

Your immense life and accomplishments are an example of what is possible through Self-mastery. You symbolize the mountain—while I am still an anthill. How can I possibly make a difference? I will start by expanding my awareness and opening my heart to myself, and then to all of life's manifestations.

What about the everyday level of temptations I am exposed to, the external bombardment of negativity and idle chatter that is at times harmful? As always, your words came to my rescue:

"I do not want to frighten you by telling you about the temptations life will bring. Anyone who is healthy in spirit will overcome them. But there is something I want you to realize. It

does not matter so much what you do. What matters, is whether your soul is harmed by what you do. If your soul is harmed something irreparable happens, the extent of which you won't realize until it will be too late.

"And others harm their soul even without being exposed to great temptations. They simply let their souls wither. They allow themselves to be dulled by the joys and worries and distractions of life, not realizing that thoughts, which earlier meant a great deal to them in their youth turned into meaningless sounds. In the end they have lost all feeling for everything that makes up the inner life."[5]

Knowing you studied the life and work of Goethe, leads me to believe you knew the universal process of being tempted by the darker forces in order to transcend our lower nature. Goethe's *Faust* enters my thoughts again, when I hear the word temptation. In *Faust*, the lower emotional forces tempt Dr. Faust, and he sells his soul to Mephistopheles in return for recapturing his youth hoping to win the love of Margarete. It describes the struggle of the spirit of man and man's journey as seen from a mystic's viewpoint. Temptation is a large part of the tests we must endure, overcome and use, in order to know ourselves better. Goethe knew a lot about the life of the soul. In his play, now turned into the book Faust I & II translated into English, I read his words at the very beginning, under the heading, *'FAUST A Tragedy'*. His dedication is as follows:

"Once more you hover close, elusive shapes
My eyes but dimly glimpsed when I was young.
Shall I now try to hold you captive?
Do these illusions still attract my heart?
Nearer yet you crowd! So be it! Do your will
As forth from mist and fog you rise about me—
The breath of magic that surrounds your train
Stirs in my breast a youthful strength of feeling.
Images of happy days accompany you,
And many dear familiar shades emerge,
First loves and early friendships too,
Like ancient tales whose words are half forgotten;
Pain is renewed, lament reiterates
Life's perplexing labyrinth
And names kind friends, cheated of joy by fortune,

Who have disappeared ahead of me.
The souls for whom I sang my early songs
Will never hear the songs that follow;
Those many friends are all dispersed,
Their first response, alas! Is long since muted.
My tragic song will now be heard by strangers
Whose very praise must give my heart misgivings,
And those to whom my song gave pleasure,
If still they live, roam scattered everywhere.
I feel the spell of long-forgotten yearning
For that serene and solemn spirit realm,
And like an aeolian harp my murmuring song
Lets its certain tones float through the air.
I feel a sense of dread, tear after tear is falling,
My rigid heart is tenderly unmanned—
What I possess seems something far away
And what had disappeared proves real."6
Johann Wolfgang von Goethe

This is one of the most moving passages I have ever read. I understand the anguish this man had experienced, the anguish he expressed is the anguish of every soul that is searching and finally breaking through. Did this story leave a deep impression on you in your youth? It took Goethe 60 years to complete Faust. He too now walks among the immortals as his work lives on to inspire us...

Jesus, when going to the mountain was faced with the same temptations, not once, but three times. However, he saw through the shallowness and illusion of temporary worldly riches, the glitter of false appearances and false power. He was able to resist and conquer the baser instincts we are born with and will eventually learn to conquer and transcend. He exposed the illusion we all so desperately cling to; the false sense of identity, which is the present personality guided by the small ego, which makes promises that never lead us to peace.

Seen in this context, yes, you are absolutely right, Jesus was a *supernatural* being. Yet, let us remember that he too was a human being... His power stemmed from knowing Truth, using this Truth fearlessly and justly, and in the process he became a *Master of Himself.* He was able to identify with his God-self, his Divine nature and his words are still showing us the way today, two thousand years later. He taught that **Love,** charity and a selfless kindness are the keys and the way, and you my dear friend—listened. I recently read this passage in one of the magazines I receive monthly:

Do it anyway
. People are often unreasonable, illogical, and self-centered; — Forgive them anyway.
. If you are kind, people may accuse you of having selfish ulterior motives; — Be kind anyway.
. If you are successful, you will win some false friends and some true enemies; — Succeed anyway.
. If you are honest and frank, people may cheat you; — Be honest and frank anyway.
.   What you spend years building, someone could destroy it overnight; — Build anyway.
. If you find serenity and happiness, they may be jealous; — Be happy anyway.
. The good you do today, people will often forget tomorrow; — Do good anyway.
. Give the world the best you have, and it may never be enough; — Give the world the best you've got anyway.
. You see, in the final analysis, it is between you and God; — It was never between you and *them* anyway.

Kent M. Keith

As I read these words again, I see that you and your teachers, Jesus and Goethe, could just as easily have said them. Goethe was a man of many interests and talents. As poet, he fearlessly explored the spiritual aspect of his own nature. Just like you, he was filled with a sense of responsibility, a sense of gratitude, a sense of wonder and curiosity.

Teachers of a Higher Wisdom, including you, who walked this path before us, are our signposts on our life journey. You knew of an aspect of our nature that is yet to come into full fruition. It is hidden from us until we grow into a fuller awareness. This state, or level of awareness is often referred to in our literature as 'The Kingdom of God". You wrote a book about this called '*The Mystery of the Kingdom of God.*' What is this next Kingdom, also known as the Fifth Kingdom? Could it be a new state of being—a higher vibration—a higher level of consciousness? Is this our true inheritance? Do we have to earn this inheritance or is it our natural birthright? Once we understand this, I mean really *understand* it, is the next step naturally to act and live accordingly? Will we now want to manifest it somehow and some way in our current life? I begin to see the importance of your vast life in a new light. Is this Kingdom to be found not on earth but on a higher plane of vibration? Can this higher vibration be felt only inside?

If the Kingdom of God is to be discovered inside each and every one of us, do we need another human being in the way of a priest or rabbi to interpret it for us and to save us? I see now that this can never work. In order for me to re-discover my soul, I have to listen to 'It'. To believe that someone else has the answers and can save us is the fallacy! The caterpillar is not *saved* and then becomes a butterfly.

You were what I call a mystic. Being a man in touch with his spirit essence, you allowed this essence to guide you, giving you the courage, the will, the strength and stamina to succeed against all the odds stacked against you. You were fearless in your pursuit of Truth. Truth remains, long after all is gone. For you it became a Living Truth...

The study of Theosophy is not a religion. The word THEO originates from the Greek word symbolizing God—and SOPHIA symbolizes wisdom. The study of *Divine Wisdom* goes beyond yet it includes every religion.

You knew that all religions are only man's quest to understand the process of this internal transformation. It is our attempt to understand this power—this essence—and because of the unique differences in experiencing this power, there are many different concepts that have developed over time, creating all the different religions. The churches and temples of today are institutions created by our own *human* interpretations, each grasping a fragment of the 'One Truth'. Each one is somewhat corrupted and influenced by the human need for power and control. Did humans change this truth along the way to make it fit their needs and their level of comprehension at the time? If these institutions are helpful in soul growth, there is a benefit. If they instill a deep sense of reverence and quietude, increasing our connection with the divinity in our selves, I see the value. If, however, the responsibility for our happiness, growth and well being is shifted to Jesus, and the now so popular bumper sticker *'Jesus Saves'* is misunderstood, our soul growth will be slowed down or stunted.

If the foundation of religion is based on the One Presence, One Absolute, One Infinite Love, One Supreme Energy, One Spirit, and each individual being is taught that he/she too has a direct spiritual connection to the One, I see its value. If it subscribes to this Oneness, the Oneness of Creation and man being its main theme, then we are approaching the High Religion as taught by the Masters. You called it the 'Religion of Love.' When we recognize that it is not 'religion', but Spirituality that matters, we are able to grow beyond its narrow confines, enlarging our view by transcending religion. Spirituality is above any humanly devised organizations.

You also knew, that each individual must be free to come to his or her own conclusions, as to what is true and right. Faith does become *an experience.* With this new and exciting insight it ceases to be *blind* faith, as the truth of 'who' I really am rings as clear as a bell in the deep recesses of my heart and mind.

"I stand at the door and knock"... said the *Christ,* through Jesus the man. Until we open the door to our inner and Higher Self, the door to our heart, each soul is in evolutionary training for one reason only, and that is to become a god, a creator in his own right. In order for us to become the true perfected self-expression of the Infinite, our mind must first become disenchanted with possessions, glamour, vanity, greed, ambition and power, which fuel aggression, competition and separateness, reinforcing the me vs. them syndrome. As we begin to appreciate the higher values our soul growth is being focused. As more light is shed on our individual consciousness we become aware of being on the path and willingly contribute to our own transformation, renewing our core values. Now our 'journey home' becomes more meaningful.

This journey is now filled with greater love, greater joy, greater beauty and greater order. The deeper understanding of 'who I am', is becoming the light of wisdom for me creating inner peace and harmony. Poets have gleaned this truth, mystics have written volumes on the subject. Poets such as Ralph Waldo Emerson, Walt Whitman and William Blake have inspired us

> *"The world was created for the education of man."*
>
> *Emerson*

I begin to understand the advice of philosophers:

> *"A life unexamined—is a life not worth living."*
>
> *Plato, quoting Socrates.*

Over the years I've gone through stages of being angry at organized religions, feeling the hypocrisy of repeating empty words, insincere platitudes and seeing a very limiting viewpoint presented by our clergy. Not anymore! I now see it as a tool for eventual soul growth for those who still feel the need for institutionalized, restricted and edited information and feel a level of comfort and security in allowing *others* to think for them. If these institutions serve them in getting in touch with their soul, teaching that Divine Love is at the core of each and every human being, a certain understanding will sooner or later emerge for those who earnestly seek. I now see that some religions are falling apart all by themselves, and that some are changing from within. Could this be a sign of the times?

Anything that is not build on the rock of Truth and Love has a tendency to disintegrate. I prefer to choose my teachers by the example their life has been for me. As I examine their actions and thoughts, I choose to learn from the higher thoughts that had shaped their character. True teachers will always encourage us to become and remain free thinkers; they will always encourage the path of self-knowledge on the path to inner peace.

True teachers *never* say: "Follow me, I am the only one with the right answers." True Teachers and Masters, like you for example, have the greatest humility and lead by example only. True teachers will inspire us to think for ourselves, to educate ourselves, stimulating us towards growth, constantly reminding us that we must walk the path alone. True Teachers teach by asking questions, questions that will challenge us to think. In this respect ignorance represents darkness or evil. Light, on the other hand, is Love and Wisdom, which will allow recognition, courage, understanding and *knowing* to surface.

"Sow a thought, reap an action.
Sow an action, reap a habit.
Sow a habit, reap character.
Sow character, reap destiny."
                    Thackeray

Knowing that I have to find my own way, be held accountable for my actions, take full responsibility for my own growth, it is better not to look for redemption or salvation outside of myself. The tools needed are already at my disposal. All I have to do is to recognize them and use them. I now trust the Process.

I recognize that I've come a long way since the days of my childhood, but I also see that I still have a long way to go in the *expansion* process. The fullness of the *now* moment is all I really have to work with in order to make this journey count. I am constantly reminding myself of the advice often seen as a paradox: "It's the journey that matters, not the destination", and "that the fruits of the journey will determine the destination."

Thank you for being here with me today, inspiring me and shedding a new ray of light on my soul which is yearning to express itself through me.

Your forever grateful student, *R.*

Dear Dr. Schweitzer,

Good morning! It is 4:30 AM. I chose to play *Bach's Brandenburg Concerto* this morning. This orchestral piece is filling my bedroom with its sound and vibration. It's a cheerful piece in which the violins and the flutes appear to be dancing.

Shakespeare said that our world is a stage. It has also been said that we are all wearing a mask. In ancient Rome all actors wore real masks while performing for the public. The mask I am referring to however, is our persona or our personality. The mask, our personality, is the role we have chosen to play in this lifetime. Do we often fall into the trap of identifying too much with the role and the actor?

I now understand reincarnation and karma a little better. We choose these parts in order to polish another facet on the jewel that is the real self, our true spiritual nature. I wrote a short poem long ago, and it seems to fit the topic I am exploring.

Our Part
The world is changing fast
Yet, some things stay the same.
A quick glance, a smile—I'm cast
To play a new part in a new scene.

We're all actors with great talent
Some bold and loud
Others shy—resisting—or latent
We all pretend to know—what it's all about.

Is our core the ego? Or maybe, let's see...
That's only a word—for what I consider to be me.
Is it my name—or is it my soul
Selecting my stage parts?
RzT 1996

We take our roles in life—our parts—so seriously and will do anything to protect our façade. I now see aspects of my personality that I never really looked at before. I discovered latent talents I never knew I had. Where did these talents suddenly come from? My intuition, Universal Mind, Universal Intelligence? My soul, is becoming my guide and inspiration—and I see my body and personality as the vehicles my soul is using in this particular lifetime.

As the process of discovery unfolds for me, I am now faced with the struggle of giving up identifying with the role and the actor and I look behind the mask or behind the role I am playing. This recognition was at first quite painful and frightening. My small ego was protecting the old self, not wanting to let go, wanting to remain in control because it got very used to being in charge of my vehicle. Do I want to remain its slave, remaining in the dark, remaining fractured and separated from my Higher Aspect? Must I now make the choice? Like the butterfly I must let go of being a caterpillar in order to fly! I can't be a caterpillar and a butterfly at the same time...

Therein lies the struggle, often called the 'dark night of the soul'. It often disguises itself as doubt, self-criticism, lethargy and depression. Seen as a necessary process of growth, I will have to step through this fear and relax in the knowledge that I will find the courage and the light will return.

As I start to see the wisdom of changing, staying the same—not growing—is becoming even more painful. I also see how resisting change, being inflexible and not using this newly gained insight will stop the flow of my intuition.

Intuition, at first hardly noticeable has now become my faithful companion. Alice Bailey in her book *'Ponder on This'* first describes what intuition is **not**:

"The intuition has no relation to psychism, either higher or lower; the seeing of a vision, hearing the Voice of the Silence, a pleased reaction to teaching of a kind does *not* infer the functioning of the intuition."[7]

Then she goes on to describe what intuition **is**:

"Intuition is the synthetic *understanding* which is the prerogative of the soul, and it only becomes possible when the soul, on its own level, is reaching in two directions: towards the Monad, (Spirit) and towards the integrated and, perhaps (even if only temporarily) coordinated and at-oned personality. It is the first indication of a deeply subjective unification, which will find its consummation at the third initiation.
Intuition is a comprehensive grip of the principle of universality, and when it is functioning there is, momentarily at least, a complete loss of the sense of separateness. At its highest point, it is known as that Universal Love, which has no relation to sentiment or to the affectional reaction, but is, predominantly, in the nature of an identification with all beings. Then is true compassion known; then does criticism become impossible; then, only, is the divine germ seen as latent in all forms."
"Intuition is light itself, and when it is functioning, the world is seen as light and the light bodies of all forms become gradually apparent. This brings with it the ability to contact the light center in all forms, and thus again an essential relationship is established, and the sense of superiority and separateness recedes into the background.
"Intuition, therefore, brings with its appearance three qualities: Illumination,...Understanding...Love... These three words sum up the three qualities or aspects of the intuition, and can be covered by the word, universality, or the sense of *Universal Oneness*."[8](My Italics)

Further down the same page I read:

"...Through the intuition man arrives at the *experience* of the Kingdom of God, and discovers the nature, the type of lives and of phenomena, and the characteristics of the Sons of God as they come into manifestation. Through the intuition, some

of the plans and purposes working out through the manifested created worlds, are brought to his attention, and he is shown in what way he and the rest of humanity can *co-operate* and hasten the divine purpose; through the intuition, we recognize the laws of the spiritual life, which are the laws governing God Himself and the spiritual Hierarchy.

"The intuition which guides all advanced thinkers into the newer fields of learning, is but the *forerunner* of that omniscience which characterizes the soul."9 (My Italics)

As I review this again, I see that the word atonement really means AT ONE MENT. It is right now that your words are beginning to have a new meaning for me, and bear repeating, as I quote them again from your autobiography '*Out of my Life and Thought*':

"Thus, at the end of my first year at the university, I was troubled by the explanation then accepted as historically correct of the words and actions of Jesus when He sent the disciples out on their mission. As a consequence of this, I also *questioned the interpretations* that viewed the whole life of Jesus as historical.

"When I reached home after maneuvers, entirely new horizons had opened up for me. Of this I was certain: that Jesus had announced *not* a kingdom that was to be founded and realized in the natural world by Himself and the believers, but that was to be expected as coming with the approaching dawn of *a supernatural age.*"10 (My Italics)

Does this mean that we, meaning humanity as a whole, will be using our intuition more and more in the future? Will that be the dawn of the supernatural age? As I flipped back to Alice Bailey's book I continue to read:

"The ignorant and the wise meet on common ground as extremes always do. In between are those who are neither totally ignorant nor intuitively wise. They are the mass of *the educated people who have knowledge, but not understanding,* and who have yet to learn the distinction between that which can be grasped by the rational mind, and that which can be seen by the mind's eye, and that which only the *higher or abstract mind* can formulate and know."11 (My Italics).

On the following page I read:

"By learning to break through the glamour in their own lives and to live in the light of the intuition, disciples can strengthen the hands of Those Who's task it is to awaken the intuition in man.

"The disciple learns, finally, to substitute the intuition—with its swiftness and its infallibility—for the slow and laborious work of the mind, with its deviousness, its illusions, its errors, its dogmatism and its separative thinking and cultures."[12]

These words were written by the mystic Alice Bailey, yet I feel that you are responsible, to a large extent, for leading me to find this knowledge. How? By constantly reminding me to keep an open mind, you were instrumental in arousing my curiosity and my intuition. I started my investigation and found certain books coinciding with your thoughts that have served me well. The archaeologist in me is becoming more and more recognizable.

This brings me back to identifying with the glamour, as Bailey calls it, of our lives. Our material possessions! Do we own them, or do they own us? This is a very personal question, a question that will sooner or later arise and every man and woman must honestly answer this question for him or herself.

Castles
Everyone's journey is different
This experience—in time and space.
Making choices—identifying themselves
Through professions—lifestyles—their case?

The farmer is up early—ready to sow
The banker—concerned with money
Profits—directing its flow.
The salesman, without his effort, there is no nectar—no honey.

We all contribute without being aware
Some less—some a little more
Through our choices—our projections
Leave an imprint on the sand.

Nature's rhythm we can't avoid
The next wave—when high tide is coming
Washing away
Just to start over—again.

Our castles are only an illusion
Something we keep only for a while
Seeking experiences—learning
Next time—to identify—a little less?
RzT 1996

We are only the guardians of these things for a very short time. Why then do we place so much value and emphasis on material acquisitions? Aren't we trying to fill an emptiness or void? This feeling of spiritual emptiness can never be filled with material objects or possessions. Castles aren't bad or good, it's our *beliefs* about the value of castles we must change. True royalty and nobility is found only in our spiritual nature. To me you were a *real* king. A real king serves his subjects without loosing anything. In this respect *service* is an inherent part of the magic and power. Your power is still radiating throughout the world today.

As I continue to write these letters to you I am experiencing a healing. Could it be that the act of looking behind the mask I chose to wear this time around, enables and helps me to remove layers upon layers of false beliefs?

What you call a *supernatural age,* is the recognition that humanity will eventually wake up to its true Divine nature. Yes, we are all evolving, perhaps not in a linear fashion, but on several levels at the same time. Our physical body is the last to register this evolution.

The process starts in the mind. Since our thoughts create our reality, our feelings—our destiny—we will eventually manifest all we have previously only thought about in our physical world and our bodies. 'As above so below' is conceptually perfect, becoming a reality.

My truth and how I experience it currently, will not be a truth accepted by everyone; it is truth only, if it resonates with something in the heart. It serves as a constant reminder for me that all is in a constant state of flux, or in a *constant state of change.* Your deeper insight is startling, yet so true:

"In everything you recognize yourself. The tiny beetle that lies in your path—it was a living creature, struggling for existence like yourself, rejoicing in the sun like you, knowing fear and pain like you. And now it is no more than decaying matter—which is what you will be sooner or later, too."13

This is the Truth, the uncomfortable Truth we will all be faced with sooner or later. Why do we so cling to the illusion of our body? The life force that animates our existence is the same in everyone. Isn't life itself, or the will-to-live—God?

This has been a very long letter and I must go and apply myself in the physical world. I now return to my tasks at hand, having absorbed a bit more than I had anticipated. Thank you.

Tonight I will be playing the role of mother. It is Sunday, Mother's Day, and my two sons are taking me to a roller coaster in Fort Lauderdale. It's been years since I last rode a roller coaster. They too look forward to this evening and know how much I love to experience the law of gravity. This morning they said, "Let's enjoy this before we take you out to dinner, so you won't throw up." Good advice!

Dear Dr. Schweitzer, in closing I would like to express my gratitude to you for helping me to grow and teaching me the value of taking full responsibility for what I think, feel and do. Looking in the mirror is a painful experience, however, it is also a liberating experience. In ordinary language I can only term it as the experience of *letting go*. It is the experience of just *being*, of letting others *be*, knowing we are not that different at all, we are all ONE, choosing to experience life in many different and diversified ways—creating our own reality—with each experience.

We are all on the path, some are a little ahead and some are still at the bottom of the mountain, scared to look up. You have taught me to be gentle and kind to all pilgrims.

There is no right or wrong path—there is only the path, also described in esoteric terms as 'The Way'. As I leave you today, I want you to know that my heart is filled with gratitude for the light you have become, which is not only illuminating my way, but also illuminating my mind and heart.

Your devoted and grateful student, *R*.

Good morning, Dr. Schweitzer,

Today is Tuesday, my day off. The roller coaster ride was wonderful. I experienced a spontaneous happiness last night. My two sons, now grown and leading busy lives, took time off to spend the whole evening with me. We laughed and talked about old times. What is this temporary fleeting moment we call happiness? I just opened the book and came across your words giving me more insight:

"It is reason which helps to get beyond the trivialities of our daily life. We become concerned about all that is happening, with all the questions that beset our times. It makes us participate in this world and feel personally what is happening on earth... Our happiness or unhappiness is not determined by what happens to us in everyday life. However favorable our circumstances, however successful our enterprises, however much envied we are by our fellow men, we still may not be happy. For peace alone is the source of happiness. The more our reasoning throws us into the turmoil of life's problems, the more we yearn for peace. We are led up the mountains until the glaciers begin to glitter before us. Then reasoning bids us to climb still higher, still further into the light, still further into peace and quietude."[14]

Are we are all seeking Higher Ground? What do we find at the top of this metaphoric mountain? Is it liberation and Peace? Who resides there? The souls of Masters such as you, who have evolved to a higher state of being? Jesus described it this way.

"Among those born of women there has risen no one greater than John the Baptist, yet he who is least in the Kingdom of Heaven is greater than he." Matthew 11:11

Jesus knew about the levels on the ladder of evolution and you understood his words. As a student, did the revelation of the true meaning of these words inspire you to write your now famous book *"The Mystery of the Kingdom of God"*? These findings were still on your mind as you wrote your life story in the 1930's. Half way down the paragraph I read your words again, showing me your full comprehension of Jesus' words:

"As a man in the condition into which all men enter at birth, the Baptist is the greatest of all who have lived. But members of the Kingdom of Heaven are no longer natural men; through the dawning of the Messianic Kingdom they have experienced a change that *has raised them to a supernatural condition* akin to that of the *angels*. Because they are now supernatural beings, the least among them is greater than the greatest man who has ever appeared in the natural world of the age that is now passing away. John the Baptist does, indeed, belong to this Kingdom either as a great or humble member of it. Yet his greatness, unique and surpassing that of all other humans, lies in the fact that he became *incarnate in this natural world*."[15] (My Italics)

This quote speaks to me of evolution. During each lifetime we progress through trials of initiations moving closer towards our ultimate purpose which is Self-mastery. You called the spirits, guides and teachers all around us '*angels*.' You knew that these messengers were hoping to make us aware of the *true* meaning of Love. Your whole life exhibits the fact that you *knew*.

Is *knowing* enough? What must I do with this knowledge, once I understand it? Do I now have to manifest this truth in my life? The process is called a 'Journey of Awakening' because metaphysically speaking we are asleep to the fact that we **are** a soul or an individual spark of a still larger Soul or the Oversoul. Everything that is alive, still lives within something greater. In my body for instance each molecule lives within a cell, many cells live and form my organs, my organs live and form my body.

I first experienced a glimpse of a different kind of love back in 1996.

Love
Love, the way we know it—romance—so sentimental
Ships passing in the night—behold
This meeting of two souls, so instrumental
Recognition—an instant desire to hold.

Will they be together for life?
Be each others teacher
See themselves—with the other's light?
Shining—molding—learning—come nearer?

Why are they together?
Love birds—man and wife
Are they really close in spirit?
Or is lust the main force—the drive?

This union is meant to be—for better or for worse
Perhaps, experiencing through climax—creation.
That moment of ecstasy and release
Receiving and giving—at the same time.

Don't cling—don't grasp—let it be
Observe the wonder of it.
Can I now I see—that the Love I seek
Is really in me?
RzT 1996

We are always crying out to be loved. Each song has the same refrain. Love is an emotion we all love to feel, expecting happiness as a result. Do we accept that at our core we *are* love.

Most of us suffer from *reverse* thinking. At the risk of repeating myself, I say again that an example of this is the question: "How many people will love me?" When the question must be: "Why don't I value and love myself? How large is my ability to love?" How can I possibly love anyone, if I don't love myself? How can I give something I don't have? How can I devote myself to anything or anyone if I don't first have and nurture *self-devotion,* Which now becomes soul-devotion.

As I look at the list of symptoms I typed the other day, I see what love is *not.* This leads me to recognize that as long as I harbor any of the false beliefs and emotions, which are the **cause** *of* all symptoms, I am not capable of experiencing the 'real' me the 'I AM Love'. What we normally think of as love is conditional upon the object of our affection living up to our image of what he or she *should* be like. Then we can love them. That is selfishness—not love. We get married and then begin to find fault with and get busy trying to change the person we married.

Why do we lack the courage to see ourselves in the light of this truth, shining a light on all of our other *self-denying* beliefs and character traits? What keeps us from doing anything about it? Our small ego is conditioned since childhood, taught to believe in separateness and competition, which keeps us acting out and living according to its limiting belief system. It keeps us stuck.

We don't love ourselves! Can I love someone who is hateful, arrogant, jealous, fearful, rude, needy, weepy, manipulative, materialistic, critical, judgmental, unforgiving, stingy and depressed? Yes, because love is not conditional. The recognition that we have a shadow side to our human character is fundamentally important. Once I am aware that the shadow is fear based, can I own it, heal it and transform it through courage and love.

The psychologist, Carl Jung, had transcended the field of psychiatry as taught by his mentor Sigmund Freud. Jung called our dark side *'the shadow side'*. It is the part of us that is energized by repressed feelings of anger and old hurts. He explained how if not recognized as such, and brought to the surface, that its energy can and will be projected onto others. Then the faults I see in other people are really the mirror image of my own. My task is to "own my own shadow."

Jung had discovered the field of the 'collective unconscious' and in this respect he was a great visionary, a rebel who just like you was not afraid to explore the unknown and think outside of the box. He looked behind what we normally look at, to find the *cause* of our pain and struggle. The cause can only be discovered once we understand that we **are** a soul. In this way, he too became a physician of the soul. His quest to 'know himself' led him into new and previously unexplored territory. I must correct myself here. It wasn't so new to the Eastern way of thinking. The Western mind is only now catching up in recognizing this. He discovered that astrology can be of great value, once the influence and the attributes of the heavenly bodies we call planets, moving through the eternal sky is fully understood. He re-discovered what the ancient astronomers and astrologers must have known and recognized thousands of years ago. For instance the Egyptians were very occupied with the movement of stars and the meaning and influence of the various constellations, as was Gallileo and Pythagoras before him. Gallileo, a mathematician, astronomer and physicist discovered that the earth revolves around our sun and that it is not the center of our universe. Being considered a heretic, he was persecuted and put under house arrest by the Inquisition in Rome for discovering and presenting a position that was opposite of accepted thought at the time. He also said that the "Book of Nature is written in mathematical characters." This leads me to see that when Truth becomes uncomfortable it is denied.

What we call God is the Impersonal Divine Love encompassing all of creation, including sinners and saints alike. This divine impersonal Love, like a wise father allows his children to experience the full consequences of their choices knowing this is part of the maturing process and can't be avoided. We must experience what it feels like to be separate, feel what it means to work against the Universal Laws, feel the pain and suffering in order to understand and grow. On the other hand, these immutable and absolute Laws also allow us to experience and feel the flow of energy that results from aligning ourselves with them. The choice must be ours.

The seat of the 'lower case' ego is in the solar-plexus, right above the navel. That's where the false 'I' is hiding. It is the seat of our emotional mind. Why does it help to know this? Because I can now lift my energy and thoughts to my heart area, represented by my heart chakra. It is not coincidental that we identify the heart with love. This magical center is the seat of our soul, *the center of all healing* and therefore the *magical center of transformation.*

My thoughts, once passed through the heart, have no choice but to change. They are then influenced by the healing force coming from my soul, which recognizes the power of unconditional Love. It now becomes the battle-ground, or struggle, between my lower tearful self, and my Higher Self, which is pure and unconditional Love. Isn't this the Love or energy emanating from the Bhuddi or Christ consciousness? Are my soul, my heart and my mind, the vehicles the Higher Self or Spirit uses to accomplish this?

In order for me to practice what I have learned, I must pass my thoughts through my heart center and watch how it changes my feelings, raises my awareness, as it burns away the old lower energies. In the heart center is the spark, which once ignited becomes the flame of transcendence leading me *naturally* to transformation.

This 'Inner Light' is making much more sense to me now. This light is present in each and every one of us, we are just too scared to look at ourselves and release all the negativity we carry around. This negativity or *fear* hides our 'inner' light or inner power. Fear and ignorance go hand in hand, keeping us stuck on the emotional roller coaster of happiness and unhappiness—pleasure and pain— which in turn, is keeping us from growing and awakening to the beauty of our true nature, our soul connection to our Higher Self. Once we surrender to the guidance of our Higher Self and reach beyond the duality of appearances, the struggle is over and peace is experienced.

During the afternoon lecture on Pythagoras I learned that the great Master would require each new student to spend 5 years in the study of astronomy, physics, science and mathematics. A student had to practice being silent for an established period of time. Thus he weeded out those who were not as yet ready for the larger mysteries of life.

Pythagoras, a metaphysician, mystic, philosopher and teacher around 550 BC, stressed that the beginning of all growth and transformation is "Know Thyself". He knew that the process of evolution, the growth of the soul, is at times a very painful experience. Buddha taught that all attachment causes pain and suffering. When we experience and are filled with a feeling of deep contentment and genuine gratitude, our cup is experienced as full instead of empty. That's when we feel truly alive!

Is the impersonal and *androgynous* power we call God expressing itself through us? What a great new concept to expand on. Dr. Albert Einstein has given us an inside view of what our universe consists of, coming up with the formula E=MC2. Seen from this angle there is no matter, only energy vibrating at different frequencies, the densest or lowest vibration of frequency being matter. How many of us take the time to contemplate the deeper meaning of this? He demonstrated, that energy can not be destroyed. It can only be transformed or changed, something many ancient teachers knew thousands of years ago. My question now is: "Does Spirit or consciousness create matter?"

"When the student is ready to listen, the teacher appears!" In this way the process becomes a very natural process of unfolding from within. The teacher is actually already there. But we can only recognize him or her when we reach the next stage of our development. Then it becomes obvious that all we have to do, is look or become aware of what has always already been there. It helps to admit that we don't know. This will open the door for something new to appear. Pretending to know keeps the door to our wider perception closed.

Are the Sages, Saints and Masters human beings who have perfected their four bodies through the experiences of many lifetimes? Do they exist on a higher vibration which our ordinary eyes can't as yet perceive? Do they form the Spiritual Hierarchy? Are they the beings you called angels?

Are they like our older brothers, ready to give us a helping hand, providing we make the necessary effort? Our free will to create and to learn our lessons will never be interfered with, since these are the necessary opportunities we need to grow in understanding and wisdom. No one is allowed to interfere in this process not even the Masters. First and foremost, we must admit that we are in need of help. Only when we admit that we are lost, will we look for and pay attention to a signpost. As we surrender our small ego and our small *human* will, they will respond showing us there is a Higher Will at work. Our vibration will become finer, more in tune with their vibration. Our soul will begin to resonate with this higher vibration or frequency. Their response will depend on our genuine effort, our interest, and the energy we expend towards *self-inquiry*, including our sincere *intention* and desire to understand.

Transformation will occur on an individual basis, the moment we take full responsibility for our lives. Humanity can only advance as one person at a time, *owns his/her own shadow* and heals him or her self, and recognizes the crucial part each and every one of us plays in creating peace. That's when I begin to see myself as being a part of a much larger whole.

Many of the ancient mysteries dramatize the human being coming into earthly existence, being tested by life itself and graduating through these tests, returning transformed into a higher state of being. The ancient mysteries reveal and describe this process of evolution. Thus, every successfully completed assignment or test is a stage of growth or initiation. Thus we are born again—or transformed.

This process of transformation was taught in the old mythologies of my history classes in grade school, but I had no idea of the significance of these dramas, and how they related to an *inner* experience.

The temptations are all around us, and it seems easier at times to remain in the darkness or 'Hall of Ignorance', instead of becoming aware of the help and the light available all around us as well. Learning to create a better balance of our Higher and lower nature, and recognizing the Power of Love as a higher Truth are two great accomplishments. Is it necessary to merge the left brain of pure analysis and reason (intellect) with our right brain (intuition)? It is only then that we experience wholeness and love instead of fear.

We all choose certain experiences, often very painful ones, in order to become aware. The process starts or is initiated by asking some of the vital questions. Such as "Who am I?" "What am I doing here?" "Where am I going?" and finally, "How do I get there?"

Each self-conscious individual will eventually ask these questions. Some will ask them sooner and some later. Some will delay the process for another life. As we start the learning process our intuition will be aroused. As we learn to trust our intuition, our own experiences will begin to guide us.

Thus we are awakened to a new Reality. This greater or new field of Reality or Actuality transcends thought. Do we grow in spiritual maturity by conquering or mastering our lower animal mind, and our animal instincts? Is this the *preparation* for our next stage of development? Isn't this the drama of life and transformation? Is that why Carl Jung was called an alchemist? He dared to look and explore the hidden (occult) side of our nature. The gold created by the alchemist becomes an inner process. As we burn away the grosser parts of our nature, we begin to expose and live from our true nature—which is our soul. It stands to reason therefore, that we must become masters of our body, mind and emotions, before we can master anything else. The ultimate Reality is the ultimate Truth. As humans we experience this Truth as Love. The more truthful we are, first with ourselves and then with others, the more Love we have at our disposal. Again, it's all relative! Being true to yourself, your soul, is a command that has reverberated throughout eternity. I must live my incarnation the best way I know how, with my present level of awareness. Life is not about success or failure, but about doing our best as I see that the unseen forces of cause and effect govern life!

Many ancient cultures share similar myths or tales of the evolution of man. At times we note a change in consciousness, at times the effect does not manifest outwardly but in dreams. All we think about and entertain in our consciousness will manifest. Initiation is a process through which we evolve spiritually. Beyond happiness and unhappiness we find 'peace', which is a soul quality.

I see now how the process works. You had mastered yourself. Being an example is all that a teacher can be. You remind me that I must walk the path—alone—yet I am not alone. You are in a way my older brother, someone who has been through the process of awakening, transmuted the pain and is now living in spirit form lending us a helping hand. Your life has become a perfect example of what a man is capable of accomplishing in one lifetime. You performed magic, which once understood is part of the natural Universal Laws that govern our existence, and not magic in the usual meaning. Magic is based on scientific and metaphysical laws. You were *true to yourself* in the deepest sense of the meaning, allowing the God part of you, *your Spirit* to shine through.

With deep gratitude in my heart I remain,
Your devoted student, *R.*

Dear Dr. Schweitzer,

I can't help but wonder how we humans would react if Jesus returned to earth today, exhibiting the same qualities and stressing the same values he did then. I dare to examine these values again. Jesus was a pacifist—he did not believe in war. Jesus embraced the ordinary people, the less fortunate ones, seeing injustice and corruption all around him. He used allegories to teach the masses, such as, "It is easier for a camel to pass through the eye of a needle, than for a rich man to enter the Kingdom of God." This speaks of detachment from material values and *turning* to the more meaningful, the more lasting spiritual ones. His life demonstrated the value of sacrifice and the value of service to humanity. Money and wealth are not good or evil. Money can be used to manipulate and control, or to educate and heal the less fortunate.

Jesus did not discriminate. He spoke of Love as a living Power and often reminded us of the brotherhood of all of mankind. He embraced the homeless, the sick and the sinners. He did not lift weapons against anyone, he taught equanimity and fairness. He taught harmlessness and gentleness. Jesus inspired, by being an example. He did not fear death. His life in a way depicts a journey—the symbolic journey of every human being—the journey of every soul. He was a wandering Jew, who's home is nowhere—yet everywhere. Jesus taught us to see through the glamour of material possessions, knowing they can and often do enslave us. His life is still seen as a mystery by those with limited vision. What would we do to a man who preached these values today? Would we put him in prison for speaking against, or exposing the motives of the ruling classes? Since he was the ultimate pacifist, would he

be persecuted for his words? How would Jesus view the gilded
churches and edifices build in his name? How would he view the
wealth and riches of the Vatican? Would they charge him with
heresy? I wonder...

I feel that you were an old soul, a giant spirit, manifesting in
your last life as Albert Schweitzer, returning to teach us who we are.
The name bestowed upon you at birth is therefore perfect.

Albert, means noble and bright—Adel—also means Royal. As
I feel myself changing, I also like my name better. Was my soul
trying to show me the way seventeen years ago? Were the poems
becoming a road map of my future development?

Why didn't I get it before? I wasn't ready! As I look at this poem
I see that some light had become visible six years ago.

Light
Light though dim, is still burning
This deep desire to be happy and free
My road is rocky—still learning
That nothing in life has a guarantee.

We search for security, comfort—mystique
Without letting anyone know
Our desires hidden—secrets in our hearts—intrigue
Our struggle through sun, wind and snow.

Allowing fear to direct is easy
When facing this world alone
Open your mind—spirit—shall I keep this role—maybe?
Or—has the time arrived to atone?

Time to hire a new director? Get on a new cloud?
Time for more light from inside
Faith—removing the shadows of doubt,
Will I take the new part offered—in stride?

Be strong, have courage and trust
Are we all slaves?
Or is this struggle for freedom a must?
To be alone, use the pain—to overcome—thus saved.

Find your Self—discover the joy of contribution
Be the light—help shine on others—just a few
Look—feel their pain—their disillusion
Allow them to see themselves—anew.
RzT 1996

    I felt a chill pass down my spine while reading this aloud, before sharing it with you. Is that what is in store for me? Do I have the strength and courage to guide others? I find it hard to believe at the moment, however, I do believe in being flexible and do not want to write the script for the rest of my life. I'd rather watch it as it unfolds naturally. I am more open to all new experiences, able to face the painful ones with a new courage, knowing they have the most to teach me.

    Looking at myself has been the most painful, and at the same time the most liberating experience in my life. Call it what you will, it is what it is—a paradox.

    I admit to being a novice, and recognize that the more I think I know, the more I know that I know nothing. I can only speak for myself and try to relate what I have experienced. As I take the necessary steps, albeit baby steps, I find myself moving in a different direction. I find myself looking inside the mystery, by examining and seeing the duality that is myself, and embrace it all. Will I be able to transcend this duality in this lifetime? I feel closer to you now than I've ever felt before, and I thank you.

I see a magic formula unfolding:
Want to create more love? BE loving.
Want to create more peace? BE peaceful.
Want to create more tolerance? BE tolerant.
Want to create more patience? Be patient.
Want to create more abundance? BE generous.

    This doesn't mean try or become, it means BE IT. Change the INNER and the *outer* will change. By **being** it we have transformed it. This creative power resides in each and every one of us, without exception. It is the gift you give yourself.

    As I look at my computer clock I see that it is only 10:30. I still have time to go to the beach and digest this new information quietly—alone. It is the middle of May, the thermostat is edging up to almost 90 degrees so I must be careful of the stronger rays of the sun this time of the year. Dear doctor and teacher, I say 'Auf Wiedersehen', which means until we meet again, here in my secret closet where my computer is perched on a narrow desk. Thanks for being my angel!

Your completely devoted and grateful student, *R*.

Dear Dr. Schweitzer,

The beach was wonderful today. I listened to the gentle rhythm of the surf and felt the warmth of the sand under my body. I listened to the sounds of the seagulls. All this filled me with a sense of peace, inspiring me to write to you again this afternoon.

Several organizations were created in your name after you passed over and returned to Spirit. The French arm of this organization is called 'Association Internationale de l'Oeuvre d'Albert Schweitzer de Lambaréné' shortened to (A.I.S.L.). It is an arm that connects all organizations formed world wide in your name. This organization is represented in Poland, Germany, Czechoslovakia, now called the Czech Republic, Austria, the Netherlands, Taiwan, Japan, Switzerland, Italy, and the United States.

I can see that you were a World Citizen in the truest sense of the word. In Kaysersberg, the village of your birth, I picked up a booklet last September called: 'Friends of Albert Schweitzer.' I took it to the beach with me earlier today and read it again, finding out even more about all the different aspects of your nature. This little booklet contains your words in the form of quotations, some of which I had never read before.

It confirms everything I have been finding out about you, and the purpose of your life. I thought for the longest time that you had only partly discovered the mysteries, as they were taught in the Ageless Wisdom Teachings. I suspected your wisdom, and knew you operated on a higher level of consciousness than most ordinary men. You were indeed completely aware and quite extraordinary in your knowledge of the ancient teaching as I am learning it today, rediscovering on my own, the wisdom of *'Know Thyself and you will know the Gods.'*

From this point of view we are all gods in the making, in other words we possess the *potential to create*, although as of now, on a much smaller scale.

You had found the power of the will, which is synonymous with purpose. *A will that is manifesting from the heart, not just the mind, tempered by Pure Reason, Love and Truth.* You certainly had found some of the answers to the most profound questions we will ever be faced with in our lives. You had transcended the duality of the personal self.

You were less concerned with your personal happiness than with the purpose and usefulness of your life! The purpose, as I now see it, is revealed very clearly and brilliantly. Your life is teaching me the value and power of Love, Compassion, Gratitude, Forgiveness, Tolerance and that there is a great underlying unity at the core of all life. This idea will lead us to the threshold of understanding what it means to have '*Reverence for Life*', because all life is what we call God.

Dear doctor, you are a true healer and I allowed you to become the physician of my soul. The idea just came to me recently, while reviewing these letters.

"So many people gave me something or were something to me without knowing it...I always think that we all live, spiritually, by what others have given us in the significant hours of our life. These significant hours do not announce themselves as coming but arrive unexpected."[16]

What knowing you has done for me, what you have given me spiritually by making your life your argument, came unexpectedly and can't be expressed in words. Where before I was too lazy and lethargic to think and contemplate my own nature, I am now finding it myself—and able to heal myself through the unity of mind, body and Spirit.

I think about the many pop-psychologists making the rounds of talk shows today. Unless they point straight at our own nature, instead of blaming parents and society for all the confusion and sorrow in the world, what good are they? Do they serve to awaken us, or do they keep us asleep? Do they empower us or do they keep us dependent and helpless? Who are our role models of today? What do they have to teach us?

I am sure that the arrow of criticism will be directed my way for being so candid, but I have learned not to take things like that personally. Adverse reactions will be a given, considering most people hide behind blaming everyone else for their behavior and lack of understanding. Incomprehension seems to afflict the masses of the population today, and I will have to accept what IS. Some people find comfort in sameness and mediocrity, never wanting to exercise their right to think on new levels. Most people enjoy wallowing in the past, reliving their painful childhood, blaming and lashing out at everyone in sight. Every victim story is the same!

I have already experienced, that a certain *truth* about psychological insights makes a lot of people very uncomfortable, especially those people who are still reliving past hurts and are stuck in the blame game. The past is over and gone, yet people make it alive for them day in and day out, replaying the same tape over and over again. In other words, they are not living in and aware of the power of the present moment. Blaming someone else has created a firmly established habit and is so much easier than taking a long look in the mirror. This way, when their marriage is shaky or on the rocks, they will always have someone else to blame. People may pretend to be spiritual, but when it comes to forgiveness they hide behind their false sense of self, justifying every manipulative action. To those people I say: "Take a look at the wounds one last time, open them and allow the poison to come out." Allow Love to be the healing agent.

I hope that the generation of my children and grandchildren will have the courage to break through the barrier of ignorance and self-deception. Until then, I admit to feeling somewhat isolated. Sadly, as much as these words are meant to help heal, they may be misunderstood.

I personally find it helpful to seek out the mystics, teachers who have walked in our shoes, who are our older brothers in a way. Like you, they know the predicament, the struggle we are presently facing. True teachers know the duality of our existence; they also *know* the healing energy of Love and Compassion.

I wonder what state our earth would be in if the mystical esoteric knowledge housed in the Library of Alexandria had not been destroyed. Would we have more respect and reverence for the life giving force of our sun, for instance? Without it's life giving energy we could not exist. I am not surprised at the ancient ceremonial sun worship. The sun's love is impersonal—it shines on everyone equally. While reading Evelyn Underhill's 'The Essentials of Mysticism' on the beach yesterday, I came across the following passage right at the beginning of her book:

"We will begin, then, with the central fact of the mystic's experience. This central fact, it seems to me, is an overwhelming consciousness of God and of his own soul: a consciousness which absorbs or eclipses all other centers of interest. It is said that St. Francis of Assisi, praying in the house of Bernard of Quintavalle, was heard to say again and again: "My God! My God! What art Thou? And what am I?" Though the words come from St. Augustine, they well represent his mental attitude. These are the only question he thought worth asking; and it is the question which every mystic asks at the beginning and sometimes answers at the end of his quest. Hence we must put first among our essentials the conviction of a living God as the primary interest of consciousness, and of a personal self, capable of communion with Him."[17]

Has the time come for us as a civilization to see the value in this, finally waking up to our potential and power? I glanced at a prayer and look at the photo of a statue of St. Francis of Assisi on my bedroom wall, a photograph I took about a year ago of a statue while walking through the garden of the retreat I attended. I now read his famous words again. St. Francis, a mystic with vision, understood the power of correct prayer, he also saw the Oneness of all of creation leaving us his legacy, also known as the Prayer of Saint Francis of Assisi:

Lord make me an instrument of your **Peace.**
Where there is hatred—let me sow **Love**
Where there is injury—**Pardon**
Where there is doubt—**Faith**
Where there is despair—**Hope**
Where there is darkness—**Light**
Where there is sadness—**Joy.**

Divine Master—grant that I may
Not so much seek to be consoled—**as to console;**
Not so much seek to be understood—**as to understand.**
Not so much seek to be loved—**as to love;**
For it is in the giving—**that we receive**

It is in the pardoning—**that we are pardoned;**
And it is in the **dying—that we are born to**
ETERNAL LIFE.

For me personally, the above represents a scientific equation, the formula for seeing beyond the personality, a formula we will eventually understand and use in our lives. I can see that this was 'your way' as well. I now see his prayer as a tool, an example of *right* thought revealing and creating a new attitude. It expresses a change or reversal of mind and heart. It's a prayer of invocation. Did St. Francis know we are all channels for this divine energy and able to align and to unite with it?

After all is said and done, the ultimate mystery is the death of the physical body, when our soul leaves the limiting confines of the physical vehicle behind.

Personally, for me the challenge is in living, learning and being truly alive. I become alive by *responding* to my innate ability or talents, the gifts that reveal themselves in my uniqueness, in my individuality and in the recognition that we are all souls on a journey and that our essential nature—is LOVE.

In order to experience the *eternal* life we must all eventually die. Death is nothing to be afraid of since it is only a transformation in consciousness, a transition from limited reality to infinite Reality.

In the booklet I picked up last September, I read on the last page, and I quote:

'What a mark of progress it would be if, in present circumstances, every one of us devoted three minutes each evening to contemplating thoughtfully the infinity of planets in the starry heavens, and if, in a funeral procession, we reflected upon the enigmas of death instead of pacing slowly, empty-headed, behind the coffins."18

Being a spiritual philosopher you had recognized the duality of our existence:

"To ensure the reproduction and survival of each species, Nature provides remarkably well-adapted equipment. But Nature does not seem in any way to incorporate this purpose in any vast total plan. She produces both a marvelous creative force and also a destructive force—an incomprehensible, bewildering mixture

of sense and nonsense, of absurdity and reason. That is the nature of the Universe."[19]
"No-one can henceforth fail to know the amount of misery that exists all over the world. Man must also learn what the spirit of humanity is capable of undertaking and achieving in its struggle against this misery."[20]

You certainly did your part. Not only did you act on your convictions, by deciding to serve humanity in the jungle of Africa and healing the physically sick, you also educated us with your wonderful words of inspiration. Your words are filled with passion, they are words of hope, words of compassion, words of healing, words of courage, words of motivation, words of wisdom, words of truth and words of power. Your words, an outgrowth of *correct* thinking, serve to constantly remind us of who we really are. Thus you have helped us to recognize our soul, which helps us to awaken to the Reality of our spiritual nature.

This brings me to another way for overcoming depression, which is negative self-focus creating a certain level of lethargy. People who have a hobby or an interest they are passionate about, are seldom depressed. Whether this interest is gardening, sewing, music, reading, painting, writing, photography or the building of model-airplanes, does not matter. For me this is very important since a hobby allows me to completely loose myself in some sort of artistic or creative expression. While indulging in a hobby I replace all negative thoughts with creative ones. Most of these activities cost very little, but they allow us to see ourselves differently. We begin to experience our own creativity, which is a spark of divinity, albeit a small part.

You, more than any other teacher up to date, have gently guided me back to myself, helping me to recognize my spiritual nature. Thank you so much,
Your grateful and devoted student, *R.*

Dear Dr. Schweitzer,

It is nearing the end of May and the newscasts are full of reports of the Taliban planning their retaliation for our bombing of Afghanistan. Last night I heard it discussed that this time the targets will be more devastating than the destruction of the World Trade Center. What has happened to humanity as you knew it? You lived through two world wars. You witnessed the inhumanity of war. I recognized that the only thing that keeps us from knowing all this is the fact that we are asleep. I was struck by the idea that we all collectively suffer from a case of amnesia, not knowing who we really are. Who was it that stated: "I searched for the enemy, and discovered it was us!"

If we are identifying only with the negative and destructive aspects of our nature, our fearful lower self, which is concerned with ambition, control, manipulation, money, greed and self-promotion, aren't we constantly reinforcing our feelings of separation, a separation from our true self? The promise of Jesus is clear and definite when he said:

"I will not leave you comfortless; I will come to you. Yet a little while, and the world seeth me no more; but ye see me: because I live, ye shall live also. At that day ye shall know that I am in my father, and ye in me, and I in you."[21]

In this respect we are all children or a part of God, yet we ignore this higher aspect of our nature. The early Christians knew the deeper esoteric meaning of the words I quoted above! Are you aware that the Dead Sea Scrolls were found in 1947? Are you aware that the translations are still being argued over and discussed by scholars today? Are you aware that they had been withheld from the general public for centuries? Are you aware that they were written by a Hebrew sect known as the 'Essenes'? What about the missing or deleted gospels discovered in the desert of Egypt in 1945, now stored in the Nag Hammadi Library, including the *'Gospel of Mary Magdalene'* and 'The *Gospel of Thomas'*? Scholars have now called them the *'Gnostic Gospels'*. Could the information contained in these writings give us a glimpse of the true meaning of Jesus? These books have now been translated and are available to everyone.

True Christianity must be looked for, beyond tradition and outer observances. Esoteric or mystical Christian teachings, as taught by Paul the Apostle, stress that the **inner life** is 'real' and beyond illusion, and that a spiritual discipline and meditation are fundamental aspects of the true 'Christ' mind. Religion's true purpose is steeped in mysticism, and it seems to have become veiled, but not lost.

Recognizing 'Christ' as a higher level of awareness now makes sense to me. We are all on 'Jacob's Ladder', the ladder of evolution. There are many levels of evolution, many manifestations and beings below the human level. So, there must be many levels or beings above the human level. As above, so below... In esoteric literature these are referred to as the spiritual Hierarchy or the Brotherhood, residing in the Fifth Kingdom or the Kingdom of God, entrance to which is barred until we evolve to a higher spiritual level. All of the ancient teachings, from the Osiris legends, to the philosophies of Socrates, Plato, Buddha, Pythagoras, Zeno, and Marcus Aurelius, refer to initiations, rites or tests that must be mastered, before one is allowed to see this Kingdom.

Religion is the *exoteric* method of teaching the masses of humanity, teachings found in parables and allegories. An esoteric school for the true seekers of wisdom and knowledge; those earnest in spirit, pure in heart and intention, seeking an unveiled spiritual perception is not really found on earth. The esoteric wisdom is comprehended differently. The inner or esoteric mysteries cannot be taught. They are only recognized on the *inner* level. Plato used questions and myths to explain what can't be explained with words. In this way his students would be encouraged to think for themselves. That's why myths and parables are so powerful.

The true purpose of religion seems to be to quicken our human evolution. Yet, its meaningful teachings are watered down and diluted to the point that it offends my intellect to make God a vengeful being, promising hell fire and purgatory for sinners. Not only that, the many other contradictions offend the minds of the more evolved. Why don't we have the honesty to admit that the 'God' we are really seeking to know and we so often refer to, is beyond our current level of comprehension, something we are not equipped as yet to fully understand?

Perhaps we have failed to look beyond these teachings, failed to look at the true source of religion by looking at the church as the authority, *human authority*, rather than 'Christ.' Having said this, I will re-read you book '*The Mysticism of Paul the Apostle*' perhaps understanding it on a deeper level the second time around. This often happens to me, and proves that we comprehend more as we grow in awareness. Many Christians have lost touch with their true heritage, the wisdom of esoteric Christian teachings, which like the ancient teachings of India and the Orient are transcendental and mystical in nature.

I see us as a bunch of hyperactive ants scuttling about in a competitive fashion trying to amass more of everything. As we frantically try to keep up with the Jones', amass more wealth expecting happiness through self-gratification, we are becoming spiritually bankrupt. We constantly complain about our state of affairs, yet avoid the one and only thing that will teach us part of the mystery, which is—to look into ourselves—unveiling our inner self, becoming more familiar with our spiritual nature.

We all too often cling to the false belief that our material and physical possessions will finally bring us happiness, peace and love. Where is that promised happiness? Where is the Kingdom of God? Where is the Promised Land? Where is Heaven? Where can we find Nirvana? Are we truly honest with ourselves?

What would happen if we all of a sudden realized that God is growing through our ability to love?

If 'As above, so below', is a fundamental fact in the Law of Nature, then God is also growing—expanding—as we are expanding in consciousness. Since our universe consists of different levels of vibration, some will encounter this higher vibration by raising their own vibration and some will not. Those who do, will become aware of another Reality, become more receptive, able to manifest a greater awareness.

Is there a message we must pay more attention to if we are to grow in consciousness? I can only speak for myself as I ponder and grapple with some of these profound questions. Peace must be experienced one person at a time. Peace has to start with me—right here—right now!

How can I change? First of all, by recognizing and acknowledging my own divinity. I AM a soul, a part of the Divine, which through experiences grows in awareness and strength. As a soul, I don't fear or suffer from lack of anything, except growth. My soul is eternal and immortal, only my personality is time bound and only as a personality do I experience suffering. The anchor of my soul is in my heart center—my Power center—my Love center.

In order to grow spiritually I must acknowledge and understand this energy, the Energy and the Power of Love and acknowledge the part it plays in my life. I have a physical, an emotional, a mental and a spiritual body or vehicle. My breath is distributing energy throughout my physical being. This energy is very powerful, but only useful to the degree it is applied.

On the spiritual level this energy manifests as strong will. On the mental level the energy manifests as focus and attention. On the emotional level it manifests as passion, feeling, desire or interest, and on the physical level it manifests as vitality.

You expressed this energy perfectly. You had a strong will, were able to focus your attention, driven by your inner passion and desire to serve and were filled with an unusually high level of vitality and devotion. We do have a choice as to how we use energy. It can be used for either destructive or constructive purposes depending upon our level of awareness, and our moral and ethical discernment. It is our soul that is affected by how we use this energy.

Freedom from the *illusion* that creates pain and suffering, can only be found in focusing on the ethical and constructive growth of our soul, not in allowing it to wither away in darkness. The ancient teachings, no matter of what religion or tradition, command us to pay attention!

If we as a species are to survive and flourish, our heart and mind must be healed. Our Universe and every manifestation on our planet, is a living entity. I can see this life energy in every cloud, every star, in every flower and tree, and in every baby's face. We are all light beings, pilgrims on this path together, part of this tremendous Love/Light energy, manifesting as the *will* to live.

My heart center is a major center of light and transformation, because it allows me to feel empathy and to identify with someone else's pain and suffering. It allows me to see the world through someone else's eyes, walk in their shoes for a while, even if only for moments. It allows me to feel that we are all connected. It allows me to forgive. It allows me to recognize that the spirit in you, is the same as the spirit in me.

Finally, I understand what is meant by 'I AM THAT I AM.' I am a part of the source we call God. That's my true identity. We are all part of the same essence walking the path of soul or spiritual growth through evolution. Jesus' words: "Seek ye first the Kingdom and all else will be provided by spirit." "Love thy neighbor as thyself..." has a whole new meaning for me now. Jesus, like all teachers tried to show us the way, to help us to understand 'who' we are, souls on a journey towards a higher level of awareness and perfection. He taught that Love is a Power. You, my dear teacher, understood the deeper meaning and took the message of the Christ personally and applied it to your life. You truly understood what Love is and what it is not.

You have brought me to the place where I see who your teachers were. You had allowed these Beings to inspire you, just as I am allowing myself to be inspired by you. As I remember the summer of 1985, I just read the last poem entered into my first book '*Our minds are like parachutes, they only function when open...*' entitled 'Love' and see now that I can substitute the word *Love* with *Life* in the title.

Life
LOVE—is our sole reason for living
    Or else we'd be a tree.
LOVE—is kind and ever forgiving
    The real source—of our energy.
LOVE—is in every living creature
    I can see it in you and you in me.

LOVE—if pure, has no boundaries
    Try to control it, you lose.
LOVE—is there—always
    To replenish—your soul.
LOVE—does not come in fractions
    It's ALL, always whole.

LOVE—it has no beginning and no end.
    It is infinite.
LOVE—is very spiritual
    It is the essence of your soul.
LOVE—to think you can hide or deny it
    Is sheer folly, because it is LIFE—it is EVERYTHING.
RzT Aug. 1986

As I remember it now, this was written at the end of my stay in Georgia. Who inspired this? Was it you, or was I at that moment a channel for a higher energy because my heart had opened? Had I become more open due to the therapy I had undergone that afternoon in Georgia? Had my heart chakra been balanced and did I begin to heal from the inside out from that day forward?

I had experienced transcending my mind and had used my heart to think. Is that what attracted you into my life? Is that the secret?

A lot of other things are beginning to make sense to me now, since the heart center is the seat of our soul connection.

As long as we are the slaves of our mind and not its master, our disorders will continue to manifest themselves through pain, suffering and disease. This discovery, or shall I say re-discovery, since certain ancient teachers of higher wisdom have known this all along, is not so new. I just did not know it then. Are we finally shedding some light on the physical, emotional, mental and spiritual nature of man?

Oh my, this life of mine is certainly taking a different direction than I had originally thought possible. It is best not to plan too far into the future. It is wise to be open and receptive to change every moment of my life. As I become more open I give thanks to you, my dear teacher, for helping me in my search, allowing me to uncover something very fundamental. I guess my deep desire, as a child to be an archaeologist has been satisfied on some level. Thanks to you and all the other teachers whom I have encountered on my path.

When I first heard that Albert Einstein had discovered and pronounced that time only exists in our three-dimensional world, I could not comprehend the meaning. I could not get my rational or analytical mind out of the way enough to understand this. What on earth did he mean by that? Of course time existed, as I glanced at the clock.

It's only lately that I have experienced more of what he meant. I discovered for myself that this was a big clue. I actually began to understand this back in 1985. Even though the times I could stay in that *now* moment were very few, I knew something magical had happened. I experienced my creativity for the first time. I experienced *being*—a state that is beyond time and space.

Those moments were unbelievably different, in that I started to write poetry, and felt a surge of energy and elation like never before, similar to a 'high' without drugs. Was it bliss? But it did not last. The moment I looked back, I fell into the roller coaster of pleasure and pain. However, I did not forget those divine moments of utter peace and joy. How could I? The experience had left me changed forever.

Yet, why did it leave me for so many years? Now, I realize it did not leave me at all, I left it! This state of being—this presence—is always there. We just don't pay any attention to it.

I must have needed to experience some more pain in order to grow, wake up and let go. I guess that is part of the mystery, another part of the puzzle. I found that during states of agitation and stress, followed by frustration and mild depression I did not bother to meditate. Looking inside had not become firmly established. It had not yet become a regular habit.

It was easier and less painful back then to blame others, protecting my own small ego, in the process prolonging its domination. The only problem was that the ego created separating thoughts and was of no help to me whatsoever in these situations. We have become so used to believing that the ego is our true self, that it is very painful to let go of its influence, redirecting its attention and power, surrendering to our true nature—the higher Ego.

Once we surrender, a symbolic death occurs, and our true self or higher self, often called the 'Christ Self' or the 'Buddhic Self' is born. This transformation is often referred to as a process, or the result of an *inner* not an outer revolution. Dropping the 'R' in revolution, it becomes the 'evolution' of man. It becomes the evolution of consciousness, as we begin to experience the *super*-conscious. Isn't that what you discovered back at the turn of the last century when you wrote, and this I feel bears repeating again:

"Jesus had announced not a kingdom that was to be founded and realized in the natural world by Himself and the believers, but that was to be expected as coming with the approaching dawn of a supernatural age."[22]

For instance, where in the English version of Matthew 3:2 Jesus supposedly said: "Repent thee..." in the German version it says: "Andert euren Sinn..." which means, change your minds, which to me also means change your attitude. I now remember reading that Jesus kept saying that we will eventually have the power to do what he had done, and more. All we have to do is recognize the Power of Love—recognize Truth—and have faith that everything is happening the way it should, for our maximum learning. *The Kingdom of God is within'* takes on a whole new meaning when viewed from this perspective. "You will do even greater things" said Jesus... If we are to believe those words, what is in store for us is quite astounding!

What Jesus was saying seems to me: "Become like me" or "Be like me." This, the modern Christian Church has turned into: "Believe in Jesus." On closer examination I see a huge difference between these two statements.

After re-reading pages in your book *'The Mystery of the Kingdom of God'*, the light is finally dawning as I begin to get a glimpse of what you had discovered and experienced. You had tried to pass this discovery on to us exactly one hundred years ago. You were a visionary!

You had discovered that *if* Jesus really existed, he was an example of a man who had developed tremendous powers by the purification of his vehicles, thus increasing his level of consciousness to pure Awareness. This increase in vibration allowed him to see beyond the duality of our material existence, which can only be described as an illusion. Yet, it looks and appears real to us, because it is the instrument of our growth. Few would listen to your revolutionary ideas and thoughts. The historical Jesus of religion is not the true Jesus. Religion would like us to believe he was a God, when in fact it looks like he was sent by or overshadowed by a Higher Being. You made your *life* the argument, showing us by example, what a human being is capable of creating, when this Truth is lived! The 'Christ impulse' or principle is a *living presence* in each and every one of us.

Humanity was not ready to link u. Perhaps we were not evolved enough? You decided that your contribution as a doctor of medicine would heal the physical bodies of so many who were suffering. But you healed much more than the physical body. Your words reached and touched many souls. You were so much more than an ordinary physician, you were a metaphysician, and a mystic.

You are among the few who understood what it is all about. You understood that all of life is sacred, because Life is what we call God. Life is Love. You saw that everything is filled with the same God Consciousness. In this way the animal kingdom, the plant kingdom and even the mineral kingdom are part of this ONE consciousness. Granted all is manifested on different levels, on different vibrations, but only the human can say the words: "I AM." Just like each cell in my body is an integral part of me, I AM Part of a much greater Being.

One of the greatest contributions of your friend, Albert Einstein, is based on our understanding of the theory of relativity. We as humans will never know ABSOLUTE TRUTH—only relative truth. The truth we experience in our daily life is relative to our level of understanding, our level of evolution, our level of awareness and our level of spiritual growth.

Great mystics, seekers of Wisdom and Truth, had sought out this knowledge eons ago. It had been preserved in the most ancient writings known to man. It is found in ancient Egyptian hieroglyphics, in the Indian Vedas, the Upanishads and the Bhagavad-Gita and yes, our Bible. I must keep in mind that these were written by humans and filtered through a human level of consciousness. Depending on the purity of the channel, it can be crystal clear or somewhat distorted, depending on the inner development of the scribe or prophet. All is a reflection, as above so below... Is the lake calm and like a mirror, or is it full of ripples caused by emotions and agitation, causing a distortion?

Similar teachings were also discovered in the writings of the ancient Jewish ascetic sect, the Essenes, whose writings were found in the Dead Sea Scrolls in 1947. Were these sacred texts hidden from the rest of humanity, by the monks of secret orders in order to protect them from being profaned or abused? Did they rightly suspect that humanity was not ready? Are we ready now? Have we evolved?

The Tibetan lamas also preserved this ancient knowledge. It was presented in the way of 'stories' and 'myths' throughout the ages. It was recognized and taught by Plato and Pythagoras, by Socrates and Cebes, by the Neoplatonists, by Krishna, by Buddha, by Jesus and Mohammed, and by all Enlightened Ones who had experienced and walked this path before us. These texts are sacred and their true meaning, often shrouded in allegory and symbolism, can only be deciphered by using our inner vision—our intuition.

As I mentioned in earlier letters, I discovered that the only thing that is ever *real* and exists, is the *now moment*. Everything else either refers to the dead past or exists in the imagined future, in other words only in our '*minds*'. To remind me to live in the 'now' moment, I haven't worn a watch for the last few years and do not miss it. Everything I create or think about in the present moment will later manifest as my future. Everything around me shows me what time it is. It is time for us to wake up from this dream, this illusion of separateness. We are all inter-connected on the Higher Ground of Spirit.

Dear doctor, I must admit during moments of reflection, which these letters have been for me, that we all grow in stages. Infants and children are dependent. During our youth we are codependent. As adults we mature and seek independence. The next stage is acquiring the wisdom needed to fully become aware that we are all inter-dependent since we are ONE. Only then do we see ourselves as an integral part of the whole, the ONE life—we call God. All the experiences, gathered during each of these stages, are natural and necessary for our growth. Acquired learning must be tested. If it touches a place in our hearts and we resonate with it, it is right and true for us. If it doesn't, then it is someone else's truth not our own.

We change when we are ready to change. We light the candle when we are tired of the darkness—not a moment sooner. The teacher appears when the student is ready. You hear the next message when you are ready to hear it. So—in this respect all is in perfect order. We learn wisdom in stages, biting off pieces and digesting it slowly. Yes, I can see that it is ALL part and parcel of our learning process, our evolution. The question remains, how can I make my mind the servant of my soul?

By seeing things the way they really are, with the innocence of a child; by being spontaneous and natural; by being myself at all times; by being open and willing to communicate my deepest feelings, since hiding in any degree keeps me stuck in the illusion of separateness from other people; by perceiving everyone, including myself as a being on the path towards enlightenment. That is Reality with a capital R. Gratitude and contentment come when we see the beauty and perfection of each step along the way.

I am very grateful for these sessions with you dear teacher. It is time to leave you for another day, although you creep into my mind more and more during my hours away from the computer. When faced with a difficult situation I often find myself wondering, 'How would Dr. Schweitzer respond to this situation?' That's when out of nowhere the correct solution or response seems to manifest itself for me. As I become more open to accept that I am worthy I open myself to the energy of Love; I must allow it to touch me and allow it to fill me and flow through me; and I accept that I am still open for more learning.

I have described you as a mystic. Yet, you didn't hide in a cave and pray. You applied yourself to the best of your human ability, leaving us to ponder the source of your energy, the source of your compassion, the source of your love for truth and your love for life. The healing power of Divine Love acted through you! With love in my heart I remain,

Your grateful and devoted pupil, R.

Dear Dr. Schweitzer,

The month of June has come to an end. Today is July 4th. I just returned from watching a beautiful sunrise and was inspired to say a prayer of thanksgiving on the deserted beach. To accompany my writing this morning I chose Siegfried's Rhine Journey, from the *Ring of the Nibelungen* series by Wagner. I can almost picture Siegfried steering his boat down the river towards the ocean at sunrise. As another day dawns, and the sun is about to appear again, the hero of this drama is filled at first with a sweet melancholy, followed by peace, accompanied by incredibly beautiful and moving music. This is followed by a sense of joy, which Wagner's music depicts very triumphantly, engaging every instrument.

As I think of Independence Day I reflect back to a year ago. On the retreat I attended last June we were asked to pick a word that represents a goal we will endeavor to aspire to during the next year. I had made my goal independence. My teacher mistakenly spelled it Independ*ance* while writing this word on the blackboard. Was it a mistake? Thank you Dr. Robert!

What did it mean for me at the time? A lofty goal not within my reach, or is it something I will experience while still in my body this time around? My heart tells me *that it is a state of mind*.

Where is my will to be found? My mind, for years has fostered the illusion of being separate. Now my heart tells me that we are all connected. I can see the dilemma very clearly. Since my mind has led me astray before, it is logical for me to begin to trust my heart. Where do I begin the lesson of thinking with my heart?

How do I begin to communicate? By listening! By listening and being quiet I begin communicating with my soul; by using conscious discrimination as to what thoughts I *allow* to enter my mind and which thoughts to act on in conscious awareness; by recognizing the difference between my ego talking, and the silent whisper of my soul; by embracing my weaknesses as well as my strength. I can use solitude, meditation, observation, study, reflection and contemplation as my tools. Our true nature will reveal itself as a part of the infinite unknowable essence.

I am not attached to the outcome of my life anymore. I just go with the flow... Detachment from physical possessions becomes easy as I simplify my life, shedding some of the unnecessary objects and adornments, remembering that all I need to exist is always supplied, namely food if hungry and shelter if cold. Everything else has lost its glamour and glitter. Yes, it is nice to have a comfortable home, but it is only an added blessing I give thanks for every day. Trust, is another attribute I will now incorporate into my daily existence. The trust I am referring to comes from an inner faith that I am being guided. A certain purpose will be revealed to me eventually, a purpose, only known to the Masters of Wisdom.

I must practice patience and do my best in whatever I chose to do. The rest will take care of itself. There are no mistakes, only learning experiences. We are all in the process of growing spiritually. The Divine Will, will be merged with my will, *to the extent that I open myself to its healing energy*, allowing me to fulfill my destiny as a soul, learning and growing through my human experiences.

My challenge ahead is clearly to allow the Power of Love to guide and inspire me the way it has inspired you. To focus my attention on the good and positive of each experience, allowing love and light to shine on my thoughts. The thoughts that create my life, my reality and my destiny, are all I really have.

The negative thought patterns will dissolve by themselves due to the lack of energy I give them. The rest will unfold exactly as it should. I am reminded just now of the admonition given to us by another wise Being, Zoroaster, also known as Zarathustra:

"Think purely, speak purely and act purely."

The simplicity of this advice, I know you would agree sounds so simple, but living it, is the challenge. In closing this chapter of my life, my eyes are filled with tears as I end this year of writing to you on this day, July 4th, 2002. As I open myself to many new experiences ahead and my inner life becomes more dominant, I have more compassion for others—and myself. As I am being renewed with Love, I am becoming more and more free, liberating myself, one step at a time from the prison of fear.

Having opened my heart and mind to you in these letters and writing this journal has been very liberating for me for several reasons. My attempts at discipline are being tested. Writing to you has been an exercise I will look back on with deep joy and satisfaction. My mind is more still, my emotions are calmer, and I feel more connected to you and other teachers. I feel deep gratitude and experience joy, contentment and peace more often. I have become aware that all I really have is the present *now* moment. All else is an illusion, created by my lower mind.

Surely there will be many other trials and tribulations just ahead on my path, which will need to be acknowledged and understood. However, all these trials will be new learning experiences, and most probably will be associated with growing pains due to some addiction and residue of fear. Does this kind of pain always accompany the quest for freedom, and is it most acutely felt just before liberation? Only by walking through this fear will I find the courage to make the necessary changes. Today, as we celebrate Liberty and Independence I have finally decided to begin the journey of liberating myself.

Lady Liberty will be surrounded with fireworks and salutations this evening in New York. The memory of the traumatic events of 9/11 will be on many people's mind. What lies ahead for us all is not for us to know. We know that hate can't be healed with hate, and I sometimes wonder how you or Mahatma Gandhi would handle the world crisis we find ourselves in today. Isn't evil just another word for ignorance and darkness? How can we shed a new light on our problems—find new solutions? By seeing the world as a whole and all of us as her children. How do we teach sharing? Is it not by sharing? How do we teach kindness? Is it not by being kind? How do we teach love? Is it not by being loving? How do we teach wisdom? Is it not by becoming wise?

Peace starts with me, right here—right now! No one can do it for me, and I can't do it for someone else, no matter how much I love another person. All I can do is be compassionate and understanding, and be of service where needed.

An old concept, the concept of sharing will be a good first step in our rehabilitation, reminding us of our humanity. Our education is our own responsibility. I don't just mean the learning as presently taught in our schools. Yes, those are the tools necessary to function in our society and our world, but I am also referring to self-education, to seeking a higher knowledge beyond what is presently taught in our schools. Learning about life skills, learning about the spiritual aspect of our nature. In this we are alone, and each soul must take responsibility for its own growth. This kind of higher knowledge is recognized as we, one person at a time, begin to examine our own life.

Some people have seen you as detached, cold, autocratic and selfish, perhaps even non-emotional. However, I see it as something quite different. I see and feel your inner passion, your dedication and your quest to help educate humanity.

We are approaching a New Age and will look to teachers like Plato, Pythagoras, Socrates, Krishna, Jesus, Buddha and you as Beings of a highly developed consciousness. They all in their unique way showed us the way. Will we become more receptive to listening? That is the big question before us today.

In closing I would like to read you a paragraph written by someone about you. I found this passage in the footnotes of your book entitled, 'Pilgrimage to Humanity'. This book is a compilation of your lectures on Goethe, Bach , Human Culture, and your life in Africa. On the bottom of page 73, the footnote relating to the title of the chapter 'The Unknown One' reads as follows:

"In the rich spiritual life of this remarkable man (Schweitzer), the character and ethics of Jesus is the dominant note. Jesus' personality and life-view are his, even though the metaphysics of the Nazarene is far different from his own. Though it is certain that Schweitzer's ethical achievement is the most praiseworthy of all the many activities which constitute his inner life...., it is also certain that the similarity of his motives are those of Jesus, which he often accents, this is the most noteworthy aspect of his psychological personality."[23] (Oscar Kraus, *Albert Schweitzer* **(Prague, 1929), p. 51.)**

Yes, the spirit in which you worked is the spirit of Jesus. You, like Jesus, and all great teachers who have walked on this earth before, were 'messengers' for the rest of us who are still struggling. You and all the rest of the messengers sent to humanity, would be the first to concur that the messenger is important, however, it is the *message* that remains long after the messenger ceases to exist in a physical body. The message if true—is Eternal.

I know that inner peace is never found in chasing after something. Inner peace is achieved by accepting myself exactly the way I am, right now, unconditionally, without constantly judging or criticizing myself. As I accept all my idiosyncrasies, all my quirks and hang ups, I give myself permission to *just be*. The power I need to change myself is then fully recognized and within my reach. As I open my heart to *myself* and forgive myself, I can now forgive others, in the process freeing myself from judging and criticizing others, who are just like me—searching—and I see others as fellow pilgrims on the path. Yes, forgiveness is the gift I give myself.

Inner peace is experienced when I completely **accept** what **is**, every moment of my day. I experience *just being*, when I go inside, and in meditation, still my rational mind. This is not easy, for we can't stop thinking, but we can become still and calm enough, to become the observer of each thought, then allow it to drift away gently. That's when we create a space for pure being, found in the space between the multitude of thoughts.

Before I am able to love another being, I must first love and respect the divinity in myself, my real Self, my soul. Before I am able to experience freedom, I must allow others the same freedom, the freedom of thought and expression. Love shows me that there is unity on a deeper or higher unseen level, despite our great diversity in outer appearances. No two people are exactly alike in their experiences and soul growth while on earth. A feeling of absolute gratitude for everything envelops me at moments like this, as I give thanks to you for coming to my rescue, lending me a helping hand that day so long ago.

This kind of love and gratitude for goodness and beauty, is not found in chasing the rainbow, it is found in experiencing the beauty of the rainbow without any further thoughts of any kind. In that moment I am so grateful for having had the experience without clinging to it or needing it to last. That's when I recognize that I AM love—that my love is endless and boundless—that I can afford to give this love freely without expecting anything in return and 'I AM THAT I AM' is finally understood.

"Some signs of *self-reflection* are beginning, however, to make their appearance. Here and there we discover a recognition that a philosophy must again be sought which will offer men a meaningful world-view."[24] **(My Italics)**

All I can utter at this moment is *'thank you'*. Thank you for being the light on my path, thank you for being my inspiration, thank you for all you have given to humanity. Thank you from the bottom of my heart. As I go on my way, knowing I am not alone makes my journey easier. You and all great teachers are always ready to help us in moments of doubt and confusion, showing us the way back home, the way back to our divine nature. All we have to do is tune into a different or higher channel.

In closing these letters, I would like this poem, recently given to me by a friend to be my final tribute to you:

If

If you can keep your head when all about you are losing theirs
  And blaming it on you.
If you can trust yourself when all men doubt you,
  But make allowances for their doubting too;

If you can wait and not be tired by waiting,
  Or being lied about, don't deal in lies,
  Or being hated, don't give way to hating,
  And yet don't look too good nor talk too wise;

If you can dream and not make dreams your master,
If you can think and not make thoughts your aim,
If you can meet with triumph and disaster,
  And treat those two impostors just the same;

If you can bear to hear the truth you've spoken,
  Twisted by knaves or make a trap for fools,
  Or watch the things you gave your life to broken,
  And stoop and build them up with worn out tools;

If you can make one heap of all your winnings,
  And risk it on one pitch and toss,
  And lose and start again at your beginnings,
  And never breathe a word about your loss;

If you can force your heart and nerve and sinew,
  To serve your turn after they are gone,
  And so hold on when there is nothing in you,
  Except the will, which says to them "hold on!"

If you can talk with crowds and keep your virtue,
  Or walk with kings—nor lose the common touch,
If neither foes nor loving friends can hurt you,
  And if all men count with you but none too much;

If you fill the unforgiving minute
> With sixty seconds worth of distance run,
> Yours is the Earth and everything in it,
> And—what is more—you'll be a man my son!
>   *Rudyard Kipling*

Yes, you were a man in the truest sense of the word. To me you were a man who had transcended fear. The world beholds you with awe and reverence. To me your message is eternal and therefore appropriate to any age. 'Know Yourself' must be my first step, the first rung on the ladder to obtaining a higher view.

Will I ever be able to experience life from this soul level? Will my life from now on reflect some of these higher character attributes? Will I become my own authority, become self-reliant and take responsibility for my own change of attitude, thus liberate myself? I guess that's up to me! You, my dear teacher, have proven to me beyond the shadow of doubt that it is possible. Any small start is better than no start. I fully realize that it's not about failure or success; it is about doing my best. I've let go of comparing myself to someone else. After all, the tenth grade is not better than the first grade. It is only different... Both are needed to complete the curriculum!

And finally, thank you for the healing prescription of LOVE. It is Love that is healing me at this moment as I recognize that I don't need to look for or yearn for respect from others, all I need—is SELF-respect. Thank you for teaching me that I don't need to seek the approval of others—all I need is SELF-approval. You have helped me to understand that I don't need someone's love, because in my deepest essence I AM Love.

Thanks to you, I learned that if I live only in my head and dwell only on intellectual ideas, I become too detached. On the other hand, if I live in my emotions only, I can become too sentimental, too attached and too possessive, creating a suffocating atmosphere for my loved ones, which is the opposite of love and freedom. Wisdom is Love applied intelligently or Intelligence applied lovingly. Walking the middle road is my goal, as it creates more balance and with it brings harmony into my life. Thank you for coming to my rescue!

While waiting for the sun to rise this morning, for a few moments I saw the pink and orange sky dotted with soft clouds reflected in the shallow surf, where the ocean meets the shore. My heart is filled with a deep gratitude that is so hard to transpose into words.

I know I've talked to you a lot about *my truth* during the past year. Whether other human beings will see it as truth is not for me to say. As for me, if it resonates with something in the deepest recesses of my heart, I know it to be true. Again, I am reminded that we can't know ABSOLUTE truth, we as humans can only know a truth that is relative to our own experiences and our own awareness. After all is said and done, our reality is our own creation.

As I contemplate the meaning of true Independence and Freedom today, I will think of you... Where, and how, will I find *my* Lambéréne? I wonder...

I trust that the opportunity to be of help in some way will present itself, since I sincerely ask to be shown the way in which I can make a contribution When I am ready to see it and prepared to act on it.

There is a deep yearning for peace in my heart. Now I know what Deepak Chopra meant to convey When in 'The Gift of Love' he quoted the words of the mystic poet Rumi: *"Outside the ideas of right doing and wrong doing, there is a field, I'll meet you there."*

Beyond all appearances, I see a field where opposites merge into one. A field becoming a sea of unconditional Love, a field of flowers and majestic trees, a river of colors and rainbows, a vision of mountains and streams filled with deep and abiding beauty, filled with the love coming from nature itself. This field reaches and expands beyond words. It is a field of peace where souls meet and where the lover meets his/her Higher Self, the beloved. "Yes, my dear teacher, I'll meet you there." "Namaste."

May peace be with all beings.
Your forever grateful student, *R*.
July 4th, 2002.

Sources Chapter 9.

1. P.26 *The Words of Albert Schweitzer*, Norman Cousins.
2. P.61 *The Words of Albert Schweitzer*, Norman Cousins.
3. P.60 *The Words of Albert Schweitzer*, Norman Cousins.
4. P.54-55 *The Words of Albert Schweitzer*, Norman Cousins.
5. P.62 *The Words of Albert Schweitzer*, Norman Cousins.
6. *Introduction to Faust*, Wofgang von Goethe
7. P.222 *Ponder On This*, Alice Bailey.
8. P.223 *Ponder On This*, Alice Bailey.
9. P.223-224 *Ponder On This*, Alice Bailey.
10. P.9-10 *Out of my Life and Thought*, Albert Schweitzer.
11. P.224 *Ponder On This*, Alice Bailey.
12. P.225-226 *Ponder On This*, Alice Bailey.
13. P.42 *The Words of Albert Schweitzer*, Norman Cousins.
14. P.65 *The Words of Albert Schweitzer*, Norman Cousins.
15. P.9 *Out of my Life and Thought*, Albert Schweitzer.
16. P.61 *The Words of Albert Schweitzer*, Norman Cousins.
17. P.2 *The Essentials of Mysticism*, Evelyn Underhill.
18. P.27 *Albert Schweitzer, World Citizen*.
19. P.27 *Albert Schweitzer, World Citizen*.
20. P.7 *Albert Schweitzer, World Citizen*.
21. St. John 15:18-20
22. P.9 *Out of my Life and Thought*, Albert Schweitzer.
23. P.73 *Pilgrimage to Humanity*, Albert Schweitzer.
24. P.7 *Pilgrimage to Humanity*, Albert Schweitzer.

With deep gratitude I acknowledge the authors of the following books, and list a bibliography in alphabetical order:

Albert Schweitzer: Man of Mercy, Berrill, Jacqueline, 1956, Dodd, Mead & Company, New York, NY.

Albert Schweitzer—Thoughts for Our Times, Anderson, Erica, The Pilgrim Press, 1975, New York, NY.

Albert Schweitzer, World Citizen, Christian, Jean, 1990, Editions La Nuée Bleue, DNA, Strasbourg.

Astara's Book of Life, Earlyne Chaney and Robert Chaney, Astara, Upland, CA.

Conversations of Goethe, I. Eckermann, Johann Peter, 1998, Da Capo Press, Inc., New York, NY.

Cosmic Consciousness, Bucke, Richard Maurice, 1923, E. P. Dutton & Company, New York, NY.

Faust I & II, von Goethe, *The Collected Works,* Volume 2, Wofgang Johann, 1984, Princeton University Press, Princeton, NJ.

Life's Little Instruction Book, Brown Jr., H. Jackson, 1991 Rutledge Hill Press, Inc., Nashville, TN.

Memoirs of Childhood and Youth, Schweitzer, 1997, Syracuse University Press, Syracuse, NY.

On the Edge of the Primeval Forest, Schweitzer, Albert, 1956, Collins Fontana Books, A & C Black Limited, London, England.

Out of my Life and Thought, Schweitzer, Albert, 1998, the Johns Hopkins University Press, Baltimore, MD.

Pilgrimage to Humanity, Schweitzer, Albert, 1961, The Philosophical Library Inc., New York, NY.

Ponder On This, Bailey, Alice A., 1971, Lucis Publishing Company, New York, NY. London, England.

Practical Mysticism, Underhill, Evelyn, 1915, E. P. Dutton & Co., Inc., New York, NY. 2000, Dover Publications Inc., Mineola, NY. Published in Canada by General Publishing Company, Ltd., Toronto, Canada.

Secret Wisdom of the Great Initiates, Chaney, Earlyne, 1992, Astara's Library of Mystical Classics, Upland, CA.

The Light Within Us, Schweitzer, Albert, The Philosophical Library Inc., New York, NY.

The Spiritual Life, Selected Writings of Albert Schweitzer, edited by Charles R. Joy, 1947, The Ecco Press, Hopewell, NJ.

The Quest of the Historical Jesus, Schweitzer, Albert, 1998, The Johns Hopkins University Press, Baltimore, MD.

The Words of Albert Schweitzer, Cousins, Norman, 1984, Newmarket Press, New York, NY.

Twelve World Teachers, Hall, Manly P., 1965, Philosophical Research Society, Los Angels, CA.

Wittgenstein's Poker, Edmonds, David and Eidinow, John, 2001, Harper Collins Publishers Inc., New York, NY.

About the Author

The author was born in post-war Germany. At the age of 12, she and her mother emigrated to Canada, where she later married and raised a family. A successful career in real estate followed.

In 1984 during a period of turmoil and inner struggle she started searching. She began her spiritual quest by immersing herself in the study of religion and philosophy. She became fascinated by the spiritual philosophy of one of the world's greatest thinkers, the philosopher and humanitarian Dr. Albert Schweitzer.

She was intrigued by his philosophy of *'Reverence for Life'* and his statement: **"I have made my life my argument."**

Her quest for freedom and a keen sense of curiosity led her to search for truth in metaphysics and the Ageless Wisdom Teachings.

She has written 3 children's books, two books of poetry and articles for spiritual magazines. She has lectured about the life and writings of Dr. Schweitzer and is leading discussion groups based on the works and teachings of other spiritual teachers including: J. Krishnamurti, Don Miguel Ruiz, Rudolf Steiner, Mabel Collins and others.

In the introduction to her current book she admits that looking at her self has been the most painful and yet, the most liberating experience of her life:

"My best and most *formative* schooling, seen only in hindsight, has been life and the many experiences that were presented to me on my path. 'Know thyself...' is the message, the path and the way."

Printed in the United States
35014LVS00003B/37-135